Social Policy of the European Economic Community

Social Policy of the European Economic Community-

Doreen Collins

Senior Lecturer in the Department of Social Policy and Administration, University of Leeds

A Halsted Press Book

JOHN WILEY & SONS · New York

331.11
C 712

First published in 1975 by Martin Robertson & Co. Ltd.,
17 Quick Street, London N1 8HL

Published in the USA by Halsted Press,
a division of John Wiley & Sons, Inc., New York

Library of Congress Cataloging in Publication Data

Collins, Doreen.
  Social policy of the European economic community.
  "A Halsted Press book."
  Bibliography: p.
    1. Labor policy—European Economic Community countries. 2. Migrant labor—European Economic Community countries. 3. International economic integration. I. Title.
HD8380.5.C64   331.1'1'094   75-22282
ISBN 0-470-16583-9

Set by Trade Linotype Ltd. Birmingham.
Reproduced and printed by photolithography and bound in Great Britain at The Pitman Press, Bath

Contents

Tables

Acknowledgements

I should like to thank Miss Williams of the European Communities' Information Centre, London for her help in the early stages of preparation and the staff of the Bodleian Library, Oxford for their general assistance. Mr Wellesley-Smith of the library, University of Leeds also gave me valuable help. My colleagues, Dr and Mrs Fry and Dr Hartley provided constructive suggestions for which I am most grateful. None of those mentioned can, of course, be held responsible for the contents of this volume.

I also wish to thank the University of Leeds for its grant towards the cost of this publication.

Abbreviations

AVT	Accelerated Vocational Training
CAP	Common Agricultural Policy
CECA	Communauté Européenne du Charbon et de l'Acier
CEE	Communauté Economique Européene
ECSC	European Coal and Steel Community
EEC	European Economic Community
Euratom	European Atomic Energy Community
GATT	General Agreement on Tariffs and Trade
gdp	gross domestic product
ICFTU	International Confederation of Free Trade Unions
IFCTU	International Federation of Christian Trade Unions
ILO	International Labour Organization
m.u.a.	million units of account
OEEC	Organization for European Economic Co-operation
PEP	Political and Economic Planning
u.a.	units of account
UNO	United Nations Organization
WEU	Western European Union

PART ONE

The Application of the Treaty

1 The Treaty of Rome

1 Introduction

The multiplicity of international organizations which now exist in Western Europe bears witness to the fertility of ideas concerning new forms of political arrangements. Two of the most novel are the European Coal and Steel Community (ECSC) and the European Economic Community (EEC). Both derived their impulse from the belief that it was necessary to take a definite step towards arrangements which would contain greater supra-national powers than those of the traditional international organization based on state co-operation. Both chose the field of economics and both have claimed to possess a social policy: indeed one section of the Treaty of Rome carries this as its title. The purpose of this volume is to examine the nature of the social policy functions of the EEC, and to consider the exercise of social responsibilities during the period from 1958 to 1972. Specifically, the focus is on the application of those treaty responsibilities defined by it as falling into the social category together with the commitment to the free movement of working people. It is not concerned with the question of whether the existence of the EEC has led to greater prosperity, since the purpose is to shed light on the contribution made to policies devoted to human well-being rather than on the process of political decision making or on the economic achievements of the EEC. The first task is to be clear about what constitutes social policy under the treaty before embarking on an account of the work which the Community has carried out. Furthermore, I have devoted attention to the arguments made within the Community structure for the development of social responsibilities and this leads on to a discussion of the possibilities for further action.

In recent years member states have given signs of a greater willingness than hitherto to allow the Community to play a more effective part in the pursuit of the broad goals of social progress. This is a reflection of the obvious fact that the European area has undergone great social and economic change since the late 1950s. At the present time much discussion is taking place on questions of a broadly social nature, such as the treatment of migrants or the development of collective bargaining at European level. These issues were not of prime importance when the

3

Community was being established. A major lesson to be derived from the account of its activities hitherto is that social responsibilities cannot develop through a process of natural evolution but require a political development in the Community itself. The founders did not provide the Community with the basic essentials of social policy in the form of a responsibility for defined social ends matched by resources devoted to their achievement. In consequence it has barely begun to consider how to formulate viable social objectives and how they might be executed, or to face the question of resource redistribution. This is the task of the future, but it is to be hoped that an understanding of what has happened in the immediate past will throw some light on the difficulties involved in undertaking such a vast commitment.

Although ideas concerning European integration go well back into the past, the starting-point for the setting-up of the EEC need be no earlier than the mid-1950s. The great post-war hopes of a European federation had faded, the attempt to create a European Defence Community and an associated Political Community had failed. The enthusiasts for European unity looked again at the example of the six countries that had created the ECSC. A number of ideas were canvassed at the time for further international authorities responsible for the control of agriculture, posts, raw materials and similar matters, but in the end the choice fell upon the general economic field combined with a sectoral approach. The new initiative developed from a speech made by the Dutch Foreign Minister, Johan Beyen, in April 1955, in which he expressed the view that the time was ripe for comprehensive economic integration amongst those countries willing to accept supra-national organization and provided measures were included to protect members against unfavourable economic and social repercussions.[1] This was not the first time that M. Beyen had floated such an idea but his previous attempt had been thwarted by French opposition to general economic integration. The problem, therefore, was to devise a scheme which would contain sufficient safeguards to overcome French fears of opening her economy to competition.[2] Thus from the start a basic issue was posed concerning wage and social security levels as well as social legislation, in terms not of their normal justification but of their effect on relative competitive positions. Whilst France in the ensuing months showed that she was in fact prepared to go ahead with proposals for greater unity, if only as a means of dealing with the German problem, her need was always to ensure that 'Europe was not created by the process of destroying France'.[3]

The Beyen speech led rapidly to a meeting of the Foreign Ministers of the six countries of the ECSC at Messina in June. The French argument was presented by M. Pinay, who stressed the importance of the levelling-up of wage rates and social security benefits, of deciding on the height of the common tariff to be erected against the rest of the world, of establishing a fund to help industry in backward regions convert itself to more modern forms of production and who argued that general agreement must be obtained before any one state adopted currency convertibility.

The French case was not, however, the only one put forward. A joint Benelux memorandum[4] had developed M. Beyen's ideas into a strongly held position linking further supra-nationalism with general economic integration in the form of a common market, as well as the specific organization of the transport and energy sectors. The former would require the suppression of obstacles to exchange, the harmonization of general policies in the financial, economic and social sphere, safeguard clauses, the creation of a readaptation fund and the setting-up of appropriate institutions. The German view was different again. Whilst her political interest in reacceptance by the West and therefore of meeting French fears remained strong, from an economic point of view she preferred a grouping which would be as loose as possible, allowing for her exploitation of fresh markets, and which ideologically veered towards her own attachment to a liberal market system rather than to dirigiste views. The German position[5] continued to reflect a deep division within Germany itself and particularly between Chancellor Adenauer and his Economics Minister Dr Erhard, who personally symbolized differences in the German attitude to the question of what economic concessions to make in order to ensure the appeasement of France. Although Germany accepted the need for a common authority for certain functions and the creation of a fund to help deal with the problem of regional disparities, her real economic interest lay in the gradual introduction of a common market including a steady increase in freedom for capital and labour movements together with rules to ensure fair competition. She had no wish to impose French social charges on her generally low-cost industry.[6] Dr Erhard himself was strongly in favour of general integration on the basis of free exchanges but against the growth of a new bureaucracy. It was unrealistic, he thought, to suppose it possible progressively to hand over national responsibilities to a supra-national institution since the totality of functions could not be split into different competences. The equivalence of wages and social charges was not a pre-condition of the market but a function of the productivity differences which create a market, and social harmonization was thus at the end not the beginning of integration. 'Sicily is not in the Ruhr.'[7] During the negotiations Germany also took the opportunity to pursue a project of particular interest to her, namely the Europeanization of her young people, and inserted into her official memorandum the need for a European University and for encouraging increased movement amongst young workers.

Italian interests were also influenced by special factors. With the ending of hostilities she had consistently favoured moves towards greater political unity in Europe as a framework within which she might link herself with the Western democracies and for which she was prepared to accept a high degree of supra-nationalism if not outright federalism. Her support was, therefore, part of a deliberate policy of Western alignment. Closer economic co-operation appeared the way to stimulate the development of her economy and to ease her unemployment problem through migration.[8] The achievement of these aims was seen as lying through the creation of a system which would aid them positively and not simply through the abolition of controls. In particular it meant the need to retain appropriate protection for Italian industry and a supply of capital for development, as well as a free labour market and aids to help workers take advantage of new opportunities. Her negotiating position thus included an argument for the need to harmonize taxes and social security contributions, for a European fund to retrain and resettle workers changing employment as well as an emphasis upon ensuring that the mechanics of the free movement policy were properly worked out.[9] Her interest lay in a forward-looking political structure, including Great Britain if possible, a common market including a free labour market but with an adequate degree of supra-national institutions to ensure specific forms of help and, finally, safeguards for particular economic problems.[10]

Underlying the Messina Conference there were therefore considerable differences of view, notably over the desirability of more supra-nationalism and whether the new organization should veer towards a liberal or controlled economic system. Since, however, neither Germany nor France was anxious for further international controls on the ECSC model, discussion moved away from this issue towards the means of achieving the broad economic ends of any new arrangement and the solution of the problems inherent in the creation of a common market.[11] General agreement was reached on the broad aim of taking a further step towards European unity by means of economic integration including the creation of the appropriate common institutions, the co-ordination of social policies and the gradual fusion of national economies. Integration was to be pursued in the energy and transport sectors as well as through the introduction of a common market in stages. It was agreed that further study should be given to the problems of the pace at which obstacles to free trade might be eliminated, the harmonization of financial, economic and social policies, a safeguard system, the gradual establishment of the free movement of labour, the rules of competition, the institutional requirements of a common market, the creation of a European investment fund, the co-ordination of monetary policy and the setting-up of a readaptation fund. In the social field it was considered necessary to study the progressive harmonization of rules concerning hours of work, overtime and holiday pay. The resolution therefore closely followed the

Benelux memorandum developed to meet the requirements of other negotiators, but it was noted in France that, whereas the Benelux statement had suggested that harmonization of social provisions was indispensable, at Messina the agreement was only to study the problem to see if this was in fact so.[12]

An inter-governmental committee, under the presidency of M. Spaak, was set up to pursue further the question of methods of achieving closer economic integration and to report on the other matters raised.[13] It began work in Brussels in July 1955 with four expert working groups: the first for the common market, investment and social problems, the second for energy, the third for atomic energy and the fourth for transport and public works. It was the Spaak report which laid the basis for the twin projects of the European Economic Community (EEC) and the European Atomic Energy Community (Euratom). It is thus necessary to turn for a while to a consideration of this report with particular attention to its social provisions.

During the course of the Spaak discussions the Foreign Ministers met again to consider progress. France once more expressed her fears concerning the possible effect on the French economy of the lowering of protective barriers, but accepted that the co-ordination of social and economic policies together with the creation of readaptation and investment funds would meet many of her difficulties. French opinion, however, continued to be exercised by the problem of social charges, especially that of equality of pay for men and women.[14]

The major theme of the Spaak report was that of the economic advantages of the larger market, notably the bigger productive base and the increased division of labour it would bring. The resulting increase in economic strength would enable Europe to acquire a political and economic stature comparable with that of the United States and the USSR. The report believed that a common market would constitute a more effective way of achieving this end than a free trade organization based on the principle of international co-operation and that its aim should be to establish an area with a broadly common economic policy, strong enough to ensure economic expansion, increased stability, a rapid rise in the standard of living and the development of harmonious relations between members. The creation of a common market would require a number of collective measures, an end of restrictive practices and a degree of co-operation between states to ensure monetary stability, economic expansion and social progress.

Three major questions were identified as requiring convergent action. Firstly, the abolition of obstacles to free trade; secondly, the establishment of agreed rules of competition including joint action to deal with balance of payments difficulties, monopoly control and the effects of state competition; thirdly, the means of developing Europe's resources through helping regional development, productive reconversion of industry and manpower and the free movement of capital and labour. Firms, labour and regions would require help in adapting themselves to the changes progress demanded. Through the co-ordination of economic policies, basic investment in underdeveloped regions and the absorption of mass unemployment, factors currently an economic burden might be turned into an asset.[15]

The key to the creation of the unit was considered to be the setting-up of a common market in stages and the reduction of tariffs. This constituted the most clearly developed aspect of the report and later of the treaty itself. It was accepted that this would require a long period of development during which a convergence of monetary and social policies would gradually occur. A definite transition period and safeguard clauses should be incorporated. For the immediate future, rules in a variety of fields would be required to control those areas which could no longer be left to governments, but general economic policy would still largely be handled at national level. A Council of Ministers, normally working on unanimous vote, would therefore be necessary to co-ordinate national policies. Additionally other institutions would be required to supervise the transitional period and to administer common measures, but the report did not discuss these features in detail.

The common market would require the elimination of customs barriers and quotas, the establishment of a common external tariff and should be applied to agriculture and to the supply of services. The former presented special problems because of its social structure. It was essential to preserve the industry on the basis of the family farm for the stability it gave to European communities, but ways would have to be found for dealing with the consequences of the large-scale intervention for its protection which states had developed. Services, too, caused difficulty. A vast range of occupations was covered by the term and priority could be given in a liberalization programme to those which were directly concerned with the creation of a common market. Many distortions arose because of national discriminatory rules based on residence and nationality which should be removed except in the case of public appointments. In the case of the liberal professions whose exercise depended upon the possession of a university qualification, the organization should move towards a common basis for education and training as soon as possible and common rules should be introduced by the end of the transitional period.

The report contained two sections concerned with the introduction of common policies. These were of prime importance for a discussion of social policy. The first is that which deals with the problem of establishing a competitive system. It was considered necessary to have rules against dumping, to deal with monopolies and state aids. These last should not distort competition and, this being the criterion, the Spaak report argued that it would be unnecessary, because irrelevant, to interfere with arrangements giving help to individuals not in the productive sector. Redistributive benefits used as an instrument of social policy should remain entirely a matter for states. The only aspect from which such arrangements might affect a common market would be when benefits in kind were distributed and these should not discriminate according to the source of origin of the goods concerned. Exactly the same argument was applied to public aid given to establishments such as schools, hospitals, research centres and charities. Aid given to regions to prevent excessive urbanization or to maintain social and economic equilibrium should be permitted and there should be temporary exceptions allowed to the rules to cover problems such as the protection of marginal firms during the transitional period or the continuance of special forms of compensatory aid.

The Spaak report then turned to the problem of distortion of competition caused by the effect on costs of national legislation. It considered it unnecessary to work for complete cost harmonization. Economies carry different costs for public expenditure, whilst social security schemes and wages reflect differences in productivity which receive compensation in the conditions of exchange. Since trade occurs because of cost differences arising from factors such as variations in natural resources or productivity levels, it would be absurd to try to impose a system of uniform costs. A common market should make free movement of factors of production, possible for it was this that would bring about the necessary alignment of costs and specific action would be necessary only in particular cases.

Firms in a labour-intensive industry would in theory benefit when sited in a country where social security costs fell significantly on general taxation compared with those in states where it was largely financed by contributions, but their total competitive situation would be affected by many other factors as well. A number of specific distortions could exist, such as the incidence of direct or indirect taxation, the financing of social security, price regulations, equal pay policies, rules concerning hours of work, overtime and paid holidays. Such problems would need further examination should they be found to affect competition adversely. The Commission of the common market should, therefore, study such questions with governments and make proposals to overcome difficulties when these were discovered. If distortion resulted from collective bargaining agreements, governments would have to try to get employers and unions to adopt new rules; if from legislation, they should attempt to alter it and, in default of such accommodation, the European executive should be able to protect disadvantaged industry.[16] Although not a condition for the functioning of a common market, unified taxation systems or ways of financing social security might well facilitate the free movement of goods and people, but changes should only occur with the unanimous consent of the members. The Commission might, however, be asked to make proposals. There would be a spontaneous tendency in a common market towards similar levels in working conditions and wages which would be encouraged by trade union pressure. Such alignment of standards would help to encourage manpower movements. However, the great diversity of economic factors, of working conditions and of factors making up the totality of living and working conditions would make it extremely difficult to impose rigid rules or to expect a timetable to be kept for their application. It would, therefore, be better to give the Commission the power to make proposals at favourable moments, but to make action dependent upon unanimity in the first instance and to provide safeguards until the position was clarified by experience.

A special section of the report was devoted to the development and full utilization of European resources. For this it suggested the creation of two funds. The first would be an investment fund able to help large-scale projects, the modernization and reconversion of firms, particularly infrastructure projects, and would be particularly active in areas of labour surplus. To provide better employment facilities on the spot was the more efficient and humane way of helping workers in such regions. The second fund would be concerned directly with aid to workers, aiming to help them become more mobile and thus maintain their employment stability through taking advantage of new job opportunities. Changes in employment would be a real factor in increasing productivity and in raising living standards. The report did not suggest, however, that the general common market should introduce a system of aid on the same lines as that undertaken for the coal and steel industries, since it was considered impossible to relate loss of employment to the effect of the common market, neither could the benefits be superimposed upon those already existing. It was thought preferable to try to move towards the adaptation of unemployment aid schemes to include the principles of retraining and the need for job change. This would itself be a progressive development and would help the free movement of labour.[17] It therefore proposed a fund, made up by states in proportion to their wage and social security bill but excluding the coal and steel industries, which should be used to help the social changes brought by the more effective economic unit. It should pay half the cost of retraining and resettlement of workers if firms closed down entirely or partially and of waiting allowances if a firm intended to reopen. There might be cases where, for social reasons, it was desired to stagger closures. The fund should help pay wages in such circumstances provided they were part of a re-employment plan. Such projects should be subject to qualified Council support. Through this help the fund would give a general stimulus to states to introduce manpower training schemes and better unemployment benefits and it would thus encourage a greater similarity of arrangements which might ultimately merge into a unified system.

Benefits would be automatically linked with wage levels and re-employment costs, although the details concerning conditions and amounts of benefits could be left to be determined by the Commission, subject to Parliamentary approval. All states should gain as well as contribute because the fund would be dealing with the broad consequences of productive changes resulting from the competitive system of the larger market which should bring an increase in productivity, more efficient use of labour and higher living standards. The necessary controls over the fund's work would have to be operated by states themselves. Workers supplying services, artisans and farmers should be brought into the arrangements as the common market began to include them or as states decided it was necessary.

Going with the introduction of the common market and as part of the effective utilization of resources should be acceptance of the free movement of labour. The self-employed should be included, sector by sector, as part of the arrangements to liberalize the supply of services. The report warned against assuming there would be large-scale movements of manual workers, whom it considered immobile and for whom difficulties of social integration and housing presented considerable obstacles. Neither did it favour viewing emigration as a solution to the unemployment problem because of the drawbacks imposed on areas from which the young and active members of the labour force had gone. It preferred to consider the possibilities of creating employment in regions of labour surplus through reconversion projects and the introduction of new industry.

However, it realized that geographical mobility of labour would continue and argued that no special restrictions should be placed by states on migrants, although measures should be taken to prevent their use as cheap labour. There was a common interest amongst states in the absorption of surplus unskilled workers and arrangements should be made to increase the annual intake under safeguards to prevent swamping. Structural unemployment should be eased by the investment aids, the free movement policy and the readaptation proposals of the new scheme.

It will be seen, therefore, that the Spaak report was not concerned primarily with the creation of a supra-national edifice but with a common market based upon a system of controlled competition as the first move towards a more fully integrated economy.[18] Social policy did not figure as a major element but, in the first instance, as a factor in costs affecting competition. A wider view was, if anything, deliberately excluded by the argument that social policy in its basic redistributive sense is irrelevant to the field of production. Even in its consideration of social policy as an employers' cost the report was less than precise, accepting that too little was known about its effects for it to be possible to lay down a great deal in the form of uniform rules. There was, however, a positive, long-term section to the report. The development of resources was not considered solely from the economic viewpoint but in the knowledge of the limited prospects available to many working people and of the importance of giving them greater opportunity in a future of increased economic change. Although confined to a consideration of the labour force, its arguments here fell far more within the social policy tradition of providing a fuller life for human beings than can be said of the earlier sections. It is significant, however, that in its statement of the broad and distant goals to which Europe should aspire it saw only the need for co-operation in social progress. If, therefore, one wishes to consider the Spaak report as a social policy document it is not one which foresaw any large transfer of responsibility to a supra-national field. It accepted that adjustments affecting costs might prove to be necessary whilst its major promise lay in the contribution a common market might make to better employment opportunities.

The Foreign Ministers of the six countries met again at the end of May 1956 to endorse the document, which thus became the basis upon which detailed negotiations were conducted. The records are not yet publicly available, but it seems clear that states continued to support those policies in relation to social issues which most nearly touched their interests. M. Pineau expressed again the French difficulty over the freeing of her economy and suggested that any reduction in customs duties and quotas should be directly related to a policy of equalizing the social charges of industry.[19]

Formal negotiations opened on 26 June in Brussels and by the autumn of 1956 France had begun to press her two major aims. The first was to protect her industry and the second to ensure that her overseas territories received the benefits of the common market. In relation to the first, she argued that France must not be penalized because of her more stringent legislation on social costs and that the other five states should be prepared to align their costs at the French level. This should apply to equal pay, overtime and holiday pay. Additionally, she requested the right to retain certain controls over imports and exports, safeguards for her balance of payments and that the passage into the second stage of the transitional period should be made dependent upon adequate progress having been achieved on social cost harmonization. A compromise with the German view was arranged in November when Chancellor Adenauer agreed to a temporary maintenance of French subsidies and to the insertion of an equal pay obligation into the treaty, but France did not obtain such full protection in relation to her other costs. Considerable flexibility in the application of the first stage of the common market was written into the Treaty of Rome and with this France had perforce to be satisfied. Henceforth she concentrated on obtaining support from her partners for special aid to her overseas territories.

Meanwhile Italy had reason to be pleased with the firm adoption of the policy for free labour movement.[20] This was not a major issue in the negotiations. Germany had begun to realize she would shortly start to suffer from a shortage, particularly of skilled men,[21] whilst France and Belgium were already aware of scarcities. Some fears were expressed in France concerning an excessive influx of Italians and of German refugees but it did not reach serious proportions and both German and French employers had accepted the free labour policy by the end of 1956.[22] The investment fund, too, was expected to be of particular benefit to Italy and some compensation for her contribution to the fund for overseas development, whilst the social fund was expected to help her problem of labour mobility. Italy, too, received recognition of the need to co-ordinate the work of the investment fund with the development of the South and special escape clauses concerning the abolition of her tariffs were agreed.

II The Treaty of Rome

The Treaty of Rome was signed on 25 May 1957 and entered into force the following January. Far less supra-national in tone than its predecessor, the Treaty of Paris which had established the ECSC, it concentrated upon the measures necessary to introduce a common market and the procedures to be fulfilled during the transitional period. For many issues it but briefly sketched the shape of future policies where it was little more than an agreement to agree at a later date. Although on a larger scale than the ECSC, the new organization had nothing to say on defence, foreign policy or domestic administration and left the ultimate form of the new European grouping shrouded in uncertainty. It must not be forgotten, however, that its purpose was, in the deepest sense, political, intended to obtain for the area an international position commensurate with its achievements. 'The essential objectives of the Treaty of Rome are strictly positive in character', intended to lay the foundation of a new economic and political collaboration and to create the conditions for the establishment of one vast economic area going far beyond a mere customs union.[23] The act of signature was dynamic. It began a process of fundamental change, the end of which could not be foreseen. whose implications would only gradually unfold and which would be much affected by the importance attached to the arrangements by the members. This was reflected in the two-stage process of working established by the treaty. The initial transitional period,[24] itself divided into three stages, allowed for the creation of the customs union and the necessary objectives and mechanisms for its achievement were laid down in considerable detail. The treaty had also, however, to look forward to the time when economic integration itself was the policy to be undertaken and for this more positive stage it was unable to provide more than general guidelines. It is unfortunate, therefore, that the term 'common market' has become popular, for it directs attention solely to the first, and easiest, step whereas the real testing time for the Community lies in the present and the future.

The institutions of the EEC followed a similar pattern to those of the ECSC and from the start the European Assembly and Court of Justice served both bodies. States were represented by the Council of Ministers which, under the Rome Treaty, became the effective decision-taking body. Thus, in a system whose treaty provision was impossible to foresee, the position of the member state was closely safeguarded. Whilst the Ministers of Foreign Affairs often attended Council meetings, other ministers constituted the membership according to the subject matter under discussion. Representatives from the Commission also went to Council meetings and played an active part.[25] The Council was supported by the Committee of Permanent Representatives, established under Art. 151, to whom matters were often referred by the Council for further discussion and which was consulted during the process of formulating proposals thus ensuring that Council decisions were fully sensitive to national interests. Nevertheless, the Council was not originally conceived simply as the forum for the promotion of state aims, and the periods of their single-minded advocacy have been those of deterioration and difficulty for the Community through the operation of the Council as 'an international conference at which national delegations are negotiating with each other, whereas in reality it is one of the government organs of a Community of 180 million inhabitants which must be guided efficiently in the same way as any one of our member countries'.[26] Decisions in the Council were taken by different forms of voting procedures. Certain matters were reserved for unanimous voting, in others a majority vote (twelve out of seventeen) was required and in yet others a qualified majority vote (twelve out of seventeen including the votes of four members) was necessary. Most decisions were taken on the basis of a proposal made by the Commission and thus technically required the application of the simple majority rule, but decisions were always taken by unanimity if at all possible[27] which was found more satisfactory than forcing decisions on unwilling participants. Although one of the purposes of the introduction of stages into the transitional period was to allow for the progressive use of majority voting by defining more narrowly those fields which would still be subject to unanimity, the French boycott of the Council in 1965–6 brought into the open the fear of moving into a period in which the achievement of common agreement as a preliminary to decisions would no longer be thought necessary. In consequence, although majority voting remains, there continues to be the unwillingness to apply it to a matter considered to be a vital national interest to any member.

As in the case of the ECSC, the novelty of the new arrangements lay in the executive. The Commission was appointed by governments, although members were to be entirely independent of them in their allegiance, being answerable only to the Assembly and collectively responsible for decisions reached by majority vote. Although its responsibilities were carefully circumscribed, the Commission was in a real sense the main-spring of Community actions for it took the initial steps from which final decisions resulted. The right of proposition to the Council, and thus the determination of the form and time of proposals, gave the Commission a vital part in the decision-making process, so that the treaty structure was an ingenious compromise between the decision-making capacity of international institutions and of national governments, care-fully designed to harmonize action in a wide range of economic affairs and to allow the interests both of the Community and of its members to be represented. That its right of initiative was an essential ingredient of its position was always obvious to the Commission, which did not view its proposals as an attempt to compromise between opposing individual or national views but as 'an autonomous political act by which the Commission, speaking with complete independence, expresses what it considers to be the general interest of the Community'.[28] On the other hand, the Commission was not itself an executive structure except in limited ways. It was dependent upon action being taken by national administrations or other appropriate organizations with conse-quent problems for it of oversight, enforcement and inspection. There was no 'European administration' in a true sense. Together, however, the Council and Commission represented arrangements which took a definite step towards international government. 'If the Communities were to be reduced to a vague inter-governmental organisation, their effectiveness would be immediately and irretrievably jeopardised.'[29] How far the structure created in 1958 will prove adequate to deal with a future of more positive integration is, of course, another matter.[30]

The Commission was entitled to collect any information necessary for the discharge of its duties and for the carrying out of necessary checks whilst, under Art. 155, it was responsible for the execution of the treaty, could formulate its own recommendations and give opinions on matters within the scope of the treaty, could take decisions, participate in those taken by the Council and Assembly and execute powers conferred on it by the Council.

Both Council and Commission could act by means of a number of processes. Regulations had direct, general application, were self-regulating and of immediate application. Directives were binding in result but the precise form of their application and enforcement was left to members to decide, since their implementation might depend upon amending laws or administrative arrangements. Decisions were binding upon the addressees, who might be states or individuals, and all three procedures had to state the reasons for their enactment. Recommendations and opinions might also be issued, a procedure which was freely used in the social field, but these had no binding force. As well as taking decisions in Council, members might at any time act as normal participants in the international community and accept other forms of international agreement and an inter-governmental resolution or declaration was on occasion passed by members meeting in Council.[31]

Administratively, it was the practice for each Commissioner to carry responsibility for a particular field of work and to be supported by a small group of his fellows. Whilst there was some reorganization of responsibility from time to time, and notably with the merger of the executives in 1967 and again with the reduction of the number of Commissioners in 1970, certain portfolios were held long enough by the same man or the same nationality for them to become, to some degree, stamped with a particular identity. This is particularly true of social affairs. The first Commissioner to carry responsibility was Signor G. Petrilli of Italy who, upon his resignation in 1960, was succeeded by his fellow countryman, Signor L. Levi-Sandri, who maintained his office until 1970. At this point tradition was broken and responsibility passed to M. A. Copeé of Belgium, who had been a Vice-President of the ECSC since 1952.[32] A special division of the Commission was responsible for social affairs. This was itself divided into sections dealing with social policy, manpower, the social fund and occupational training, social security and social services. After the merger of the European executives, the division was strengthened by the addition of two new sections dealing with health and industrial safety respectively.[33]

The work of the three Communities[34] was closely linked, and from the start their executives needed to collaborate in order to deal with matters of common interest, to prevent overlapping and to allow one to work on behalf of all where possible. This meant joint meetings and information exchange at the level of Presidents, Directors of Services and below, collaboration in surveys, studies and calling of conferences and the pooling of expert knowledge.[35] In 1958 an inter-executive group for social affairs to carry out such tasks was created.[36] Many contacts were established, too, with other international organizations. The treaty referred specifically to the maintenance of relationships with the United Nations Organization (UNO), the specialized agencies, the institutions of the General Agreement on Tariffs and Trade (GATT) and other international organizations, and to co-operation with the Council of Europe and collaboration with the Organization for European Economic Co-operation (OEEC). For the purpose of this study some of the more important links lay with the International Labour Organization (ILO) with which arrangements existed for technical collaboration and regular consultation on matters of common interest, and joint efforts were made to make the best use of legal and statistical information.[37] Furthermore, special arrangements were formed with the *Centre international d'information et de recherche sur la formation professionnelle* set up in 1961 by the Council of Europe and the ILO with the help of the OEEC. This functioned largely as a documentation and information centre.

A major difference between the Treaties of Paris and Rome is to be found in the financial arrangements. The Commission was given no levy-raising power. General financing was on the basis of a fixed percentage scale but it was foreseen that the Community would ultimately command its own resources, notably from the imposition of a common customs tariff. The same principle applied, although in different proportions, to the financing of the European Social Fund. It was not until the end of 1969 that a new agreement was finally reached concerning the financial arrangements. This enabled the Community to turn progressively to a position in which it would have its own finances derived from import levies, customs duties and the proceeds of national value-added taxes so that it would become effectively financially autonomous by 1975 and completely so by 1978. In the meantime Community financing is supplemented by contributions from members, based on an amalgam of the original treaty scales and an impost dependent upon the size of the gross national product. Table 1.1 shows, however, that by 1972 the Community budget was still of modest size.

Table 1.1
EEC Budget, 1972
(u.a.)

Expenditure	Administration	367,690,020
	European Social Fund	97,750,000
	European Agricultural Guidance and Guarantee Fund	3,526,551,300
	Food Aid	36,823,320
Receipts	Own resources	1,851,750,000
	Share ECSC levies	18,000,000
	Member states	2,143,766,520
	Other	15,297,800

By 1957 little was left of the argument that European integration was a means to contribute to peaceful development and to overcome past rivalries. Attention had become firmly rooted in the desire to promote mutual objectives. The Preamble of the Treaty of Rome made clear that the European experiment was essentially concerned with the development of closer union through a common effort devoted to economic and social progress. It accepted that this goal both had to be seen against the broader picture of Europe's position within the international trading community and also carried the internal obligation to remove existing barriers, strengthen the unity of the economies and remove regional disparities. In Art. 2 the main task of the Community was defined as the promotion of the harmonious development of economic activities, continuous and balanced expansion, increased stability, an accelerated improvement in the standard of living together with closer relations between the members. Any discrimination based on nationality within fields covered by the treaty was banned. It is therefore clear that, despite the emphasis laid on the establishment of a common market and the process of economic integration, the treaty system cannot be considered purely as an economic institution for its social objectives are at this level of equal significance and 'the governments allotted the Community its own role in social affairs'.[38]

The attractive concept was now of a continental market which would enable Europe to reap the benefits of modern technology through the evocation of a more rational use of resources enabling industry to develop large-scale production and to afford the cost of modern capital equipment and research programmes. Increased wealth, strength and influence were thus seen as dependent on changes which an integrated economy would make possible. Size was no longer automatically suspicious and its possible harmful effects considered controllable. The new system was to be one of 'fair and healthy competition' but where a 'system of automatic implementation could not be expected to work'.[39] The assumption was of the value of a market-oriented system in which competition itself would be the basic mechanism for establishing the optimum use of resources. The restraints to prevent a debasement of competition were spelt out in general terms and were intended to be exercised for the sake of making an effective competitive system work rather than to supersede it. Rules of competition therefore banned arrangements such as restrictive practices, agreements, excessive concentration and price fixing unless they were specifically approved. The treaty recognized special needs requiring positive policies, as in the sphere of regional, sectional and labour problems, and insisted that members consult with each other and with the Commission on economic policies. Additionally it established certain safeguarding and protective mechanisms, including the possibility of extending the first stage of the transitional period, the protocol which allowed France to continue with import charges and export aids, and the insertion into the treaty of clauses designed to harmonize the social costs of employment.

One of the more permanent provisions which qualified the competitive system concerned the possibility of continuing state aids. Although in general these were forbidden, certain forms were acceptable. Aid of a social character given to individuals was permissible as long as it did not discriminate on the basis of origin of the product where benefits in kind were given. Thus any social service benefit, such as orange juice for babies, was a matter for state discretion provided there was no national monopoly of the supply of orange juice. This point was basic from the point of view of national social policies since it implied that there was no obligation under the treaty to adjust national welfare provision carried on state subsidy of any sort unless a specific requirement of the treaty so demanded. This was clearly stated by the Commission in reply to a Parliamentary question on the French scheme of aid to the economically weak. There was no obligation even to inform the Commission of such aids.[40] Help given in response to natural disasters or similar emergencies and aid to regions of West Germany necessitated by her division were all permitted under the treaty, whilst other forms of aid might be so allowed. These included aid to underdeveloped regions, for the promotion of a project of common European interest, for the remedying of a serious disturbance in a member's economy and to facilitate the development of certain activities or regions provided this did not conflict with the common interest. In practice the Community took a relaxed view of those aids designed to permit the adjustment of particular industries in the initial stages, so that Italy was authorized to continue to help its sulphur, raw silk, lead and zinc industries and Germany to place a temporary tax on bread coming from the Netherlands.[41]

In particular the importance of aid for regional development was recognized. Although the emphasis in the treaty was on the temporary, selective nature of such aids, a growing awareness of area disparities led the Community to develop its interest in measures to encourage the socio-economic development of backward regions. By 1961 the Commission had already recognized the importance of measures to promote the economic and social development of Sardinia, to improve the regional balance in Luxembourg and the industrial development of Algeria as well as the importance of grants to aid the modernization of French industry. It had also set up a working party to discuss the role of state aids in economic development.[42] Community concern shifted, therefore, towards the possibility of standardizing the practice of state intervention rather than forbidding it, since government aid was recognized to be important in order to minimize the adverse consequences of decline or to give new, promising industry a start.[43] Such policies, through their impact on the overall quality of life and, in particular, on the employment possibilities open to individuals, illustrate the difficulty of disentangling economic and social aspects in relation to both goals and techniques.

Distortion of competition can also arise from the existence of national legislation designed to regulate particular problems. Such provision was extremely varied in content as between the six members of the Community, and its removal or change often a threat to some internal interest. Laws on patents, trade marks, company registration, taxation or, in the social field, industrial safety, social security, the control and sale of pharmaceutical products or entry into certain professions will serve as examples. Art. 100 allowed the Council, working unanimously on a Commission proposal, to issue directives to ensure the necessary approximation of national legislation and administrative procedures. Where amending legislation was in consequence required, both Parliament and the Economic and Social Committee had to be consulted before such directives were issued. The Commission was given the responsibility to work to get agreement between members where their legislative and administrative provisions caused distortions and to prevent new state action having this result, but if the Commission failed to get agreement the Council might issue the necessary directives to ensure the elimination of distortion. The difficulty of interpretation of Art. 100, notably over the meaning to be attached to 'approximation' and the insistence upon Council unanimity, meant little use was made of it.[44] As far as social policy was concerned it remained of potential rather than actual importance, enabling legislation to be changed if it had a direct influence on the establishment or functioning of the common market.[45]

The creation of a single market consists, however, of more than the removal of existing barriers, whether these are in the form of impediments to trade, the alignment of import duties or the more subtle obstacles arising from anomalies in taxation and legislative systems, from market sharing arrangements or even the establishment of the conditions for the effective movement of the factors of production. Since the common market, in the sense of the abolition of final duties on trade in industrial goods and the imposition of a single import tariff, was not achieved until 1968, only then did it become possible to look forward to handling more fundamental problems. Such basic tasks are only preliminary to the positive creation of a unity directed by a degree of common rules and policies. Here the treaty was but a limited guide. Although it referred to the need for economic expansion, a high level of employment, the raising of the standard of living, price stability, maintenance of confidence in the currency and equilibrium in the balance of payments, it had little or nothing to say on such matters as overall economic or monetary policy or industrial development. Transport, agriculture, regional development and social affairs were all singled out for special attention in the treaty, but often in very general terms, so that the creation of definite policies to implement the treaty not only required positive acts of will but were unlikely to be seriously considered until after the customs union was established. The treaty was less than clear on the subject of the control of the economy as a means to achieve its objectives and the system was sufficiently flexible to embrace the French interest in planning and the German social market economy.

The creation and execution of social policy was not only to be affected by the economic framework of the treaty but by its political aims, the strength of its political institutions and their evolution once the system had begun to operate. Although the form of future political organization was obscure, the treaty was clearly directed towards the ultimate aim of unity and created institutions designed to achieve a balance between national and Community decision taking as well as between democratic, governmental and industrial interests. Whilst subsequent crises amply demonstrated national political sensitivity, the system contained an impulse towards policies formulated on a European base rather than a fusion of separate national approaches. 'Wherever the Treaty is applied, whether in general economic policy, in monetary policy, in policy relating to economic trends, in energy policy, in social or agricultural or transport policy . . . the Community must be the expression of a policy consciously intended to be European.'[46] The ultimate supremacy of the political objective was reiterated in the 'Action Programme' of October 1962 in which economic developments were clearly seen as subordinate to the larger aim of political unity. 'What we call the economic integration of Europe is in essence a political phenomenon . . . and integration of the economic and social aspects of national policies is aimed at in the Treaty of Rome as a means of achieving political unity in Europe.'[47]

III Social Policy in the Treaty of Rome

The main references to social policy are to be found in Part Three, Title Three of the treaty. This is introduced by a statement of broad purpose which echoes the Treaty of Paris. Under Art. 117 members not only accepted the general objective of raising the living and working conditions of the labour force, but that progress should contain their greater equalization, 'permettant leur égalisation dans le progès'. It was stated in the treaty that this would occur as a result of the operation of the common market which would itself favour the harmonization of social systems, from the procedures of the treaty and the approximation of legislative and administrative provisions. In the light of the negotiations and of the Spaak report it seems clear that this statement is a fusion of a number of themes concerning the relation of a common market to the social charges of industry. It recognizes the French position that these may be important, but takes no firm stand on whether it is necessary to take direct action on the matter and appears to have arisen, as in the case of the ECSC, for defensive, industrial reasons. Unfortunately for the evolution of social policy as a welfare goal, the result was that the key article was both obscure and lacked any definite means of achievement. No guidance was given on the extremely complex matter of the definition of equalization of living and working conditions or on the major issue of whether more importance should be attached to the automatic working of the common market or to conscious action under the treaty as a means of attaining this end. Neither did it contain specific directions to members concerning the timing or the sale of action nor lay down procedures for the Community institutions to follow. This looseness, especially when compared with many of the economic clauses, created an area of uncertainty which enhanced the importance of the role of the Commission in seizing opportunities for the articulation and development of social goals, but at the same time enabled blocking action to be taken by members on the grounds that proposals were beyond the scope of the treaty. It cannot be claimed that the European system accepted a clear obligation to ensure that all social advantages are uniformly available throughout the Community area whether for reasons of competition or otherwise,[48] and the absence in Art. 117 of a timetable, which was so useful a device for maintaining momentum in other policies, should also be remarked.

> These hesitations precisely reflect the dual preoccupation of the authors of the treaty; to provide a social policy but to put up a definite barrier to anything which might sanction, whether on the argument for the equalisation of social charges or in the name of a social ideal, a demand that any progress in any part of the common market should automatically be translated into a community norm as though it were a single state.[49]

Such omissions in the treaty, allied with the pride of place given to the pressure of the market as a causative factor under Art. 117, produce a sense that the ideological basis of the treaty veers towards a belief that the competitive system will itself determine both the alignment and the improvement of such standards. Economic developments are powerful forces making for a similarity in many social standards and 'one can assume that the influence of European integration will be towards a convergence of living standards and will certainly not be felt in the opposite direction.'[50] It is possible to argue that Art. 117 does no more than direct attention to the need to consider the removal of artificial restrictions which have grown up over the years as part of national policies. This indeed presents an immediately obvious approach to the social action of the Community. Significant differences in real labour costs, the growth of fringe benefits, the relative burden of social security falling on the employer rather than on the general community can all be viewed from the standpoint of their effect on competition between firms in different parts of the Community. The difficulty is that such interpretation is inadequate if Art. 117 is to be taken as the foundation of policies deliberately designed to improve living and working conditions.

Art. 118 placed responsibility on the Commission to promote close collaboration between members in the social field and particularly in relation to employment, labour legislation and working conditions, elementary and advanced vocational training, social security, protection against occupational accidents and diseases, industrial hygiene, trade union legislation and collective negotiations between employers and workers. In order to do so, the Commission was directed to act in close contact with members through the promotion of studies, the giving of opinions, the organization of consultations both on problems arising at the national level and on those of concern to international bodies. Before giving opinions, the Commission was under obligation to consult the Economic and Social Committee.

Close collaboration under Art. 118 did not imply the necessity for subsequent action. No follow-up procedures were included and thus the treaty left members free to decide whether any matter was to be taken further by the establishment of rules under the Rome Treaty or by other forms of international agreement. Neither treaty pressed the possibility of the European Communities formulating precise standards in fields such as factory safety or social security coverage. Whilst the imposition of such rules might be done under the Treaty of Rome through the approximation of laws procedure, it is somewhat surprising to note that no thought was given to the possibility of issuing recommendations, regulations or directives in order to develop the process of standard-setting for the subject matter of Art. 118 which had been of international concern for many years. The limitation of executive procedures to the ability of the Commission to give opinions seems weak indeed. The willing acceptance of responsibility by the Commission at the start increased the likelihood of controversy about both ends and means under Arts. 117 and 118.

> The European Commission realises that it bears particular responsibilities in this [i.e. social] field and intends to neglect no sphere in which it may prove possible to 'promote close collaboration' . . . and it will use all appropriate procedural methods . . . the Community will be judged by a large part of public opinion on the basis of its direct or indirect successes in the social field.[51]

The Council was entitled to delegate responsibility to the Commission to establish common social measures and particularly in relation to the social security needs of migrants (Art. 121). A further responsibility of the Commission was to make an annual report on social developments within the Community area to the Assembly, whilst the latter was entitled to invite the Commission to draw up reports on any particular social problems.

Art. 128 directed the Council, on a proposal of the Commission and after having consulted the Economic and Social Committee, to lay down the general principles to serve as the basis for a common policy of vocational training. Here again the absence of a definite implementing procedure and the limitation of responsibility to general principles must be accounted a serious weakness in the light of the potential importance of such principles to the creation of an effective labour market.

So far, therefore, the conclusion must be that social affairs were approached with extreme caution. Here were fundamental clauses whose content was either weak or imprecise. It can only be concluded that major responsibility was left with national governments in a field which, at the time, was itself not clearly demarcated. Certain articles of the treaty, however, carried a more precise obligation for members or gave the institutions of the Community greater power. These dealt with matters of a practical nature requiring immediate attention or better understood as a result of the experiences of the Coal and Steel Community. On the one hand are those provisions designed to protect French interests. Under Art. 119 members agreed to apply the principle of equal pay for the same work; in Art. 120 they accepted the need to maintain the existing equivalence of paid holiday schemes and in Part Two of the special Protocol concerning France empowered her to take protective measures to safeguard industries penalized by overtime payments. 'Nevertheless such provisions, notably the commitment to equal pay, the hope of harmonization of social legislation and social security systems, of the maintenance of paid holidays were in the Treaty as a means of protecting the economic position of France.'[52] As is now known, the argument later proved wrong. French industry did not suffer through the introduction of the common market but was psychologically stimulated by it and, encouraged by French governmental action, did extremely well. No use was made of the Protocol and studies began to show that the argument about social charges and their effect on competition was not as straightforward as had been assumed. French labour costs were not the highest in the Community at its start[53] and it may be that the original arguments were insufficiently sophisticated. The total labour charges per unit of identical product cannot always be measured precisely and social charges may themselves depress wages in compensation or be passed to the consumer in varying degrees. Their crude comparison is not, therefore, very helpful.

A fundamental creation of the treaty was the European Social Fund. 'The social fund is the major instrument of Community social policy.'[54] Drawing on the experience of the Coal and Steel Community, the Treaty of Rome accepted the importance of a European instrument which would assist workers in employment difficulties but which would not be confined solely to helping those whose problems were directly attributable to the introduction of the common market. There is no such limitation to be found in the treaty itself. Art. 123 stated that the purpose of the fund was to improve job opportunities through increasing both the availability of employment and the geographical and occupational mobility of workers through the provision of grant aid to them in the form of retraining and resettlement allowances as well as for temporary maintenance if employment were reduced or suspended consequent upon the conversion of the firm to other types of production. The fund was entitled to reimburse half the cost of approved schemes. Retraining allowances were to depend upon showing that a new occupation was necessary and had been followed for at least six months; resettlement allowances that a move was necessary and that six months' work had been undertaken. Tiding over allowances were to depend upon the re-employment of the worker for at least six months and the prior approval by the Commission of the conversion plan.[55] Applications were to be made by members on behalf of their own re-employment schemes or those carried out by approved bodies and were thus necessarily retroactive. Art. 126 provided that the ending of the transitional period should be the time for a thorough reappraisal of the role of the Social Fund. Thus, working on the basis of an opinion of the Commission and after having consulted the Economic and Social Committee and the Assembly, the Council was entitled to rule by qualified majority vote that assistance in the original form should no longer be granted or, by unanimous decision, that new tasks be given to the fund. In the first possibility there are perhaps traces of the notion that the fund was designed to offset the problems involved in the introduction of the common market, although experience illuminated the importance of developing its responsibilities more widely. Money for the fund was to be raised from the members according to a separate scale. Although its budget passed through the same procedures as the main Community budget, Council votes were weighted directly in relation to the finance provided. Administration was placed in the hands of the Commission assisted by a committee of thirty-six members representing government, trade unions and employers' organizations in equal numbers. This committee was entitled to take the initiative in making known its opinions and had to be consulted on more important questions.[56] The detailed rules for the fund were passed by the Council, acting on a qualified majority vote, on the basis of a proposal of the Commission and after consultation with the Economic and Social Committee and the European Parliament.

A formative influence affecting the social policies of the EEC consisted of the application of the principle of the free movement of the factors

of production to the working population. This was done, not as part of
the social clauses, but by Part Two, Title Three of the treaty. The primary
obligation was to establish free movement of labour by the end of the
transitional period through the abolition of nationality-based discrimination between workers in matters of employment, pay and other labour
conditions. This meant that, subject to residual limitations on grounds
of public order, security and health, workers should be able to accept
offers of employment anywhere within the Community; be allowed to
travel in order to accept such jobs; to stay in a member state to work
on the same terms as nationals and to remain in another member state
after having been employed there subject to conditions to be later
determined by the Commission. Employment in the public service was
exempted.[57] In order to implement these provisions the Council was
directed to issue rules intended to cover a number of important questions.
These included the development of close collaboration between national
labour exchanges, the gradual elimination of administrative obstacles to
labour movement and of those special restrictions imposed on non-
nationals within member states which impeded free movement or free
choice of job and the establishment of better machinery for bringing
together notices of vacancies and unemployed workers bearing in mind
the necessity to avoid flooding an area or industry with an influx of
cheap labour. Such arrangements implied at the very least the need for
the Commission to establish means of co-ordinating the work of employment services, of encouraging a degree of standardization in their working
arrangements[58] and of ensuring a regular exchange of information on the
employment situation. It hoped, however, that such arrangements would
not prove exhaustive.[59] Furthermore the Council, acting unanimously
on a proposal of the Commission, was responsible for initiating appropriate action in the social security field so that migration might not be
impeded and in particular for the adoption of a system in which
established social security rights would be maintained and benefits be
payable within the territory of the Community.

Under Art. 50, states agreed to encourage the exchange of young
workers within the framework of a common programme. Unlike Art. 48,
however, this provision started slowly for it did not contain such detailed
instructions for development. It was limited to the broad statement of
principle and the first programme was not adopted by the Council until
May 1964.

Free movement of labour was not confined to wage-earning employment although the self-employed were dealt with separately and under
complicated provisions. On the one hand was the principle of the right
of establishment allowing individuals to set up on their own on the same
terms as nationals (Art. 52). This principle was to be progressively applied
through a general programme for the abolition of existing restrictions

accepted unanimously by the Council before the end of the first stage.

The treaty gave certain guiding lines for the application of this principle which is an important aspect of a system designed to establish genuine competition and to encourage industrial specialization. Priority treatment had to be given to those activities likely to make a particularly valuable contribution to the development of production and trade; people who had migrated as wage earners were to have the right to stay on to take up a non-wage-earning activity; members accepted the need to arrange for the right to acquire land and buildings and to abolish all practices preventing or restricting free establishment. Such a principle runs straight into questions of occupational entry and notably that of the relative stringency of qualifications for particular posts. It raises fundamental questions of the organization and degree of control exercised in branches of industry and in the professions and the treaty therefore demanded that national authorities extend their knowledge of existing conditions in which activities were carried out over the whole Community area in order to define the problems and deal with them with the necessary degree of competence. Activities involving government action were excluded, and national controls, exercised against foreigners for reasons of the public interest, security and health, were still permitted with the intention of bringing co-ordination between national rules through directives issued by the Council, acting unanimously on a proposal of the Commission and after consulting the Assembly, although as from the second stage of the introduction of the treaty system the Council might act on minor issues by qualified majority.

On the other hand were the articles dealing with services where restrictions on supply were to be progressively abolished during the transitional period (Art. 59). The purpose here was to cover those circumstances in which the provider of a service might live in one member state whilst the recipient lived in another. Examples are highly specialized consultancy services, whether of an industrial or professional nature.

Implementing directives for the programmes were to stem from the Council on a proposal of the Commission and after consulting the Economic and Social Committee and Assembly. Such directives were to be agreed unanimously during the first stage and thereafter by qualified majority vote.

The problems involved in executing the principles of the right of establishment and the right to supply services are clearly closely related and the two programmes were normally dealt with together by the institutions of the Community. However the wide range of activities involved, and the implications in the professional, business and agricultural fields, made these principles highly complicated in application and progress was slow.

The provisions affecting the labour force are clearly of the utmost importance for the development of social action. The treaty did not limit itself to the suggestion that the abolition of barriers to free movement, such as less attractive employment and promotion opportunities, inadequate protection against arbitrary dismissal or inability to benefit from services when unemployed or old, was a necessary expedient at a time of manpower shortage. Rather did Art. 48 imply that the elimination of discrimination was inherent in the type of free movement which the Community wished to encourage. Similarly the clauses concerning the self-employed and the supply of services implied far-reaching changes in national policies towards professional and business activity. The treaty, therefore, did more than establish the principle of a free labour market. It attempted to pinpoint the main barriers to its effective operation through the removal, in the first instance, of forms of discrimination based on nationality and the use of the national base as the unit for social security and for the exercise of self-employment. It accepted that free movement in such fields raised complex questions of education and training and the recognition of skills which could only be dealt with gradually. However, for many of these matters, decision depended upon a unanimous vote of the Council and therefore remained under effective national control.

In comparison with previous labour treaties, whether of a bilateral or multilateral nature, the provisions of the Rome Treaty appear as a more advanced form of international activity. Not only was it simpler to proceed by regulation than through the negotiation of new international agreements but, by adopting the principle of a free labour market as a positive goal, it elevated the principle of equality of treatment of alien workers with nationals and the adoption of measures designed to overcome the immobility of the working population to the imperative level.

Two economic sectors, namely agriculture and transport, were singled out for special attention in the treaty and, following the example of the Coal and Steel Community, social considerations were incorporated as a necessary ingredient of a common market and the creation of an effective Community policy in these fields. In each case the treaty accepted that the formulation of policy was more than a question of the simple dismantling of protective barriers and would include the establishment of development policies compatible with the wider framework of the EEC and which would necessitate consideration of broad social issues.

The European Community was established at a time when the size of farms and social structure of agricultural areas often remained typical of a pre-industrial age in which, despite heavy protection, rural incomes failed to keep pace with those earned in the towns and environmental, educational and social facilities in rural areas lagged seriously.[60] The creation of a common market in farm produce was to be paralleled by the creation of a set of marketing arrangements and the need to introduce a common agricultural policy by the end of the transitional period. Of fundamental significance for the well-being of the agricultural community was the acceptance of the belief that the efficiency of agriculture left much to be desired and demanded, *inter alia*, a smaller agricultural population and a more rational use of land. The scale of the problems involved in changing the structure of the agricultural population, improving the skills of the labour force and enlarging the scale of farming units meant that such developments would only occur gradually and would require the continuation of grant aid. Within such a context, however, the agricultural policy included the aim of ensuring a fair standard of living for the agricultural community especially through increasing earnings and emphasis was placed in the treaty upon the co-ordination of efforts for vocational training, research and the dissemination of technical knowledge.

Similarly, the treaty envisaged the creation of a single transport system based on common rules for international transport and the right of firms to operate on the territory of other members on agreed terms, provided the standard of living and employment levels of workers were protected. State grants might be continued under certain circumstances.

Regional policies have become increasingly important in industrial countries with greater realization of continuing severe disparities in living standards between areas within the national state. The experiences of the Coal and Steel Community drew attention to the concentration of socio-economic problems in particular areas due to their heavy dependence upon mining and ancillary occupations, and their influence is to be seen in the references in the Preamble of the Treaty of Rome to the need to diminish regional disparities and in the concept of equalization of living standards of Art. 117. Modern economic developments often appear to accentuate rather than diminish regional differences and the creation of a single trading area could be expected to increase this tendency by allowing even easier concentration of industry and population in the industrial heartland leaving peripheral areas such as south-west France or southern Italy to further decay. It 'seems safest to assume that the regional disparities produced by the operation of these forces in the past will increase rather than diminish'.[61] No specific section of the treaty was devoted to regional policy although it is a major field in which economic and social objectives merge closely with each other. There were, however, a number of references to regional issues. Certain clauses on agriculture have an applicability to the problem of regional disparities, notably the desire to obtain a fair standard of living for agricultural populations, the possibility of grant aid to farms handicapped by structural or national conditions or within the context of regional economic development programmes. Similarly, Art. 80 refers to the possibility that states should continue to protect their transport industries as a necessary part of regional economic policy or to cater for the needs of underdeveloped and other areas. Neither did the treaty necessarily forbid aid given by states to promote the economic development of regions where the standard of living is abnormally low or where there is serious unemployment or to develop regions or industries. The treaty also created a European Investment Bank to contribute to the balanced and stable development of the Community through helping to finance projects designed to aid the less developed regions, projects of modernization, conversion or development necessitated by the common market and which were beyond the internal facilities of the member states and projects of common interest to several members for which existing financial capacity was inadequate. The authors of the treaty were therefore keenly aware of the importance of the regional issue which bears an obvious and necessary relationship to the improvement of social well-being, although they stopped short of giving the institutions definite power to develop regional policies. However the recognition of the need for European, in addition to national, policies strengthens the suggestion that adaptation to economic and technological change, in order to ensure its utilization for the human goals of improvement, is a recognizable theme of the treaty.

These aspects of the treaty provide the foundations for the pursuit of social goals by the European Community and it can be seen from this brief discussion that these foundations are by no means fully comprehensive or clear-cut. The Preamble refers to the improvement of living and working conditions as the essential aim of the treaty, but its detailed provisions do not substantiate this claim. Art. 3 sets out those basic fields of action for the Community which are considered of outstanding importance and it bears no direct reference to social policy at all but only to the creation of the Social Fund to increase employment opportunities. Important as this is, it falls a long way short of the modern concept of the range of social need. However Art. 117, which presents the framework for the social policy of the treaty, despite its obscure meaning and lack of implementing procedures, clearly states the social goal of improved standards. Secondly, one may detect the thread of protection against the social costs of change which the treaty might be expected to exact which runs through the agricultural and transport policies, the possibility of state aids, the use of the Social Fund and the very conception of gradual transformation and adjustment which underlay the introduction of the new system. Finally, it seems proper to suggest that a more long-term philosophy of social concern lies behind the agricultural clauses and the recognition of the need for regional development.

The emphasis upon man in his working environment rather than upon the totality of his social needs is marked. It is found not only in the creation of the Social Fund but again in the interests listed in Art. 118. It is of great importance, too, to remember that Community responsibility here was to promote collaboration with, and between, members in the social field, not to elaborate a single Community policy in these matters for which direct powers of intervention did not exist. The role of the Community is better thought of as broadly educational and promotional; functions which could be developed both through the means listed in Art. 118 and supported by the information produced in the annual reports submitted to Parliament. Whilst, therefore, at a superficial reading, social policy might appear to have equality of place with other titles of the treaty, the system in fact protected itself against any argument that progress in one state or in one particular field should necessarily be generally adopted.

The Community had more strength where definite programmes of action were laid down. This is most obvious in the case of the free movement of labour whose importance was reflected in precise obligations and in the identification of three major social problems requiring solution in order to achieve a single labour market. These were the removal of discrimination, the creation of machinery for filling jobs and the maintenance of social security rights. A less compelling but still important programme related to the right of establishment and the supply of services. The creation of the Social Fund with definite responsibilities and the obligation to establish common principles of vocational training are further evidence of the seriousness of social purpose in particular respects.

It is clear, however, that there were different degrees of urgency in the treaty objectives which were to be pursued in a variety of ways; 'The treaty sometimes uses the supra-national and sometimes the inter-governmental method; sometimes Community rules and procedures apply and sometimes those which depend on inter-state co-operation.'[62] It seems that a partial vacuum was left by the treaty in the field of social affairs. In the main, this meant that member states retained great independence. Collaboration only was demanded of them under Art. 118, whilst equal pay and the maintenance of paid holiday schemes were responsibilities of members and were not subject to Community programmes. Similarly it was the application of members which activated the grant-aiding system of the Social Fund, although the Commission thereafter was a major determinant of action. Community policies themselves were, of course, subject to the delicate and complex balance established by the treaty whereby European decisions were a blend of national and Community interests, but even here the maintenance of the unanimity rule in the Council can be found in many social matters. Social security for migrant workers (Art. 51); the general programme for the establishment of the self-employed (Art. 54 (1)); directives to initiate the general programme during the first stage (Art. 54 (2));[63] the co-ordination of certain legislation under this programme (Art. 56 (2),[64] Art. 57 (2));[65] the giving to the Commission of duties to implement common measures (Art. 121); the new tasks for the Social Fund at the end of the transitional period (Art. 126); any proposal requiring the approximation of laws (Art. 100) and Council agreement on the justification of state aid (Art. 93), are all examples here.

Where little guidance was given by the treaty the onus was upon the Commission to create policies if anything was to be done. The institutions

> far from being merely the machinery for executing a series of technical measures, . . . form a dynamic element which will bring about the progressive approximation of national policies and, later, the application of a common policy. In this matter the Commission is assuming a special responsibility. It is an independent body capable of taking a broad, objective view of the Community's problems. As guardian of the Treaty, it is first and foremost responsible for thinking out and formulating the main lines of the action to be taken.[66]

It is important, therefore, that the Commission held the view that social policy was an end in itself, rather than a by-product of economic development, for which the Commission itself would be required to develop action, since the autonomous character of social policy is by no means obvious from the treaty and the discussions which led to it. The Commission's early policy statements were quite definite. It 'cannot conceive that the Community has not got a social purpose', whilst in the development of policy the key concept would be that of harmonization through raising the level of the lower and not through retarding the progress of the more advanced.[67] In any case it 'would be inconceivable for the Community to be created and to establish itself in an atmosphere from which social preoccupations were artificially excluded while in its six constituent States these preoccupations, in the widest sense, constantly played an important and growing role in their politics and economics'.[68] In similar fashion, the Commission argued for a progressive development on the basis of Arts. 117 and 118, together with a liberal interpretation of the latter, 'the problems listed in Art. 118 being in no way exclusive'.[69]

There was, therefore, considerable room left for tension in the social field between the members and the Community, notably with the Commission, and the social history of the Community has often shown this in operation. It was typical of this difference of approach that Signor Levi-Sandri, speaking to Parliament in 1965, should claim that Art. 118 did not mean that inter-governmental co-operation was the exclusive form of operation but that the Community must use the possibilities offered by other articles of the treaty.[70] The social policy envisaged by the treaty was a tender plant. Its practical limitation to labour questions, the provision of clear-cut policies only where these were intimately interwoven with economic demands and the continuing importance attached to the right of the national state to take decisions suggested that the European system did not obtain the ability to develop policies adequate to pursue its claim to further progress.

IV Co-operative Principles

The recognition that social policy, dealing as it now does with the broad needs of the population, must be able to draw upon knowledge of the views and aspirations of the people at large combined with the need to obtain support from the public, and particularly from European labour organizations, in order to ensure the effective working of the Community as an economic entity and to enable it to fulfil its potentiality as an instrument for moving towards a more integrated Europe. 'A dynamic social policy, not subordinate to other considerations of Community policy, is needed, not only to gain the support of all workers in the building of Europe, but also to . . . improve the living and working conditions.'[71] Unfortunately the practical expression of democracy in the form of an effective Parliament[72] did not follow and, on the score both of limited responsibility and of remoteness from the democratic process, a grave institutional weakness remained within the Community. Many had hoped that the Assembly of the ECSC, although originally little more than a symbol of the need to associate the people with the growth of the new Europe and of the determination to ensure democratic forms, would prove to be the embryo of a federal Parliament. One of the major criticisms of the European structure has always been the lack of power held by Parliament and the relatively little attention paid to the problem of extending its importance. However, its obligation to debate the reports on the activities of the Communities at least proved a means whereby knowledge about their working was spread amongst national parliamentarians and into national environments. Although its power was limited, Parliament nevertheless achieved a certain influence in the field of social affairs through the active use of the procedures available to it.[73] The ability to question the executive and to extract full oral or written replies was fully used whilst both the executive and Council possessed the right to attend meetings of Parliament and to speak if they so wished. The working groups and standing committees which produced written reports on a wide range of topics provided the main body of delegates with material upon which they could base their arguments and demands. They provided, too, a method of continuous contact with the work of the executive on a day-to-day basis since experts normally attended meetings to explain policies. In practice Parliament or its appropriate committee was often consulted in advance of decisions. This machinery was in constant use in the field of social affairs. Most important here were the active Social Affairs Committee[74] and the Committee on Health Protection, which amalgamated in 1967, but much discussion of social affairs inevitably took place elsewhere because of the social implications of other developments.[75] Through such contact and through its supply of material to Parliament, the Social Affairs Committee was able to exert constant pressure in favour of the extension of Community responsibility in the social field as, indeed, the executive wished to see. 'Wherever possible the Commission will obtain an opinion from the Assembly and will act on the suggestions made to it by this body concerning the preparation of reports and studies, as specifically laid down in the Treaty in respect of the social field.'[76] It would be wrong, therefore, to dismiss Parliament as negligible, for with the establishment of good working relationships and the willingness of the Commission to co-operate it played a more important part in policy formation than can be deduced from the treaty, whilst its function as a goad to action is well illustrated in the area of social policy.

Considerable attention was also given in the new system to the need to associate a wide range of interests with its operation. This was in any case a practical necessity, since national arrangements were not uniform, were inter-related with provisions lying outside the scope of the treaty and were dependent upon a complex interplay of issues and interests. Since so much of the work of the Community was necessarily indirect, its capacity to work with responsible institutions was to be essential. Neither could social decisions be practically sound unless formulated with the participation of those they were designed to benefit.

The Treaty of Rome continued the pattern established by the ECSC with an Economic and Social Committee designed to represent a wide range of occupational interests and modelled on the pattern of national economic councils.[77] It differed from the ECSC consultative committee, however, in that under the Treaty of Paris representative organizations put forward recommendations for membership whilst under the Treaty of Rome this duty lay with member states who presented to the Council a list of acceptable names from which the choice might be made. The Council was entitled to consult European organizations before making its choice but this was not done. The treaty allowed for the committee both to split into specialized sections[78] and to set up sub-committees. An important limitation on its activities arose from the fact that it was only activated by the reference to it of questions by the Council or the Commission, either in circumstances as directed by the treaty or by the general right to consult the committee whenever it appeared appropriate. Attempts to develop the status of the committee beyond the consultative by giving it a right of initiative met with no success. Furthermore, publication of its reports depended upon the decision of the two major institutions.[79]

Its field of coverage was nevertheless wide[80] and the committee was in practice often asked for an opinion on social matters when this was not legally necessary.[81] Furthermore, the practice of submitting both majority and minority opinions meant that the Council and Commission had a full spectrum of the views of a variety of economic and social interests.

The committee contained 101 members chosen so as to give equal representation to the employers, workers and the general interest.[82] Not only was personal standing high ('There are highly influential experts and representatives'),[83] but members sat as individuals receiving no instructions from their organizations although 'in practice they speak on behalf of the categories they represent',[84] thus cohesion within the committee occurred on the basis of interests and not nationality. Employers and the trade union members acquired the greatest degree of solidarity, whilst the general interest, representing such varied groupings as the farmers, the liberal professions and the consumers, found it more difficult to speak with a single voice and to achieve maximum effectiveness.[85] It was, therefore, valuable not because of its political strength but for its professional knowledge and its opinions, which, being recognized from the start as providing 'important food for thought',[86] both warranted and received serious attention.[87] Despite the obvious weaknesses inherent in its position stemming from its passive role and its limited representational basis, the committee retained its importance as a forum for the discussion of issues and as a means of bringing industry and labour into direct contact with Community developments.[88] It is by no means irrelevant to the development of firmer views concerning the nature of social policy that both Parliament and the committee proved their capacity to evolve views based on criteria other than the national interest.

On the other hand, the formal ability of the Commission to establish other means of communication with industry and labour was less certain and it will be seen that there were times when members objected to the efforts of the Commission to establish direct links. Since it possessed no independent income, no powers comparable to those of the High Authority to aid research, to insist upon information or to effect and publish studies, its position was necessarily more vulnerable than that of the earlier executive. A comparison of Arts. 118 and 152 of the Treaty of Rome with Arts. 46, 48 and 55 of the Treaty of Paris shows this clearly. The vacuum was filled by the multiplicity of pressure groups which established themselves in Brussels and by the creation of a series of advisory committees and working parties of both a tripartite and bipartite character, to which the Commission attached considerable importance. 'In the social field in particular, both sides of industry are consulted before the European Commission adopts the final text on any proposals in a problem of importance.'[89] The mutual interchange of views and information, the joint participation in discussion and the development of systematic co-operation constituted an attempt to inject a realistic note into the workings of the Community and at the same time operated as an informal check upon it. Right from the beginning, under the ECSC, intensive co-operation between the High Authority and national governments, employers' and workers' associations, consumer groupings and individual employers had been undertaken in order to get the system established.[90] The Commission, in its turn, continued to attach importance to constant meetings with experts, senior officials from national administrations, as well as to wider conferences in order to associate as many groups as possible with the work[91] and such arrangements, both formal and informal, went some way towards maintaining contact between the executives and broad currents of opinion. Despite these efforts, however, the European institutions remained in a position remote from the ordinary citizen in a way which appears particularly undesirable for social welfare policies whose purpose is to make an impact upon individual lives and which made the avowed purpose of the Commission to win support for the process of European integration more difficult.

The similarity of social thinking in the Paris and Rome Treaties is obvious. In the first instance, it may be said that the European Communities identified consequences of the process of economic integration for which they should carry certain responsibility as the converse of the attempt to direct economic life into alternative channels. A deliberate process designed to expose industries to unaccustomed competition could be expected to reveal not only weaknesses and inefficiencies but the effect on costs and patterns of production of tax and welfare systems developed within the national framework and ultimately related to forms of protection for particular social groups. The effect of the revelation of such differences in costs, although only a matter of speculation at the time of the creation of the Communities, the impact of the dismantling of economic barriers in particular industries or frontier areas, the long-term impact on occupational structure, production methods and industrial location were seen as matters requiring compensatory actions by the body instigating such changes however beneficial their ultimate impact on total material prosperity.

The acceptance of responsibility to provide a degree of compensation for such effects, and the recognition of inequalities at least as between regions and of the need to accept the pluralist nature of society are all broad social considerations which represent a transference to the Communities of concepts widely accepted within national states.

The European Communities did not receive a responsibility to control wage levels, but they were given a direct role to play in the improvement of industrial conditions both through the encouragement of research and the promotion of international collaboration. The Treaty of Rome, in particular, carried forward-looking goals of a promotional rather than compensatory kind. The importance of a high employment level was accepted, although this could have been put more forcibly, whilst the Treaty of Paris simply contained more general reference to the growth and continuity of employment. Other social goals, notably the free movement of labour, the development of occupational training policies and the provision of cash benefits for the working force were closely related to this end. The first of the goals stood in the Treaty of Rome in its own right as an extension of the concept to be found in the earlier system.

The most fundamental objective of both treaties was that of the improvement and equalization of living and working conditions, although neither treaty was sufficiently bold to develop techniques strong enough to deprive members of their autonomy in social affairs.[92] The encouragement of international collaboration in welfare matters, the pursuit of regional development and the recognition of sectoral policies were the principal methods foreseen, but as long-term, imprecise treaty themes rather than as concrete policies.

As far as can be ascertained, it seems possible that the main reason for the insertion of the principle of harmonization was the fear of certain employers and unions of low-cost competition. In fact, the weight of specialist opinion has always supported the view of the Spaak report that equality of costs is economically unnecessary in an international competitive system.[93] In general, it is not those countries with high wages and the more advanced forms of labour legislation that experience greatest difficulty in international competition in so far as such phenomena are associated with a productivity rate more than adequate to take care of the extra cost. 'Nowadays we know that the importance of differences in labour costs as factors affecting international competition has been greatly exaggerated, that by and large the high labour cost countries have not encountered any special difficulties in selling their goods abroad.'[94] Neither is there any clear indication from the statistics of ratification of the International Labour Code that much equalization of standards has occurred amongst states which are trade rivals.[95] Debates during the 1950s on the social implications of the desire to develop freer trading patterns in Europe generally agreed that there was no overall economic case for unifying the social charges imposed on employers or the number of hours worked. The ILO discussion on the matter felt that, in the absence of any move to equalize all tax burdens, it would be illogical to single out any particular cost, such as social security financing, for special treatment and possibly positively unwise to attempt to harmonize such payments without considering the broader economic effects of any new grouping.[96] In any case, so little was at that time known concerning the

relative burden of wages, social charges and taxation by industry throughout the common market area that it was impossible to determine the
effect of such differences on future trading patterns. States did not follow
identical policies concerning costs borne on the general revenue and the
capacity of employers to pass costs on in higher prices had also to be
considered.[97] The general conclusion of the ILO study was that the
creation of a free trading area did not of itself demand a uniform social
policy although 'important general social advantages would be attained,
if general agreement could be reached on certain broad principles of
economic policy' such as the approximate stability of national price
levels.[98] However special cases no doubt existed, such as the financing
of social security schemes for miners and the need for a transitional
period to allow the less efficient firm to adjust. 'An economy that has been
protected . . . for 100 years cannot open its frontiers at a single stroke.'[99]
Finally, certain workers would clearly suffer loss of employment and,
although this was not expected to be severe or on a large scale as a
result of the introduction of the common market, it was right that
compensation measures be undertaken.[100]

The experience of the High Authority, which helped to draft the
Treaty of Rome, bore out the arguments of the ILO. Its opinion was that
it was unnecessary to obtain prior harmonization of wage, labour and
taxation policies but believed the new treaty should be more flexible than
that of the ECSC in order to give the Commission room to manoeuvre in
order to find the necessary range of control.[101] The general view of the
time was that overall harmonization was not a pre-condition for economic
integration. Although the concept of equivalence of labour standards
was valuable, 'since common standards of social policy can help to
reduce the opportunities for unfair competition, give some security to
industries competing on world markets and (more generally) facilitate
economic integration and freedom of movement for capital, goods and
manpower,'[102] yet it cannot, in isolation from other common policies and
in the present state of knowledge, demand acceptance for reasons of
economic necessity although special problems requiring joint action may
be identified. Within the limits imposed by the obligation to ensure that
any increase in labour costs does not outrun that of productivity, 'there
does not seem to be any economic necessity for international harmonization of social policies in general'.[103] The overwhelming interest of the
time was in the presumed economic advantages the new system would
bring.[104] Neither was the Treaty of Rome as protective as the Paris
Treaty had been in that it contained no safeguards against wage cutting.
By implication it left responsibility to the trade unions to prevent adjustments to the new situation occurring through labour losses and gave
scope for greater union activity at European level to protect any group
against gross exploitation and to insist upon the abolition of anomalies

in the forms of labour protection then existing.[105]

In short, the treaty was given a limited view of social policy, did not always express it without ambiguity and left uncertainties for future resolution. Its dedication to social improvement did not incorporate adequate powers for the institutions to develop policies which would extend the scope of social competence beyond the field of working conditions or allow a growth of responsibility in those fields which had been identified as of proper concern. Although ideologically the Treaty of Rome was similar to the Paris Treaty, the conditions under which it was to operate were different. The ECSC was primarily concerned with the social problems presented by the declining fortunes of the coal industry and its creation was coloured by memories of unemployment and war. The EEC, on the other hand, was influenced by the excitements and possibilities of the creation of a larger economic unit prepared to accept the consequences of technological change and large-scale productive processes for the sake of higher productivity. Its scope was far larger for it affected the total population rather than the workers in two industries and the treaty itself contained provisions which were potentially far-reaching in scope. On the other hand, the capacity of the Commission to pursue social ends was more circumscribed than that of the High Authority through its lack of an independent income and the absence of a right to make contact with unofficial bodies, call for information or support research, whilst the imprecision of the terms in which much of the treaty was formulated was an inherent weakness. These factors meant that much of the effect of the new system in social affairs would be felt indirectly through the changes of attitudes which constant consultation and co-operation might effect with consequent adaptations of national structures.

The following account is essentially descriptive of the social tasks faced during the years from 1958 to 1972. Although the later years were preoccupied with the problems involved in the merging of the institutions of the ECSC, Euratom and EEC, with the completion of the customs union and the possibility of enlargement, yet the 1970s opened with real hope that social questions might become of greater significance to the European system than hitherto and be given the attention their complexity demands.

2 Employment

I Manpower in the EEC

One of the most striking social changes in the European Community area in recent years has been the increase of total population. By 1972 190·8 million people lived in an area whose population had increased by nearly 22 million since 1958.[1] Superficially this makes the group appear one of high population density whose urban people require similar, sophisticated services to maintain effective living standards, but in fact it displays significant differences in density, occupational structure, industrial strength and living patterns.

Whilst in 1958 there were 39·3 million young people under fifteen, by 1970 there were 46·1 million. Germany had over 3 million more, France over 1 million and Italy nearly 2 million more. Those over sixty-five had similarly increased. In 1958 17·46 million people had reached this age and by 1970 23·6 million. The elderly population in Germany had increased by 2·8 million, in France by 1·6 million and in Italy by 1·2 million. By 1972 young people constituted 24·1 per cent and the elderly 12·4 per cent of the total population. In contrast, the civilian labour force only grew from 72·36 million people in 1958 to 74·6 million by 1972 and as a percentage of total population had actually declined. It was a period, too, in which the labour force enjoyed conditions of high employment. An overall unemployment rate of 3·4 per cent for the Community in 1958 had become 1·4 per cent in 1969 although rising to 2·2 per cent in 1972. The most striking change was in Italy where an unemployment rate estimated variously between 6 per cent and 8 per cent in 1958 dropped to 3·7 per cent in 1972. Variations in regional rates remained important however. Districts such as the Saar, Lower Saxony, Bavaria, the Mediterranean areas, northern and south-western France, southern Italy, the north of Holland and the south-east of Belgium were particularly badly placed. High rates of juvenile unemployment were found in Italy, France and Belgium in 1970, whilst Germany and Belgium were troubled by unemployment amongst the elderly.

A noticeable feature has been the fall in the number employed in agriculture from 16·2 million in 1958 to 8·4 million in 1972. Whereas 20 per cent of the total working population was employed in agriculture in 1958, by 1980 the percentage may well be only 10 per cent. This fall has been matched by, and has largely caused, the decline in self-employment from 23 million in 1958 to 15·5 million in 1972, but it may be remarked that the growth of the tertiary sector is bringing some increase in self-employment of a different sort. Although only in Germany, Belgium and the Netherlands had over 80 per cent of the workers achieved employee status, the Community average for 1972 was 79·2 per cent. Great stress, too, was placed upon the need for workers with skills who could find employment in the new technological industries, in personal services and mechanized agriculture,[2] as the decline in mining, textiles, shipbuilding and similar old-established industries was matched by the growing demands in chemicals, mechanical engineering, electricity, plastics, motor-car and aeroplane construction and public administration. White-collar jobs increased in proportion to the whole. In the Netherlands they rose from 18·5 per cent of all jobs in 1955 to 27·1 per cent in 1967, whilst in Germany white-collar and civil service posts accounted for 29 per cent of jobs in 1950 and 34 per cent in 1968.

A dominating feature of the social landscape was that of manpower shortage, the number of known vacancies being estimated at over three-quarters of a million by the end of the 1960s and subsequently remaining at that level.[3] The general buoyancy of the economies, together with trends towards longer schooling and life expectation, helped to ensure both labour scarcity and a relatively small-sized working population in relation to dependent groups. Shortages were met by pressure to absorb groups on the margin of the labour force, notably women, by labour migration from outside the Community and from Italy to areas of demand as well as by changes in the occupational pattern. These phenomena in turn required greater consideration by public authorities and employers of social and human factors, including those connected with the assimilation of foreign workers and of measures to turn the available unskilled workers into trained personnel. For governments, therefore, it was very much a period which led them to appreciate that, beyond the well-recognized aims of avoiding mass unemployment and alleviating the particularly stubborn problems of the regions of declining industry, manpower requirements demanded attention to methods of achieving the 'optimal utilization of the labour force'[4] through improved organization and transparency of the labour market, measures to maintain economic growth and the promotion of occupational and geographical mobility.

The measures taken by governments during the 1960s to deal with the needs of the unemployed were noticeably more sophisticated than those adopted by states in Western Europe prior to the Second World War. Whereas in the past it had been difficult to do more than provide inadequate cash benefits for persons living in conditions of severe privation, the emphasis in recent years has been towards ensuring a reasonable adequacy of living standards through increasing the number of workers covered by income maintenance schemes, better benefit levels, longer periods of support, an increasing element of state assistance and help with re-employment through better labour placing and retraining facilities.[5] However, in order to take advantage of the existing opportunities, a high degree of mobility was often required, new skills had to be learnt and fresh family patterns established. Full employment did not necessarily mean the continuance of the same job, the opportunity to transfer to identical work or even vacancies in the same locality. Social and human problems thus acquired a new importance as part of the policy of maintaining the unemployed as members of society and their reintegration into the labour force. It must be remembered, too, that new opportunities were often beyond the reach of those who wished to work but who could not meet the ancillary conditions. The image of the mobile working man, not overburdened with family responsibilities and with infinitely adaptable skills, is highly unrealistic. It certainly does not fit the elderly, the worker with some degree of physical or mental handicap or the man with domestic responsibilities. Any public agency wishing to foster high levels of employment is inexorably driven to concern itself with a wide range of human problems and to develop the appropriate skills to enable it to do so. It requires detailed knowledge of industrial trends and job opportunities, and skilled assessment of training needs and of the capacity of individuals to undertake learning experiences; it may need to promote supportive social services to ease geographical if not occupational mobility and encourage flexible attitudes on the part of employers.

If, however, from the point of view of economic efficiency, the labour force is required to accept a high degree of mobility, from the human point of view it often has no wish to do so. One of the more difficult problems for any political authority to determine is the balance of wider job opportunities in places where reserves of labour still exist. The help given to workers to move can now be seen to contribute to scarcities of housing, educational and social services and to make heavy emotional demands on newcomers from agricultural areas or from abroad. Less attention has been given to the depopulation, imbalance of age and family structures and run-down of social facilities which result in those areas from which workers have gone, although the growing interest in job creation as part of regional development may bring greater awareness of social problems which are already acute.

Prior to the formation of the EEC, the decline of the coal mining areas had presented the question of support for labour mobility. States were compelled to find ways to soften the adverse consequences by introducing measures to find lodgings, help with removal costs, deal with the effects of family separation, maintain incomes at previous levels of earning or protect special social security benefits and holiday rights traditionally enjoyed by miners.[6] The Treaty of Paris enabled a good deal of help to be given for such measures, although it was a less effective instrument for bringing in work than for helping workers to move despite the belief of the High Authority that this was the wiser course. The Communities were no more immune than their members from the basic socio-economic dilemma that the aim of economic expansion often conflicted with social and human considerations by drawing workers into the areas of high concentration. If the Treaty of Paris reflected the assumption that this was the major solution to the problem of unemployment, the EEC Commission was early aware of the need to establish an equilibrium. It

> could not accept the principle of an employment policy whose implementation was likely to hinder both the general expansion of the economy and the economic and social progress of the regions and sectors affected by this expansion. Nor could the Commission accept a concept of economic and social integration under which the prosperity of certain regions and sectors would be paid for by an aggravation of the economic and social imbalances within the Community.[7]

The Treaty of Rome possessed neither a dedication to full employment nor a basis for a manpower policy. As the common market began to take effect under buoyant conditions it increasingly became obvious that the limited approach which had emphasized the absorption of unskilled labour, primarily through migration, was insufficiently sophisticated for the new conditions which had brought changes in the type of employment available, overfull employment in some areas and the continuation of unemployment in others. However, the habit of considering questions of demographic and industrial change on a supra-national rather than a national level did not at first exist, and it was 1967 before the first attempt at economic programming brought the concept of a European manpower policy into the forefront of serious Community debate. Until then the Community was more concerned to execute specific policies of labour mobility, job creation and vocational training as ends in themselves to fulfil the obligations of the treaty rather than as a coherent policy of manpower use. Both Parliament and the Economic Social Committee considered the treaty weak in this respect and urged the importance of Community efforts to ensure the full utilization of manpower.[8] If the process of monetary and economic integration develops it will become more difficult for states to pursue full employment independently and the need to transfer the obligation to the European level correspondingly more compelling. 'Full employment is valid for all or for none.'[9]

Thus the Commission found the expansionist economic philosophy of the Treaty of Rome inadequate by itself to deal with the manpower problems with which it was confronted. It was soon to be found stating that:

> In view of the existing imbalance on the labour market of the Community where, despite scarcities recently felt in some countries, structural unemployment and under-employment persist in certain regions and sectors, the Commission considers that it is essential to pursue an employment policy which can facilitate the harmonious development of economic activities and general economic expansion by means of various measures of a social nature.[10]

The severe unemployment problems in coal mining areas, the lack of opportunity in agricultural regions and the general slackening of employment opportunities which became increasingly obvious after 1965 reinforced the Commission's viewpoint. Such facts challenged the assumption that the creation of the European Communities would automatically improve employment and exposed the inability of the EEC itself to take economic measures to improve the employment situation. When challenged, the Commission could do no more than refer to the recommendations issued to states on guidelines for economic policy during 1967 in view of the decline in economic activity.[11]

The rise in the unemployment rate, however, prompted the Council to take more interest in labour matters. 1967 saw more attention being given to ways of improving co-operation between national employment exchanges.[12] On 29 July 1968 the six members agreed they must work more closely together to try to produce a better balance in the labour market since action by individual states was bound to have repercussions on other members. They considered unemployment rates might be lowered through more effective employment services, measures to improve mobility, more attention to vocational guidance and occupational training and a greater variety of aid directed to the unemployed themselves. In consequence they accepted the need for a drive at Community level to improve knowledge about employment rates by sector, to establish uniform job definitions and Community statistics, to prosecute the free movement policy and to broaden the use of the social fund to aid retraining and geographical mobility.[13] Considerable anxiety concerning unemployment problems was expressed by Parliament in the spring of 1972.[14] It was closely connected with the realization that the incidence of unemployment was very unevenly spread over the Community, with Italy and France bearing by far the greater share and a high proportion concentrated amongst young people.[15] Job loss amongst migrants meant that, although they theoretically had equal rights to help from the host country, in practice they often returned home thus swelling the ranks of the unemployed in the areas of traditional emigration.[16]

In a longer perspective, however, the over-riding characteristic of the period was one of labour shortage. Although by the end of 1971 there were 2·1 million unemployed compared with 1·7 million a year earlier, this was still a considerably better rate than when the Community was set up in 1958 and the emphasis which was being given to questions of dislocation such as redundancy, lack of alternative employment in areas of industrial decline and of under-employment in agriculture rather than to absolute unemployment figures was a reflection of a generally more sophisticated and complex situation. Economic necessity encouraged states and employers to look at manpower as a single Community entity as it became a bottleneck to expansion. This was the background for the progress of the Community from its exercise of responsibility to operate treaty clauses designed to bring offers of, and requests for, work together or to ensure the abolition of discrimination against free movement of labour to a realization of the need to assess future labour requirements and to consider the exploitation of Community reserves, their training and effective use.[17]

The EEC began life with a lack of familiarity with the notion of a European labour force and with little knowledge of the facts in each individual country. It was in a position, however, to study industrial trends over the whole area and to draw attention to developments taking place between regions and economic sectors both through its own studies and in conjunction with national labour officials, individual experts and representatives of trade unions and employers' federations. The Commission therefore began to consider the possibility of preparing manpower forecasts with suggestions of how to meet problems of shortages and the difficulties of under-employment. It also saw the need to study the practical measures involved in issues of vocational training, regional development and mobility of manpower, so that much of the Commission's work during the period was confined to essential groundwork such as studies of the decline in agricultural employment, rates of increase in other sectors, under-employment, regional disparities, problems of the building, textiles, shipbuilding and electrical engineering industries, the employment of women as well as of the functioning of national labour exchanges. Its reports on the manpower situation repeatedly drew attention to the need for vocational training and retraining, for states to give encouragement to firms to settle where labour reserves existed, to labour transfers, mobilization of labour reserves and the problems of employing foreign labour.[18] Parallel activity, it thought, would be needed to adapt the work of national employment exchanges so that the collection and use of employment statistics might be standardized and improved and uniform job classifications adopted in order to improve knowledge of the employment situation. Additionally it would be necessary to use procedures for the filling of vacancies which would express the growing reality of the Community labour market. Better notification of jobs and of the unemployed at regional, national and European level was required and more knowledge about the operation of the members' employment services. Detailed collaboration between labour exchanges was thus necessary which the Commission called for in its manpower reports and was able to encourage to a limited extent in the form of joint discussions on matters such as forecasting methods, the use of computers for information processing, job classification and joint studies of manpower problems.[19]

In February 1960 a specialist working party was set up whose report remarked on the labour shortages of Germany, Luxembourg and the Netherlands and the reserves still existing in Italy.[20] It suggested the possibility of short training courses for adults, of about four to six months duration, as well as improvements in arrangements made for migrant workers. It emphasized that the future was likely to be one of labour shortages with wide divergencies in employment opportunities between areas.[21] It was the first medium-term economic programme of 1967, however, which marked the formal recognition of manpower as an element in economic development for the Community area. During that year the Council approved a plan to improve collaboration between the members through the use of more effective methods for the exchange of information, joint discussion of problems and increasing the work of analysis and comparison of national training programmes for employment officials and exchanges of trainee personnel. At the same time it agreed that in future it would hold regular meetings to discuss labour trends within the Community on the basis of the Commission's reports on manpower.[22] This did not, however, entirely meet the dissatisfaction with the lack of importance traditionally shown by the Council to employment questions and a number of moves were made to improve communication between employers, unions and the Community. In November 1969 the Commission held a conference with unions at Luxembourg. The same month formal recognition was given to the French and Italian Communist union organizations which thus began to participate in Community affairs for the first time whilst, somewhat reluctantly, the Council agreed to call a general conference on employment to be attended by governments, the Commission, employers and unions.[23] This took place the following April and effectively established the principle that national employment policies must be brought more closely together. The importance of associating employer and worker organizations with developments was recognized by the Council decision of May 1970 to create a consultative standing committee on employment as a continuing forum for co-operation in order to ensure that the need for studies, better forecasting and proper attention to vocational training should not in future be so easily overlooked.[24] It was expected that the committee would be an important means of ensuring that problems of employment received their proper attention as the measures for economic and monetary union were introduced, thus repairing a major structural and conceptual weakness in the original arrangements.[25] The Commission, in particular, attached considerable significance to this move as a way of bringing an improvement in the former patchy methods of consultation and of encouraging members to consider employment policies as part of their wider schemes for sectoral and regional development.[26] By the end of the period it had moved into a position of arguing for the adoption of an active employment policy. Specific elements therein included the need to prevent the aimless return of the unemployed migrant, the creation of jobs in peripheral and single industry areas to prevent forced migration and a consideration of employment questions when Community decisions for industry, agriculture or the regions were under consideration.[27] Specific proposals for common rules to be followed by members in the case of redundancy were formulated subsequently, with the aim not only of helping individual workers in times when firms ran into difficulty but of starting to enforce common standards on multinational companies.[28] These suggested that firms should be obliged to notify public authorities in advance of dismissals of more than ten workers and to consult with union representatives when such a policy was being discussed. Public authorities should then be able to insist upon a delay in the dismissals to allow employment services time to find new jobs and to apply for aid from the social fund. If the dismissal of over fifty workers was contemplated, more stringent rules were suggested including a phased programme. Proof of the need to eliminate jobs, the giving of adequate notice, of proper consultation and sufficient protection for the disabled worker were included.

Although the formulation of an effective manpower policy had thus only just begun to develop, a great deal of attention was devoted in earlier years to those specific questions recognized as important at the time of signature of the treaties. Of these, far and away the most important was the policy designed to effect the free movement of labour (see chapter 4). This provided the basis for the Community's *entrée* into manpower questions and the establishment of the concept of a common labour policy. If in the early years this could be seen as making a contribution to fuller employment by removing the obstacles to labour migration, it did much to demand uniformity of job classification, better collaboration between employment exchanges and to show the need for knowledge about migration rates in different industries, potential demand, the importance of different types of skills and for speedy and efficient methods of notification of vacancies and available labour. Questions such as the nature of qualifications required for particular posts, the desirability and practicability of their standardization or the possibility of improving existing labour reserves to meet the jobs available became issues inevitably raised as a consequence of the free movement policy. The obligation to ensure that employment services were in a position to meet the demands for labour at a national and a Community level and to co-ordinate their work perhaps provided some substitute for a common employment policy.[29]

At the same time, labour movements showed up the one-sidedness of considering migration without paying due attention to problems of regional development, the limitations on the structure of the social fund which prevented it from favouring measures to improve job opportunities on the spot[30] or of giving sufficient help to training schemes. Inadequately qualified labour was not effectively available for many of the vacancies, so that a major question recognized by the Commission in 1958 was the role it might play in the development of vocational guidance and training schemes.[31] The following section is devoted to this question. Here it is sufficient to suggest that an effective employment policy must give some thought to occupational training to ensure its match with industrial changes and that not only young people but those already working, who wish to move into skilled jobs or up-date existing qualifications, are adequately provided with courses and maintenance. The development of skilled work meant that matching particular vacancies to particular individuals was becoming more necessary, so that the provision of vocational guidance, a facility in which labour exchanges have traditionally been lacking, came to be seen by the Commission as one which it should encourage. Successive steps were taken through comparative studies of systems, a joint conference of government experts held in 1962, a programme for collaboration between national authorities and, finally, a recommendation to states in 1966 arguing the case for close Community co-operation in order to obtain improvement in services.[32] Such measures did not constitute a fully European system. They fell into the category of close collaboration between national systems dedicated to a larger and common end. The importance of this should not be under-estimated as increased contact between national institutions, greater experience in co-operation, the growing uniformity in job definitions and statistical classification, valued for their practical worth, helped to create a habit of thought prepared to share the responsibility of maintaining stability and high employment levels with European institutions, which is likely to become more necessary in the future if labour movements continue to increase.

II Occupational Training

The progressive application of the principle of the free movement of labour and the growing familiarity with the concept of a European manpower policy both suggest that it would have been logical had occupational training policies possessed a central position in the social activities of the European Community. In fact this was not so. It was not that their importance went unrecognized by the Commission, but that the treaty had not given them sufficient attention. The Commission, as the High Authority before it, was fully conscious of the need to develop policies designed to improve existing training levels and to make mobility within the area more possible, not in isolation from the work of the members but by giving more effective expression to the growing concern of industry and of national governments with questions of vocational training. The treaty did not enable the executive to exploit fully what it believed to be the opportunities of the time.

The demands made by modern industry on human beings do not only compel it to pay more attention than was once necessary to ways of recruiting and maintaining an efficient labour force, but carry the implication that any community concerned to ensure employment opportunities must accept the responsibility to provide the means of acquisition of those skills without which men cannot secure or maintain a place in the working force. 'A possible employment policy, which is closely linked to a medium term economic programme, is largely conditioned by occupational training suitably adapted to current needs.'[33] The consequent involvement of firms and public authorities in training procedures has wide ramifications. At one time vocational training could be viewed as a once-for-all process at the point of initial entry into the labour market. Relatively few workers moved into supervisory posts and the problems thus presented could be overcome by short training courses. Today training is becoming more of a continuous activity as new technical developments demand periodic re-education or the need for workers to move into new specialisms. More than technical skills, however, is often needed nowadays, for new jobs may require the ability to plan and to organize work rationally or contain supervisory, management or teaching responsibilities. The activities required by this new situation can make more sophisticated demands on human beings and mean that, in addition to teaching technical skills, industrial training is likely to be more concerned than before with the process of developing the human personality. In turn, these changes mean the adoption of new teaching techniques dependent upon the involvement of the student, particularly if he is adult, rather than reliance upon older, didactic methods of instruction. This broader conception of industrial training does not fit comfortably into the traditional view of it as an adjunct to a firm's main role, which sometimes meant that it was given but a grudging existence to comply with legal requirements. Nowadays training is often an undertaking essential for efficiency whose cost is likely to grow[34] and in which the educational system, with the financial support of the public authorities, no less than industry is involved. In this way industrial training can be considered as a force which stimulates social and cultural change for, as standards of skill rise, training facilities tend to become more obviously linked with educational processes aiming at the wider development of the human being. The Commission's interpretation of policy followed this line of reasoning.

> Finally, in an action of this scope, the qualitative improvement of the labour force will imply a coherent effort for the cultural improvement of the whole social milieu extending far beyond the field of occupational training in the strictly technical sense. This is a task which by its very nature cannot be dissociated from fundamental changes in living and working conditions.[35]

By this argument the Commission asserted its right to participate consciously in a process which it believed was contributory to the broad stream of equality of opportunity and not merely to the Treaty of Rome.

> The aim of these proposals [of the common vocational training policy] is to give people the desire and the means, through improved methods of teaching, to exercise and develop their abilities, to make full use of their vocational capacity and to profit intellectually, morally and socially from their work. . . . This common activity is of special importance to agriculture.[36]

All states in the Community had a long-standing interest in questions of vocational training particularly in relation to the young worker. In recent years they have shown 'a unanimous agreement on the necessity for a renewed effort, from both the public and the private sector, in the field of the vocational training of labour'.[37] Systems of training varied considerably, however, particularly in relation to the question of whether they should be seen as an educational or an industrial responsibility. At one extreme was Germany, where the training of most adolescents was the responsibility of the employer, who provided a well-organized and understood training experience supplemented by part-time school instruction. At the other was Belgium, where most occupational training was carried on in educational institutions, both public and private, as an extension of full-time education with an industrial or technical emphasis. French arrangements, although relying heavily upon the educational system, lay within these two extremes. Artisanal occupations maintained an apprenticeship system, but the majority of young people entering industry and commerce attended schools to which employers made a financial grant. Training for agriculture was the responsibility of the Minister of Agriculture and adult training centres of the Minister of Social Affairs.

A fundamental issue of the 1960s was the question of whether the greater flexibility demanded by modern industry requires that young people in future should receive a more thorough grounding in the fundamentals of their trade with the expectation of using this as the basis of more specialized training throughout working life. France, in particular, has laid great stress on the importance of a general level of training upon which more specific instructional courses may be built according to particular occupational requirements and which will enable workers to change careers during their working lives. The argument has been that each person should have 'a totality of general or technical knowledge sufficient to impart to their vocational training the necessary character of polyvalence, because of the constant changes taking place within employments'.[38] The introduction in 1962 of the *Certificat d'aptitude professionelle* (CAP) for the 'general mechanic' qualified to take one of a variety of jobs gave practical expression to this view.

In addition public policies were turning towards accelerated vocational training (AVT) for adults. This is essentially concerned to train unskilled or semi-skilled workers to undertake more specialized activities and a considerable development of such programmes occurred. 'Originally planned as a means of meeting temporary and occasional emergencies, AVT is now widely regarded as an important element in a manpower policy aimed at full employment and a balanced labour market.'[39] These schemes, too, had different administrative patterns and policies concerning examinations and certification, but normally provided grant aid during training. All experienced considerable difficulties in finding enough instructors, who themselves need frequent retraining in order to keep in touch with the latest industrial processes. One example of the recognition of the importance of adult retraining is to be found in the French legislation of 1963 which created a supreme employment committee to advise the Minister of Labour on matters of retraining and placement for both areas and jobs threatened by serious disequilibria in opportunities and in labour supply. At the same time, new allowances were introduced for workers who required retraining after redundancy or who needed aid with resettlement costs. Special allowances were introduced for the over-sixties.[40]

A further growth area in the field of occupational training was that of vocational guidance, whose importance is closely related to the development of specialization of work content, more frequent job mobility and greater awareness on the part of individuals of the opportunities that are available to them. It is not just that people now require more individual counselling in order to match their abilities and aspirations to the appropriate job. It is also increasingly difficult to obtain effective and up-to-date information about careers and training opportunities, so that advisory schemes with various functions are being incorporated into employment services. 'Vocational guidance has developed, particularly in more recent years, in the context of national policies for education, vocational training and employment.'[41]

The fall in the agricultural labour force was a particularly obvious example of the need to retrain workers for other types of work as well as to provide those remaining on farms with mechanical skills. Legislation in both France and Germany was devoted to this end.[42] Meanwhile the lengthening of educational life, attempts to improve the quality of instruction as well as the growing number of jobs in middle management were creating a demand for vocational training which would match the higher expectations of the trainees and devote more attention than hitherto to the development of personal qualities rather than concern itself exclusively with the inculcation of technical skills.

The provision of effective opportunities for occupational training thus represents a field in which the economic and social objectives of the European system had a great deal in common. The free movement of labour, the exchange of young workers, the improvement in the standard of living, the maintenance of employment levels and the harmonization of social policies all demanded consideration of this issue. Discussion on a Community basis was encouraged by the growing interest in economic forecasting and by the recognition that manpower was likely to be a limiting factor on economic growth. The generally high level of employment and the demand from industry for the skilled worker turned attention to the possibility of finding ways to absorb the remaining numbers of those unemployed through lack of jobs, who were marginal to the labour market or who required training or retraining as an initial step towards employment. The readaptation programmes submitted to the High Authority in its early years at once showed up the importance of training as a means towards re-employment[43] and later experience confirmed this.

The economic drive towards effective utilization of labour provided some compensation for the lack of direct commitment to full employment as a social goal of the European system in its effect upon the establishment of occupational training policies. Possession of a job remains a key requirement for human satisfaction and, although recognition of this fact was but implicit or partial in the treaty, the Commission did not fail to recognize the importance of the employment situation from the human viewpoint. 'Employment is probably the major problem of social policy. It is not only a question of ensuring a job to all workers but of providing the means of appropriate vocational training and, indeed, of ensuring the stability of employment.'[44] Since modern industry increasingly demands skilled labour, the development of industrial training policies, whether for the young entrant or the retraining of the worker in middle life, for dealing with the special problems of the married woman, the elderly or the physically handicapped should be significant as a means of maintaining and stabilizing employment and of contributing to the general standards of the working population; 'The common policy of vocational training will in the future be an essential factor in the achievement of the basic social ideal underlying the treaty, namely to move towards a constant improvement in the living and working conditions of the people.'[45]

Severe disparities in training levels are bound to prove an obstacle to labour mobility, may well affect adversely policies designed to improve employment opportunities in lagging regions and can play their part in maintaining variations in living standards. From an early stage the Commission began to stress the importance of occupational training to the general economic development of the Community and to the achievement of balanced regional developments. 'From this angle, a common policy on occupational policy training must necessarily be considered as the linch-pin of the Commission's future action in the social field.'[46] The *Action Programme* of 1962 also singled it out for special comment.

> The Commission attaches fundamental importance to the implementation of the common policy . . . [This] will also enable a common employment policy to be defined and put through. As things are at present . . . an effective policy on vocational training, co-ordinated with other Community action (social fund and freedom of movement), will exercise a decisive influence on the geographical and occupational mobility of labour within the Community.[47]

The development of skills is, at first sight, closely related to another objective of the treaty system, namely the establishment of the free labour market. The persistence of labour shortages during the period led to the search for workers, either trained or trainable, and encouraged interest in appropriate training schemes. However, it is now clear that such measures are not in themselves sufficient to overcome the severe social, cultural and linguistic barriers to mobility. Experience under the Treaty of Paris, which linked the notion of the international labour market to the provision of definite skills, demonstrated that the number of those ready to take advantage of the new arrangements was in practice very small.

Despite the publicity given to problems of migration, a perspective must be maintained. In 1965 the percentage of EEC nationals in relation to the total of employed persons was about 2 per cent in France, 2 per cent in Germany, 3·5 per cent in Belgium, 0·5 per cent in the Netherlands and 24 per cent in Luxembourg.[48] In 1967 the total labour force of the Community was 74 million but the number of new work permits issued to its citizens for work elsewhere was 111,361.[49] Thus, although the growing interest in trained labour from beyond the frontier meant a greater realization of the need to look at the differing standards of qualification recognized for jobs of particular grades, in numerical terms the period suggested that work to improve training levels may be less important in encouraging labour mobility than in creating the possibility of modernization and change at local, regional or national level.

The major reference to occupational training in the Rome Treaty was the direction to the Council to formulate the general principles for the implementation of a common policy capable of contributing to the harmonious development of the economies both of individual states and of the common market. It also figured in Art. 118 as a matter for collaboration and in Art. 41 as a means of developing a common agricultural policy, but was not specifically mentioned as a means of promoting free movement of labour, the exchange of young workers or of ensuring a high level of employment. There was thus no systematic consideration in the treaty of the close inter-relationship between occupational training and its broader goals.[50] The meaning of Art. 128 was in any case unclear. Although the Council was directed to determine general principles, by the use of majority voting, nothing was said about the extent to which they should be binding, about their implementation or whether the execution of a common policy should be placed in the hands of Community institutions or left to members. Neither was the extent to which the Social Fund might be used to develop occupational training obvious from the treaty. As will be seen in section IV of this chapter, the grant-aid provisions under Art. 125 were narrowly drawn and the legality of the right given to the Council under Art. 1 of Regulation 9 to allot to the fund schemes designed to implement Art. 128 remained untested.[51] Controversy concerning such issues hampered the introduction of Community policies.

Vocational training was, however, recognized as important in the development of the common agricultural policy. The objectives under Art. 39 included the optimum utilization of factors of production, including labour, and the need to ensure the agricultural population a fair standard of living and an increase in individual earnings. Under Art. 41 provision was made for an effective co-ordination of effort in the spheres of vocational training, research and the spread of technical knowledge, including the joint financing of projects. For many years, however, the Community interest in agriculture was almost exclusively concerned with the adoption of price structures to the neglect of modernization and reform. It was not until 1972 that it began to take seriously the possibility of encouraging the amalgamation of small farming units and easing the transition of farmers either into retirement or into other forms of employment.[52] Advisory services for farmers are to be built up and the Agricultural Guidance and Guarantee Fund permitted to contribute a proportion of the cost of training and employing advisers as well as of the cost of training farmers themselves, although it is expected that the reformed Social Fund will ultimately take over the second function.

Recognition of the importance of vocational training determined the Commission to begin at once to encourage the exchange of information and to collect material concerning national training systems in order to formulate a European policy. On 3 October 1961 a first proposal was sent to the Council for discussion.[53] It argued that the justification for a policy of occupational training was not solely the response to the demands of industry but a means of encouraging the general and intellectual development of the individual. To meet such needs, vocational training policies should be of an advanced and comprehensive nature no longer allowing an artificial break between the ending of general education and the beginning of occupational training, but designed to establish close links between the educational and training systems. Opportunities throughout working life should be provided and every worker offered a chance of advancement. 'The progressive approximation of standards . . . must equip workers with equivalent skills so that they can pursue their trades in any country of the Community.'[54]

These general principles were set out as the broad guidelines for members upon whom they would be binding. However, the document did not in any way envisage a standardization of arrangements and accepted that the modes of implementation of the principles would be left largely to the discretion of members, whose schemes would necessarily be adapted to the occupational standards actually operative in different regions and industries. The document urged the need to survey future labour requirements in different sectors of industry both within members and within the Community itself, drew attention to the shortage of vocational guidance facilities and the importance of increasing the number of better qualified instructors. The general principles should also serve as the basis for the development of concerted, and indeed common action under the stimulus of the work of the Commission. The proposals hoped for some ironing-out of levels of training, examinations and curricula through more contact between those operating national systems and considered that curricula for teacher training might well be harmonized. In these ways, levels of training would be brought progressively into line, a series of occupational monographs could be published and reciprocal recognition of qualifications established. Specific European action could be taken to deal with special problems of widespread concern, such as training for farm and transport workers, provisions for special skills or special groups such as women, the handicapped, the young workers on exchange programmes, supervisory grades, teachers in training and the provision of vocational, linguistic and social preparation for migrant workers, perhaps through modern organizations. Such special programmes would require joint financing.

The draft claimed an important role for the Commission whose responsibility it would be to determine the priority of objectives, to follow up their implementation and to ensure their effective co-ordination. An on-going programme of study and research should be established and the Commission should collect and disseminate information which members should be obliged to supply. It should have the right to take any special steps necessary for specific occupations with labour problems, with the active participation of members and would assist in the work of manpower forecasting and the harmonization of training standards. The draft recommended that the Commission should be aided by an Advisory Committee with equal representation of national administrators, employers' organizations, existing bodies responsible for vocational training programmes and trade unions.[55] Nevertheless, it did not clear up all confusions. It remained uncertain how widely the proposals were intended to range both in coverage of workers and course content, whilst the major question of whether the principles were legally binding was still unsettled although the Commission argued that they must commit states so that, although members would retain a wide freedom of action, in the long term there would necessarily be progress towards greater uniformity.[56]

After discussions by Parliament and the Economic and Social Committee and further debate by the Council, the proposals were finally adopted on 2 April 1963 in compromise form. Main discussion had revolved around the problems of the extent of the Commission's competence in implementation and the joint financing of agreed projects.[57] The Commission and Italy alone took a strong European line. They argued that Community institutions should be at least partially responsible for executive action and that the Commission should therefore have the right to submit proposals to the Council which should result in regulations or directives. Since these would automatically be applied, they would ultimately be an effective way of creating a Community system. France, Germany and Belgium, on the other hand, argued that all members must first agree before common action was undertaken and that the Council had no power to draw up implementing devices. Agreement was ultimately reached that the Commission might propose appropriate measures to the Council or to members, but the suggestion that Community procedures should be used in order to implement such proposals was not adopted. France and Germany were also antagonistic to the Community financing of occupational training projects. The Benelux group believed the future possibility of this should be provided for and only Italy, together with the Commission, was in favour of immediate action.[58] In consequence the reference in the final text to joint financing was extremely cautious.

The final principles[59] thus represented a considerable watering down of the original proposals. They were, in the main, a victory for national autonomy, showing that states were not prepared at that stage to envisage a significant transfer of power to the Community. Their exact standing remained somewhat obscure.[60] Whilst in content they went further than a mere declaration of intent and may 'be considered as having been adopted',[61] they yet did not provide the basis for a uniform policy. They applied to all those in gainful employment, including the self-employed, to the training of new entrants, the retraining of adults and to all posts up to the level of middle management. Here the programme was more limited than that of the ECSC, whose work had no ceiling of job competence, neither was a precise definition of middle management provided. Employers had opposed the broad scope of the first draft, being anxious to confine training standards to the lower grades, and the issue remained unsettled.[62] Training, it was stated, should enable everyone to make full use of his abilities, be broad enough to help to develop his capacities generally, encourage him to achieve the maximum development of which he was capable and make him free to choose occupation, employer, place of training and of work. It should not entail a harmful interruption between general education and vocational training; should encourage retraining at different stages of a worker's career, establish close relations between different kinds of occupational training and ensure that the various sectors of productive life are associated with the development of training schemes. Forecasts of the number, and type, of workers required were recognized as necessary, as was the need for permanent information, guidance and advisory services for the labour force. Such services would need to be provided in ways of which people could take advantage.

The policy recognized that actual programmes would be drawn up and implemented by the members. 'When speaking of a common training policy, we do not have the intention of creating a uniform system of training in the member countries.'[63] Nevertheless the Commission was specifically given the right to propose measures, to collaborate closely with members in the production of studies and in research projects to ensure that the common policy was put into effect and to promote employment opportunities and labour mobility. It also had the right to consider what vocational training measures were used, to make recommendations to members concerning them, to encourage the signing of bilateral and multilateral agreements and to undertake follow-up studies. It was also responsible for ensuring an effective exchange of information so that teaching methods and training remained up to date. Members agreed to assist the Commission to obtain the necessary information for such purposes. The Commission was also made responsible for promoting the direct exchange of experiences and for arranging visits and seminars.

The principles recognized the importance of adequate training for teachers and supervisory staff and members agreed to take action to eliminate deficiencies. Attempts at harmonizing instructor training were to be made and special attention given to measures to obtain better qualified staff in less favoured areas and in the associated states.

The common policy was aimed at a gradual narrowing of differences in training levels, and the Commission agreed to draw up a summary of requirements giving access to different levels of training by occupation with the intention of reaching the stage of mutual recognition of qualifications. Members and the Commission agreed to support the notion of European competitions and tests. Members and the Commission might join together in drawing up programmes particularly directed to accelerated training for adults to meet changes in occupational and regional requirements. Particular attention should be paid to special problems and steps to execute the objectives of the common policy might be financed jointly.[64]

On the basis of this statement of principles, the Commission drew up a general action programme in addition to one for agricultural workers as a group requiring special attention. By October 1964 these programmes had been submitted to the Advisory Committee, endorsed by it the following March, thereafter adopted by the Commission and sent to the Council for information.[65] Considerable emphasis was placed on consultation procedures and on the exchange of experience as a means of obtaining greater uniformity in standards of training, developing exchange schemes and helping to improve teacher training. Subsequently the Commission developed an active programme of visits, seminars, studies and documentation of its own as well as supporting nationally arranged activities.[66] In 1964 it recommended that customs duties should not be levied on educational material imported for use in training courses and in July 1966 a further recommendation dealt with the need to improve vocational guidance services.[67] This argued for the development of free public services, which should be easy to use, supplied with adequate staff and finance and recognize that guidance is not an isolated operation but a service that workers may need to use on several occasions. It pointed out that rural areas were often particularly badly served and urged co-operation between national services to exchange information on facilities provided for the young worker, for adults and for migrants.[68]

The drive in the early 1970s towards more effective employment opportunities reawakened interest in common vocational training standards. A new set of guidelines was accepted by the Council on 26 July 1971[69] which was intended to allow the Commission to develop more precise programmes to encourage training suitable for modern industry and to assist specific programmes to help workers in backward regions. It appears to see one of the major tasks of the Community as being to help with the improvement of teaching techniques and of the supply and quality of teaching staff as well as with an active information service.

At the start of the vocational training programme the Commission had been instructed to draw up lists showing the requirements for entry into training at different levels. It decided to start first on jobs within the building and certain metal-working trades where migration was significant, known shortages existed and where existing trainings and skills were thought to be similar. Progress towards the alignment of standards, however, proved very slow, not least because of the growing interest in polyvalence which, since it stressed the common elements of different, but related, occupations as the basis for training, tended to be unfavourable to the establishment of common standards trade by trade. By 1970 the only occupation for which the Commission had managed to establish a European base was that of skilled machine-tool operator in metal-working trades. After long discussion this was sent to the Council in 1969 and approved the following year. A recommendation was sent to states on 29 September 1970.[70] The aim was to establish basic training and proficiency standards which members might use as a guide for their own training levels and accept as deserving of recognition if obtained elsewhere. Members were asked to keep the Commission regularly informed of their actions. It was hoped that the scheme would serve as a 'basic prototype for methods of alignment and reciprocal recognition'[71] but further action has been extremely limited. Whilst studies of possible minimum standards of training have been undertaken in building, transport and agriculture, no definite decisions have been taken although the importance of the alignment of training levels was reiterated in the 1971 guidelines.

Experience with crash training programmes was largely confined to the need to use foreign labour to fill immediate shortages of manpower, but the Commission had little more concrete achievement to show than the High Authority had previously. In October 1960 a special working party of government experts met in Rome to establish a programme of rapid training for Italian workers. A scheme to train 9300 workers to fill vacancies in France, West Germany and the Netherlands, mainly in building and metal processing, was agreed upon. The Italian government reserved places in its occupational training centres and the receiving countries and the social fund bore part of the cost.[72] Few of the workers migrated for they obtained jobs in the north of Italy where most of them preferred to go. In 1965 the Commission made another attempt. On 30 June[73] it submitted to the Council a scheme to train 3000 Italians for work in the Community, mainly in the building, metallurgy and hotel industries, on the basis of joint financing under principle 10 of the vocational training policy. The suggestion met with grave difficulties[74] and was finally accepted only as a matter for inter-state agreement which members could finance individually. An opportunity to establish a precedent thus foundered on the unwillingness of states to finance programmes from which they did not expect to benefit and their greater readiness to accept inter-governmental rather than Community action.[75]

III Exchange Schemes

Under Art. 50 members became committed to develop exchange schemes for young workers. This principle sprang in part from the belief in such visits as a means of creating a European consciousness[76] but was favoured by the Commission also for its likely impact on the development of common training standards and, indeed, was only thought valuable within the context of a common occupational training policy.[77] Earlier bilateral and multilateral agreements, notably under the Brussels Treaty, although evidence that importance was beginning to be attached to the principle, had led only to a small number of exchanges and from the start the Commission was anxious to get a Community programme going.

> It does not seem possible to hope for a common policy of occupational training in the early stages; instead it will be necessary to look for co-ordination of national policies. This could cover, among other things, exchanges of information between governments and between enterprises and joint schemes of occupational training. No time must, however, be lost in initiating the study of the bases on which a common policy can be built. The European Commission plans to establish forthwith a first programme for young workers to spend a period of apprenticeship abroad.[78]

The first programme, submitted to the Council on 22 February 1962, included suggestions for Community measures to encourage exchanges, improve their quantity and quality, to set up national advisory committees and to allow for supplementary finance from the Community itself.[79] It was hoped, also, to see a more effective multilateral agreement replace existing bilateral arrangements.[80] The unwillingness of members to allow the development of Community-organized schemes or to see control pass from national hands determined that the programme was only to be accepted in modified form remaining under the control of the Council.[81] Rather than a true joint policy, states retained basic responsibility and no system of Community financing was established. Existing bilateral agreements were not merged into a general plan, although it was agreed that they should be operated in the spirit of the programme and with an improved system of international collaboration, not being invoked where their terms were less favourable. Under the new scheme it was agreed that trainees would benefit from the same forms of protection, work under the same conditions and receive the same social security benefits as nationals. The role of the Commission was to improve the mechanics of the exchanges. It became responsible, in collaboration with governments, for making information available for employers, workers and youth groups generally and for improving communication both at national and Community levels. In consequence it became active in developing discussion with governments on the working of the scheme, considering such questions as the possibility of increasing its scope and improving reception arrangements; in establishing contacts with interested bodies; in the production of brochures and similar explanatory material and in the arrangement of joint sessions of organizers and participants.[82]

A procedure was laid down for regular meetings between national representatives and the Commission to discuss matters of common concern and to simplify the administrative formalities involved. A standard application form for use by all members was agreed.

States agreed to set up national consultative committees to bring together interested parties, to develop channels of communication both internally and with the Commission and to encourage the development of schemes. In practice such arrangements varied considerably and, despite pressure from the Commission, there was delay in establishing such machinery.[83] Furthermore, states agreed to provide information concerning the number of places, the participating industries and the number of available scholarships. They accepted the obligation to cover the cost of fares, lodgings, of making wages up to the normal level and of contributing towards the cost of language instruction. The competent national authority remained responsible for the selection of applicants on the one hand and for the determination of the number of available places on the other.

The agreement covered trainees of either sex between the ages of eighteen and thirty who had already completed a basic training and who wished to take paid employment abroad to improve their vocational, cultural and linguistic skills for a period of six to eighteen months with the possibility of an extended stay.[84]

Between January 1965, when the first programme became operative, and July 1968, 5051 young people had participated in the exchange arrangements and on 3 December 1968 governments agreed to step up places to encourage young people to come forward. In July 1970 the Commission sent states a further memorandum intended to enlarge the programme[85] and this has since been done. Ideas for the development of the scheme have included its extension to wider categories of persons and the possibility of supervising the growing volume of vacation work undertaken by students in order to protect pay and conditions.[86] Details for the first six years are shown in Table 2.1.

This scheme had considerable practical value. Most exchanges derived ultimately from private initiative and the co-operative and standardizing procedures facilitated arrangements, whilst organizers were continuously exposed to information about developments and opportunities.[87] There was, however, no impetus towards the establishment of Community schemes in which the flow of exchanges was determined by Community criteria and supported by Community finance. Indeed states ensured that the programme remained one of orthodox international collaboration.

Table 2.1
Exchange of Young Workers, 1 January 1965 – 31 December 1970[88]

Receiving country	Sending country						
	Belgium	Germany	France	Italy	Luxembourg	Netherlands	Total
Belgium	—	162	48	106	—	—	316
Germany	21	—	1356	719	5	131	2232
							5282*
France	69	5286	—	425	18	1237	7035
Italy	3	20	20	—	—	12	55
Luxembourg	4	7	9	3	—	2	25
Netherlands	5	76	140	103	1	—	325
							15,270

* cannot be classified by country of origin.

In retrospect the achievements of the Community in the field of occupational training appear surprisingly limited for a period in which there was both widespread interest and belief in it as a cause as well as a consequence of economic and social development.[89] The Treaty of Rome had not provided an adequate legal base, and neither economic pressure nor the recorded view of the Commission that it was an issue of fundamental importance for the future development of the EEC[90] made up for this in relation to concrete policies. The work of the executive contributed to the general clarification of the role of vocational training under conditions of rapid change and made plain its belief that access to training and to guidance must be made available to everyone if the right to work is to be meaningful. The inter-relationship between regional development and training was especially stressed. Smooth international collaboration was encouraged by its work. Activities to improve the interchange of ideas and experiences, to document processes and national developments and to encourage exchange schemes will also have had a general educational impact which is itself valuable in a period of rapid industrial change. The work of the Commission gave a new fillip to programmes for the exchange of young workers and showed that it was possible to establish a common basis for certain trades. Its contribution to actual places on training courses or to the production of more teachers must have been negligible and it is clear that no effective European policy of training was created. Indeed this was not a serious aim, for 'putting a common policy into operation does not necessarily require that existing vocational training schemes be fundamentally modified but rather that common objectives must be formulated and attained'.[91] There was little sign, either, of the 'co-ordination of national policies' of which the Commission once spoke[92] and national patterns of training and qualification remained intact.[93] Whilst it seems logical to suggest that Community solutions are valuable, notably to enable industry to make the best use of migrant labour, the larger problem is still that of improving general training standards for workers who are going to remain within the national, if not the local, environment. For this the educational process is the more important. If 'the potential links between free movement and training have yet to be forged',[94] it would appear that neither the original enthusiasm to achieve equivalence of standards as a policy objective[95] nor the practical pressure arising from the demand for skilled labour was in practice strong enough to overcome states' reluctance to allow the Community to play a determining role through the issue of binding instructions or the financing of joint schemes. Strict uniformity seems more likely to arise either from economic pressure or as a slow evolution from the work of raising standards generally with an emerging consensus as to the desirable content of particular vocational trainings.

IV Protection Against Unemployment

The one concrete mechanism created in the social field was the European social fund and it was thus rational that the Commission should have considered it as one of the more significant features of the Treaty of Rome. It was hailed as the 'cornerstone in the edifice of social security'[96] and as the first 'supra-national joint guarantee for those living in the European Economic Community'.[97] Arts. 123 and 125 of the treaty substantiate the claim of Signor Levi-Sandri that the fund was the institutional expression of Community solidarity which, under circumstances where employment opportunities between areas in the Community were significantly different, required redistribution policies in some form.[98] However, although Art. 123 was phrased rather grandly, in practice only Art. 125 was applied and this meant the adoption of policies which were narrowly conceived and rigidly executed. 'The Council has prudently put the emphasis on Article 125 of the treaty, which is relatively restricted, rather than on Article 123 which gives the fund wide scope'.[99] Thus a full development of the possibilities under Art. 123 did not occur.

Art. 125 contained the duty to reimburse states for half the cost of expenses previously incurred in providing retraining schemes and resettlement allowances for the unemployed and of stand-off payments for workers whose employment was temporarily suspended during conversion works so that their income might be fully maintained. The basic rules for the implementation of the scheme were provided in Regulation 9.[100] Schemes receiving aid had to be accepted as meeting the objectives of Art. 125 with the exclusion of those designed to aid public employees or eligible under the Treaty of Paris.

The unemployed eligible for resettlement and retraining allowances were defined as those over the age of sixteen registered with an employment exchange and currently unemployed. Workers between the ages of sixteen and eighteen years had to be registered as unemployed for three consecutive months before being eligible. Those seeking self-employment were excluded, but both wagearners and the self-employed classified as 'under-employed' were within the scope of the regulation provided they were registered as looking for work under contract. Those off work because of a conversion scheme who required vocational retraining were also included. A later amendment[101] clarified the concept of underemployment and extended it to cover family workers in the agricultural sector provided the owner of the farm was eligible for help.

Considerable controversy always surrounded this definition of the unemployed and particularly the exclusion of those aiming at self-employment including those so classified but under-employed and not wishing to enter work under contract. It at once excluded the possibility of improving the productive skills of many of the agricultural population. Nevertheless, the amendment led to a considerable increase in the number of retraining applications.[102] It also became obvious that persons suffering from sickness or physical handicap were often excluded from the definition of the unemployed, but this problem had a more positive outcome. The dividing line for employment purposes between the sick and the well is notoriously hard to draw in that a person may be unable to fulfil the strict requirements of a wage earner whilst being capable of a degree of productive work. Many people have been able to help out on family farms who were unable to withstand the full rigours of paid employment, while the general ageing of the labour force is likely to increase the number of those capable of some work but not necessarily of a full-time job. Often such people are only capable of light work, are not mobile and have only limited employment opportunities. In consequence they may not be registered at the employment exchanges at all, yet with retraining and careful placement are capable of maintaining their position in the labour market. The Commission had always pressed for a wide definition of the unemployed worker[103] and in May 1963 the Council accepted a new regulation[104] which made it clear that those who had lost their previous jobs because of physical or mental incapacity and who required occupational retraining before being fit for productive employment should also be included in the definition of the unemployed for purposes of grant aid. This relaxation proved of considerable practical importance. By 1965 21 per cent of repayments for retraining schemes concerned the handicapped[105] and in 1967 42 per cent of aid was directed to them although they formed only 12 per cent of the men retrained.[106] This development is of the utmost interest for the extension of social policy, for if the concept of occupational retraining for the handicapped were to develop to include medical, rehabilitative or social care the way into some of the major forms of social welfare would lie open to the Community.

Additionally, the regulation defined approved occupational training and laid down conditions for the receipt of grants. It had to be carried out in a definite, pre-established scheme aimed to provide the appropriate qualification for a new job, including the improvement of existing skills. Normal training schemes intended for young people were excluded. It was necessary to show that workers had been unable to find employment without retraining or moving elsewhere and that afterwards they had had employment within the Community for the specified period in the job for which they had been retrained, where applicable. Originally this was for at least six months during the twelve months following the end of the retraining course or after resettlement. In 1963 the rule was relaxed by Regulation 47/63/CEE to allow the time limits to be extended to cover the period of military service in the case of retraining schemes. Finally, by Regulation 37/67/CEE, the twelve-month period was extended to eighteen months in cases of special difficulty since it had been found that there was some tendency not to apply for aid for areas of limited employment opportunity. The amendment was first proposed with the Italian sulphur miners particularly in mind but drawn more widely in the event. A considerable range of allowances was covered. It included subsistence allowances, accommodation and travelling, contributions to social security and unemployment benefits paid to trainees as well as the running costs and wages bill of training centres. Resettlement grants covered travelling expenses of the worker and his dependants, furniture removals and other costs, including a separation allowance up to a maximum.[107]

Conversion of a firm to new production was also to be covered by the social fund provided it led to a temporary suspension of workers requiring a 10 per cent reduction in hours or a 50 per cent fall in the labour force. However, a somewhat arbitrary limitation was introduced by the need to show that a new, not a related, or the same, commodity was subsequently produced. The scheme was designed to maintain payments at the rate of 90 per cent of wage levels, whether based on time or piece-work, including bonuses and other approved payments. Workers were required to be registered as seeking wage-earning employment but were eligible for retraining bonuses if this was a pre-condition of their re-employment. Grants were made retroactively, provided the worker had been back at work for six months, applications being submitted via the national government within twelve months following completion. Conversion schemes required prior approval by the Commission but no proposal had been accepted by 1970.

Each member was required to make an annual estimate of the total assistance likely to be required and to submit requests, in due form, for schemes actually completed within the appropriate time limit. Originally this was fixed as six months after the end of the twelfth month following the end of a retraining course or resettlement. Under Regulation 47/63/CEE the time limits for requests for aid were increased to eighteen months after the end of the calendar half year within which retraining ended and to twenty-four months after the end of the calendar half year in which departure occurred for resettlement. By Regulation 37/67/CEE the time limit for requests with respect to occupational retraining in areas of special difficulty was extended to twenty-four months and by the time necessary to cover military service in all retraining schemes. Only training schemes run by approved agencies qualified for aid. These ranged from central and Länder governments to autonomous bodies acceptable to national authorities who recommended names for inclusion in the Community list.[108]

By the financial arrangements for the fund, France, Germany and Belgium agreed to pay relatively more, and Italy and the Netherlands rather less, than in the case of the general expenses of the Community budget.[109] This confirms the early view that the fund was intended in part as a redistributive agent, since Italy in particular might reasonably be expected to call heavily upon the fund whilst paying less of the cost than either France or Germany. Grants paid out during the period up to 1967 suggest that this result was to some degree obtained although subsequently Germany became the main beneficiary whilst the French share fell sharply. It must also be remembered that those benefiting may not always have been nationals of the applying member. A common procedure was for Italy to bear the cost of aiding emigrants up to the frontier, the receiving country to support travel costs thereafter and similarly in the reverse direction when workers returned home. Furthermore, migrants might be trained after arriving in the host country. Thus Italians, as opposed to Italy, will have done better than the figures in Table 2.2 suggest. The percentage received by states may be compared with the percentage contributions to the fund listed in note 109. The table also shows the significant gap between application and reimbursements in part due to the slow administrative procedures of the Commission.

Retraining proved more expensive than resettlement. During the period from 1960 to 1973 1·7 million workers benefited from grants actually reimbursed, of whom 999,000 had been trained at a cost of 316 million units of account. Resettlement often meant little more than half the cost of a railway ticket to the frontier and, although 1968 saw a striking increase in the number benefiting from resettlement grants as the Italians returned home in a strained employment situation,[110] the later years were notable for the growing emphasis placed by members on retraining schemes.

The expenses of the fund grew steadily. During the first fifteen months

Table 2.2
Grants from the Social Fund, 20 September 1960 – 31 December 1973[111]
m.u.a.

	Type	Grants applied for	% total incomes applied for	Grants paid out	% total paid out	Workers covered by paid-out grants
Germany	retraining	170·4		134·6		172,826
	resettlement	4·6		3·4		259,912
	total	175·0	43·8	138·0	42·2	432,738
Belgium	retraining	12·8		10·9		15,069
	resettlement	·003		·003		20
	total	12·8	3·2	10·9	3·3	15,089
France	retraining	48·9		44·2		50,481
	resettlement	2·6		2·3		98,486
	total	51·5	13·0	46·5	14·2	148,967
Italy	retraining	138·2		113·2		744,780
	resettlement	5·0		4·3		355,523
	total	143·3	35·9	117·5	35·9	1,100,303
Luxembourg	retraining	·04		·016		97
	resettlement	—		—		—
	total	·04	·01	·016	·05	97
Netherlands	retraining	16·1		13·4		16,066
	resettlement	·06		·04		390
	total	16·1	4·3	13·4	4·1	16,456
Community	retraining	386·6		316·5		999,319
	resettlement	12·4		10·0		714,331
	total	399·0		326·5		1,713,650

they amounted to 5·8 million units of account, 4·7 million spent on retraining; by 1970 they had reached 37 million units of which 36·3 million went in retraining. In 1972 grants were 54·8 million units of which 53·9 million were for retraining. Of 167,036 workers benefiting in 1970, 133,587 were retrained.[112]

The cost of applications rose rapidly. In 1965 they totalled 8·2 million units and in 1970 46·2 million. Whilst some of the increase must be an inflationary cost, retraining expenses rose noticeably from 1966 onwards as a result of a number of pressures in which a better quality service, higher cash benefits and a greater willingness to train those with less favourable employment prospects were probably the most important factors. Only in Italy was it possible still to produce a considerable number of retrained workers relatively cheaply.[113]

The industries into which retrained workers went varied considerably, but a steady influx into building and mechanical engineering occurred and an increasing number entered electrical engineering and service industries.[114]

Nevertheless the fund, as it operated until 1972, was too weak to be viewed as more than an embryonic Community system. It contained an in-built tension between its broad aims and the mechanisms of its operation which left the onus of work in the hands of the members. The procedures were activated only by applications from governments with the function of the Commission limited to retroactive payments which could not be withheld from schemes meeting the technical requirements. There was, in fact, no 'fund' as such; members met the cost of grants according to the proportions laid down in the treaty. A cumbersome administrative procedure coupled with long delays in repayment[115] was no way to encourage applications from areas or firms unaccustomed to training or conversion schemes or work of an experimental nature whose success was uncertain. It seems likely that there is truth in the criticism that the only work supported by the fund was that which would have been done anyway[116] and that members succumbed on occasion to the temptation to submit sufficient applications to ensure, over time, a rough balance of payments and receipts.[117]

A number of negative decisions may also have hindered the evolution of the fund as an effective instrument of European employment policy. This is illustrated, firstly, by the lack of use of conversion aid.[118] Secondly, the long drawn-out negotiations to provide the sulphur miners of Sardinia with help were complicated by the reluctance to develop the use of the social fund. The Italian sulphur industry at first remained isolated from the introduction of the common market pending an agreement on rationalization which would allow it to survive on a reduced basis. The miners, of whom there were about 2500, formed 'a typical case of need created by the common market'[119] for whom little alternative employment was available. Underlying the difficulty experienced by the Community in formulating its aid programme was not the unwillingness to accept responsibility but disagreement over the way help should be given.

In November 1962 member states, meeting in Council, created an *ad hoc* Liaison and Action Committee to discuss what should be done in order to incorporate the sulphur industry gradually into the common market through a reorganization of the industry and consequent redundancies. Its report recommended a number of compensatory measures and on 8 May 1964 the Council asked the Commission to submit detailed proposals for action to give effect to them. This report was submitted in November 1963 and discussed with the Italian government, which broadly agreed its terms.[120] The Commission's suggestions were sent to the Council on 15 April 1965, being designed to provide a variety of aids primarily through the use of the social fund suitably adapted[121] in order to allow retraining and resettlement schemes to qualify for Community help more readily and for the payment of cash grants on terms equivalent to the most favourable developed by the Coal and Steel Community. In addition it suggested the development of the vocational training policy in order to enable aid to be given to help the children of elderly miners obtain training for other jobs.[122] Art. 235 of the treaty could, it thought, be used to cover interim benefits which the provisions of the social fund did not cover and for which states might make a special contribution under Art. 200. In sum, then, the proposals consisted of a draft regulation enabling the Community to contribute to a variety of measures to be undertaken by the Italian government to aid the sulphur miners. Firstly, that it should contribute half the cost of redundancy payments to consist of monthly benefits based on previous earnings, subject to a maximum, for those who lost their jobs; grants to those leaving the industry voluntarily and monthly payments to those aged between fifty and fifty-five years until they either obtained a new job or became eligible for pension at fifty-five. Secondly, that the rules of the social fund should be relaxed in order to allow resettlement and retraining schemes dealing with the sulphur miners to receive advance rather than retrospective payments and to lift the requirement that a new job be found within six months of aid being given. Finally, that 1500 scholarships be given for vocational training, including 150 for gifted children to stay on at school and fifty for university or other higher education for the children of miners aged forty-five or over who were receiving unemployment benefits. It was estimated that about 4200 workers would be eligible for aid at a cost of 5·6 million units of account.

After discussion by Parliament and the Economic and Social Committee, the proposals were further modified and passed by the Council to the Committee of Permanent Representatives. Severance payments equivalent to the full basic wage and family allowances were suggested for workers under fifty-five years for a maximum of twelve months. A monthly allowance payable to workers aged between fifty-five and sixty was to be based on 50 per cent of previous earnings. Suitable workers aged under fifty-five years were to be eligible for special retraining courses and to receive a monthly allowance equivalent to both former pay and severance benefits. Arrangements for the vocational training of children applied to all miners irrespective of age.[123] However it became clear[124] that some members were unwilling to prejudge the question of the development of the social fund to cover new types of work and thus the Council's decision of 21–22 December 1966 was based upon Art. 235 and not upon the use of the fund itself. As previously noted, minor amendments to the operation of the fund, which had originally been proposed to aid the Italian sulphur miners, were accepted in February 1967. The Council refused, however, to accept the suggestion of advance aid. The agreement allowed for aid to be paid in Italy, via the Community budget, of up to 4·2 million units of account to cover half the cost of aid given to unemployed miners and scholarships for their children on terms to be agreed between the Italian government and the Council.[125] These were made final on 12 May 1967[126] and so, ten years after the signing of the Rome Treaty, aid could finally be granted. By 1972, however, the project had still not been completed owing to the reluctance to close the mines until alternative employment was locally available and subsidies from the Italian government were continuing.[127]

Strict evaluation of the work of the fund up to 1972 is difficult in that Community aid was limited to schemes already, in one sense, a proven success. It laboured, however, under considerable difficulties. Remoteness from actual operations made technical control difficult. Art. 24 of Regulation 9 laid down that the Commission should receive all necessary information and be in direct contact with operating agencies, and Regulation 113/63/CEE[128] laid down the detailed methods of examination and verification of projects. The Commission examined books and documents on the spot but, since it was concerned with material submitted in support of schemes already an historical experience, the system was difficult to monitor.[129] A great deal necessarily devolved on the care taken by national governments in recommending inclusion on the approved list for training centres and in checking the operation of all schemes.[130] Other types of evaluation, such as long-term follow-ups to see if resettled workers sent for their families, obtained housing or were integrated into their new communities, were not called for. Much less, therefore, was the Commission in a position to influence the major lines of policy, such as the balance between retraining, resettlement and conversion; the type of, or methods used in, retraining; to encourage retraining in areas of greatest need or to evaluate schemes in terms of their worth either to the Community or to those workers it was trying to help. The one built-in exception was the need for the Commission to give prior approval to a conversion scheme, but this possibility was not used.

> But the Treaty did not allow the fund either a direct grant function or the possibility of using its own initiative. It was thus impossible for it to stress the readaptation of workers in their home areas rather than resettlement elsewhere. This choice remained the responsibility of governments.[131]

Related to this passive role was the rigid structure of the fund. Its work was limited to those already unemployed or under-employed to the exclusion of the self-employed. It was effectively prevented in the first case from anticipatory retraining or resettlement aimed to ensure a smooth changeover from one job to another and in the second from contributing to greater efficiency in a wide range of jobs especially in agriculture. The first ten years of the common market were characterized by rapidly developing employment opportunities, whilst the future appeared to be one in which labour would both be in overall short supply and moving away from agriculture into the industrial and service sectors. The great need was therefore for the social fund to be used flexibly, not only to meet problems of redundancy and prolonged unemployment, but to help to shape the working force into an instrument to meet economic demands. For this it needed to be able to switch its aid easily between one group of workers and another, to adapt its work to fit in with that of other agencies dealing with related problems of regional development and to undertake preventive action in the form of training, retraining and resettlement before rather than after the worker became unemployed. The rapid retraining of workers who, although in work, yet required extra skills to work new processes and operate new machinery was a case in point. However, few such schemes run by members appeared to fall within the scope of the fund[132] whose more orthodox interpretation of unemployment also prevented its use for the support of vocational training schemes on a large scale. As a European agency it needed to see the area as a whole and to regard its work from the vantage point of the overall employment situation rather than from within a specifically national context. It was, therefore, irksome to be required to fit in with a state's prior determination of whom to help and how and of the re-employment considered necessary. Although from the start the Commission saw the fund as a stimulant to a balanced and dynamic labour market to which its greatest contribution would be through the assistance it might give to occupational mobility,[133] the original arrangements often prevented it from aiding those groups who would appear to be strong claimants of aid from the standpoint of industrial change, including those already in employment needing new skills, those on family farms or married women whom the labour market wished to absorb. There was some justification for this in 1958 when there were over 1·7 million unemployed in Italy alone for whom retraining schemes and travel grants were of obvious and immediate benefit and it was natural to stress that the Community had a mechanism for providing compensation for need directly attributable to the introduction of the common market. The comment of Professor Hallstein referring to 'a compensation fund financed by all member countries to meet what might be called the social cost of the Common Market' expresses this viewpoint.[134] The limitations became more obvious as new employment problems were identified. The persistence of areas of hard-core unemployment, shortage of skilled manpower in other districts, the surplus agricultural population and the need for greater efficiency on the part of those who remained on the land all pointed to the need to concentrate help in certain areas, to integrate it with agricultural and regional policies and to devote time to special projects.

The need to reform the fund to enable it to play a positive part in the creation and operation of a European labour market in which human resources were effectively utilized through a positive encouragement of active re-employment policies therefore became a major element in the social policy of the Commission. This required a new formulation of its role, above all through schemes to anticipate unemployment, to encourage vocational training as a means of occupational mobility and to fit the work of the fund into regional development plans. To become a European instrument in any effective sense it required to operate as part of the overall European context, serving the needs of the area as a whole. Socially this required that the fund should function in relation to the harmonization of living and working conditions through measures such as the concentration of its effort in poorer areas, the stimulation of modern retraining methods and greater support for the social needs of migrants. Since, however, nothing was said in the treaty about such matters, change was dependent upon the agreement of members to allow the work of the fund to develop. The desire of the Commission to see this was not in doubt; 'There has been some intention of using the European Social Fund as a weapon against unemployment, but it should not be forgotten that its main task was to make labour more mobile within the Community.'[135]

In 1963 Parliament argued for a revision of the operation of the fund to enable it to develop a common vocational training policy, to extend its coverage to those aiming at self-employment and to forestall loss of employment. The *Action Programme* took a similar stand, hoping in addition that in the future the fund would not be limited to reimbursing governments but be given the right to take the initiative through the establishment of pilot retraining schemes. 'Initiative 1964' contained further suggestions to improve the working of the fund by taking up the general question of its role in maintaining high employment levels, its possible contribution to more effective regional policies and to improving the living conditions of migrants and their families. It argued that the concept of resettlement might be developed to embrace all adjustment problems not only for humane reasons but because the better educated and qualified workers of the future would not submit to the crude forms of migration common in the past. Thus the full potential of the fund was not realized, since greater emphasis was placed on specific schemes designed to reabsorb those already unemployed rather than to develop employment opportunities for the labour force as a whole. A reconsideration of functions was required and from 1965 the Commission began to turn its energies in this direction.

Art. 126 foresaw the need to reconsider the role of the fund at the end of the transitional period, leaving open the possibility that it might be wound up or given new tasks by the Council. The preparation of proposals provided the opportunity for formal consideration of the new context within which it was operating, and a scheme of reform was submitted to the Council in January 1965 containing a number of specific proposals designed to draw the boundaries of the work more widely by enabling the fund to play a greater part in promoting geographical mobility and in assisting schemes for regional development. The reform was seen in terms of extending the existing functions of the fund so that it might deal with advance training and grant-aid services for migrants, and be more active in training schemes and in maintaining the labour force pending regional development. Associated with the suggestions was a proposal for a regulation intended to help farmers and family workers wishing to change their occupation in areas of agricultural change, by means of building and running training centres and through grants to students between the ages of sixteen and forty-five years successfully re-employed. A final proposal related to the provision of grant aid to allow for the training of advisers to the farming community on occupational prospects.

Initially such ideas were received 'with great reserve by the Council of Ministers'[136] and long delays in decision ensued. It had been hoped that acceptance might be won by the realization that there was something for everybody in the plan. Italy would benefit from the improved aid for migrants and the special help for the impoverished regions, other members from the wider scope for retraining assistance.[137] Dissensions between members and later between members and the Commission over the latter's role prevented acceptance,[138] and it was not until 1967 that it became generally accepted that change would be necessary although disagreement still persisted over its form. At the December Council meetings, which included a general debate on the future trends in social policy, an agreement in principle on the extension of the fund was reached. It appeared inopportune, however, to take concrete decisions at a time when the enlargement of the Community was under consideration,[139] and differences of view concerning the future role of the fund continued. Further debate in Council, on 29 July 1968, revealed their continuance and led to a new referral of the issue to the Commission for a reconsideration of the role of the fund in the 1970s in conjunction with the Committee of Permanent Representatives.[140]

The proposals of 1969[141] stressed the importance of reform in order to help workers adapt to changing employment needs, notably the expected losses in agriculture, textiles and coal and steel, the corresponding growth in other industrial sectors and the need for a technologically advanced labour force. They 'would transform the fund from a mere accounting mechanism into a powerful instrument of social and economic policy and so provide the Community as a whole with an instrument which has already proved its worth in the more limited setting of the Treaty of Paris'.[142] The fundamental change was the argument that it was necessary to allow the Community scope to decide on schemes for grant aid and no longer to confine it to support of those wanted by governments which led to a medley of unco-ordinated projects. In the future Community priorities should be established and schemes coming from governments should be presented as part of a wider programme of reform. It would be important to relate the work of the fund to the regional and medium-term economic policies, to anticipate that it would be on a far larger scale than hitherto, to retrain workers in advance of change and to give the Community control over the resources of the fund so that members were not under pressure to ask for what they had put in. Community grant aid should be a variable proportion of a project according to requirements and scope should be given to the support of research and experimental programmes.

By the end of the year the political climate had at last improved. The Hague Conference of Heads of State or Government held in December 1969 agreed, *inter alia,* on the desirability of reforming the social fund 'within the framework of a closely concerted social policy'.[143] On 27 July 1970 the Council finally agreed to reform and adopted the text the following November.[144] This marked the formal recognition by members that the existing arrangements were inadequate to allow the fund to play its part in helping the labour force to adjust to changing socio-economic conditions and to ensure that workers have suitable employment opportunities. Whilst the aim of the reform was to enable the fund to act more flexibly in order to fit in with Community objectives, eligible projects were classified into two groups to meet differences of view concerning what the new priorities should be. The first consisted of those schemes designed to support general Community policies or to obtain a balance between the supply and demand for manpower as determined by *ad hoc* Council decisions on a qualified majority vote, taken as needs are recognized within the development of general policies of industrial development. Such broad Community decisions must necessarily often require geographical or occupational mobility from labour for which the social fund should in future be able to provide assistance. The second was made up of plans aimed to help with particular difficulties whether affecting industries, firms or regions such as local shortages of skilled workers, chronic unemployment or under-employment in an area and the rehabilitation and specialized training of groups such as the handicapped, elderly, women and young workers. Approval is given by the Commission to particular schemes.

Determination of the relative importance of these two groups of projects caused great difficulty. Opinion was divided between those states with shortages of industrial labour which felt priority should be given to schemes designed to ease their recruiting problems and Italy who argued vehemently for preference to be given to backward regions and particularly agricultural ones, going so far as to vote against the credits for 1972 as a protest against their inadequacy.[145] The question of whether the fund is to aid an industrial or a regional policy remains unsolved and the relative priority of needs is likely to continue to be contentious. It was originally agreed that aid designed to serve Community policies should steadily increase in importance, although structural difficulties should claim at least half the available money during the early years on the understanding that the matter should be reviewed after five years. In fact the agreement for 1972 represented a considerable victory for the Italian thesis, since 7·5 million units of account were earmarked for the first group compared with 35·5 million for the second. Furthermore, 60 per cent of the latter was to be directed towards the agricultural regions.[146] Additionally, 55 million units were needed to aid projects under the old arrangements and 250,000 units for studies and pilot projects.[147]

In order to encourage the submission of well-thought-out projects in the regions, requests must now be shown to be part of a set of measures aimed to provide a constructive solution to employment difficulties[148] and are submitted for prior authorization so that, although a great deal will still depend upon the individual state which must activate the arrangements, the Community should be able to influence the quality of the decisions made and avoid the earlier position in which it found itself reimbursing states for schemes it considered to have little practical value. Although projects are submitted by states, those run by private organizations as well as by public and semi-public bodies can now benefit. The former have their arrangements financed by the national government and the social fund in equal amounts but must also make a financial contribution themselves, whilst the latter two groups are eligible for a 50 per cent grant from the fund.

The types of aid available have been specified in considerable detail.[149] They fall into several main groups. Firstly, those designed to help occupational mobility through aiding training schemes, the employment and training of teachers and instructors and through providing individual allowances for trainees themselves. Secondly, aid can assist geographical mobility through meeting travel and adjustment costs, including the integration of the migrant and his family into a new social and working environment. Thirdly, the fund can help with special schemes to aid the elderly and the handicapped find employment, fourthly, with guidance and information services and, finally, provide certain wage supplements as in the case of the less-developed regions or for certain categories of the elderly. All those normally engaged in wage-earning activities become eligible, not excluding nationals of non-members, whilst certain groups of the self-employed are, or may be, covered. Currently this last provision relates to the handicapped and those in agriculture in conditions falling under Art. 5 of the Council decision dealing with particular difficulties.[150]

The financing of the fund underwent fundamental reversal. It became part of the total reform of Community financing accepted by the Council in January 1970[151] so that the fund will progressively obtain its own income. The amount, however, will still need to be determined as part of Community decision and much will therefore depend in the future upon the willingness of the Community to devote considerable sums to the fund. The Commission has estimated that during the 1970s at least 250 million units of account should be spent by the Community on readaptation projects directed to those leaving agriculture and the declining industries alone.[152] Over a quarter of a million people may need help in leaving farming and a large exodus from textiles and clothing industries is also anticipated.[153] The allocation for 1972 was far below this figure, although it does not compare unfavourably with the average of 30 million units a year for the 1960s. Neither does it necessarily follow that the most backward regions will receive the most money in absolute terms since, temporarily at least, reimbursement is on the basis of real cost and training expenses in Italy are comparatively low. If, therefore, the social fund is to be a real stimulus to the elimination of structural unemployment, it is essential to co-ordinate its work with that of other agencies designed to diversify the types of employment and to raise the general standards of amenities in a region. A further difficulty of the new arrangements stems from their complexity. The distinction between projects designed to further Community policies and those intended to eliminate barriers to its harmonious development is a confusing one, whilst members of Parliament have criticized the extreme detail of the regulations on the grounds that the rigidities implied are not the best way to go about obtaining a more flexible system for the future.[154] Decisions to aid schemes in agriculture and textiles have been taken by the Council under Art. 4 rather than Art. 5, thus perhaps reflecting the Commission's desire to place aid within a European context and to encourage a diminution in the use of Art. 5 whose mandate appears more firmly rooted in the older arrangements. It is, therefore, important not to assume too readily that the Community has even yet provided itself with a means of ensuring effective aid to workers needing help to maintain or improve their position in the employment structure.

Taking the experience of the two Communities up to the beginning of the 1970s, it seems clear that a European authority can find a constructive role in helping to alleviate the human problems of unemployment. In both cases the way in was through the ability to provide financial aid and it seems therefore that it is through the terms upon which this is granted that any positive influence must largely depend. The fact that time was needed before the volume of applications built up to any scale points to the value of establishing direct contacts between the European executives and firms or local authorities so that a proper understanding of schemes can develop, encouragement and advice be given and a full exploitation of facilities achieved. The involvement of the High Authority in job-creation schemes was more constructive than the non-activation of the conversion aid of the EEC, as it is hard to believe that there was no case which could have benefited from help from the latter. Experience of both schemes demonstrated the difficulty of confining activity to one simple facet of need. The logic of events pushed both executives into looking at unemployment protection as one function of a much broader, positive activity consisting of job creation and the maintenance of employment and which had a strong preventive aspect. This ultimately bore fruit in the 1970 social fund reform. In similar fashion the concept of resettlement merged into a comprehensive definition of the human needs of migrant workers. The growing emphasis on forward planning, on preventive work and labour skills suggests that a broadly based, and adequately flexible, instrument would have great scope when working from a European rather than a national basis, able to undertake preventive and anticipatory work, cover the whole range of occupational activity and develop effective qualitative controls which would move the work away from supplementation of cash benefits as an end towards a deeper appreciation of employment needs. This, however, is a task for the new European social fund which, by 1972, was only brought to the brink of fresh activity. The principle of its reform appears to allow it to operate on more up-to-date lines, but it will be essential to integrate its work more closely with that of other Community policies, notably that in agriculture which is now turning towards aids to encourage workers to leave farming, to amalgamate holdings and to farm more efficiently.[155] In the absence of a coherent programme allowing all Community aids to focus on the problems of a region, there is an obvious danger of disjointed schemes providing allowances for particular purposes with haphazard consequences and inefficient use of resources.

3 Wages and Working Conditions

I Investigations

It will be recalled that the European Commission was given no right to determine the level of wages or of social security benefits and that the Treaty of Rome expressed no clear view as to the effect on them of the introduction of a common market. Although it has been argued that greater equality of pay was implicit in the treaty in a number of ways, there were no direct imperatives to establish it as a general policy.[1] Certain forms of action, by governments or firms, were imposed or, alternatively, forbidden by the treaty. Thus equal pay for men and women was imposed and discrimination against migrants disallowed. Wage cutting in coal and steel as a form of competition had been forbidden but a similar provision was not inserted into the Treaty of Rome. No obvious method existed whereby the Community might establish a position in the determination of wage levels although suggestions were made from time to time that Art. 121, under which the Council could 'assign duties to the Commission in connection with the implementation of common measures', might be used for this purpose. Main responsibility for wage protection and improvement remained where it had always been, with national governments and collective bargaining systems.

The effect of the introduction of the common market on these arrangements cannot be described as dramatic. Long-established institutions for the control of employment conditions existed in each member and were unlikely to be deeply affected by a European organization of doubtful powers. Furthermore, the variations in national patterns, ranging from the extent to which collective bargaining was carried on at national or local level to the question of the matters that were left to collective bargaining or determined by statutory regulation, meant that 'one of the permanent problems of adjustment will be the co-existence of collective bargaining and legislation as two alternative methods of establishing standards'.[2] Both the structure of relations between employer and worker and the organization of trade unions themselves had taken individual forms. As a consequence, although general trends in labour relations were visible within the Community, these concealed considerable variations in national arrangements. If there was a tendency for collective bargaining to take place more frequently at the national level, and this was strongly developed in Belgium and the Netherlands, yet in Germany it was often still effective at the level of the local firm. Agreements might therefore be valid for the whole of an industrial sector or only for a branch of it and, although the principle that they might be extended obligatorily to the whole of an industry was accepted in all members, it was not necessarily often used.[3] Considerable use was made of legislation to establish minimum wages and holidays, but in practice higher levels often obtained as a result of collective bargaining whilst the participation of the worker in decisions had been developed further in Germany than elsewhere through the co-determination laws.

Although the determination of wages has been traditionally left to bargaining procedures, attempts to establish incomes policies have introduced new factors into industrial relations by reopening the question of the proper concern of the Community in the content of collective agreements in general and wage negotiations in particular, often as an aspect of its concern to establish conscious control or at least guidance over the fortunes of the economy itself. The interest of the state is here neither that of the worker nor of the employer since 'the critical question of current incomes policy is that of the reconciliation of the goal of achieving a greater real share of the distribution of the national revenue for employees with the economic aims of monetary stability and the provision of adequate capital for investment'.[4] Not only wages, but labour relations generally, are tending to become subjected to more critical analysis in order to establish more facts, to articulate principles of fairness, justice and comparability upon which wages may be based and to eliminate the irrational pay anomalies which are often discovered to exist within the same country. 'It is also true that within each state, levels of pay for comparable jobs vary not only from one economic sector to another but even more on a regional basis.'[5] The post-war period thus saw a considerable increase in government intervention in the labour field[6] and the redefinition of the traditional responsibilities of the three major contestants presented a continuing theme.

> The respective competences to determine wages and working conditions of the three protagonists of social policy, namely state, employers and unions, has taken many forms according to time and place. To the extent that state intervention has been developed the autonomy of the social partners has been limited.[7]

One of the results of viewing wages and labour conditions in a broader socio-economic context became the need to institutionalize arrangements for their handling and to develop a form of relationship between employer and worker organizations and the state. The Economic and Social Council in France and the Netherlands, the National Economic and Labour Council in Italy and the National Council of Labour in Belgium are all examples of institutions which were created to perform a liaison function with industrial circles and to involve a wide range of interests, not always exclusively drawn from employer and worker associations, with broad policy developments. The contrast was perhaps with Germany where the greater interest shown in participation in decision making within the firm was not, except in informal ways, paralleled by centralized arrangements.

Although the complexity of national structures over the whole field of industrial relations made any simple transfer of collective bargaining to a European stage unlikely, the existence of the Community may well have worked to some degree to encourage their greater formalization through the demand for representation in Community activities, participation in investigatory studies and the need to represent an employer or union viewpoint to governments in matters affected by Community decisions. As in the case of the ECSC, the EEC created a series of joint committees to bring representatives of employers and workers into its discussion procedures with a central industrial group[8] as well as those for specialized problems. In addition to the formal advisory committees, the Commission relied heavily on *ad hoc* bodies to take responsibility for the comparative studies in collective bargaining procedures, health and safety, the length of working hours and so on. The structure of such working parties was variable. Some represented employers' and workers' organizations, possibly with the assistance of government experts, others were tripartite in character and yet others composed of government or independent experts.[9] One of the purposes of such work was to impose standardized conceptions upon material previously neither readily available nor in a comparable form, thus providing the 'technical foundations for social harmonization'[10] which were originally lacking. The role of such committees was delicate. Involved in the discovery and discussion of discrepancies and anomalies yet established within a treaty structure claiming to work for harmonization, it was probably inevitable that the attempt would be made by unions who wished to 'level up' and the executives who wished to 'Europeanize' to develop work beyond the role of analysis, report and discussion to one of a more active nature concerning the formulation of standards and the exercise of pressure to secure their adoption.

The episode of the miners' charter showed that the ECSC was in no position to establish common working standards. The history of the EEC reinforced this lesson. There have been only two examples of this process so far. The first was the agreement reached in the Joint Advisory Committee on the Social Problems of Paid Agricultural Workers signed on

6 June 1968. This set out the terms for the working week for certain agricultural wage earners, both sides of industry agreeing to recommend the terms to their respective national organizations. The second was reached in the same committee and related to the hours of work of wage earners employed in livestock breeding upon which occupational groups reached agreement in 1971.[11] They cannot, therefore, be thought of as international collective bargaining in the full sense. The lack of uniformity in national institutional arrangements, the inter-relationship between wages in one industry and those in the same town or area, the differences in fringe benefits make the imposition of a formal bargaining system at Community level of doubtful advantage until the need for it is consciously felt. There has, therefore, been little sign of the maturation of the Commission's hope that it would be able to develop collective bargaining at a European level.[12] However, the growth of the multi-national company, notably in the car industry, has kept alive questions of the possibility of standardized agreements negotiated across national frontiers and of the desirable pattern of union organization in the same way that discussions on the statute for a European company have presented the issue of worker participation in management as a norm for the area as a whole.[13]

The signature of the Treaty of Rome brought a renewed interest in comparative studies of labour costs and it was the economic aspects of wages that first aroused attention. An immediate consideration was the question of overtime upon which members had expressed the view that the first years of the common market would in any case bring about an equalization of standards. This problem, which loomed so large at the time of signature of the treaty, never became serious and France did not require to exercise her right to take protective measures. 'It thus seems that this chapter is closed.'[14] However the deepening of the integrative process shifted attention away from the immediate impact of the dismantling of tariff barriers towards the significance of common policy formation notably with the production of the medium-term economic programme. National struggles to fit accustomed methods of wage determination into the framework of an incomes policy similarly drew attention to the question of the factors which do, or should, affect wage levels. 'Lastly, the Commission considers that there can be no full social policy that will enable the whole population of the Six to benefit from the progress to be expected from the customs union and of economic union unless appropriate wage policies are framed either on the national or on the Community scale.'[15] Thus the early interest in the relative position of competitors extended to include studies of much wider topics including the relation of wages to productivity, wage drift, the relativity of wages and the total stake of the worker in the growing economy.[16] These more sophisticated wage studies made the maintenance of a distinction between fact-gathering and analysis on the one hand and active policy making on the other more difficult.

As with the ECSC, the early problems of making wage studies were considerable in view of the lack of comparability in existing national statistics which used different base years, definitions of industries, workers and wages. It was therefore clear that it would be necessary to mount fresh investigations on the basis of newly determined Community criteria. The work of the Commission was established by Regulation 10 passed in May 1960[17] on the basis of Art. 213. This drew attention to the impossibility of making international comparisons on the basis of existing information and to the need for new work utilising uniform definitions and methods of collection of material. Investigations were to be carried out designed to shed light on both manpower costs and workers' incomes by looking at direct wages, compulsory and voluntary social charges in all firms employing fifty or more manual workers in certain chosen industries.[18] Labour costs of other employees were collected separately. The investigation was to be carried out in two cycles, covering 8 million workers. In phase one, wages in fourteen industries were to be studied in 1959, in eight industries in 1960 and a further thirteen industries in 1961. In phase two, the work was repeated from 1962 to 1964.[19] The inquiries showed the similarity between labour costs of the same industry wherever operating, often more marked than the similarities between industries in the same country.[20] The 1959 inquiry showed that in most industries Germany, France and Belgium formed a group of relatively high-wage countries whilst the Netherlands and Italy tended to have rates 15 to 20 per cent less, but there were important exceptions as in the Italian rubber industry. The differences between the highest and the lowest wage rates declined from 20 per cent in 1959 to 18 per cent in 1962; for the second group of industries from 23 per cent in 1960 to 22 per cent in 1963 and for the third group from 23 per cent in 1961 to 18 per cent in 1964. The Italian level had made notable improvements by the time of the second cycle.

The material also made possible a comparison of real incomes of workers performing comparable jobs in different parts of the Community.[21] A comparison of the figures for a married man with two children showed that, in real terms, such a family was best off in France except for the brewing and malting, pulp paper and paper board and shipbuilding industries, where Luxembourg and Belgium had higher standards for this size family. The Italian two-child family did least well in seven industries but reached second place for workers in the rubber industry. It was, however, beaten by the French family because of the good family allowances, which also brought the Belgian family near to the Italian level. The larger Italian family, however, did very badly in comparison with those abroad. In five industries the German family with two children held the lowest place.[22] By 1962 the most favoured position was still held by the two-child family in Luxembourg where the wage was earned in brewing. The French worker had lost ground in wool spinning and cotton to the Dutch and Belgian workers, but remained at the top of the list in eight industries. The family in the Italian rubber industry had been overtaken by the Belgian.[23] Family budget surveys have also been undertaken.[24]

These few illustrations show how complex a procedure is involved in attempting to make comparisons, much less to draw any firm conclusions from them. Although a closing of gaps in wage levels seemed to occur, the effect of the common market thereupon is entirely obscure and the attempt to make a comparison of real levels, allowing for charges on income, social benefits of various kinds and different living patterns, is, of course, very much of an abstraction.

In 1964 a new regulation was adopted enabling the Commission to organize a further survey of manual workers' earnings, on a sample basis of 2 million workers in industry in October 1966, designed to throw light on differences in wage structures resulting from factors such as the age and sex pattern of the labour force and the size of individual firms.[25] Further wage studies were agreed in 1966, including a special inquiry into wage costs and wages in transport.[26] Two million workers in industry were sampled and the results indicated the wide variations between the wages of skilled workers and average wages from one country to the next, varying in manufacturing from 7 per cent in Germany to 16 per cent in France.[27] In all countries the level of earnings varies with age; the earnings of workers under twenty-one years are low and wages reach a peak between the ages of thirty-five and forty-four years except in Italy where the peak is reached for the sixty-year-old workers. On 19 October 1971 the Council agreed to a new set of wage surveys to determine the structure and distribution of wages in industry for both manual and non-manual workers with the intention to repeat the work in 1974.[28]

In 1960 a conference on technical progress and the common market was called by the three European Communities and as a result information was compiled on paid holidays, overtime, labour law, dispute conciliation, wage agreements and similar topics. Such studies and reports led to the accumulation of a vast store of material available for the use of national organizations, but for the institutions of the Community a clear distinction had to be drawn between such investigations and a policy designed to eliminate any disparities they might disclose.

II Equal Pay

In regard to one aspect of pay, the Treaty of Rome was much stronger. The provisions of Art. 119, which had figured as a practical expedient rather than as a principle of social justice, imposed a greater obligation upon members by committing them to the introduction of equal pay by the end of the first stage of the common market. Its importance can be seen from the fact that, in 1959, women constituted 36·4 per cent of the active population in Germany, 24·8 per cent in Belgium, 33·4 per cent in France, 27·2 per cent in Italy, 27·5 per cent in Luxembourg and 21·3 per cent in Holland.[29]

The effective execution of a policy of equal pay is a highly complex matter. It depends upon the extent to which other factors, such as the provision of training facilities, promotion procedures or the availability of job opportunities work so as to favour and improve the position of women in the labour force. Attitudes of employers, and workers of both sexes, to problems of women's employment are deeply embedded in the socio-economic conditions of a country, so that the application of an implementing policy cannot be left as a question of legal form, important though this is, but requires a readiness to accept the consequential changes in the labour market and in the status of women in the community generally that are necessarily involved.[30] To remove the artificial and irrational disabilities that surround the employment of women implies enormous changes in attitudes, traditions and education, makes it hard to assess the existing degrees of inequality between industries, the scale of the problem presented to the various sectors of the economies or the likely effects of the introduction of such a principle upon the relative position between one state and another. The difficulties are heightened for an international organization committed to the principle yet possessing limited powers of control and execution whose members may rely upon informal bargaining techniques to ensure its application.

The principle of equal pay has long been accepted amongst civilized nations, finding expression in Art. 427 of the Treaty of Versailles and more recently in Art. 23 of the Declaration of Human Rights and Art. 4 of the European Social Charter. In 1950 and 1951 the ILO adopted a new convention, No. 100, and resolution, No. 90, on the matter. Nevertheless, the members of the Community entered the common market with different commitments to the principle of equal pay. In France and West Germany its application stems from the constitutional provision of equal rights for men and women while Art. 37 of the Italian constitution specifically refers to the right to equal pay for equal work. No specific right existed elsewhere but Belgium had ratified the ILO Convention and Luxembourg did so in 1967. Belgium had, however, established equal pay in the public services and Luxembourg gave women public servants 90 per cent of the male wage rate together with the right to retire five years earlier. Resistance to the idea was probably greatest in the Netherlands, which entered the common market with considerable disparities between male and female wage rates and a heavy reliance upon female labour which promised to make the introduction of equal pay an onerous affair. Allied to variations of intent and indeed application was the sheer paucity of knowledge concerning the existing degree of inequality between men and women in different industries, the scale of the problem presented to various sectors of the economies of the members, ignorance of the likely effects of introducing such a principle and of the relative position between state and state.

Early discussions in the Community were directed towards the provision of a clear definition of Art. 119 since members were not willing to follow the ILO's wide phraseology of equal pay for work of equal value. On the other hand, the suggestion that Art. 119 should be confined to those jobs held indiscriminately by men and women would have limited its scope unduly. This claim was made, and opposed, from time to time.[31] In view of the very real difficulties it is not surprising that here, in contrast to the unexpectedly rapid progress made in the common market itself, the obligations of the treaty remained unfulfilled. This unsatisfactory position was recognized by the Council on 12 May 1960, whose declaration of that date on the speeding-up of the implementation of the common market contained an annexe on social policy which referred to the Council's wish to hasten measures in the social field notably in the fields of vocational training, free movement and equal pay.[32] The Commission was asked to formulate more detailed suggestions for its application and these took the form of a recommendation to states on 20 July 1960 together with an explanatory letter from the President.[33] The Commission's view was that sex should not be used as a criterion either for job classification or for the fixing of wages, but that other factors such as seniority, qualifications, age or family responsibilities could legitimately affect the level of pay. The economic yield of the worker should only be taken into account in piece-work calculations so that employers might not argue for lower wage rates on the grounds that greater protective measures made women more costly or that more frequent absences from work necessarily lowered productivity and therefore justified different wage scales. Minimum wages, whether fixed by law or by contract, should apply to both sexes and no individual contract between employer and worker should incorporate pay differences. A later amendment gave the Commission's view that the term 'equal pay' covered pay and emoluments but not social security benefits provided within the context of social security schemes.[34] The recommendation urged the application of the principle to all pay received in return for work done, that states should press for its implementation through discussions with employers and workers on its ramifications, through encouraging industry to include it in negotiated collective agreements, if necessary withholding official approval, where this might be required, of those that ignored the matter. Equal pay should be ensured in the public services and states should organize appropriate supervisory measures keeping the Commission informed of developments.

The replies received from members to the inquiries instituted as a result of this recommendation were unsatisfactory: 'no country can point to a practical initiative taken by it prior to 30 June 1961 by virtue of the recommendation.'[35] The approaching end of the first stage of the common market on 31 December 1961 meant that it was becoming urgently necessary to take action. The Council therefore decided that a special working party should be created to collect and analyse information on the position in each member and study possible methods of ensuring effective application.[36] Its first report suggested women should be given a right enforceable in the courts, that governments should insist upon clauses in collective agreements to apply the principle wherever they had a right to do this. It urged industry to become more active in the matter.[37]

During the remainder of the year it became clear that it would be impossible to expect a complete, immediate application of Art. 119, but to move into the second stage of the transitional period without at least a serious step towards its fulfilment would violate the treaty. 'It is clear that Article 119 constitutes a legal commitment of a precise and formal nature.'[38] Member states, at the Council meetings at the turn of the year, resolved therefore to apply the principle by the timetable procedure.[39] They agreed additionally on the need to abolish all discrimination based on sex in wage fixing and recognized that in practice wage equality meant the removal of other forms of disability surrounding women's employment. Members also accepted the need for enforcement and, although accepting that the particular methods would have to be decided internally in view of the differences in wage settlement procedures and the varying appropriateness of forms of control, agreed to look for ways of overcoming the practical difficulties and of finding a way of giving women a right enforceable at law. They also agreed not to accept for extension any collective bargaining agreement which did not adhere to the timetable and to accept the restrictions on labour policy referred to by the original recommendation of the Commission. If it were reported that a firm or sector were seriously disadvantaged by continuing discrepancies members would consult with the Commission on the action to be taken. Members agreed to co-operate with the Commission in activities designed to make the timetable work, such as inquiries into wage structures, wages paid and methods of job classification.

The application of the principle, however, continued to cause considerable difficulty. Discussion continued on whether it could logically be limited to work done indiscriminately by men and women: 'not all members are inclined to extend the principle of equal pay to female employees beyond "mixed" jobs.'[40] Belgium continued to reserve her position on the interpretation of the phrase 'equal work':

> The resolution [of 20 December 1961] is the latest attempt to find a solution to the problem. It can only be considered as an interpretative agreement since it has not the same characteristics as the treaty, namely ratification and consent. The resolution is a political engagement of a community nature.[41]

Job reclassification so that women's jobs were the lowest paid was reported from Italy, Belgium and Germany, this being a well-recognized consequence of the introduction of equal pay if nothing is done to prevent it, for it goes 'hand in hand with the implementation of the principle of equal pay'.[42] The Belgian government at least argued that it had no power to control this.[43] A number of collective agreements were accepted by the Belgian government for general extension despite the fact that they maintained disparities and, in some cases, retained the restrictive interpretation that the principle applied only to jobs done freely by either men or women: 'certain agreements maintaining discrimination or only applying the equal pay principle to identical jobs in the same firm have received the right to general enforcement.'[44] As might be expected industries in which a large number of women were employed, such as textiles, were slower to remove the disparities than occupations where men and women did the same jobs, while the undervaluing of work done mainly by women as a result of inadequate job evaluation, down-grading through reclassification and payment of higher rates to men by individual employers were all reported.[45] Women were still banned from certain posts. In October 1967 the question was raised in the European Parliament whether the Belgian government was correct in advertising certain posts in the civil service as available for men only, but it was pointed out that Art. 119 did not cover job recruitment and that, although the action was against the ILO convention No. 111, this had not been ratified by Belgium.[46]

In 1962 the Commission drew the attention of members to the continuing failure of some states to apply the principle and commented upon the general lack of enthusiasm shown by governments, employers' associations and trade unions to take the steps open to them to ensure it.[47] The Parliamentary resolution of 1964[48] referred to the need for the Commission to take steps to thwart attempts at non-application through the down-grading of women's jobs and their reclassification as 'light'. It urged members to insist upon the implementation of the timetable and to amend their laws if necessary so that women might possess an enforceable right, but despite such concern the Social Affairs and Public

Health Committee remained of the opinion that not all the appropriate steps had been taken by states to ensure the application of the principle, neither had the timetable been successfully completed; 'in the eyes of the European Commission, the question of equal pay is far from being controlled.'[49]

During the period there was a decline in disparities between the male and female rates. 'In all members, female rates are going up more quickly than male rates'[50] and this was also the opinion of the Commission: 'negotiated wages for women have generally risen more than those for men; separate wage scales for women have nearly vanished from collective agreements.'[51] However, within a generalization which must necessarily be extremely broad there is room for many anomalies, and a considerable danger that the argument be used to justify reliance upon a natural process of economic development so that special attention to the question is unnecessary. The 1966 wage survey attempted to compare male and female rates matched for groups of workers identical in age, professional qualification, size of firm and system of wage payment. This suggested that in textiles, food and clothing differences ranged from 13 per cent in Italy to 28 per cent in the Netherlands, while in the electrical industry differences of under 15 per cent were found in France, Italy and the Netherlands and about 20 per cent in Germany and Belgium.[52] Even the Commission's reports on the subject, which were based on official returns, accepted that equal pay was in practice far from having been achieved.[53] Legal protection developed in Germany and Italy and in October 1967 Belgian women were given a right of legal appeal.[54] In France and Luxembourg the legal right was only partial, whilst in the Netherlands such protection depended upon the point being covered as part of a legally enforceable collective agreement.[55] It had not been firmly established whether Art. 119 was automatically self-executing within members or whether it placed an obligation on members to take appropriate action and the matter awaited an individual appeal to a national institution from which it could be referred to the Court for an authoritative opinion.

The experience showed that the power of the Commission to exert effective control over the situation was severely limited. National methods of wage fixing, the importance attached to an incomes policy, the degree of labour organization and of unionism amongst women, the methods of wage enforcement and relationships between industry and government were all factors affecting the degree of acceptance of the principle and the capacity of each member to ensure that it was effectively executed, yet these were not questions over which the Commission had more than an indirect and tenuous influence. Action to apply, and enforce, equal pay policies depends a great deal upon employers and workers themselves, for these are the people who are directly in touch with the realities of the situation and who can take up individual cases, thus setting in motion the machinery of legal redress or of attracting attention sufficient to ensure Community pressure on the state concerned whether through action by the Commission or publicity in the European Parliament. Despite the efforts made to keep in touch with events through the special working party, it was not easy for the Commission to know the true facts of the situation; certainly the simple collection of facts concerning pay is not enough to determine if the principle is being violated. In reply to a question of M. Troclet in Parliament in 1966 concerning the results of a French inquiry into wage rates showing considerable discrepancies between male and female earnings, the Commission had to admit that it was impossible to use such material to determine whether Art. 119 had been violated because no allowance was made for factors such as age, length of service, quali-fications or hours worked.[56] This must raise not only the issue of whether the Commission's original interpretation was too lenient but the further question of how far it is practical to single out the question of equal pay without positive policies to overcome the attendant problems associated with women's employment.

Nevertheless the contribution of the Community was positive. The establishment of the principle and the recognition that it had to be taken seriously were the first steps towards changing the attitude of employers and in forcing states to take action designed to implement it. Thus the most important single move in getting the principle off the ground was the resolution of the members in 1961 which gave the Community a firmer base from which to work. Henceforth the central core of the Commission's activity was educational, in the sense of publicity, both for the principle and known violations,[57] fact-gathering seminars and meetings on its application and the encouragement of employers and unions to adopt the principle.

> Whilst it is the case that a number of gaps still remained by 31 December 1964 it is also true that the persistence of the Commission in this field has been useful since definite progress has been achieved in the majority of members and the combined efforts of governments and the social partners have contributed in particular to the more rapid growth of female wages compared with those of men.[58]

However the resistances to equal pay are very strong. Although equal pay policies have been accepted in France since 1945, a survey of the late 1960s found unskilled women workers 20 per cent worse off than male colleagues and female executives and senior technicians perhaps 85 per cent worse off than men in the same jobs. The average discrepancy in wage rates was over 33 per cent.[59] It therefore seems unrealistic to suppose that a European policy can be more than a contribution and a slow, painstaking one, to its attainment.

III Industrial Health and Safety

The protection of workers through the imposition of special rules covering the employment of vulnerable groups such as women and children, through the insistence upon minimum standards of safety and medical supervision of those working with dangerous substances, through recognition of the right to compensation for industrial injury or disease and to the necessary medical care: such matters constitute the older forms of state intervention in industrial activity for social ends. Changes in techniques and processes which bring new hazards, turnover of personnel and new developments in medicine imply that constant re-evaluation of the field is necessary through research programmes, the application of up-to-date preventive measures and the supervision of arrangements made. The general population, too, is at risk from health hazards, ranging from air pollution to radio-active contamination of milk or harmful food additives, and the problems of sampling material, determining permitted levels and measures of control are questions which seem prime candidates for investigations and decisions at European level. The Communities have been instruments for making an additional contribution to such work, not least because of their ability to extend people's horizons through the interchange of experience and to draw attention to anomalies and gaps in national coverage on the basis of international comparisons. Their work cannot be unique since public and industrial health problems have long been the concern of national governments, but they can stimulate interest and activity. Since the ILO has a long history of study and educational programmes, much of the work of the Communities was carried out in conjunction with it, for example through the International Information Centre for Industrial Security and Hygiene at Geneva.

At first sight the field of industrial welfare seems a particularly suitable one in which to move towards a degree of uniformity of provision through the imposition of European standards.[60] The long-standing practice of protection, experience in defining standards objectively and the broad similarities of industrial processes in use suggest that the resulting human problems are likely to require comparable solutions. Finally, it would appear advantageous for a Community anxious to promote mobility of goods and of labour to insist upon identical standards of safety and protection, not only from the human viewpoint but also to prevent unnecessary obstacles to trade and a rise in industrial accidents resulting from ignorance of legislation and established procedures. Differences in national standards of industrial health and safety have normally been considered by the Commission to be liable to affect the policy of liberalizing goods and services.[61] All three Communities had a direct interest in the promotion of such work, and Parliament was particularly interested in the possibility of greater harmonization of standards, notably in relation to industrial safety, and in the role of the Communities in accident prevention, arguing for the 'absolute necessity for the three Executives to lay down a common programme of action' and later questioning the possible use of Art. 235 or of an inter-governmental convention to step up the work.[62] In February 1967 it strongly urged the Commission to develop measures, such as arranging more regular meetings at European level, in association with the ILO; the use of directives and recommendations to establish a greater standardization of industrial protection; the setting-up of a committee to lay down definite Community standards and to consider new forms of protection as they became necessary; the formulation of a regulation on the common use of security signs in view of labour migration; the strengthening of the Industrial Health and Safety Division of the Commission and the publication of research results.[63] Studies and consultations, Signor Levi-Sandri had argued in 1965, were leading to a programme ultimately aiming at a European system of industrial health expressed in the form of directives and recommendations.[64]

In contrast with the High Authority, the Commission received no direct instruction to develop and support research in the field of industrial safety. It was not until 1962 that an Industrial Health and Safety Division was created within the Commission[65] but even so its work was hampered by lack of funds for which no special allocation had been made in the treaty.[66] It was, therefore, dependent upon collaborative effort under Art. 118 and the extent to which it might set up study programmes and work of an educational nature thereunder. A wide range of topics was in fact considered, including the social and economic aspects of occupational disease, industrial safety, personnel training, the influence of human factors in the prevention of accidents, national legislation on accidents and diseases, rules governing industrial medicine and its organization, the causative agents of diseases giving rise to compensation. Work on the standardization of statistics on industrial accidents and disease as well as on the organization of the exchange of experience and literature was undertaken. Later studies included those on pressure chamber work, heavy agricultural work performed by women, reduction of noise in factories, protection of workers against noise, inoculation of workers exposed to special risks and a survey of qualifications demanded from experts and technical inspectors, normally in association with other international and European organizations. From 1965 a yearly study programme was run for senior factory inspectors, doctors, lawyers and engineers to enable them to see work elsewhere in the Community. Better knowledge 'facilitates approximation of the different concepts and helps to speed up the work'.[67] Meetings of government experts were held regularly.

A particularly important function was that of undertaking work to encourage safety-mindedness through arranging meetings of national safety experts and the exchange of educational material. A seminar was called in June 1966 at the request of the Health Protection Committee of Parliament to discuss possible action to make workers more safety-minded, to consider the establishment of safety standards and instruction therein and the particular problems of migrant workers who were at special risk as a result of language difficulties, job dissatisfaction and often absorbed in cultural readjustment. The same year saw a special conference on the possibility of standardizing electrical equipment as a safety measure.

About half of all industrial accidents are caused by lack of individual protection[68] so that measures which can overcome this are of particular value, whether this means increasing the understanding of the individual, improving protective devices or redesigning machinery or processes to eliminate hazards. The notorious non-use of protective appliances by workers often has good grounds. Equipment may be badly designed in itself such as a crash helmet which is too heavy, inappropriate for the particular job as in the case of a thick glove which prevents essential dexterity, or have unfortunate side effects as when protective spectacles distort vision. However perfect, the use of such appliances is always under some degree of human control and it may therefore be more satisfactory to redesign machinery or to introduce new working processes so that the hazards are eliminated. Other work which the Community could well support includes investigation of the psychological state of workers and the level of personal relations at firm level as factors in accident causation, and the educational campaigns in school, industry and agriculture particularly those directed at young people when they start work. Parliament has also suggested that the standardization of protective material, including clothing, and its proving on a uniform basis would be of considerable benefit to the Community,[69] and in June 1967 the Council agreed that members should co-operate both together and with the Commission in the standardization, checking and testing of individual safety equipment.[70] At the same time it agreed to see co-operation develop on the standardization of safety signs and notices, again of great convenience for migrants and for the use of imported machinery. Many experiments with the use of colours and symbols have been undertaken with the employment of foreign labour particularly in mind. Even this is not as simple as it sounds, however, for the meaning to be attached to a particular colour can still admit of misunderstanding as the common use of red to denote stop, fire, or danger demonstrates.

During 1964 and 1965 the Commission began the process of the harmonization of safety standards requiring the adaptation of existing rules. On 3 August 1964[71] the Commission submitted to the Council a draft directive on the introduction of standardized control of the manufacture and use of the cartridge-operated stud driver, on the grounds that lack of uniformity constituted a barrier to trade and to the free supply of services which could be eliminated if states would accept an authorization provided by a fellow member and provided the safety of the operator was guaranteed by standardized devices. Two further directives were submitted to the Council on 10 May 1965.[72] An outline directive concerned the classification of dangerous substances, the use of symbols to denote danger and the nature of the risk involved in the use of particular substances, and gave advice on the handling and identification of such materials. The second related to the classification, labelling and packaging of certain dangerous substances aimed to eliminate discrepancies between national rules. This latter directive was accepted on 27 June 1967[73] but the time limit for the application was successfully extended. Further plans for directives covered questions such as the manufacture, inspection and approval of components of tubular steel scaffolding and its use and electrical equipment carrying fire risk especially where likely to be widely used by foreign labour.

Clearly this is not work which has a definitive end. The Commission was continually involved in the work of evolving improved protective standards for the use of dangerous machinery or substances and providing better protection for migrants and this remains true today. By 1972, little had been done for agriculture, although a European safety code on the farm was considered necessary by the Commission, which recognized the value of continuing co-operation between members on educational techniques to ensure that workers maintained proper safety standards even where, as on small farms, the employer had few resources to spare for industrial safety.[74]

Additionally, in the field of industrial health and safety, the Commission worked on an ambitious programme of recommendations designed to establish minimum standards in fields of particular importance. All states have recognized the vulnerable position of the young worker in industry and have developed schemes of apprenticeship and vocational training as well as special arrangements for medical supervision and for working hours. The early forms of protection of child labour, developed from the middle of the nineteenth century, were largely concerned with gross abuses such as excessively long hours of work and the employment of children in dangerous or otherwise unsuitable occupations. The passage of time has extended social responsibility so that the young worker has increasingly obtained a privileged position in the labour force. The minimum age of starting work has increased as has the upper age limit for eligibility for special protection; regular hours of work up to a maximum are generally laid down and night work forbidden or limited. Rules concerning rest periods and paid holidays are often more generous than for adult workers and the pressure to keep up on the assembly line or in the work team modified. Patterns of apprenticeship and vocational training are well established, including periods of educational attendance and obligatory systems of medical supervision, whilst states enforce their regulations by both legal sanctions and factory inspection. As is to be expected, however, states vary considerably in the exact forms of measures taken and nowhere is protection entirely satisfactory.

A tripartite working party began to study the matter in 1961 and its report[75] demonstrated not only the extent but also the variability of national measures of control. Gaps in protection were particularly obvious for young people employed in agriculture, building, family firms, domestic work and home work. This report led to a recommendation from the Commission aimed to establish basic minimum standards to be applied in all branches of activity, with strictly defined exceptions.[76] Similar action was attempted to encourage higher standards of protection for the working mother. The tripartite group considering the general questions of protection of women at work gave special consideration to this question, producing comparative material which demonstrated that, although forms of control existed everywhere, there were wide variations. In France and Luxembourg protection extended to all types of work, but elsewhere agriculture, domestic and outwork were wholly or partially excluded. Legal limitations on hours of work or night work either did not exist or, where they did, were variable, although all forbade employment in underground, dangerous or unhealthy occupations. Compulsory maternity leave varied from six to fourteen weeks as did further leave for the nursing mother, if permitted. Cash benefits under social security ranged from twelve weeks to five months at amounts between half pay and full wages, whilst other types of cash grants existed in addition. All provided medical care for the confinement.[77] The Commission therefore drafted a recommendation designed to fill the gaps which was adopted in 1966 but no further action has been taken upon it.[78]

Industrial medicine was another field to which the Commission addressed itself in the form of a recommendation to members. Although this was based on the work of the ILO, it represents an example of an attempt to assert those 'higher and more exacting standards'[79] deemed appropriate for advanced nations rather than allowing minimum and maximum standards as the ILO has done. It followed the latter's lead, however, by assuming that today industrial health services should be interpreted on a wide scale in the belief that proper consideration of the health of the worker requires attention to the general standards of hygiene and amenity with adequate services such as canteens, washing facilities and protection against accidents, smoke, dust and fumes. On this view, industrial medicine includes proper training and supervision of workers for the jobs they are to do and the machinery they are to use and participates in activity to improve the conditions of work, whether this means better standards of building and equipment, the use of processes attuned to human capacities and needs as well as the elimination of dangerous products.[80] In scope, therefore, the recommendation opened a new field of industrial medicine by going beyond the traditional field of minimum health protection into preventive work including the identification of occupational hazards, worker training and retraining, the psychological and physiological study of jobs and research as well as traditional medical surveillance and care. A recommendation on industrial medical services was adopted by the Commission in July 1962.[81] 'The purpose of the recommendation of the Commission of the EEC is to get states to give a legal base to industrial medicine in the firm'[82] although the variations in existing conditions meant that only the principles and not the details could be laid down at European level. Existing differences in the pattern of services and in their range suggested, however, that benefits would result from 'a system established on a legislative rather than a purely discretionary basis'[83] since where such a system existed in practice the worker was better protected and the responsibility of the employer clearer; 'experience does indeed show that in those countries there exists a higher density of services and more industrial doctors'.[84] Such a system should also provide better, and more harmonized, conditions of work for doctors, thus contributing to the establishment of greater similarity of conditions required by the Treaty of Rome under Art. 57 (3). For such reasons states were asked to take the necessary legislative and administrative action to establish services allowing for details to be filled in by collective agreements.

Following a symposium on industrial medicine held in 1964[85] which stressed the need for special training and the development of collaboration between factory doctors, engineers, chemists and social workers, three studies were prepared on the establishment of regional centres and institutes of industrial medicine, the status and role of the factory doctor and the organization of medical services in small firms. It was clear that considerable variation existed in the number of industrial doctors employed, whilst only in France and the Netherlands did an obligatory qualification exist. Germany in particular has been criticized for allowing firms to flout the directives of the Ministry of Labour on the employment of factory doctors,[86] and the constant delays experienced by the Commission in obtaining information from members on industrial medicine is no doubt indicative of their lack of interest in the subject.[87]

A further extension of medical services was envisaged by the recommendation from the Commission on 27 July 1966 concerning extra protection for workers exposed to particular hazards in all industries other than those covered by Euratom which has its own norms.[88] The previous year it had been queried whether the Commission intended to utilize Art. 101 to ensure the necessary medical control, but it had been considered that the balance of advantage was in favour of a recommendation.[89] This argued that, where it is known that a health risk exists, periodic medical checks are valuable not only for the health of the individual worker but as a means of helping to control incidence. Once again states had accepted the principle but applied it in various ways or in respect of different risks and the Commission argued for the establishment of a uniform list of risks against which workers should have similar and obligatory medical protection.[90]

A move parallel to that urging the development of industrial health services was the attempt to establish a uniform list of occupational diseases and the right to receive compensation and treatment for them. In the Community, where the same industrial processes are widespread, there seems no logical reason why a disease, identified in origin in one country, should be refused such classification elsewhere, yet of eighty diseases known to the area as of occupational origin only twelve were established in all members in 1962.[91] They therefore appeared as a suitable subject for an early step in harmonization.[92] Furthermore, there was a real risk that migrants might often find themselves ineligible for compensation, since this normally depended, *inter alia*, upon detailed rules concerning the length of time worked in particular occupations. Broken service was likely to prevent them proving a period of employment adequate to establish the occupational origin of a disease unless rules operative in member states were standardized.

The establishment of a list of diseases and causative agents has long been considered the most satisfactory way of identifying those conditions which warrant compensation, so that Commission policy was directed in the first instance towards obtaining acceptance of a standard list of forty-four diseases where a known causal relationship existed and which might be used as the basis for national legislative protection by standardizing rules concerning the length of exposure to risk, definition of diseases and their relationship to particular occupations. It was hoped that such a list might encourage states to consider such diseases as eligible for compensation, even when they had not yet received proper legislative cover. A secondary list was annexed to the recommendation of diseases whose occupational origin was not yet fully established, so that the submission of returns might lead to a strengthening of the evidence and thus their full acceptance if appropriate. By its recommendation[93] the Commission also wished to obtain greater statistical uniformity, improve the exchange of medical information and encourage the development of preventive measures. States were asked to inform the Commission of additions to their national lists of occupationally determined diseases.[94]

The recognition of an industrial disease leads logically to the question of compensation for the victims, but it was not until 20 July 1966 that the Commission was ready to send a recommendation dealing with the conditions governing the payment of benefit.[95] Rules concerning the type and length of work done, the time limit for the onset of the disease and the relationship of work to illness are all factors which are used to determine eligibility for compensation and where uniformity of practice appears a reasonable goal. The new recommendation was designed to suppress the most restrictive limiting conditions, to give more freedom to doctors to establish cause and effect by providing the possibility for workers to obtain compensation for a disease which in the individual case was occupational in origin without the necessity for a state to classify it as occupational in all cases, to increase the chances of migrants receiving compensation when exposed to the same risk in two countries between which differences in legislation existed and to incorporate special arrangements for agriculture into the general rules.

A further development came as a result of the Commission's study of long-term invalidity in social security systems. Since benefits can be viewed as compensation for loss of health, absolute loss of earnings or loss relative to occupational status or for a mixture of all three, it is not surprising that this revealed considerable variations in the level of compensation given. A draft recommendation was accepted by the Commission on 12 January 1966 which suggested the adoption of two broad categories of total and partial invalidity based essentially on medical assessment rather than loss of earning power, but no further action had been taken on the matter by the end of 1972.[96]

The value of the Communities in the field of industrial welfare was positive but limited by the failures of the Commission to prosecute its views to the logical conclusion of a formal act. The peak of the Commission's activity was reached during the period from 1966 to 1967 with the recommendations on the protection of young people, industrial medicine, payment for industrial disease and the acceptance by the Council of a directive on the labelling of dangerous substances. Additionally the extra study, research and educational work which resulted from its efforts can be accounted as a gain in a field which receives little publicity or glamour. The attempts to establish uniform standards of welfare provision, however, were more difficult to prosecute since the Commission was in no position to impose rules. The executive therefore depended upon the willingness of members to give effect to European standards as part of their own internal policies. It is interesting to note that no use was made of those mechanisms of the treaty whose activation depended upon members, such as Arts. 100 and 235, and that even the issue of Commission recommendations was on occasion postponed. Despite this extreme caution, the Commission remained optimistic that its aim was the establishment of a European system of industrial health and safety.[97] The limits of power meant that the best chance of success for the executive was to make its work valuable to members through giving new stimulus and encouraging research and education, so that it would commend itself by its obvious worth. 'Governments', the Commission congratulated, 'have given full support to the Commission's activities concerning approximation of legislation on industrial health and safety.'[98] The future was to show that this goodwill was severely limited.

4 The Movement of the Working Population

I The Wage Earner

The Treaty of Rome placed the provisions concerning the free movement of labour within the context of the mobility of the factors of production. Their implementation proceeded relatively smoothly during a period when manpower shortages worked to absorb people who might otherwise have remained unemployed in those areas where they were born because of a lack of available jobs. The ability to move to obtain work reflects very closely upon human welfare and the task of the European Community was to establish for its territory a right taken for granted on the national level. The principle of the free movement of the working population was thus seen by the Commission to possess a dimension beyond that of an economic imperative, being an ingredient of that social unity at which the treaty was aimed through giving expression to the notion of European citizenship and of the human right to take action which appears good to the individual.[1] The conception of free movement under the Treaty of Rome was not, argued Signor Levi-Sandri, entirely explicable in the narrow sense of enabling unskilled workers to escape from regional poverty, but also made a contribution towards a higher form of political union in which, with respect to the fundamental activity of employment, men are placed on an equal footing.[2]

The Community area has long been affected by the complex labour movements of Western Europe resulting from the disturbances of war or political upheaval and by the more traditional seasonal migrations and frontier crossing with which the Continent is familiar. It is not that the Community has created unique problems but that its logic is to be additionally concerned with two facets of migration. In so far as it occurs in order to enable men to escape from unemployment and lack of opportunity at home, then the adoption of the free movement principle should have made such relief easier. Italy, as the only member with a stubborn unemployment problem, was clearly the one most likely to benefit from this point of view and she has been the state most anxious to establish that unemployed workers from the Community should be offered jobs in preference to applicants from elsewhere.[3] However, in

99

recent years Community labour has been less mobile and, as industry has developed in Italy, her unemployed workers have increasingly consisted of those requiring considerable help and training before being ready to fill vacant posts whether in Germany or elsewhere. A further, more complex, problem of labour quality was beginning to arise which, although recognized as an issue,[4] was never properly faced by the Community in its first period. Both the free movement of labour policy and the resettlement aid from the social fund in practice placed greater emphasis upon the traditional type of movement of the unskilled worker than upon the more sophisticated services which public authorities are now developing.

If in the future employment opportunities continue to develop in the Community and come to depend increasingly upon skills, the right to move in search of work will be part of the human wish to use one's abilities in a constructive way. Labour movement based on a reasoned decision by an individual to seek his social betterment is very different from mass movement designed to enable men to escape from regions of dire poverty, but assumptions held by public authorities sometimes appear slow to adapt to the changing characteristics of this complex social phenomenon. In 1967 the Commission noted the growing trend towards spontaneous rather than organized migration, even in countries, such as Italy, which have been traditional suppliers of unskilled labour and where established recruiting offices existed.[5] In part this may have reflected the fact that workers were becoming better informed, more selective in their approach to work and more competent to make their own arrangements, in addition to the development of more efficient co-operation between employment exchanges so that workers were no longer solely dependent upon firms' recruiting schemes. The comment of the Storch report in 1964, that mass movements encourage one to think that migrants should be permanently condemned to the lower-grade jobs, is also relevant in its implication that more selective choices require that attitudes towards migration should change at the receiving end as well.[6]

Migration policies reflect these underlying factors. Traditional state policies were minimally conceived in order to deal with questions such as the volume of migration according to the demand for unskilled labour, the protection of nationals against competition or the insistence that firms accept basic social responsibility for their migrant workers. When migration is less forced and more a matter of individual choice, more complex issues are likely to assert themselves. In the first instance, in order to allow those who are still impeded by the lack of opportunity in their native areas to take advantage of jobs offered elsewhere, some means of enabling them to acquire the necessary skills is required. In consequence a free movement policy has logically to be closely linked with the aim of improving occupational mobility and knowledge of available opportunities whether at home or further afield. For an organization such as the EEC this at once raised the further question of the policy balance to be obtained between job creation in areas of unemployment to provide opportunities within the competence of the existing labour force and encouragement to geographical mobility.

> In a speech last December to a conference on regional economies, M. Marjolin, the Vice-President, emphasised that labour mobility, of which so much is being heard now, is a very different thing from forced migration. Mobility he understands as freedom for workers to move from one industry to another *within* the same region, aided by training and of their own free will.[7]

But a worker with a marketable skill cannot be treated as a second-class citizen by the host country if he is to stay, and the ease of communications of today will expose this situation more readily than in the past. Traditional arrangements for recruiting labour are therefore giving way to more intricate policies, which include the need to attempt to remove social, political or economic disabilities experienced by non-nationals. To place the migrant in a position of comparability with the indigenous inhabitant may in fact require that he receives more attention, care and services than the latter. Positive policies may need to range from those designed to promote family integration into the host community to those concerned to ensure labour efficiency by ensuring language proficiency and knowledge of administrative and trade practices or working processes. Equality in the work situation may not only require ways of ensuring the migrant is not used as cheap labour but that his pay, conditions of work and opportunities for training and promotion are the same as those of the indigenous worker. From the viewpoint of social policy, therefore, the principle of free movement of labour, although essential, is limited. Legal provisions to establish rights may need to be supplemented by special aid to overcome the manifold social and human difficulties which surround migration.[8] Although the term 'integration' is not used in the Treaty of Rome, yet acceptance of the principle of free movement, equality of treatment and permanent residence makes little sense without an implicit acceptance of such a concept. Regulation 1612/68, by referring to the complete equality *de jure* and *de facto* of everything relating to the actual carrying-out of a wage-earning occupation and to the integration of the family into the new environment, overtly accepted that this is so.

However migration cannot be looked at solely from the worker's side. A rapid turnover of labour because migrants are anxious to return home with a little cash in hand must dampen employers' enthusiasm for active training policies. At the same time foreign workers are inefficient if they lack the ability to communicate on relevant matters and both technical and safety issues may be prejudiced. Vocational training and induction schemes often need to be specifically adapted in order to take account of linguistic shortcomings, different training methods and national attitudes. Employers must mount recruiting operations and, if intending workers are to be given some realistic understanding of what is involved in the projected move and some preparation for it, work has to be done in the country of origin. Arrangements for, and during, the journey, settlement on arrival, family movement and repatriation are all issues which will arise at varying times.

A further complicating factor results from the varying pattern of migration. Long-term movement presents different issues from short; single workers face different problems from those faced by families; mass recruitment of unskilled labour requires different handling from the employment of a qualified worker for a particular job. Whilst the migrant family may require help with housing, language, schooling arrangements and cultural adjustment, better forms of help for the short-term worker may be ways of ensuring he can send money back home, that his family is not in need and that his own housing needs are adequately met. Family migration often exposes the basic weakness of the newcomer, who is both a stranger and a member of the unskilled working class. Since it is more likely to be on a long-term basis, effective integration into the life of the community becomes a wide-ranging affair, involving cultural disparities, schooling facilities and job opportunities for other members of the family. At this point the human problems of immigration have extended beyond the realm of the employer and become a question for the community as a whole.

The provisions of the Treaty of Rome concerning free movement were drawn on a wider scale than for the coal and steel workers. They were divided into three sections. The first was that of the mobility of the wage-earning population, the second was the need to ensure the same right to the self-employed whether performing an entrepreneurial or professional activity and the third the provision of facilities so that services might be supplied across frontiers. Most success was achieved during this period in relation to the first group.

It will be recalled that the policy for the free movement of wage earners consisted of three parts. Firstly, the abolition of discrimination at work, secondly the right to accept employment, to move about freely for employment purposes, to continue to stay in a state during both employment and retirement and, thirdly, the establishment of appropriate machinery in order to make labour movements effective. It was intended that this policy should be progressively implemented so that discrimination against foreign workers would be gradually removed through the adjustments of national legislation to a Community timetable.

EEC action was not new. It followed other international attempts to create a freer labour market and developed from the bilateral agreements of the post-war world based on the principle of reciprocity and close control. Western European Union (WEU) discussions had already taken up the question of a common classification of jobs and had led to a multilateral convention to ease the position of trainees, but most progress had been made by Benelux from 1956 onwards. Under these early arrangements governments retained wide protective powers over matters such as public order, health and the priority of the national labour market, but a good deal of experience in administrative co-operation was obtained. OEEC had also been interested in removing obstacles to the movement of workers and obtained agreement on questions such as the collaboration of employment services, the limitation of the priority of the national labour market and the easing of restrictions on people's right to continue to live in countries where they had held jobs. Nevertheless the first *Social Exposé* commented on the severe control of labour permits that still generally obtained except between the Benelux countries.[9] Action by the EEC was largely conceived in terms of liberalizing the issue and renewal of labour permits, improving machinery for bringing supply and demand together and lifting restrictions on employment.[10] Steps were not taken until after careful study of existing conventions and national practices and after discussion with government experts and trade union officials. Technical studies included investigations into possible methods of easing restrictions, eliminating disparities and discrimination; the compilation of material to show existing entry regulations and rules concerning employment, family residence, the possession of passports, visas, labour and residence permits. Special studies were done, too, on the position of frontier and seasonal workers, the means of transferring wages and the social security rights of migrants.[11] A draft regulation was submitted to the Council in July 1960 and sent both to the Economic and Social Committee, which approved it in November, and to Parliament, whose recommendations led to some strengthening of the provisions on the Commission's power, the process of liberalization and the role of employers' and workers' organizations.[12] The regulation was adopted on 16 August 1961[13] and remained operative during the period from 1 September 1961 until 31 December 1962. Technical questions were dealt with in an accompanying directive, which was considered a more suitable instrument since administrative arrangements varied between states. Practical complexities can often act as barriers to migration, and the purpose of the directive was to simplify such questions by obliging states to provide a passport or comparable travel document, valid for five years in EEC countries, to enable their nationals to accept offers of employment and receiving states to issue labour and residence permits, not to ask for a visa and the like.[14]

Regulation 15 marked the first major step towards an effective labour market, in a wider sense than the purely economic, by dealing with four basic questions. In the first instance, lay the problem of the extent to which national priority over other members and Community priority over non-members was to be established. Additionally, however, attention was given to the application of measures to ensure equality of treatment and the prolongation of employment in the host country and to resolve family matters. Jobs were reserved for the national labour force for three weeks and then made available to the nationals of other members. However, following arrangements previously developed under OEEC, employers might apply immediately by name for individual workers on the grounds of special skills or family ties. Members agreed to send to the Commission details of areas and occupations both deficient in, and experiencing a surplus of, manpower and, in the case of the former, employment permits were to be issued automatically. A general obligation rested on members to allow their nationals to accept posts elsewhere in the Community. In these ways there was a definite step towards the unity of the labour market, at a time when buoyant conditions might be expected to make states less anxious to protect national priority but sensitive to the need to prevent a rapid influx of labour looking for work with consequent difficulties of job competition and social strain in areas already attracting large numbers of people.

The question of whether Community nationals should themselves receive preferential treatment over migrants from elsewhere was less easily established. The principle was of most interest to Italy but other members were not anxious to interfere with their recruiting arrangements in Spain, Portugal, Greece, Yugoslavia and elsewhere. However the realities of the situation meant that tensions at no time became severe. Art. 43 of Regulation 15, which dealt with the matter, was not entirely precise. States agreed to pursue employment policies which took account of the labour situation in other members and, provided the employer concerned was indifferent between one group of workers and another, to give preference to workers from members with surplus manpower in the occupational skills required. The claim that it was accepted from the start that one aim of the Community was to absorb its labour surpluses seems therefore somewhat excessive.[15] Parliamentarians were less certain of their approval of the situation. In 1961 M. Rubinacci referred to the limited value of Art. 43 and the need to reaffirm the principle of the priority of the Community labour market so that it might be put fully into operation.[16] A serious difference of view almost at once developed over the meaning of Art. 43, reflecting Italy's aim to help her surplus manpower and Germany's wish to be able to continue recruiting in third countries. The Commission took the view that the article imposed a definite obligation on members to consider the unemployment problems of the others by giving vacancies in the first instance to Community workers qualified to fill them. This it held to be more than a recommenda-

tion but a definite legal obligation which prevented states from system-
atically ignoring the availability of Community labour. This view was
communicated to the German Federal Minister of Labour and Social
Affairs although the Commission also recognized that exceptions, as in
the case of Austria, might be possible although it would wish to approve
them.[17] In 1965 members reaffirmed their intention to encourage
preferential recruitment of surplus workers from the Community.[18]
Additionally, nationals of members were exempt from arrangements
limiting the number of foreign workers permitted in any country.

Workers became progressively freer in relation to employment in their
new place of residence. After one year of regular employment they were
entitled to have work permits renewed for the same type of work, after
three years to take up any other form of employment for which they
were qualified and after four years, in most cases, to move between jobs
on the same terms as those permitted to nationals. Periods of work
completed before the entry into force of the regulation were partially
eligible for consideration. Other issues directly relating to the principle
of equality of treatment in the working situation were also considered.
It was agreed that migrants should receive the same treatment as nationals
in respect of all conditions of work and notably in respect of pay,
dismissal and trade union membership. Eligibility for union office, being
an internal matter for the union, was omitted from the regulation. The
right to vote for workers' representatives in appropriate bodies in so far
as these came under public control was agreed. This was of particular
importance in Germany because of both the widespread use of representative bodies and her position as a major importer of labour. The
right to use employment services was accepted, although this proved not
always easy to arrange without prior agreement on acceptable qualifications for jobs and uniformity of job classification. Any discriminatory
clauses in collective agreements were abolished and no special criteria
might be laid down for the Community worker to fulfil before being
recruited. Agreement was reached on the need for free transfer of wages
and savings.

It cannot be overstressed that these were legal requirements which in
themselves, although important as a first step, could not deal with the
manifold problems of socio-economic reality. The application of uniform
criteria for dismissal such as age, seniority or length of service impartially
to Community and national worker alike may be very hard to make in
the face of the antagonism of local workers although it may be pointed
out that, if a length of service rule penalizes, an age rule often benefits,
the migrant. The legal right to be treated equally and to receive help
from employment services does not overcome the hard facts of un-
familiarity with the local arrangements. A migrant may easily assume
his employment prospects are poor and that he had therefore better go

home thus worsening the prospects in those areas where jobs are normally short. Employment services in reception areas thus need to be adequately skilled to help migrants find new jobs but such services have in practice been used mainly by the children of migrants settled for a considerable period[19] and the Technical Committee has attempted to consider the effectiveness of services for those migrants made redundant.[20]

The position of the worker's family was also considered. The spouse and children under twenty-one years had the right of entry and members agreed to encourage the admission of other dependent kin, subject to the worker having a 'normal' dwelling. His right of equal access to housing was laid down. The spouse and children had the right to take up paid employment and children to be admitted to state schemes of apprenticeship and vocational training provided they were resident within the territory. Such arrangements were an important first step, but limited in practice being particularly weak in that no concept of enabling families to take advantage of such right was at that time incorporated. M. Troclet's description of the provisions as *'une heureuse liaison entre le droit familial et le droit social'* seems a little precipitate.[21] The continuing lack of housing facilities in areas of high employment presented one of the more difficult problems for the migrant family and this the regulation left to member states. It was, in consequence, dealt with in differing ways. France operated a liberal entry policy but by doing so encouraged the creation of sub-normal living conditions, Holland insisted that migrants had been in the area for a year before being eligible for the waiting list for low-cost housing, whilst employers often provided facilities in Germany. Such requirements often acted either as a brake on family immigration or as an incentive to illegal entry.[22]

It was clearly necessary for changes in national employment services to occur in order to operate the new system and make the labour market a practical reality. Jobs had to be defined in a comparable way, uniform levels of skill laid down, effective and useful information about personnel supplied, and co-operation in the collection of information concerning employment trends in the Community established. For such reasons a system of institutional collaboration was required. Members agreed that their central employment offices would henceforth co-operate closely together and with the Commission for which specialized administrative sections would be created. Contacts would be developed at regional level also. Employment services became responsible for the collection and distribution of information about labour movement and obstacles thereto, for making a quarterly return of employment trends by industry and area, for providing an overall assessment of the labour situation and for making any necessary studies to further the free movement of manpower. The Commission, in co-operation with members, was also given the duty to instigate or undertake studies relating to employment trends. A special

European office for the co-ordination and balancing of employment supply and demand was created within the Commission to establish regular contacts with, and encourage the smooth working of, national machinery and to collect and analyse national data. Each quarter it distributed a list of regions and occupations scheduled as having a shortage or surplus of manpower and provided both quarterly and annual reports on the clearing operations which formed the basis for a broader view of employment policy and enabled the Commission to ensure that the arrangements were properly applied. It also produced standard classifications for jobs, criteria for assessing labour needs and, along with member states, arranged exchange visits and study courses for the personnel of employment offices. It was given two supporting committees. The technical committee represented governments whilst ECSC and Euratom sent non-voting members.[23] Its duty was to assist the Commission in administrative affairs through helping to improve co-operation, carry out the necessary studies, establish uniform criteria for fact collection and arrange exchange programmes. A major task was to establish a comparative glossary of trades within which migration proved to be most frequent.[24] It compiled a comparative dictionary of occupations and helped to establish definitions of jobs so that labour movements in occupations such as building or hotel work could be assessed more rationally. Through its auspices the Commission arranged study courses, in-service training and information meetings for officials, for welfare workers working with migrants and for representatives of employers and workers. In May 1966 it held a fact-finding session for officials from Ministries of Home Affairs and Justice especially concerned with entry and residence problems and the operation of the restrictions deriving from the clauses relating to public order, health and safety. Secondly, in order to associate governments and employers' and workers' organizations with the work, a consultative committee of thirty-six members was created with particular responsibility to consider questions of free movement in relation to national manpower policies. It was given the right to study, to recommend and to give opinions notably on the exchange of information concerning labour trends, the movement of workers, vocational guidance and vocational training, housing for migrants and social assistance for them. This committee was active in discussing the substantive issues connected with free labour movement. Examples of its work include the examination of the employment aspects of the medium-term economic policy, the discussion of measures to maintain optimum employment levels and of co-ordinating national policies at Community level. Specialized studies were done of the integration of the migrant worker into the firm, reception arrangements for migrants and ways of informing workers of their rights, and the committee played an active part in the creation of the more liberal proposals subsequently introduced.

The Commission was given a special role in developing courses of vocational training, particularly accelerated vocational training, in order to meet manpower deficiencies. In co-operation with members it was entitled to ascertain needs, to contact appropriate bodies and to consider the desirability of organizing courses designed to enable workers to move from one state to fill vacancies elsewhere. Members agreed to keep the Commission informed of agreements made between themselves on the organization of such courses. As has been seen, however, these courses were not very successful. Following the rejection of the 1965 proposal that three thousand Italians should be trained in a Community scheme, France offered to train 150 Italians in her own centres on six-month courses in construction work, provided they agreed to stay to work in France for one year. Again the results were disappointing.[25]

Frontier and seasonal workers, entertainers and musicians, were initially dealt with separately. In the first group long-established labour patterns had given rise to a variety of international arrangements which gave such workers rather more favourable treatment than it was wished to give to migrants as a whole. The Commission presented proposals to the Council on 28 February 1962 which attempted to define both frontier and seasonal workers and to lay down provisions for them. In brief, frontier workers were defined as those who returned home every day or at least once a week and who lived and worked in defined neighbourhood frontier zones. These were normally limited to a depth of fifty kilometres from the relevant frontier, unless previous bilateral treaties had defined the area otherwise.[26] Here national priority was to last only for one week with the possibility of obtaining named workers with no delay. After one year's work the right to automatic renewal of a labour permit for the same occupation was given, after two years the right to carry on any paid employment as a frontier worker, after three years the right to carry on the occupation last exercised anywhere within the Community and after four years any post on the same terms as nationals. Seasonal workers were those who went to work elsewhere in the Community for a maximum of eight months. If workers were to be recruited under a quota system for certain specific tasks in agriculture and the food industry no waiting period for the notification of vacancies was imposed, whereas for all others a two-week priority might be established with the possibility of issuing labour permits automatically for regions of labour shortage or for a named worker. After eight months a seasonal worker was to be entitled to the renewal of his labour permit for the same occupation, after two years for any seasonal supplement for which he was qualified and after thirty-two months for any occupation on the same terms as nationals. These proposals became merged into a generalized regulation passed in 1964. Entertainers and musicians were originally subjected to more restrictive conditions in that individual offers of employment might only be made in the case of highly paid persons.[27]

On 1 May 1964 a new Regulation, 38/64/CEE,[28] replaced Nos. 15 and 18 and incorporated the arrangements for frontier and seasonal workers. New directives were also issued. Directive 64/240/CEE[29] liberalized questions relating to the issue of relevant documents. The issue of work permits themselves was transferred to the regulation so that standardized procedures became part of Community law, but the directive simplified the issue of other documents, abolished the need for residence and work permits for stays of under three months and dealt with similar matters. Directive 64/221/CEE[30] applied to both the free movement and free establishment programmes and was designed to co-ordinate the rules restricting travel and residence on the grounds of public order, safety and health which previously had been unevenly interpreted and enforced. It was made clear that such rules should not be used as a means of economic protection. Illnesses which would justify refusal to allow entry were laid down under broad headings. Those dangerous to health included infectious and quarantinable diseases, tuberculosis and syphilis. Those which might be considered a threat to public order or safety included drug addiction and serious psychoses. Subsequent contraction of such illnesses should not, it was considered, be used as grounds for expulsion. Restrictions on entry or sojourn should be founded on reasons exclusive to the individual and be of a serious nature – for example, the expiry of a passport or identity card was not in itself serious and criminal convictions should not necessarily be considered adequate reason. Any decisions against the individual should be taken speedily and he should be told of their nature unless state security was involved. Although no formal right of appeal was established, decisions were only to be taken after proper discussion by the appropriate machinery, including consideration by a body other than that having power to issue or renew a permit, to which the individual should have the chance to speak for himself. He should have the same right to protection against purely administrative acts as that held by nationals. States were given six months to conform to these arrangements.

Underlying the acceptance of the new regulation there had been lively debate on the questions of the priority of the national and Community labour markets, of workers' participation in works councils and of the right of the migrant to equal access to housing provision.[31] Over such matters the regulation was a compromise. Priority of the national labour market was further curtailed. Any Community worker had the right to take up wage-earning employment if the job had been notified as vacant subject to the right of a member to suspend the rule in a specific region or occupation on account of a surplus of local manpower. Such suspension had to be notified, and justified, to the Commission and if a job remained unfilled for a fortnight labour permits for Community nationals had to be issued. In certain cases the two-week local priority rule could not be applied at all. Exemptions included frontier workers, some specialized personnel, workers staying less than one month, entertainers and musicians over a particular rate of pay, workers receiving individual employment offers and migrant and seasonal workers who had already completed periods of work.

In practice not a great deal of use was made of the power to protect the national labour market. France reserved the jobs of labourer, office worker and shop assistant during the first year of operation and the provisions were used in 1965 and 1967 by France, Belgium and the Netherlands.[32] France made particular use of the restrictions.[33] In 1968 Germany, Italy and Luxembourg made no use of the safeguard clause, limited use was made of it by the Netherlands and France, whilst Belgium protected certain jobs in mining areas.[34]

More effective steps were taken to create a Community labour market. In addition to the quarterly notification of labour surpluses, members were required to keep the Commission effectively informed of their national arrangements and to make appropriate returns of job vacancies and employment trends. Direct regional and local co-operation between employment offices was strengthened. Out of such information the Commission was to compose an annual report on the labour markets to serve as the basis for employment policies and for attempts to absorb, on a priority basis, Community nationals left unemployed. A further report analysing the success of such arrangements was also to be made. An important extension of co-operation provided for members to be notified in advance of expected surpluses of both manpower and jobs so that they might have first chance of filling vacancies. Thus, although the regulation contained no definite commitment to the principle of the priority of the Community labour market and, indeed, recognized that it could not be applied entirely,[35] these arrangements went a considerable way towards its acceptance.

The regulation still only applied to wage-earning occupations but included workers accompanying the supplier of a service, or those providing a service on such a person's behalf, if such activity had been liberalized within the context of the general programme covering such matters or was carried on under the provisions of national legislation. The possibility of increasing numbers of people becoming eligible with the liberalization of the arrangements for the supply of services was clearly envisaged. Both Parliament and the Economic and Social Committee had urged that the new regulation should be extended to refugees and stateless persons, but the Council refused to accept this. Instead a declaration of intent was attached affirming the concern of members and expressing their willingness to consider such applications on the same terms without undertaking a definite commitment to do so.

Conditions of working were further eased. A work permit was valid for the whole territory, subject to restriction in the case of areas of surplus manpower, limited to a particular employer for one year only, valid for at least one year with the possibility of extension and issued and renewed automatically. Permits could, however, be issued for defined periods to allow entry for a specific job and were not then automatically renewable if a surplus of local manpower existed. Longer established workers and those transferring to wage earning from self-employment were entitled to permanent work permits. Migrants received the same rights as nationals in relation to changing jobs after two years instead of four.

The provisions designed to ensure equality of treatment at work were elaborated and strengthened. The migrant now received the right not only to vote for, but to become, a workers' representative on works councils if he had worked in the firm for three years and fulfilled those conditions imposed on all candidates. His right to benefit equally from vocational training courses was made clear and the clauses concerning housing became stronger and more positive by giving the migrant the same rights and advantages as nationals with regard to housing access.

Considerable attention was paid to family needs. The definition of the family was extended to include dependent ascendants and descendants of the worker and his spouse, although entry of dependants was still restricted by the possession of housing considered adequate by local standards. A man's wife and children were given the right to seek employment. Members now agreed not only that the children of migrants had the right to utilize educational and training facilities but that they should be encouraged to do so.

A major step resulted from the Council meetings of May 1966 at which it was agreed to complete both the customs union and the policy on free movement on 1 July 1968. The first set of proposals was submitted to the Council in April 1967 [36] and after the usual process of discussion issued in Regulation 1612/68 of 15 October 1968 and its accompanying Directive 68/360/CEE. [37] The regulation makes clear that what is intended is the abolition of all discrimination based on nationality; the acceptance of a fundamental right of the worker and his family to make a free choice of work anywhere within the Community and to have the same opportunity to obtain work as nationals; the need to ensure both legally and in practice equality of treatment at work and in access to housing and the protection of family entry as well as measures to ensure effective social integration. It recognized that better mechanisms are still required in order to give workers effective information, to enable states to notify the Community speedily when certain areas run into employment difficulties and to arrange for temporary suspension of migration as a last resort. Finally, it accepts that close links exist between the free movement, employment and training policies and that the co-ordination of states' employment policies is necessary.

The importance of this as a policy statement can hardly be over-estimated with a labour force in the Community of 75 million who are eligible to benefit from these provisions. The problem for the future is to make them a reality.

The principle of the Community labour market was developed in a number of ways. All Community nationals have the right to take up jobs and to receive the same priority in placing in jobs as the indigenous population (Art. 1). State rules which submit offers of employment for non-nationals to special arrangements or rules which establish quotas do not apply to Community nationals and employment exchanges must give them full assistance in job-hunting. Direct contacts between workers and employers may be freely made and workers are free to enter a country for three months to look for work.[38] No special work or entry permits are now required, a residence permit valid for five years, automatically renewable and valid for the whole territory of the host country, must be issued, and temporary loss of work or sickness is insufficient reason for the revocation of such documents. Secondly, the right to protect the national market no longer operates in its old form. Procedures are neces-sary, however, both to pursue ways of matching supply of, and demand for, labour and to ensure the protection of the local position thus giving effect to Art. 49 (d) of the Rome Treaty. When a member is conscious of a threat to the living standards and the employment level in a par-ticular area or occupation, its duty is to inform both the Commission and its fellow members, who are then responsible for making the difficulties as widely known as possible in order to discourage new migration without the necessity to suspend the formal right of entry. States may also ask for the suspension of procedures whereby existing vacancies are notified throughout the Community area and it is for the Commission, subject to appeal to the Council, to determine what is to be done. In this way effective protection of local markets has passed away from the control of national governments. Thirdly, the quicker and more effective measures for notification of vacancies and available manpower, the agreement to study employment questions jointly, to provide proper information about living and working conditions in receiving areas can all be expected to strengthen the structure of the labour market particularly over the long term. Monthly returns of vacancies unlikely to be filled from the national labour market and of persons willing to migrate are made both to the European Co-ordination Office and to the members' employment services in order to obtain greater transparency in the labour market. Names supplied to employment exchanges offering vacancies must be passed on to prospective employers within eighteen days with the same degree of priority granted to nationals over non-nationals and offers of employment are not sent, during this period, to non-member states unless it is believed no available labour exists within the Community. However, despite the priority given to fellow members in job notification and the holding of vacancies, it is still possible to give priority to non-Community nationals in the case of named persons, where there are special reasons for allowing preference or frontier or seasonal workers are involved. Finally, it was agreed to provide up-to-date information on labour movements and the number of placements of non-Community nationals and to take steps to improve the chances of filling available jobs with Community workers. The first report on the reasons for employing personnel from outside the area although Community workers were available reached the Council in 1970.[39] One important outstanding point was that of the mutual recognition of qualifications which was left to the Commission to pursue.

The provisions concerning equality of treatment and family needs follow naturally from what had already been established. The former is now very broadly defined. An emphasis is placed upon the worker's right to benefit from the same services of rehabilitation when unemployed, from employment training programmes and to enjoy the same social and fiscal advantages. No discriminatory clauses in collective agreements are valid. Whilst the right to join a union, vote and stand for office in workers' organizations is maintained without a time lag, bodies exercising a function under public law can be excluded pending further examination of the problem. The worker must have the same rights as nationals in relation to housing, including that of home ownership and of registration for social housing. Right to entry is given to his spouse, dependants under twenty-one years of age and ascendants for whom he is responsible and states are prepared to give favourable consideration to the admission of other dependants. Although the proviso concerning normal housing is retained, this must not allow discrimination against migrants to develop. Wives and children have the right to undertake paid work, children must be admitted to educational, apprenticeship and training courses and states are to take active measures to encourage them to do so. Certain special arrangements, notably those deriving from the Treaty of Paris or past imperial relationships, remain unaffected.

One further matter remained to be settled. It will be recalled that the right to continue to live in a state after having been employed there was subject to implementing regulations to be drawn up by the Commission. The question does not appear to have received serious consideration until 1965 with the setting up of a study programme,[40] and discussion proceeded to determine rules covering the period of residence and employment necessary for eligibility by workers and the extension of such a right to family members who had entered the country whilst the applicant was still employed.[41]

On 29 June 1970 the Commission adopted the definitive text,[42] allowing for the right to be exercised either on retirement or on the onset of disablement provided certain residence qualifications were fulfilled. For retired persons, a residence of three years and employment during the previous twelve months were required, with derogations for those maintaining a home but employed elsewhere as in the case of frontier workers. Disabled persons are eligible after two years unless receiving compensation for an industrial accident or disease when no residence qualification is required. Those married to nationals do not need to fulfil residence requirements and a two-year period is allowed for workers to decide whether to exercise the right to stay. Families can continue to live in the host country after the death of the worker and may be able to do so if he dies during his working life before having established a residence right. States have agreed to maintain the principle of equality of treatment and to be favourably inclined to readmit persons who once worked in their territory for a considerable period. The key to the system is the receipt of a residence permit valid for five years and automatically renewable.[43]

It is difficult to assess the effects of these provisions. The concept of priority for Community nationals had little meaning at a time when labour shortages drove employers to recruit a long way from home.[44] The original philosophy became outmoded since it belonged to a period when fears of unemployment were everywhere greater and levels of unemployment in Italy were still significantly higher than elsewhere. Thus the elaboration of these arrangements may have had little effect upon the pattern of labour movements and did not, in practice, establish priority channels between Community members at the expense of third countries. In 1958, 48 per cent of first work permits issued in the EEC were taken by Italy and 37 per cent by countries outside the common market. By 1968, after which their issue was abolished for Community nationals, only 27 per cent went to Italy and 68·5 per cent to non-member countries.[45] It is figures such as these that underlie the continuing Italian disquiet with the effective operation of the principle of the priority of the Community labour market, since she believes she still possesses labour reserves, particularly in the form of under-employment, for which greater Community efforts should properly be made. Furthermore, should a serious recession develop the obligation to ensure the priority of the Community labour market would no doubt assume greater importance.

There is some doubt as to the precise number of non-nationals at work in the Community. Figures quoted are only approximate and the question of their more precise determination has been under discussion by the technical committee.[46] However, by the beginning of 1971 about 1 million Community nationals and 2·5 million non-Community nationals were at work in the area and these figures represent significant percentages of certain labour forces.[47] In 1972 an estimate was given in Parliament of 6·7 million foreigners living in the six members, of whom 2 million originated in these states.[48] Thus the Commission's view, held as late as 1966, that 'the steps taken to give priority in employment to workers available within the Community have helped to reverse the tendency observed in the last five years towards a decline in the number of vacancies filled by Community workers' was overtaken by events.[49] Since the majority of those from further afield are unskilled and more likely to experience a cultural gap with their host communities, it is important that the more liberal ideas developed within the Communities to benefit migrants should be applied to all newcomers whatever their origin. The refusal to admit stateless persons and refugees to coverage of the regulations suggests, however, that the road to this extension will be long and hard.

It is always possible that the development of more positive manpower policies, coupled with an effective training programme, will have an impact upon recruitment patterns. In 1966 the Commission referred to the better vocational training of young people, including girls, short courses for adult training, more vocational guidance and freer exchange of workers as being matters where measures might lead to more effective matching of vacancies and workers within the Community.[50] At the same time it must be remembered that vocational training is likely to make workers more attractive to employers at home, so that potential employers abroad may have to increase substantially the attractions that they can offer. A major problem for a more selective labour market is the harmonization of training schemes and the reference to this in Art. 45 of Regulation 1612/68 is an indication of the direction in which opinion has begun to turn.[51]

The main legal problem which still remains for Community nationals is their exclusion from employment in the public administration, of which there is no uniform definition and where restrictions tend to be wide,[52] and from participation in the administration of bodies under public law. The extent of socio-economic discrimination is, of course, another matter. Furthermore probably more could be done to ease the inevitable difficulties of adaptation, whilst the lack of housing, difficulties of co-ordination of social security schemes and differences in occupational training have all been identified as issues inhibiting the free movement policy.[53] As policies pass from formal rule making to the human problems of labour movement, it is important to keep distinct the differing requirements of the frontier, seasonal, short-term and long-term migrant, since this basic classification suggests that, with more sophisticated policies, the needs of these different groups will be recognized as diverse. However it is difficult to escape the conclusion that the result of dealing with the socio-economic problems of migration, itself necessary to fulfil the requirements of a common labour policy as well as the norms of the Treaty of Rome, may well act as the spearhead for policies designed more specifically to harmonize social levels by its exposure of existing variations.

II The Self-Employed

Chapters Two and Three of Title Three of the Treaty of Rome were devoted to the right of individuals to set up in a self-employed capacity within another member state or to supply services across frontiers. Companies constituted in accordance with the law of a member, or an associated country, may also be eligible to benefit from these provisions, whose application represents an important extension of individual rights. As in the case of the free movement of labour, the basic objective was to remove restrictions on equality of treatment with nationals by the end of the transitional period, with the exception of governmental activity. Since, however, the practice of many of these occupations is conditioned by the existence of other forms of regulation, the right would have remained largely an empty one in the absence of steps to uncover and deal with the associated disabilities. The treaty clauses were therefore complex and the establishment of this right has been of considerable difficulty. Whilst free movement for wage-earning activities was completed ahead of schedule, the programme for the establishment of a common market for other types of labour generally fell behind its target.

Although the right of establishment and the right to supply services are technically distinct, the two issues are in practice closely allied and have been dealt with jointly by the Community institutions. The main emphasis in the treaty is on the right to set up in employment in another Community member and to establish a procedure for making this right a meaningful one. The provision of services is dealt with in less detail but in similar vein and the clauses are in a sense residual in character being designed to fill any gaps remaining outside the more general policies covering the free movement of goods, capital and persons. The problem here was to cover the supply of services when the supplier is domiciled in one country and the recipient in another. No question of personal establishment therefore arises although short visits may be necessary. The growth of highly specialized services, not only in the professional fields but in agriculture, market research, machine maintenance or advisory services, makes this flexibility important both for the supplier and for his supporting staff and equipment. Goods which require to be processed or analysed must be allowed to cross frontiers freely or the recipient of services may in turn require to move to the supplier for a short period. At the time of signature of the Treaty of Rome, the supply of services was severely hampered by restrictions, apart from the relief given in a number of minor, bilateral arrangements largely dealing with frontier areas. The refusal of permission to practise, the ban on the passage of goods or the inability to pay for services rendered created a formidable barrier to effective free movement broadly similar to those impeding the right of establishment. In both cases restrictions revolved, in the first instance, around the differential treatment of aliens,[54] which effectively prevented the exercise of the entrepreneurial function in the industrial, commercial, agricultural and professional spheres. Restrictions resulted from factors such as rules requiring the possession of nationality in order to practise, refusal to recognize qualifications obtained abroad or the imposition of special rates or taxes on foreigners, especially severe rules to ensure their financial soundness, prohibitions on their making contracts, acquiring property or obtaining access to credit or the law courts. Removal of the anomalies in company law which severely affect the capacity of the individual to practise abroad, to supply a service or set up a subsidiary or branch is a pre-requisite of a free establishment policy, but it was not until 1968 that a first directive was adopted on the co-ordination of company law and a convention on the mutual recognition of companies signed.[55]

The removal of such disabilities carries serious implications for domestic policies, so the Council and Commission were given a special responsibility to encourage cross-national collaboration between competent authorities in order to broaden their understanding of the issues involved. They were also asked to ensure the abolition of practices impeding the policy, the right of migrant wage earners to remain to pursue forms of self-employment provided they satisfied the necessary conditions, that member nationals would be able to acquire and exploit land and buildings, that progressive abolition of restrictions on the right of establishment and on free entry for the purpose in fact took place, that members did not provide grants giving unfair advantage to their nationals and that members began to co-ordinate and rationalize the guarantees demanded from companies.

Such formal barriers may be reinforced by other difficulties such as the inability to play an effective part in local business life, by the impossibility of maintaining social security rights for the self-employed, of particular importance for retirement pensions, as well as by general restrictions on the transfer of payments, the movement of goods and on the entry and sojourn of people. Finally, the practice of many occupations depends upon the possession of appropriate qualifications. The implication of the treaty system was, therefore, to require consideration of existing standards of the training and educational experiences which lay behind them, the possibility of extending the right to practise to those holding Community qualifications and of establishing agreed minimum standards in order to ensure their mutual acceptability. So far it has been better able to facilitate the admission of migrants to particular forms of work than to obtain acceptance of each other's qualifications which leads directly into the question of educational and cultural levels, policies which the treaty left entirely alone. The work done so far on syllabus and training content has never been meant to establish complete uniformity but rather that students should, taking both theoretical and practical courses into account, have reached a similar level of attainment.[56] However in 1971 it was agreed that Ministers of Education should meet periodically in Council and at their first meeting in November of that year they accepted that the work on the mutual recognition of qualifications should be expedited.

This maze of restrictions required detailed study, rationalization and, where necessary, removal for Community nationals. Only certain problems could be dealt with in general terms, owing to the variety of employments concerned, the complexity of the regulations governing them and related issues which demanded attention. The problems of each occupation have had to be considered separately.

Although certain bilateral agreements already existed to cover specific and discrete matters, the Treaty of Rome attempted to create a system in which the significance of nationality would ultimately be removed as a factor in itself justifying the imposition of restrictions and in which arbitrary factors affecting self-employment had been lifted. After discussing the problems with appropriate officials from members and obtaining information concerning existing restrictions and the terms of existing bilateral agreements, the Commission set up a working party to establish priorities for occupations, to formulate the type of restrictions which would have to be lifted and to suggest methods of co-ordinating the conditions for the exercise of different posts. This quickly split into nine specialist groups made up of delegates nominated by member governments to cover the general problems arising; special regulations for various commercial, industrial and artisanal activities and ancillary occupations; agriculture, fishing and forestry; exploitation of the sub-soil, mines and petroleum deposits; banking and insurance; transport, tourism and entertainment; medical and para-medical occupations; veterinary surgeons, pharmacists; the liberal professions and civil engineering. A draft programme was submitted to both Parliament and the Economic and Social Committee before being finally approved by the Council in October and December 1961.[57] The policy was designed to deal with each type of activity in the necessary detail, to establish within broad treaty direction the order of priority in which occupations were to be liberalized, to institute studies of the problems involved and to set out procedures and timing. It was intended for completion by 1 January 1970 but 'the General Programme . . . has proved somewhat ambitious'[58] and, although directives had been drafted for most occupational groups, much remained to be done at that date.

Implementation was to be through Council directives thus enabling the means of attaining the objectives to be handled at the discretion of the members. Certain reserve powers remained. Jobs which could involve the exercise of governmental activity were excluded and the Council retained the right, acting on a qualified majority on a proposal of the Commission, to exclude other activities from the programme.

In essence, the scheme was a timetable laying down the stages through which the abolition of existing barriers relating to named sectors or trades should pass. General priority was given to the industrial and commercial sectors of the economy, especially those for which the treaty required preference to be given as making a particularly valuable contribution to production and trade. Agricultural occupations were included and where the strict control of activity existed, as in insurance or the liberal professions, a particularly long period of adjustment was allowed. Widespread restrictions in industry and commerce were to go by 1963, in foodstuffs, manufacture and wholesale distribution of pharmaceutical products, retail trade, some types of insurance, architecture, accountancy, surveying and engineering consultancy by 1965, and in retailing of pharmaceutical products and drugs, the practice of medicine and veterinary medicine and further forms of insurance by 1967. By the end of 1969 only very few industries, such as shipbuilding, the manufacture of railway equipment and forestry would remain to be opened up. A similar programme was laid down for the supply of services in these occupations. The arrangements were also designed to lift the general restrictions on entry, residence, transfer of payments and on movement from wage-earning employment into self-employment, so that Community nationals could benefit as soon as the occupations they wished to follow had been liberalized. Steps were taken to achieve these ends during 1963 and 1964. Restrictions on payment for the supply of services where this was the only limiting factor on their supply were removed first,[59] and followed by arrangements for the supervision of restrictions on entry, movement and residence aimed to remove administrative obstacles, simplify formalities and to recognize a right of permanent residence.[60] General agreement by the Council on the right to become a member of the local Chamber of Commerce and professional association, to enjoy the resultant advantages and to be eligible for office except where this entailed the exercise of public authority was achieved for some manufacturing industries in July 1964.[61] In 1967 a directive relating to certain building activities expressly recognized the right of the self-employed to join professional organizations on the same terms as nationals and to stand for office.[62]

The main attack on restrictions in industry began in 1964 and by 1970 the programme was complete for about three-quarters of activities in industry, commerce and craft occupations.[63] Three directives were passed on 25 February 1964 dealing with intermediate activities in wholesale trades in industry, commerce and crafts and included transitional measures.[64] They were shortly followed by instructions operative for extractive industries and for manufacturing and craft occupations. These covered processing operations in textiles, wood, paper, chemical, metallurgy, electrical industries, automobile and precision instrument making, private building and construction. Arrangements for direct selling either wholesale or retail were included, the latter being subject to certain conditions. Mining, quarrying, operations concerned with processing ores, prospecting and drilling (not natural gas or petroleum) and measures to liberalize direct selling in this latter group were covered. The third directive dealt with transitional measures for the first group pending further co-ordination of training levels and mutual recognition of qualifications. It laid down rules concerning the length of experience in a particular occupation which might be considered as equivalent to a formal qualification and, where this was not demanded, allowed states to protect themselves against immigration 'not attributable to purely economic motives'.[65] A Council directive of 4 March 1969 amended that of 7 July 1964 on transitional measures in certain industrial groups and removed some occupations dealing with health from the scope of the directive altogether, namely those concerned with the examination of visual and auditory organs and other parts of the human body with a view to the supply of appliances.[66] It further adopted a directive later in the month removing restrictions on exploration for oil and natural gas,[67] whilst the film industry has also been the subject of a number of directives.

Already, in 1963, two directives on agriculture had been adopted. The first allowed farm workers who had completed two years unbroken work in the host country as labourers to set up as farmers on their own account, and the second enabled Community nationals to lease farms that had been left derelict or uncultivated for at least two years.[68] The provisions were chiefly significant for persons already in practice partially integrated in the host country, such as seasonal or frontier workers, and who were often welcome in areas experiencing rural depopulation.[69] In order to help farmers improve their productivity, a directive aimed to 'facilitate trade, contribute to technical progress and generally promote rationalisation in agriculture'[70] by lifting restrictions on a wide range of service activity in agriculture and horticulture was passed on 14 December 1964.[71] It covered questions such as the provision of technical aid, services designed to improve the destruction of weeds and vermin, to help with spraying, pruning, picking, packing, the hiring of agricultural machinery and the care of the soil and was chiefly of significance for large suppliers in frontier regions. In order to ensure uniform implementation the Commission sent out three recommendations under Art. 155.

The agricultural programme was, however, intended to gather momentum from 1965 as access to credit, co-operatives and farm leases became progressively more open. Significant measures were achieved in 1967 enabling farmers to change farms provided they had previously been working as self-employed persons in agriculture for a minimum of two years, removing restrictions in national legislation adversely affecting the ability of Community nationals to obtain farm leases generally and on the right of Community nationals to join co-operatives.[72] To these was added a directive lifting restrictions which prevented Community nationals working as self-employed or supplying services in certain forestry and logging activities.[73] All these directives applied to both individuals and companies. At the end of December 1968 a further directive allowed Community farmers to qualify, on the same terms as nationals, for financial aids and tax exemptions although not social security and other statutory insurance benefits.[74] Two years later the Council widened the scope of Directive 65/1/CEE to apply to the supply of services in a very wide range of ancillary occupations including pest control, hire of machinery, plant spraying and harvesting.[75]

The plans to liberalize the award of public works contracts and those to free the provision of transport services ran into great difficulty. A first draft regulation submitted in March 1964 dealt with the abolition of laws and administrative practices preventing firms from tendering, either wholly or in part, for work of minimum value to be done for central and local authorities and other public bodies, in any member state. It aimed to do this through the abolition of restrictions on the freedom of establishment and the freedom to supply services of public works contractors and through the definition of circumstances which would entitle members, for the transitional period, to reserve contracts to their own nationals. All public work concessions and certain contracts awarded by nationalized railway systems were covered. A supplementary proposal dealt with the co-ordination of national procedures for the award of contracts. The matter was extensively debated and a revised proposal was submitted in June 1965 which raised the minimum value of contracts to be covered from 60,000 to 300,000 units of account but which excluded public works contracts awarded by gas, water and electricity supply undertakings directly operated by the state or by local authorities for the transitional period. Contracts awarded by public rail, road or inland waterway transport boards were also excluded.[76] No agreement was reached, but with the development of the common market and the debate on industrial policies it became increasingly important to incorporate public works with their vast construction responsibilities and heavy investment in technologically advanced fields. During 1970 the Commission proposed that a start be made by co-ordinating buying policies for capital goods in certain sectors, which would itself necessitate standardization of technical specifications, the provision of more public information on contracts and encourage cross-national co-operation. Discussions continued, with construction work particularly in mind, towards the elaboration of a system for contracts of over 1 million units of account which would overcome the problems of concession granting, credit availability and similar obstacles. Two directives were finally accepted by the Council on 26 July 1971 which agreed procedures whereby this might be done. They required the appropriate amendment of national laws by August 1972 for contracts of this size, the obligation to publish information in the official journal on work to be undertaken and the duty not to discriminate in the acceptance of tenders, but allowed arrangements for the protection of local sub-contractors.[77]

The Treaty of Rome laid down that the free movement of services in transport should be governed by the development of general transport policies, whilst the liberalization programme had planned that restrictions on the right of establishment in transport should be lifted by the end of the second year of the third stage at the latest.[78] The details of the arrangements were, however, extremely flexible, partly because of the need to co-ordinate them with the common transport policy and partly because of the widespread existing restrictions of the market resulting from licensing systems and quota agreements. Freedom of establishment was therefore to develop along with the alignment of legislation relating to market access and the growth of a common transport policy. Restrictions on the freedom of establishment in services ancillary to transport such as travel bureaux, forwarding and charter agents were to go by the end of the second stage, whilst the question of whether liberalization should be preceded, accompanied or followed by reciprocal recognition of degrees and diplomas was left over for further discussion. The treaty had left in abeyance the question of whether transport was to include sea and air transport or only rail, road and inland waterway and, despite the attempts of Parliament to introduce the wider definition when discussing the liberalization programme, its suggestions were not accepted by the Council.

Greater mobility must be affected by the necessary regulation of industrial and professional activity for purposes of social protection. The problem for the Community was to evolve effective rules which were at the same time appropriate to the new conditions through consideration of the effect of legal and statutory requirements and of the conditions which surround the practice of different types of jobs. The treaty arranged for the Council to issue directives co-ordinating legislative and statutory rules by the end of the transitional period. In most cases these were to be based on the unanimity rule during the first stage followed thereafter by qualified majority vote. Unanimity was retained for any matter subject to legislation in a member, for insurance, banking and similar activities and for the conditions governing the exercise of medical, para-medical and pharmaceutical professions. In the case of the latter group, the removal of restrictions was made dependent upon the co-ordination of the conditions for their practice. The need for considering similar problems in other professions was recognized in the general programme on liberalization.

The most complex aspect of these arrangements was that of achieving the mutual recognition of qualifications, since standards of education and training were not identical. The obligation was on the Council to issue directives for such recognition which required detailed negotiation and study of each major form of activity and on occasion the use of temporary, transitional measures. As a result of its work, the Commission evolved for a general guideline the view that what is required is to ensure 'an effective equivalence of training levels which can be reached through different programmes',[79] thus retaining the concept of flexibility and variety in training and allowing different methods to be used to establish mutual recognition according to the needs of particular posts. The direction in the treaty that priority should be given to those activities making a direct contribution to the development of production and trade itself helped to cause delay. The wide definition and high degree of organization of craft industries in some members, such as Germany, in contrast with the position elsewhere which allowed of the easy establish-ment of a business, led to widespread fears of the movement of workers who had not obtained the requisite qualifications at home and perhaps were incapable of doing so. The general programme established a very 'elastic formula'[80] with regard to trades and crafts including transitional measures attempting to equate experience with existing qualifications. The Committee for the crafts and small industries of the Six was most active in formulating the means to accomplish the programme without arousing fears of dilution. It will be noted that the arrangements accepted on 7 July 1964 included transitional measures to be taken by members providing effective co-ordination and recognition of qualifications. These were based on the preliminary adoption of a period of experience, whether as self-employed or in a paid managerial position, as equivalent to a formal qualification. Safeguard clauses however were inserted to protect countries having no strict regulations against an unwelcome influx of the untrained.[81]

In contrast, highly professional activities are everywhere closely controlled and the mutual recognition of qualifications 'involves the confrontation of teaching systems and standards'.[82] By 1965 work was well advanced on identifying the problems involved in the mobility of architects, engineers, general medical practitioners, dentists, lawyers, veterinary surgeons, opticians, accountants, tax consultants and pharmacists (manufacturing and distribution). Educational equivalence was considered to exist for architects qualifying from particular schools[83] and for general medical practitioners.[84] Where discrepancies were greater and it was considered that educational equivalence did not exist, as in the case of medical specialists,[85] discussions were undertaken to arrange for examinable supplementary courses to be taken before practice elsewhere might be permitted,[86] whilst transitional arrangements were required where qualifications represented standards of considerable diversity. This was considered for occupations such as engineering, chartered accountancy and tax consultancy where the principle adopted was of the possession of a qualification and a minimum number of years of practice. Proposals concerning barristers, veterinary surgeons, chartered accountants and business consultants were remitted to the Council during 1969 and 1970.

Special mention was made in the treaty of medical and para-medical activities, where the lifting of restrictions on mobility was considered particularly complex. France, Italy and Germany all reserved practice for their own nationals subject to some modifications resulting either from reciprocal arrangements as in the case of the Italian–German exchange scheme or from special arrangements made in certain frontier areas. In the main Belgium and the Netherlands required practitioners to have qualifications obtained nationally. Although the Commission argued that educational equivalence for the general practitioner already existed and therefore there was no need for rules to establish professional competence, it was still necessary to face problems of ancillary skills and knowledge necessary for competent practice: language proficiency, an adequate knowledge of public health and social legislation, the desirability of a period of readjustment by work in hospital and of professional ethical codes. Particular issues also had to be considered. German regulations demanded a period of special training before practice in the social security system was allowed; the question of the full recognition of East German medical degrees and of those obtained outside the Community generally had to be settled. This last point was of particular importance to Luxembourg since the Duchy has no medical school and in 1969 a draft recommendation was submitted suggesting that, if such qualifications for doctors and dentists were acceptable to Luxembourg, other members should recognize them also.[87] Furthermore, whilst the free establishment policy applied to the self-employed doctor, the number of salaried posts, notably in hospital, was increasing and it appeared impractical to refuse to recognize this development when considering the movement of doctors. The first proposals concerning doctors and dentists were submitted to the Council on 3 March 1969[88] and indicated the main restrictions in national legislation which would need to be abolished. They dealt, too, with the mutual recognition of qualifications on the basis of those minimum training conditions necessary to ensure effective equivalence of competence. The recognition of specialist qualifications was dealt with and the proposals required any doctor to spend six months in a country in order to familiarize himself with social and legislative conditions before being allowed to take a private patient. Community nationals wishing to practise in Germany would be required to have spent a period in work at home equivalent to the preparatory period demanded under the German social insurance system. In the case of dentists the main problem was that of the Italian training system, which required all dentists to be medically qualified and a draft recommendation suggested to Italy that she create a specialist dental training system.

In the case of nurses, opticians, dentists and agricultural engineers, the suggested procedure was to lay down minimum standards to which training schemes should conform but to leave room for considerable variation above this point. Thus the proposals for nurses laid down minimum standards of education at entry, the length of training courses, the number of hours to be spent on theoretical work covering different aspects of study, the number of hours to be spent on practical training and the need for the completion of a full-time trainee stage in a recognized unit.[89] Three draft directives for general nursing were submitted to the Council in 1969[90] laying down the conditions for the right to settle or supply services in the case of self-employed nurses; arranging for the mutual recognition of stated national qualifications whether for salaried or self-employed nurses and establishing minimum standards of training which it was hoped states would incorporate into their programmes. Similar proposals were submitted for midwives.[91]

In March 1969 the Council amended Directive 64/427 of 7 July 1964 dealing with transitional measures affecting certain groups in order to exclude particular types of optical work requiring special consideration, and later in the year four proposed directives were aimed at the mutual recognition of qualifications through laying down the equivalence of various types of training and the minimum standards to which training must conform in order to qualify for recognition in sight-testing and safeguarding the right of professional recognition. Firms working as opticians and spectacles manufacturers were to have a qualified optician on the staff.[92]

Closely associated with the supply of personal health services was a long-drawn-out battle concerning the freeing of the market in pharmaceutical products. Whilst the manufacture, import and sale of drugs was under strict national control for health reasons, the rules normally had the additional result of giving preference to the domestic supplier and there was little intra-Community trade at the start of the common market. On 26 January 1965[93] a first directive on branded pharmaceuticals passed the Council by which states agreed to introduce all necessary legislative and administrative changes within eighteen months and to apply the rules over a five-year period in order to bring goods under uniform measures of control. No drug might be sold unless previously licensed and the issue of licences was to be based on uniform criteria to establish safety, therapeutic value and the information content of labelling. In this way, although licensing was to remain a national matter, it was hoped that it would in practice become a good deal easier to sell products freely. A companion directive was designed to establish uniformity of control over the manufacture of goods and of checking procedures and to detail the evidence thereof which would in future be required when application for a licence was made. This however met with grave opposition from Germany,[94] despite an amendment to exclude a large number of products, including serums, vaccines, human blood and radio-active products[95] and to postpone the entry into force of the new scheme. States, however, took few or no steps to implement the first directive or to agree upon the second, and during 1967 the Commission submitted a timetable to the Council for the application of the rules together with a proposal for a resolution and a letter to be sent to each member pointing out its obligations and aiming at the reciprocal recognition of goods by 1 January 1970.[96] This too made no progress.[97] By 1969 only France and Belgium had adjusted their national rules to allow for the operation of the common market by the new date of 1974.[98] The lack of progress here is indicative of the reluctance of states to give up their control over health matters and of the strength of the drug manufacturers. In 1969 the Commission produced seven proposed directives as a new package deal to try to get the programme working and a free market established.[99] These were aimed to apply the free establishment and supply of services rules to pharmacy at the manufacturing, wholesale and retail stages, including drug dispensing and covering both self-employed and paid personnel. They required the harmonization of national legislation relating to the supervision and control of production, storage, distribution and selling as well as the establishment of minimum standards of training required by pharmacists. Early in the new year a further proposed directive was aimed at the approximation of legislation on standards and procedures for productive processes to encourage the free movement of goods.[100]

The Commission has tried to verify the compatability of the measures taken with the treaty and the complexities of the directives but it is largely dependent upon notification by states of action taken and of future intentions. It is difficult to establish a fool-proof system here, but the

Council achieved a declaration of intent that states would inform the Commission 'as far as possible'.[101] Infringements are taken up by the Commission either through informal channels or court proceedings[102] but, as in the case of the equal pay policy, it is perhaps through an intended beneficiary insisting upon his rights and setting local machinery in action that major progress can be made.

On 23 December 1969 the Commission submitted a proposal for a comprehensive directive on the removal of restrictions in remaining fields where no prior co-ordination of laws and regulations was required, as in many service industries.[103] In general it can be seen that, by the end of the period, considerable success had been achieved in industry, agriculture and services but in no case had professional work been subjected to firm decisions, whilst the Community system had been unable to make a significant attack on the problems of drug production. Leaving on one side the tremendous problems of commercial advantage which are involved, it is additionally clear that the programme raised social, educational and cultural problems for which the treaty as it stood was ill-fitted. In many cases it is not a question solely of the approximation of laws as a compromise agreement but of working out 'a clear picture of the *Community's* requirements in this field, in short, a concept of what economic, educational and social policy is to be at European level'.[104]

The experience of the free establishment policy suggests that any attempt to promote the movement of professional persons on the grounds of social desirability as part of a Community social policy would be likely to run into very severe difficulties. The qualified services of doctors, teachers, social workers and related personnel form an essential part of such a policy since they constitute an important element of modern living standards to whose equalization the treaty is dedicated. The exclusion of public service activity from Community programmes and the lack of progress made over the free movement of medical goods and labour suggest that it is probably more appropriate to view this part of the treaty as an enlargement of the individual's freedom of action rather than as a practical contribution to a specific Community policy. It is perfectly possible to see, however, that the health standards so painstakingly evolved by the Commission in the industrial sphere, over the control of drugs and the common market in labour could well form the basis of a Community health policy if the political will to establish one developed and that it could serve as an example for the establishment of Community policies in other social spheres.

5 Supportive Social Services

I Social Security for Migrant Workers

As social security schemes become more comprehensive over the population and provide for more contingencies, so they can act as an impediment to international labour movement. Few workers will be willing to sacrifice social security rights, to receive benefits at a lower level than those available at home or to run the risk of seeing dependants excluded from cash benefits and health services. At the same time the greater ease of international population movements, swollen by workers, political refugees and tourists, means that the international regulation of social security is a growing practical necessity. Here international control has reached one of its highest forms. Two elements, theoretically distinct but in practice much less so, are to be found. On the one hand is the notion of international standard-setting as a humanitarian goal and on the other the need to deal with the practical questions to which labour movements give rise. But for whichever purpose they are designed, international agreements are rarely simple in content. Social security schemes have developed within the national state and on examination are seen to stem from a variable use of the social principles of insurance, assistance and universal benefit as means of providing income mainte-nance and associated services. The resulting differences make international arrangements highly technical.

In so far as the early social security schemes favoured the insurance method the inclusion of foreigners presented no real difficulty, although the early German social insurance legislation discriminated between national and foreign workers with the intention of extending rights to foreigners only to the degree that this was reciprocated abroad.[1] The question today is not so much one of nationality as of territoriality, for social insurance schemes – the major form of social security concerned – do not normally include nationality requirements, which are clearly irrelevant: 'The legal provisions operative in Community members in relation to the classic forms of protection rarely contain discriminatory clauses based on nationality.'[2] The frontier may still be an important barrier, however, if the worker finds that his previous insurance history is ignored, that his family is excluded from benefit as long as it remains outside the country where the head of the household is working and that he cannot have his benefits paid to him if he leaves the country where he built up entitlement. International agreement is necessary if contributions paid to a previous insurance scheme are not to go unrecognized, if work periods rather than contribution periods are to be eligible for the determination of entitlement for those migrating from countries where such a system is used or if previous industrial history is to be considered if the migrant succumbs to an industrial disease. Most previous international experience related to the export of benefits after the worker had built up an entitlement, such as to an old age pension, and returned home after working abroad, but, with the growing ease of travel, a wider range of circumstances necessitate consideration. These include that of the worker who falls ill when at home for his holidays or who becomes unemployed and prefers to return home to look for a job before his benefit is exhausted.

Industries which are long-established employers of migrant labour, such as the French and Belgian mining industries, traditionally made the newcomers members of their social security schemes and relied upon international agreement to ensure benefits were paid when the worker returned home at the end of his working life. In consequence the worker forfeited other ancillary benefits provided for employees in the industry but not part of the official social security system. The extension of social security cover, notably by the addition of health and maternity care and by the inclusion of family members as recipients of such benefits, has meant that it has become more important to find ways to extend them to families at home or to insured persons receiving cash benefits but living outside the country where entitlement rests. Furthermore, since social security schemes are deeply embedded in the socio-economic structure, ancillary benefits may exist which, by not being part of a formal scheme, are not available for migrants. Concessionary coal or special housing for miners are obvious examples and where such benefits are continued into retirement are probably impossible to apply, or to compensate for, if the worker returns home.[3] More general examples come from the development of occupational pension schemes, so important in the modern economy but whose existence may help to depress the level of statutory pensions, or from the use of an assistance service to supplement inadequate pension levels. Since assistance schemes developed from the obligation of the community to support its weaker members, nationality and residence as well as income qualifications can exist and rules can still be determined by the locality rather than by central government.

At the time of the formation of the EEC, certain forms of unemployment pay in the Netherlands demanded residence in the commune; French old age allowances were only payable on the basis of an income test to French workers and to workers from a country with a reciprocal agreement who had worked a minimum period in France and who were resident therein, but such allowances were an integral part of the income maintenance system for the elderly. A similar system of supplementation existed in the Netherlands for a 'transitional' pension payable until the old age insurance scheme was fully mature but non-nationals were ineligible for this benefit. Neither could they draw certain widows' and orphans' pensions. In Belgium non-nationals received old age pensions worth 20 per cent less than those paid to nationals. Conditions concerning nationality, whether or not combined with residence qualifications, were also to be found in family allowance schemes and if such benefits have been introduced for demographic reasons it is unreasonable to expect them to be paid beyond the frontier. In short, the commonest difficulties seem to stem from the restriction of eligibility to nationals, as in assistance and family allowance schemes, the refusal to pay benefit outside the frontier whether for the recipient or his family, certain discrimination against non-nationals with respect to participation in internal administration, the loss of rights built up in one country with the consequent need to start afresh and lack of recognition of previous circumstances in the determination of benefits. Such examples show the difficulty of equating the position of the migrant even if he is a formal and full member of a social insurance scheme, for different social philosophies are at stake and considerable obstacles exist to the application of any principle of equivalent cover for social security needs or to methods of overcoming migration barriers.

The bilateral treaties which were used to allow migrants to take advantage of developing social security schemes worked reasonably well as long as migratory movements were small scale and followed customary routes. They still hold an important place. Such treaties require no fundamental alteration of social security systems or the establishment of common principles upon which they should be based. They are essentially measures designed to overcome a certain set of difficulties operating in a limited situation. The historical accident that social insurance for those below a defined income limit was the normal method of providing social security in Western Europe and that it was normally based on the principle of wage-linked contributions and benefits eased matters considerably by enabling problems to be considered as technical ones designed to ensure that no forfeiture of social security status occurred on migration through the maintenance of personal rights acquired through the insurance contract. Bilateral agreements between European countries are numerous and have developed the original principle by the addition of certain important rules of which the maintenance of previously acquired rights, the precedence of the legislation of the country of employment in cases of conflict and special arrangements to equate contributory and non-contributory periods of cover are probably the most important. Under the first of these a solution can be found to such questions as the addition of contribution periods, the payment of benefit to a worker who has gone home to retire and the recognition of previous industrial history in order to determine eligibility for compensation for industrial disease. The second can permit dependants outside the state to be covered on the terms laid down by the employing state and not that of residence, although levels of benefit have often been restricted to the level of the latter. As a result of these principles, social security rights can be preserved, rules for the division of the cost of long-term benefits worked out and dependants covered without demanding any large-scale rationalization of the schemes themselves.

Certain groups of workers have been singled out as requiring special consideration. The needs of both frontier and seasonal workers led states to consider cost-sharing arrangements and methods of determining benefit levels for temporary workers. If companies become accustomed to operate across frontiers, if diplomatic and consular staffs grow or the movement of professional or craft workers increases, then workers temporarily abroad for a year or two may increase in number and such questions become more numerous.

The removal of social security impediments to labour movement was a matter of concern to the Treaties of both Paris and Rome, on the assumption that effective co-ordination between existing systems would be demanded although complicated in practice by the existence within each country of a complex of general, special, statutory and voluntary schemes. Special schemes for miners, for farm workers or seamen, special arrangements for the self-employed, varying financial burdens imposed upon the state, the employer and the employee, ancillary services in the form of personal welfare and the growth of occupational welfare schemes continue to create formidable obstacles, not only to any concept of harmonization or equivalence but to equality of treatment of persons moving. The arrangements developed by the European Communities are an outgrowth from these earlier bilateral and multilateral arrangements: 'the current rules are the result of a long-standing tradition in the international law of social security.'[4] They are a step forward, however, through their greater ability to treat the area as a single unit.

The key to the policies of the EEC is to be found in Art. 48, which forbade discrimination based on nationality in relation to working conditions, and in Art. 51, which directed the Council to adopt those social security measures necessary to ensure free movement and based them on the principles of totalization of qualifying periods, the maintenance of benefit rights and payment within the area of the six members. The 'first achievement of the Community in the social field'[5] was the adoption of two regulations to give effect to the need for more effective social security cover for migrants. One of their advantages was the creation of a system more comprehensible than the network of bilateral and multilateral conventions which had hitherto existed, another the greater ease of administration than that of the 1957 convention produced under the auspices of the ECSC. Even so, large problems were left over for further consideration, notably those relating to frontier and seasonal workers, the export of unemployment benefits in certain cases and the retention of some previously established arrangements, whilst the signature of special agreements remained necessary if more favourable terms were thought desirable.

The regulations came into force on 1 January 1969[6] designed to maintain social security rights through the implementation of four basic principles. The first, and most important, was that of equality of treatment within the context of national legislations so that all migrants might be admitted to social security schemes on the same terms as nationals, the right to participate in the administration being excluded.[7] Secondly, continuity of coverage was to be achieved by adding together appropriate periods of insurance or assimilated periods in order to maintain entitlement to benefit thus surmounting the worst problems which arise when different types of eligibility principles are used as between one national scheme and another. Thirdly, the rules of the system of the country of employment were to take precedence in cases of doubt as it is, in most cases, that country which bears primary responsibility. Fourthly, the free export of benefits to workers and families anywhere within the Community area was agreed upon. This is of particular importance for retirement and widows' pensions where a judgment of the Court was necessary in 1966 to confirm the right to pension in the case of the widow of a Dutch miner who later moved to Germany.[8] An important qualification originally limited the payment of family allowances to dependants separated from the breadwinner to the maximum payable in the country of residence. A further exception to the principle of the export of benefit was made by France with regard to unemployment pay for frontier and seasonal workers. Temporary workers, however, remained covered by the legislation of their own home state for a period of twelve months with possibility of extension for a further year. By Regulation 24/64/CEE[9] it was forbidden to replace one worker by another at the end of twelve months in order to avoid the necessity for social security cover in the state of employment, a practice which has been adopted particularly by employers in building and constructional trades. It was also made clear that workers constantly on the move, such as commercial travellers or international transport workers, should be covered by the legislation of that member in which the company was registered. Generally speaking, therefore, the traditional territorial principle had been seriously qualified by the developing notion of social security as a personal right.

The regulations were concerned with schemes covering sickness, invalidity, maternity, old age, death and survivors' benefits, industrial accidents and diseases, unemployment and family allowances. Such schemes might be contributory or non-contributory, generalized or particular to certain workers, run by public authorities, semi-public institutions or professional bodies; their essential qualification for inclusion was that they were schemes established on a legislative basis to cover the appropriate contingencies and the national legislation affected by Regulation 3 was listed in Annex B. The arrangements did not apply to assistance schemes or to special arrangements for war victims. Those chiefly benefiting were wage earners but the steady extension of national social security schemes has meant that salaried staff have been increasingly drawn in. Stateless persons and refugees living within the Community were also covered, but schemes for civil servants were permanently excluded from the scope of the regulations as were established members of diplomatic staffs. Wage earners in diplomatic posts were normally to be covered by the legislation of the country of employment although if they possessed the nationality of the mission they worked for they might exercise a choice. The problems of seamen, frontier and seasonal workers necessitated their being dealt with separately in certain respects, although it was foreseen that the latter two groups would ultimately be brought entirely within the scope of the more general provisions.

In order to maintain entitlement to sickness and maternity benefits the aggregation rule was applied. However, where cash benefits related to average wages over a given period, the actual wage earned in the new country served as the basis for calculation and rules concerning the place of origin of illness could not be operated to exclude a worker from sickness benefit. Cash benefits were paid according to the rules of the competent institution, but when paid to a beneficiary living outside the country the appropriate national agency could be utilized to make the payment and it was the latter's ancillary conditions, such as medical checks, which were operative. If a worker fell ill when home on holiday immediate care was to be provided locally, although the provision of major appliances and similar substantial but non-urgent benefits required prior authorization. A later government agreement[10] accepted that any insured person and his family might be treated for health care whilst on holiday anywhere within the Community.[11] The worker who fell ill in the host country before having built up entitlement to benefit despite aggregation yet who would have qualified at home was to receive health care on an agency basis. Dependants left at home received cash benefits according to the legislation of the country of competence and benefits in kind according to the rules of the country of residence, the cost of the latter being divided.[12] Pensioners and their families living outside the country of competence, or in a country only partially responsible for the pension, were also covered for health care by the country of residence on the terms normally operated for residents and Arts. 22 and 23 of Regulation 3 laid down the principles for the determination of where the cost should fall.

Invalidity pensions caused special difficulty due to the varying rules upon which benefits were calculated and the fact that neither France nor Belgium, except in the case of the miners' schemes, made benefits dependent upon the length of time for which insurance cover had been held. Where possible the standard rule of aggregation of insurance, or assimilated, periods was applied as in the case of long-term benefits, but special arrangements could be negotiated.

A worker who sustained an industrial accident or contracted an industrial disease when outside the country of competence or who left to live elsewhere was nevertheless to be eligible for health care reimbursed by the country of competence provided he had received prior authorization in the case of permanent transfer of residence. Previous accidents and diseases might be taken into account in determining later eligibility if the new legislation took previous history into consideration. This was, of course, a particularly important provision in order to establish that the onset of a particular disease might be due to a worker's industrial history, but experience showed that many miners, particularly where they were also frontier workers, were failing to qualify for compensation for pneumoconiosis due to a continuing disregard of past periods of working experience. By Regulation 8/63/CEE[13] clearer rules of procedure were laid down for this, the major responsibility for benefits being laid firmly on the authority covering the firm where the worker was last employed and establishing rules for cost-sharing.

The principle of aggregation of periods of contribution or of employment was again followed to establish eligibility for unemployment benefit with the exception that France and Luxembourg were only prepared to accept it fully in the case of qualified coal and steel workers.[14] In the calculation of benefit rates, normal rather than actual wages in previous periods of employment might be used where necessary and families outside the country of competence were eligible for dependants' benefits. An important extension of cover enabled benefit to continue to be paid for a short period outside the competent country, thus enabling a worker to return home to look for a job while still on benefit provided prior authorization was obtained and at the price of losing entitlement in the country where benefit was earned. In such a case the country of last employment was only responsible for 85 per cent of the cost of benefit and France and the Netherlands bore less for a temporary period.

The principle of totalization was of most importance in relation to retirement benefits. Survivors' benefits were normally determined in a similar way. When the time came for a worker to retire each competent authority determined what pension would have been payable had all work been done under its auspices and provided a fraction of that sum according to the period actually spent. If the total fell short of what could have been paid by a single scheme then a supplement had to be given whose cost was shared between the competent institutions. Workers in special schemes were only entitled to have work in equivalent jobs taken into account in assessing entitlement and might therefore find that they qualified only for a pension from the general scheme. However, certain exceptions were laid down to the principle of payment of benefits anywhere within the Community in relation to pensioners. These related to those essentially transitory provisions of national legislation introducing forms of assistance payments to the elderly until such time as an insurance scheme would be fully mature.[15]

Family allowances were made payable to families remaining outside the country of work, of obvious and particular importance for Italian workers. In this case, however, the principle of the priority of the legislation of the country of employment was abandoned in favour of paying allowances up to the level of the country of residence. Children of pensioners and orphans might also draw allowances if living outside the country of competence, and, although these benefits were originally limited in duration to thirty months, by Regulation 16[16] this limitation was suppressed and under Regulation 1/64/CEE[17] rules for financial responsibility were simplified. Regulation 35/63/CEE[18] extended the payment of family allowances to children of temporary workers taking their children abroad.

Family benefits, whether in the form of allowances or of medical and maternity care, were originally limited in time to a period of three years on the grounds that family separation should not be encouraged. If a man was still working abroad after such a period it was time for him to send for his family and make a home. Difficulties of family migration, particularly of housing,[19] made it necessary firstly to prolong the period to six years under Regulation 16 and later to suppress it altogether.[20] Finally, under Regulation 109/65/CEE,[21] arrangements were made to provide for the direct transmission of family allowances in those cases where the wage earner was in default.

Despite these rules, special conventions were still used in order to provide more favourable arrangements between countries than the regulations were able to establish for the Community as a whole. This was particularly so for family allowances where a number of agreements existed allowing for their payment to families at home at the level payable in the country of competence.[22]

An Administrative Commission was created to supervise the implementation of the scheme and to ensure its uniform interpretation in members. It dealt not only with a vast range of administrative detail but with the interpretation of the regulations other than those minor matters which states could settle by direct contact. From the Commission, problems might be referred to the Court. It had to ensure the necessary translation of documents and was responsible for the design of pro formas to be used on a standardized basis throughout the Community, as is obviously essential when dealing with highly technical material for which precision is essential if claims are to be made and benefits calculated accurately. Unless institutions preferred to deal directly with each other, the Administrative Commission arranged accounting transfers. In addition it kept appropriate records enabling both accurate determination in the case of shared benefits and proper payment of benefits where families were separated. One of its most important aspects has been the provision of these clearing house functions so that benefits may be paid speedily and efficiently. Additionally, it determined the shares and repayment of costs as between national social security funds, the methods of calculation for lump sum payments, the exchange rates upon which money transfers were made and could grant advances where a delay occurred in paying benefit. A separate auditing committee was established in 1960 to deal with problems such as procedures for payments, bilateral agreements on reimbursements, or fixing average costs as the basis for determining certain lump sum payments.

Furthermore, the Administrative Commission was given a general duty to foster co-operation in the field of social security particularly in respect to health and general social action. In theory, therefore, it should not be considered solely as an executive body, although in practice much of its work has been of a technical character designed to smooth out administrative problems.[23] It became responsible for submitting proposals for the revision of regulations and could undertake any other duty within its competence. It has thus been able to set on foot enquiries to assess the workings of the scheme in relation to different types of benefit and has published a series of guides providing intending migrants with necessary information.

The Administrative Commission consisted of one government representative from each member who might be accompanied by technical advisers. Representatives from the Commission, and the High Authority in former years, attended in an advisory capacity and the ILO provided technical advice. A subsequent attempt by the European Commission to widen membership by bringing in observers from employers' and workers' organizations was not accepted by the Council.[24] The Administrative Commission had its own statutes drawn up by itself, certain decisions being taken by unanimous vote. It met monthly and compiled an annual report on its work.[25]

Members agreed to give each other all necessary information concerning the action taken by them to implement the regulations and relevant changes in their legislation. They also accepted the responsibility to work actively to ensure that the regulations work well and were obliged to accept documents and claims written in one of the official languages of the Community.[26] Documents, appeals and certificates may be submitted to a national authority for transmission to the competent authority elsewhere.

The conference of directors of social security institutions held in Florence during November 1960 under the auspices of the Community stressed the importance of each country having staff especially trained to deal with the problems of migrants, competent to interpret the Community regulations and able to act as liaison personnel with the Community and with other national institutions. The Administrative Commission has thus been responsible for training arrangements which have allowed national staff to be attached for short periods to the European Commission as well as to the social security organizations of other members.

Frontier and seasonal workers present particular problems of co-operation between social security schemes, not only to ensure that effective payments are made but because of the need to allocate responsibility for maintenance and care in a fair and reasonable manner between territorial systems whilst ensuring that workers are effectively covered. In general, long-term benefits have been proportioned on the same rules as those for migrants as a whole, but short-term benefits have required more specialized consideration and unemployment pay originally caused considerable difficulty to the Community. France reserved her position regarding unemployment benefit for both groups of workers under Regulations 3 and 4 and exempted seasonal workers from provisions enabling workers and their families to receive health care and family allowances when outside the country of employment.[27] The special problems of frontier workers were dealt with in Regulation 36/63/CEE,[28] supplemented by Regulation 3/64/CEE,[29] and of seasonal workers in Regulation 73/63/CEE,[30] which was also used to fill certain gaps in the original regulations concerning the protection of temporary workers generally.

A frontier worker, being of appropriate nationality, a refugee or stateless person, was defined as one who worked in one state yet resided in another to which he returned each day or at least once a week. Special agreements between France and her neighbours laid down that frontier areas should be limited to a depth of twenty kilometres on either side of the frontier and a later regulation listed the areas in detail.[31] A seasonal worker was defined as one who worked at a seasonal occupation for a maximum of eight months in the year and who lived in the country of employment during that period but not permanently. The principles for the payment of the long-term benefits of invalidity, old age and survivors' benefits and of death benefits laid down in Regulation 3 were applied to frontier and seasonal workers. In the case of frontier workers, cash benefits for sickness and maternity were to be paid by the institution of the country of employment either directly or via that of the country of residence. Benefits in kind were to be provided by the local body on its own terms but paid for by the insuring authority. The possibility of benefits being provided for the worker and for his family in the country of employment, should this be necessary, was covered. Maternity benefits were always to be covered by the country in which the confinement occurred. The issue of major appliances in the case of disablement was to be subject to the prior agreement of the covering institution. The procedure for applying for sickness benefit by a frontier worker falling ill at home was laid down. The country of employment was made responsible for payments for industrial accidents and disease, and arrangements made to cover the problems arising when industrial compensation depended upon payments and services being provided by the employer or a private insurance company. Journeys to work outside the country of competence but within the frontier zone were included as a protected period and transport costs after an accident paid. This was also the case for a seasonal worker. Unemployment benefits, however, were to be paid by the authority of the country of residence except in cases of partial unemployment and the responsible authority was additionally to carry the cost of health and maternity care for the unemployed. The seasonal worker returning home at once fell within the scope of the country of residence. Although the rule concerning family allowances for migrants generally was applied to frontier workers, Regulation 36/63/CEE accepted the possibility of amending agreements between states and it was common practice to pay frontier workers their family allowance at the level obtaining in the country of employment.[32]

On 7 March 1967 the Council adopted Regulation 47/67/CEE[33] which brought seafarers into the scope of Regulations 3 and 4 thus superseding previous arrangements. Workers on board ship are subject to the legislation of the state whose flag is flown with exceptions to cover cases of temporary attachment, but bilateral conventions have been particularly incomplete for seamen employed by two or more countries and beneficiaries and their families residing outside the immediate states involved have often found themselves excluded from benefits. The general provisions concerning industrial accidents, occupational diseases, death benefits and family allowances were found applicable, but special rules were required to determine the appropriate legislation to be made operative to cover sickness, maternity, incapacity, old age, survivors' pension and unemployment pay as well as to determine the calculation of benefit.

The great complexity of the subject,[34] experience of the working of the regulations and the discovery of gaps and anomalies led the Commission to recognize the need to revise the rules in order to consolidate the provisions into a coherent statement, to take the opportunity to improve benefits and to simplify procedures. The *Action Programme* had already argued the need to speed up the co-ordination of social security systems as part of the continuing process of integration and new draft proposals were submitted to the Council on 11 January 1966.[35]

> The aim of this revision was to assure the various categories of migrant workers and their families of the maximum protection against insured risks and of equality of treatment with other workers, and as far as possible to eliminate the discrepancies that exist between Member States because of the retention of a number of bilateral arrangements.[36]

The Council began to discuss the matter in September 1968 and by November of the following year had reached general agreement on the main substantive issues.[37] The text of a new regulation was agreed on 25 May 1970 but was not operative until October 1972.[38] Its objective was both the consolidation of the existing regulations into one instrument and the improvement of the benefit system. Firstly, more people became eligible for assistance by the inclusion of all those insured under a compulsory social security scheme or who were members of schemes of equivalent status including certain self-employed persons compulsorily insured in an employees' scheme. This allowed workers moving from one type of job to another to maintain their continuity of coverage and applied in particular to self-employed craftsmen from Italy and West Germany and to Italian farmers.[39]

Secondly, the terms upon which certain benefits are given were eased. Health care for the pensioner residing outside the country of previous employment is now determined solely by the law governing the relevant social security system and is no longer also dependent upon whether the legislative system of the country of residence provides such care for pensioners. The intention was that the pensioner should thus become eligible for a wider range of medical services, but it must be remembered that this can only be the case if the services actually exist. Certain pensions listed in Annex C of Regulation 3 which were originally only payable in the country where they were earned are now freely exported. Thus the French assistance allowance to elderly workers can be drawn outside France by EEC workers. A more favourable method of determining the cost of medical care for families left at home was intended to provide assistance at a higher level and a similar result should come from a new method of calculating shared benefits such as old age, disablement or survivors' pensions so that benefits up to the maximum obtainable in any one country can be paid.

A number of improvements affected unemployment pay. The previous restrictions which limited the payment of certain benefits to coal and steel workers only were lifted. Seeking work outside the country of last employment whilst drawing benefit was no longer subject to prior authorization and payments were in future to be paid at the full rate. France removed an important restriction relating to unemployment pay. Originally it was only the French state scheme of unemployment assistance that had been subject to Regulation 3, but the new rule included the scheme which had been developed in France since 1958 by industry and commerce. This, too, implied improved benefits as well as a wider coverage of persons.[40]

Family allowances were also altered for the better. With the exception of France, the members agreed to the export of all family benefits other than maternity grants and special housing allowances and to abolish the ceiling determined by the country of residence. Nationality and/or residence is, however, still a requirement for these special forms of family allowance in Belgium, Luxembourg and France. Where allowances have been introduced for demographic reasons, as in the case of certain birth grants, they have not yet been held to fall within the conditions of employment defined in Art. 48 (2) of the Rome Treaty. At best, the competence of the EEC is believed to derive from Art. 51 (b) which requires the payment of benefits to persons resident elsewhere as a means of securing the free movement of workers, but this provision is subject to unanimous Council agreement.[41] On the other hand France accepted the Italian definition of the family for allowance purposes, which includes impoverished parents as well as children.

Other changes were designed to fill in gaps which the operation of the earlier regulations had exposed. Clearer rules were laid down for cost-sharing for cases of miners' pneumoconiosis where exposure to risk had occurred in two or more countries, journeys to work included in compensation for industrial accident for all workers and arrangements made to cover cases of sickness during temporary residence and periods of transfer between one country and another. The removal of a number of bilateral arrangements perpetuated under Regulation 3 had a liberalizing effect, since these often meant a derogation from the principle of equal treatment. For example, the Italian worker returning home from Germany only received unemployment benefit at the Italian level until 1972. Migrants can now help to elect members of social security bodies provided this rule does not require changes in national legislation to alter the membership of such committees.

The regulation also allowed for the creation of a tripartite advisory committee consisting of two representatives from the governments, workers and employers of each member under a non-voting chairman provided by the Commission which was designed to associate a wider range of interests than hitherto with the workings of the Community in this aspect of employment.

That the regulations have been important is undeniable. About two million people benefit each year from the rules and annual sums around 220 million units of account have been transferred.[42] Their intention has been to establish equality of treatment between national and migrant Community workers and in this sense they have imposed higher social standards than previously existed. States increasingly rescinded bilateral arrangements which allowed less favourable terms than those in the regulations.[43] It must be emphasized, however, that the regulations have not been designed to set standards for the levels of social security benefits so that they became uniform although, by bringing schemes into close proximity, desirable minima may be suggested and the Community become aware of the more obvious discrepancies. One of the most difficult questions of comparability relates to the question of benefits in kind as, for example, the quality and duration of health care. Whilst it is now the rule that cash benefits are normally paid to the returned migrant, or to his family, in the case of sickness and maternity at the level of the country of competence, benefits in kind must be provided by the country of residence as is clearly stated in Art. 9 of the regulation. The removal of wide discrepancies of care is a question of changing the content of national legislation or of improving the provision of services as a matter of social reform and not a question of the adjustment of legal rules concerning the social security cover of migrant labour. The general process of discussion and rationalization, together with consider-ations of convenience, may ultimately have some influence on the question of uniform standards, but this process is distinct from the obligation under the Treaty of Rome to treat migrants equally with indigenous labour. Social security is, nevertheless, a rapidly developing field and the need to deal with fresh problems, even if each one itself appears small scale, at least poses the question of whether one national scheme should follow the example of another. A current illustration is that of the German legislation relating to industrial accidents which, under safeguards against precipitate surrender, allows the beneficiary to forego standard benefit in order to obtain real assets. This presents to the Community the question of whether the principle of equality of treatment demands that the migrant should be allowed a similar right to include the acquisition of assets in his home state thus in turn demanding that his national government exercise the same controls as those operated in Germany.[44]

Important issues still remain. The question of social security cover for migrants from outside the Community must, in view of their number, be considered of primary importance. If the free establishment and supply of services policy results in large-scale movement, highly complex social security problems will have to be tackled, for the great variety of voluntary insurance schemes currently existing within members, often on a professional basis, will make transferability of benefits and entitlements a difficult matter to resolve. The third major issue relates to the growth of supplementary occupational benefits whether in the form of cash payments or in kind. All agreements which result from collective bargaining are excluded from the scope of the regulation unless states decide otherwise, so there can be no automatic guarantee from the EEC that migrants will benefit from such schemes. More consideration will have to be given to the right of migrants to participate in voluntary and occupational arrangements thus bringing firms and savings schemes of a non-statutory nature into the scope of the Community.

The purpose of the regulations has not, so far, been to move towards a fundamental revision of national social security schemes on the basis of common principles, although at a theoretical level this development has attractions as the way to overcome the problems discussed in this chapter. Such a move has commended itself to the Social and Health Committee of Parliament, not only on the grounds of social justice and equality of treatment within the Community but also as a way to remove obstacles to the free movement of labour and to the development of a Community economic policy.[45] However, such a decision would be of the first order of political magnitude.

II Personal Welfare

To the student of social policy it may come as a surprise to realize that the Treaty of Rome made no specific reference to policies of family support housing or to the provision of personal social services. The constant spate of social legislation bears witness to the great concern of modern governments with these subjects, yet the treaty avoids direct and explicit reference to them. Although it may be argued that personal and family welfare is a necessary component both of improved living standards and of the matters listed under Art. 118, the institutions are not in a strong position to develop a welfare policy and there are no powers corresponding to those of the Treaty of Paris enabling the executive to provide housing finance. Experience suggests that it is difficult for the Community to develop action for which its responsibilities are not clear and, since Art. 118 is limited to close collaboration between members, the role of the Community is in turn confined to encouragement and assistance which, unless states are receptive, will be of little use. Nevertheless the Commission started with the hope that it would be able to make a definite impact.

> The European Commission will take especial interest in human relations, in social service in the true sense of the word and in the various social achievements which help to improve the living and housing conditions of the workers and their families. . . . The housing problem will be of special interest in its many aspects, including the psychological, sociological and statistical, particularly in connection with large towns and industrial centres. In order to encourage the construction of dwellings for workers, the European Commission will offer every possible assistance and will search for additional means of obtaining finance.[46]

Family problems and social services which had not been subjected to intensive comparative study were to be considered: 'our duty is to find out the facts and to draw the Member States' attention to existing problems' and give constructive advice.[47]

Improved housing is a field in which Community influence can never be more than marginal in the absence of financial intervention, but the EEC began life at a time of considerable housing difficulty when there was widespread recognition of the need for action to ensure accommodation at reasonable rents and to deal with the particular problems of the areas of war damage and slum clearance and of the mining areas.[48] In addition to the direct housing allowances to families payable in some countries such as Luxembourg and France, members were providing a variety of public subsidies to aid construction by individuals, housing associations and, in some cases, employers whilst a common object for social security and family allowance funds was, and remains, the support of housing programmes. A great post-war effort was undertaken, but by the late 1960s there were signs that the interest of public authorities in the general question of the housing of those of modest means was declining. Less action was taken to soften rent increases and the total construction of social housing fell. Attention shifted to more specialized problems such as the demands of young married couples, large families, old people and workers in new firms or in certain regions.[49]

Discussions were held with independent experts in January 1960 on methods of financing low-rent housing and followed in March 1961 by a conference on general housing policy attended by government representatives. In December 1963 a symposium was held on low-cost housing for representatives of governments, workers' and employers' organizations and family movements, whilst delegates attended from the European Parliament, the Economic and Social Committee, ECSC, the ILO and other international bodies. This symposium discussed a wide range of topics including the methods of assessing housing demand, the special problem of the necessary amount of low-cost housing, methods of determining ability to pay for it and eligibility for tenancies. Slum clearance, housing for migrants and rural housing were particular issues raised. It was followed by the start of special studies on the availability of low-cost housing, its financing, the possibility of inter-state co-operation to improve the situation and of action by the European Social Fund and the Investment Bank.[50]

The Community interest in housing was maintained in its *Action Programme* of 1962, which stressed the need for 'opinions, recommendations or proposals' to cover the housing requirements of the Community, particularly low-cost housing; housing standards, especially those experienced by migrants; improvements in rural living conditions and financial co-operation among members to subsidize housing for workers moving within the Community.[51]

At one time social work was seen largely as a charitable service for the poor, inadequate and unfortunate, but it has been steadily evolving into a much broader system of social service aimed to achieve a state of equilibrium between the individual and society and to contribute generally to social well-being; 'The purpose of social work as we see it is to help the individual to achieve the best possible personal, family and social adjustment.'[52] It is now widely recognized that it has a role to play in helping with the social problems of young people, the handicapped and the elderly in society and with the human difficulties presented by regional development policies.[53] As a result public authorities are playing a much bigger part in the provision, or the subsidy, of personal services and training schemes for social workers at various levels of competence are developing rapidly. Much of the Community's contribution has lain in the discussion and studies which it has been able to arrange for those concerned with social services and family questions.[54] Annual meetings have taken place designed to keep family policies under review. The prime value of these activities has been to help to establish better liaison between the social services of the members, between the Commission and appropriate ministries, industrial organizations and family associations and to encourage the exchange of views on common problems. In 1961 the international union of family organizations found it worthwhile to set up a European office to maintain relations with the Community.

Personal service for migrants is not specifically mentioned in the Treaty of Rome. Although there can be no doubt of the acceptance of the principle of equality of treatment for migrants, its initial interpretation emphasized problems of wages and working conditions. With the growing awareness of the many social, cultural and political disabilities of migrants, the question of the provision of welfare services for them came to be seen as a necessary ingredient of an enriched concept of equality. 'The human dignity of the worker and his family must be brought further to the foreground.'[55] The traditional migrant, moving to undertake unskilled work on a labour contract, is ideal material for under-privileged status. In the past the pressure of unemployment and of depressed agriculture has meant that migrants were often unqualified and, furthermore, ill-adapted to the disciplines of town and factory life. 'Indeed, there are men for whom Europe is neither an idea, nor a legal entity, nor a policy but a different daily reality mingled with some degree of expectation. These are *"les travailleurs qui se déplacent dans la Communauté"*.'[56] Driven from a familiar environment by economic pressures, little serious thought may have been given to the realities of the situation or the cost in family separation. Migration has often worked badly through lack of adequate preparation and ignorance of each others' requirements on the part of both workers and hosts. Many workers would have benefited from the chance to discuss the project with a knowledgeable person in order to ensure that a rational decision was made and that migration, if undertaken, was done so on a sound basis. Workers have often suffered from an unrealistic picture of the life before them, lack of knowledge of working conditions, price levels or the real value of earnings. Inability to speak the language has impoverished social contacts, prevented workers following job instructions and obtaining promotion. Social isolation has been increased for those housed by employers in hostel accommodation, by lack of leisure-time facilities and by the unwillingness of many workers to spend time and money on social assimilation since their major objective has been to return home with a nest egg and set up a small business.[57] Under such circumstances a subtle balance in social policy is required, for if leisure-time facilities and special aid are too effective they may help to maintain isolation unnecessarily but without them the migrant may flounder.

If social damage to the receiving country can easily be done by the existence of considerable numbers of partially assimilated migrants, housed communally, cut off from any worthwhile social life, unhappy, bored and listless and disliked by the community in which they live, it is matched by the existence of a crippled family unit, maintaining only precarious contact with a breadwinner. Left behind, the children grow up fatherless, income can be irregular[58] and families are often anxious over whether to sell up and join the breadwinner or wait for him to return. All too often it is only after a catastrophe has occurred that the problems of the family come to anyone's notice. Although family migration is not the answer in all cases yet more could have been done to encourage it. 'It can happen that a country which has need of labour does not wish to receive the families.'[59] Although as has been seen, the free movement policy recognized certain implications for families, such as the right of the worker to have his family with him, the right to allow family members to get work and training and the recognition of the family for social security purposes, yet to make a reality out of family migration and to ensure that it works well for those involved, positive welfare programmes, in which housing arrangements are the biggest essential, are necessary. This means state action.

To ensure reasonable standards of housing for migrants is inevitably a complex matter. They do not form a homogeneous group and may bring with them very different standards and expectations from those current in the areas in which they find themselves. Single men, or married men without families, often arrive with the intention of saving as much as possible in the shortest possible time and, by gravitating to the poorest and least desirable accommodation available, help to focus the fears of the neighbourhood on minority groups. In Germany an employer of migrant labour had to provide single accommodation; France operated a *laissez-faire* policy and whilst she readily admitted families the great majority had to find their own homes. The notorious *bidonvilles* were part of the result.[60] Holland refused family entry until adequate housing was obtained and great difficulties were experienced in obtaining this. As a consequence of the many problems, the housing conditions of workers were often of the poorest kind.[61]

Family migration, which itself may be short or long term in character, presents the chief concern. The newcomer at the bottom of the occupational ladder, unfamiliar with local ways and unacceptable to sponsoring bodies, is likely to find himself at the tail end of the queue in a competitive market, but the EEC was unable to help states overcome the very real difficulties involved in giving special help to migrants in the only effective way, namely financial aid. Allocation of resources for migrants is bound to be a delicate matter for states, but by the middle of the 1960s there was a growing appreciation of the need to allow for migratory movements in the formulation of housing plans and at least two members, Belgium and Germany, were providing special aid for housing migrants.[62]

A first attempt at the identification of the problems of migration had been undertaken by the High Authority, which commissioned a study of the obstacles to free movement in 1955,[63] but the provisions of the Treaties of Paris and Rome did not provide an adequately precise basis for the development of a full range of services to overcome them. The regulations on free movement, however, established a formal position of some importance notably with regard to the right of family entrance, the wide definition of the family which they encouraged and the increasing importance attached to the housing question in successive regulations. Regulation 38/64/CEE reiterated the need for the migrant to have a normal dwelling as a precondition for family entry but elevated to a separate article his right to equal access to housing accommodation (Art.

10). By Regulation 1612/68 the rule concerning the possession of normal housing was qualified by the clause 'unless this provision might lead to discrimination between national workers and workers from other Member States' (Art. 10 (3)), whilst Art. 9 spelt out the implications of equality of treatment in the housing field. Nevertheless severe problems remained. The regulation did not deal with the hidden forms of discrimination which can prevent property ownership; residence qualifications necessarily mean the migrant joins the end of the queue and, since low-cost housing is provided by a variety of authorities, supervision of their work and practices is extremely difficult for the Commission, which found it necessary to stress that equality, in the housing field, meant the eligibility of migrants for tenancy allocation, loans, bonuses, subsidies and fiscal advantages.[64] It is believed that many workers return home because of housing difficulties. 'The cause is often that the workers find they cannot be joined by their families for lack of housing.'[65]

With the acceptance of Regulation 15 it became possible for the Commission to argue that special financial assistance for migrants might be derived from Art. 11 (2), which states that 'each Member State shall encourage the admission of every member of a family who is wholly or principally dependent on the worker and lives under his roof', and it began to consider the possibility of using the Investment Bank and the Social Fund as sources of European finance. On 27 January 1965 a draft was sent to the Council of a supplementary regulation to allow the fund to include aid for the building of low-cost housing for workers who have moved within the Community,[66] but the matter was not pursued by the Council. However, supported by Parliament and the Economic and Social Committee, the Commission itself adopted a recommendation on 7 July 1965[67] concerned with the housing of migrants and their families and designed to mobilize a special Community effort 'to stimulate and support action in the Member States to ensure really equal treatment in the allocation of housing for workers from another Community country and nationals of the host country'. The recommendation asked members to ensure that estimates of future demand for housing included consideration of the likely number of migrants from whatever source and of their families. Such estimates should be renewed periodically especially at regional and local level. The needs of newcomers should be included in provision made for the public financing of low-cost housing or for its grant aid. Where low-cost housing was publicly controlled and allocated, a percentage should be reserved for migrants. It pointed to the lack of knowledge of actual housing conditions, discriminatory practices and of family admissions, suggesting that government departments should collect information allowing comparisons to be made of the position as between nationals and migrants. Relevant information would include questions such as the number of low-cost dwellings actually obtained by migrants in different areas, the number of workers who would bring in their families if they had decent accommodation and the rents they might be able to pay. The number of workers living in communal or temporary dwellings, huts, sub-standard or overcrowded accommodation should be ascertained.

Measures should be taken to prevent discrimination in the allocation of housing and a record kept of the results of any bilateral or multi-lateral agreements undertaken in order to improve housing, including any projects of financial co-operation between members, in order to increase housing accommodation in areas of significant migration and known housing shortage. It was hoped that the European Investment Bank would be able to participate financially.

States should aim to ensure that housing standards of migrants and nationals were equal and where communal housing for migrants existed this should be supplemented by measures to prevent segregation and to improve environmental standards and facilities. In such housing the younger workers should if possible be housed separately and be given a measure of self-government.

A migrant worker should receive precise information about housing facilities and rents when he first applied for a job. When he arrived he should be informed of the level of controlled or customary rent, the possibility of obtaining low-cost accommodation and related social benefits. Heads of families should be told of the regulations in force regarding family re-unification and of the practical possibility of finding accommodation. Where the employer provided accommodation, a clear statement should be given about its quality, rent and other charges, disciplinary rules, the period of notice upon expiry of the employment contract and so on.

The Commission asked for a wide circulation of the recommendation and a periodic report from members on the measures taken, difficulties encountered and proposals for future action. It offered its help particu-larly over plans to ensure public and private financial aid.

This recommendation met with some, though limited, response. More efforts have been made in recent years to supply migrants with better information about housing whilst they have become eligible in Belgium, France and Germany for housing allowances.[68] Grants from central authorities towards subsidized housing for migrants in the three countries were made[69] but the idea of international financial co-operation for house building was not taken up.

At the same time there was a significant increase in the development of personal social services aimed to provide help directly to migrants. A large part of this work was carried out by voluntary organizations, many of them of a religious character, who had to deal with the rapidly developing situation resulting from the considerable number of people involved, often with resources inadequate to meet standards now considered reasonable, but these arrangements came to be supplemented by more formal organizations, grant aid from public authorities and the provision of social service within official institutions. Organizations in Italy included the Catholic Association of Italian workers, the Italian Catholic Union for Emigration as well as organizations more directly connected with the Catholic Church. The establishment of a National Association of Emigrants' Families in Rome made communication between workers concerned with divided families much easier than hitherto. Similarly a degree of rationalization of working agencies occurred in receiving countries, such as the French *Fonds d'action sociale pour les travailleurs étrangers,* the Luxembourg *Comité d'assistance sociale aux travailleurs étrangers* and the Dutch *Commission de contact et de consultation pour l'assistance aux travailleurs étrangers.*[70] Belgium established a system of regional committees, whilst a network of centres existed in Germany. These arrangements meant that it was easier to co-ordinate services within countries as well as between them even though this remained on an informal level between the specialist organizations themselves. More effective training for workers was provided,[71] both the Commission and member governments financed schemes to allow for sojourn abroad and recognition was given to the need to involve migrants themselves at the local level in the provision of services.[72] Although facilities remained patchy since organizations still lacked both staff and resources, attempts had been made to identify and reach the more obvious problems. Preparatory work was developed in Italy by employment and recruitment offices as well as in work training centres, all of which were used to provide more detailed information about host countries as well as language instruction. Effective guides to Benelux, Germany and France were issued by the Ministries of Foreign Affairs and Labour and Social Insurance. By 1966 twenty social workers were attached to employment exchanges in areas where emigration was high; consular staffs had been strengthened and grant aid given to organizations providing workers abroad.[73] There have been divided opinions on the relative merits of attaching social workers to groups of their fellow nationals working abroad and of permitting the host country to provide specialized services, but one estimate suggests that sixty German-speaking Italian social workers were in Germany by the late 1960s.[74]

Grant aid was used in host countries to help unions, firms, religious organizations and lesser public authorities to provide facilities for social and recreational activity, quiet places for children to do their homework, language courses, low-cost housing, radio programmes as well as personal counselling.[75] 'As far back as 1960, the social welfare bodies in Germany contended that the biggest and toughest problem raised by immigration was that of leisure.'[76] By the end of 1966 some 281 centres, employing 500 social workers, existed in Germany in addition to part-time and peripatetic offices dealing with a wide range of questions and devoting particular attention to young people.[77]

Growing interest in migration had already led to some international recognition of the need for social services in the ILO Convention No. 97 and Recommendation No. 86 on migrant labour, while the European Social Charter referred to the modern demand for welfare services suggesting that, whilst everyone should have access to qualified social service when required, migrants in particular required protection and assistance (Arts. 14 and 19). The Commission called a conference of social workers on the role of social service in relation to migrant labour in December 1958,[78] and an early recommendation urged on states the need for improved welfare services with the possibility of increased migration as the free movement policy developed.[79] Such services, it thought, could be expected to enlarge human freedom through enabling men to benefit from wider opportunities and to avoid failure in migration through being unable to deal with adjustment problems or unexpected difficulties such as illness. The Commission argued that Art. 117, as well as the close collaboration under Art. 118, formed a sufficient basis for its promotion of activity in the social welfare field, this being defined as 'professional activity aimed to secure help and a better reciprocal adaptation between individuals and their social environment through the use of appropriate methods whether this requires the utilisation of individual capacities, relationships of an individual or group nature or the resources of the community'.

The recommendation suggested that states should be prepared to stimulate, through financial support where necessary, the provision of social services to aid migrants and their families both in the form of personal service and material aid. Such services, whether run by public or private authorities, should be freely available to migrants, including seasonal and frontier workers. The pay and conditions offered to workers providing these services should be adequately adjusted to the degree of responsibility involved and the amount of training deemed necessary. Effective services should be organized prior to departure, during the journey, upon arrival and when a migrant was joined by his family. Before leaving home the worker, and his family if need be, should have the chance to discuss the project with a knowledgeable person and receive adequate information covering the general conditions of life, housing facilities, working conditions, national legislation likely to affect him, Community provisions concerning free movement and social security. At this preparatory stage, help might be given to ease the first contacts by the provision of more detailed information about the job, lists of addresses, language course facilities, pocket vocabularies and the like.

Help should be given to families to enable them to prepare themselves psychologically for a period of separation and ultimate reunion, to maintain family links, to encourage reunion and to make sure that the appropriate social legislation was known and applied and that social security benefits were received. Linguistic preparation might be necessary and practical assistance during the journey required. On arrival, both workers and their families would require access to services where the workers spoke the migrant's mother tongue and could help with adjustment problems, administrative formalities and accommodation. Good liaison between such services and the social services of the host country would be essential so that migrants could remain in touch with necessary services. During the settling-in period, too, workers and their families need someone at hand whom they can consult in their mother tongue, who can provide them with support and encouragement, help them to become familiar with the language and customs of the new country and direct them towards membership of cultural and social organizations. Such a service should provide help to workers who want to bring in their families by helping with the arrangements and trying to ensure adequate housing facilities.

Special attention was paid in the recommendation to the problems of integration. Migrants can be classified into groups, each one of which requires individual consideration. Children, adolescents reaching the stage of employment, young girls, mothers and single men all have different needs and, although a social service organization cannot deal with educational problems in the schools or ensure that all adolescents get apprenticeship, yet it can play a part in smoothing difficulties in a particular instance and a general role in the creation of a sympathetic public opinion and in developing co-operation with other social services, schools and employers. Pilot experiments to help in the development of these services would be useful.

Social work in the country of origin is still necessary after the migration of the wage earner. Families need assistance in arranging for their move or, if long separation is experienced, in being informed of their rights under social legislation.

Stress is laid on the importance of good co-operation between social services as a whole and those particularly concerned with migrants so that the newcomers get the facilities they require. Not all their needs come from the fact of being employed in a foreign country and in many cases their problems are those of the host population.

States would need to pay more attention to the supply of qualified social workers. General social work training would need to be supplemented to ensure workers had adequate knowledge of emigration areas, its customs and people, a knowledge of the receiving country, particularly of its social legislation and administrative organization, its social and cultural arrangements, a special knowledge of working conditions and prospects in different occupations as well as familiarity with international agreements covering questions such as social security benefits and the free movement of labour. Workers would need a knowledge of work methods suitable for dealing both with individuals in need and with group activities as well as language fluency. States should arrange refresher courses to ensure workers were kept up to date and exchange scholarships would aim to help to give workers the necessary professional expertise. The Commission agreed to establish a programme of scholarships and to encourage meetings on an international and bilateral level.

Good co-operation between social services of countries of emigration and receipt is essential for the reciprocal exchange of information and to ensure that effective liaison provides continuity of care for individuals and families who are moving or returning home.

The Commission recommended that social services for migrants should normally be organized by the host country, although close liaison with the services of the country of origin would be essential. In some cases social workers from the home country are attached to groups of their fellow nationals abroad and where this solution is adopted the workers should be seen as being complementary to indigenous social services with which good liaison must exist. Such social workers should be trained for work abroad, be fluent in the language of the host country and care should be taken not to allow such arrangements to encourage the formation and maintenance of isolated migrant groups.

Governments were requested to take early action, to keep the Commission informed of developments and asked to arrange for a wide distribution of the content of the recommendation. The Commission offered its help in developing co-operation whether on a Community or multilateral plane.

These recommendations cannot be considered as adequate either to make a real impact on the human situation or to be considered as a European policy. The very large number of foreign workers, whether from within the Community or not, is now known to be the cause of considerable social tensions in many industrial cities and it seems probable that this will not be alleviated without positive action by public authorities. From the personal point of view greater mobility will include more family separation and distress, marital breakdown and individual maladjustment. In 1970 a number of Italian organizations concerned with the position of their countrymen working abroad submitted a petition to the Social Affairs Committee of the European Parliament and, whilst some of the more extreme grievances were considered unjustified, Parliament has passed a resolution recommending stronger measures to prevent discrimination and the adoption of a European charter of civil, social and human rights.[80] The complications arising for many people from the effect of their legal status on questions of domicile, nationality and family relationships require further study in a period of increasing international mobility and, for Community workers, there is now considerable illogicality in a situation where a great deal is done to give them equality of rights at work but where they cannot influence their political environment. It is to be hoped that the Commission's new study of migration will deal with some of these questions.

The economic demand for workers underlay the application of the free movement policy and no doubt it was this need that enabled states and employers to accept the rules of the treaty without great difficulty. The contrast with the free establishment policy is marked. Community institutions made great technical achievements in the fields of labour placement and social security coverage with their attendant questions of job definition, information provision, definition of benefits and administrative co-operation. They acted, too, as a stimulus to the better treatment of migrants both at the work place and more generally. Yet the period demonstrated as many problems as it solved. There remains the unresolved question of whether Community workers are to be given priority in filling vacancies, with the implication that major effort should be put into attempts to match supply and demand through much closer integration of employment services and a build-up of vocational training schemes with the deliberate intention of meeting the requirements of industrialists within the Community. Whether the EEC will still wish to emphasize the free movement policy or will prefer to attempt a regional development process enabling workers to remain more frequently in their own localities remains an open question. For the former to become an effective social reality, however, it is clear that a vast extension of policy is required. More positive manpower arrangements, including vocational training schemes and short training courses, an attack on the question of training levels and their mutual recognition, vocational guidance and services to aid social integration are all necessary if the migrant, whether temporary or permanent, frontier or seasonal, is to achieve a footing of equality with his fellows.

PART TWO

A Common Social Policy

6 Social Harmonization

I Equality, Harmonization and Equivalence

The growing interest of member states in social policy since 1958 has reflected the rapid social changes which have occurred in Western Europe. Alterations in the patterns of working and family life, the prolongation of education, growing urbanization and changes in demographic structures presented features widely familiar and it is not surprising that members reacted in broadly similar ways by being drawn more deeply into social questions or that their social policies should have possessed many common characteristics. To what extent, therefore, did the EEC itself prove capable of participating in the search for measures adequate to meet changing situations, of stimulating the laggards, of articulating the necessary goals of social policy and of ensuring that the greater prosperity of the area was devoted to fuller and more satisfying life styles for the people? Part Two of this work is devoted to a discussion of the reaction of the Community to these broader questions.

It is essential to bear in mind that the day-to-day work of the Community was necessarily bounded by the terms of the Treaty of Rome. This defined certain objects which it was the duty of the institutions to promote. Such aims were not, however, sufficiently far-reaching to form the basis of a comprehensive social policy. Even the concern of the founders of the Community with the labour force did not lead them to commit the new organization to a policy of full employment, of manpower utilization, of comprehensive social security cover or an obligatory programme of vocational training. Much less did the treaty refer to common goals in health, education or the welfare of children or the elderly. The treaty, therefore, was a narrow base from which the Community might respond to the social issues of the time and it lacked the flexibility of action and the ability to anticipate the likely consequences of socio-economic change which are the hallmarks of an effective social policy.[1] The specific developments which have been described neither added up to a coherent strategy of social policy in themselves nor provided the foundations for its natural evolution.

The objection may be advanced that, in its Preamble and Arts. 2 and 117, the treaty did in fact possess broad social goals and had, furthermore, woven into its fabric recognition of the social problems of agriculture,[2]

157

transport and regional disparities. It was on such a base that Parliament attempted to argue that social progress was the main, not the secondary, objective of the treaty system.[3] Such goals undoubtedly existed. Their weakness lay in their lack of clarity and in the absence of means whereby they might be translated into a precise and effective policy. Thus the treaty did not give the institutions a mandate for the development of social action other than that of those limited purposes deemed necessary for the creation of a common market.

The key article for the possible development of a general improvement policy was 117, by which members not only agreed to promote improvement in living and working conditions for the labour force but accepted the principle of their *'égalisation dans le progrès'*, thus retaining the policy of Art. 3 (e) of the Treaty of Paris. Despite the suspicion that such doctrines were originally inserted to cover the possibility that differences in standards might adversely affect competition, Art. 117 has often been used as the statement of the human purpose of the Community. The task 'will not only be to reduce the difficulties which might result from the merging of the economies as the result of divergencies in initial conditions, but also to strive for equalisation in an upward direction of living and working conditions of labour'.[4] Much later, in the official debate on British entry, the Secretary of State for Social Services also assumed a moral goal to be implicit in the treaty.

> It is within the purpose and the spirit of the Common Market that there should be an attempt to improve the social services all round . . . There can be no doubt both that the Common Market countries seek through the Treaty of Rome to improve their living conditions and the social services of their own nationals and that they should make progress in so doing. Article 117 of the Treaty of Rome enjoins them to seek better conditions of living, working and employment and to harmonise their national conditions upwards.[5]

Art. 117, however, has severe limitations when considered as the possible basis for the creation of a broad social policy including action in fields not specifically mentioned in the treaty. In the first place, it referred to the conditions of the labour force rather than of the general population. This emphasis upon man in his role of worker was implicitly accepted by the Commission when Signor Levi-Sandri declared that 'the problem of harmonization must include all working conditions and all those conditions of life linked to the carrying out of a job'.[6] The focus on the work situation was reinforced by the provisions of Art. 118, whose operation has been closely associated with that of the preceding article and which details the particular fields in which state co-operation is expected.

In the second place, Art. 117 was very imprecise. This lack of clarity gave rise to great debate over its meaning and accentuated the difficulties faced by those institutions which wished to develop social policy beyond the work situation. Furthermore, it laid down no direct forms of action, contenting itself with the statement that its twin objectives would result from the operation of the common market which would favour the harmonization of social systems, from the procedures of the treaty and the approximation of laws. The first is a particularly obscure statement which seems to hint that such harmonization would follow automatically from the new economic arrangements and seems to reflect the economic reasoning of the Spaak report. When it is remembered that Art. 118 spoke only of the close collaboration between states and of the possibility of studies, consultation and advice, it is clear that this, too, was inadequate as a base for action to fulfil egalitarian goals. 'All action aiming at a progressive equalisation in living and working conditions *must* be the object of a close collaboration . . . but the results can at most give rise to acts which do not bind states . . . social distortions *may* only give rise to studies, consultations and opinions.'[7]

A particularly important lacuna in the treaty was the lack of a clear statement of the relationship between economic and social aims. It was uncertain how far the underlying philosophy was that the fulfilment of the former would introduce the latter or that the social ends required equal attention and conscious pursuit:

> the debate was primarily concerned with the nature, functions and limits of such a policy. The alternative propositions were, firstly, to see in the social provisions of the treaty of Rome only those measures necessary to prevent competitive distortions and to help bring about economic integration; secondly, to view a community social policy as analogous to national social policies which, although conditioned by economic policy are not subordinated to it and on occasion may themselves be the determinant of economic policy.[8]

The phraseology of Art. 117 goes further than simple acceptance of the argument that the rapid growth of productivity arising from the international division of labour would be the main cause of better living conditions[9] without taking the step of laying down definite policies to ensure such improvement actually occurred. It demonstrates the extent to which the European movement was motivated by politico-economic rather than social goals and neglected to consider fully the inter-relationship of economic and social policies.[10] Here is further evidence that the Treaty of Rome was a better guide for the immediate task of creating a customs union than for the long-term future, for it is in a period of positive integration that it becomes more difficult to envisage either a common economic policy without consideration of its social effects or to see how common social policies might be established whilst ignoring their economic base.[11] Considered from the point of view of social policy, Art. 117 was inadequate as it stood. In consequence a considerable responsibility lay upon the institutions to undertake the task of creative interpretation and to turn the generalizations into practical objectives.

It was, therefore, of critical importance that the Commission considered '*égalisation dans le progrès*' as a genuine aim necessitating the development of a social policy existing in its own right and not as a subordinate partner of economic ends; 'The aim is to assure both economic and *social* progress . . . the objectives of a social character are placed on the same footing as those of economic character.'[12] One of the most eloquent proponents of this view was Signor Levi-Sandri.

> First of all, it must be remarked that the whole of the construction of Europe is inspired by the principles of social justice . . . notably through the reduction of the gap between the different regions and of the slow development of the less favoured. The common market is not an end in itself. It is only the base, the necessary condition for a deeper and stronger integration of the European people . . . the European ideal should not be the monopoly of restricted circles . . . but the common inheritance of our generation and our people. For this a social policy which is developing on a par with economic production and which guarantees at a community level a just division of wealth and its resulting advantages is an absolute necessity.

Social objectives do not follow automatically from the realization of the common market. Such a conception conforms neither to the letter nor the spirit of the treaty. Whilst social progress is conditioned by economic progress the latter creates new disequilibria and 'cannot automatically lead to social justice'.[13]

The insistence that the Community was fundamentally a social and political organization, rather than simply an economic one, which could not tolerate disparities 'unjustifiable in moral terms and which were anti the principle of Community solidarity which is the base of the European Community idea',[14] was the guiding motive behind the attempt to establish a social policy designed not only to remove inequalities but to raise the standard of living, unify social systems and pay particular attention to the social conditions of impoverished regions. It should, therefore, thought Parliament, be approached in a global as well as a sectoral sense.[15]

The belief that social progress constituted a fundamental aim implied the necessity for conscious control of the new economic unit in order to achieve its social ends.

> In fact it seems that one cannot entirely abandon to the natural course of events the responsibility of directing the social development of the Community in the paths of harmony and convergence laid down by the Treaty. Without endangering free competition which is an indistinguishable element in common progress, a more co-ordinated effort towards harmonisation must be proposed to member states in order to progress more surely and rapidly towards these objectives.[16]

An immediate problem thus arose. If Art. 117 was to be taken as a base for social policy, was it aimed at comparable living standards between one member and another, between workers in the same industry but different states, between workers in different regions but the same state or simply all workers everywhere? The social security conference of 1962, considering the question of interpretation, recognized that the problem might be defined as between one working group and another, between nations or between regions within nations, and suggested that harmonization would require procedures for raising the level of the lowest without preventing others improving their position.[17] It was

> a process of social improvement which is carried out more rapidly in the less favoured countries and regions and for the less favoured groups than in the case of the more privileged. At the same time, it must not put a brake on the social development of the latter but work through stimulating the social development of the former.[18]

It appears naive to suppose that the concept of equality should be limited to that of comparative national standards when the considerable discrepancies which exist within states are now common knowledge. The temptation to make crude comparisons between states on the basis of national statistics, and particularly of average incomes per head, must be resisted. From the viewpoint of social policy, the fact that the inhabitants of West Germany have had one of the highest rates of income per head is less significant than the association of wealth with the second highest rates of infant and neo-natal mortality of the six members.[19] Equally important from the point of view of the development of European social standards is the fact that the social statistics of the Community were not broken down by class, income or region so that internal differentiations might be determined on a comparative base. The weakness of social policy is thus seen to have derived from more than the inadequacies of the treaty or from a philosophy which considered labour as a unit of production; it stemmed, too, from the nature of the EEC as an organization of states and not a community of peoples. The broad sweep of social policy, the degree and form of redistribution are matters of state responsibility for which there is no effective tradition of international concern. In consequence the arguments produced by the Commission, Parliament and the Social Affairs Committee as to why the EEC *ought* to have increased social responsibilities were bound to remain, in large measure, at the theoretical level. Art. 117 incorporated a dilemma. It was the member states who retained effective responsibility to deal with internal inequalities, but at the same time they had created a Community concerned with individuals as migrants, as members of the labour force or as low-income farmers and which had been given broad goals of social progress to pursue. The claim that '*égalisation dans le progrès*' meant 'offering individuals, social groups, geographical areas and economic sectors equal opportunities to play their part in social progress'[20] was far-reaching and logical but impossible to apply.

The ambiguities of Art. 117 led inevitably to the attempt to define its meaning more helpfully. In 1961 a detailed discussion took place in the Social Affairs Committee, which concluded that no clear distinction could be made between the goals of equalization and harmonization.[21] Although harmonization was not a necessary pre-condition of European integration, the moral purpose of the treaty demanded some such goal going beyond an interpretation limited to the elimination of obstacles to, or distortions of, competition.[22] Nevertheless the interpretation was cautious. Strict uniformity in matters such as conditions of work, social benefits and wage levels appeared impractical to the committee,[23] even in the long run, in view of the disparities of standards existing between members of each of the three groups, and unrealistic in that it would be a more advanced social goal than any member state with greater experience in social policy had set itself. Different degrees of intimacy in social affairs might be postulated according to the closeness of integration achieved by the Communities. At one end of the spectrum was complete uniformity of social legislation which would leave a restricted role for the members and at the other was the straightforward co-ordination of national policies by which states took account of the needs and developments of their partners but retained their independence. Harmonization was considered by the committee to be but the first step above co-ordination and was left undefined in order to allow for evolution as the Community moved further towards integration. It recognized, however, that members would retain great power even in the stage of uniformity since the treaty had left responsibility for policy decisions to the Council.

As a result of these discussions, harmonization became the object of policy desired, not as an end in itself, but as a contribution to raising the standard of living[24] and as the means whereby the ultimate goal of equality might be achieved. In consequence the social aim became divided as discussion substituted an indeterminate concept of harmonization for the alternative possibility which would have been an attempt to harden and particularize the meaning of 'égalisation dans le progrès'.

> After all, did not Article 117 of the Treaty of Rome foresee that the progressive equalisation in living and working conditions would result, amongst other things, from the very functioning of the common market? This tendency towards the harmonisation of social systems, which is to some extent automatic, cannot be questioned but it is at the same time in part the result of the many activities developed at the community level in the social sphere.[25]

The comfort of the belief in the inevitability of improvement thus underlay the discussion of the development of Community social action which, far from taking a radical direction, emphasized the importance of a constant process of adjustment as obvious anomalies in social standards were disclosed by the process of social change or uncovered by social investigation. Harmonization 'does not mean levelling or uniformity. It would be purely utopian, even inauspicious, to attempt a unification process at community level when it does not exist nationally because of regional or sectoral particularities.' Since, however, such disparities were disappearing at national level it was desirable to find 'un moyen terme entre "spécificite" et "parité".'[26]

The view that any direct policy of equalization was impractical gained general support. The High Authority had concluded that at any given moment the standards of provision in a particular service would show considerable discrepancies over the Community area as a result of historical, economic, demographic and political forces which had led countries to emphasize one need or service rather than another and whose significance could not be isolated from the sum total of provision which made up the overall social standard for an individual. The hopes and objectives of professional organizations working for improvement would vary similarly.[27] Parliament's conclusions were on the same lines. Uniformity of social security benefits, to take one example, was an unrealistic aim, since one member might wish to emphasize family allowances, another unemployment, old age or sickness insurance and yet another more generous holidays. Members' aspirations were bound to differ and allowance should properly be made for national preferences. It should not be for the European Community but for national agencies to determine in what form increases of wealth might be taken.[28] It could, however, be argued that 'global harmonization' was a valid Community concept in which the total amount of redistribution was the same despite variation in the use to which it was put; thus a 'recherche systématique d'équivalences' was a possible objective,[29] although the mutual imposition of preferences was not wanted[30] and the aim of strict uniformity was denied.

> Harmonization does not mean making the different systems identical; it means eliminating contradictions and differences justified neither by particular requirements nor by differences in social structure. It does not mean levelling downwards or holding back the most progressive groups; nor does it mean granting wholesale the special concessions offered in given sectors, regardless of the concrete reasons for such differential treatment. Lastly, harmonization will not come from regimentation, but through close co-operation between the Common Market Commission, Governments and workers' and employers' organizations.[31]

Harmonization was, however, considered to be a double process. Firstly, the increase in living standards for the most advanced in the Community should not be held back whilst the others caught up,[32] for then the former would not benefit from the greater progress and prosperity for which the common market was designed. Social progress could not be at the expense of retarding that of the most favoured so that levelling occurred at an average level.

> The European Commission considers that Article 117 provides for the equalization in an upward direction of the living and working conditions of labour, and a functioning of the Common Market which will favour the harmonization of social systems cannot imply a levelling on a theoretical average standard of living, as this would, for example, force those countries with the most advanced economic and social development to hold up their social evolution till the less fortunate countries have managed to catch up.

Secondly, however, gaps in standards must be closed. The Commission had 'the desire to encourage and help all people in the Community to improve their existing social situation, as the equalisation provided for by the Treaty must be sought by means of more rapid progress in those areas where progress seems to be most needed'.[33] Thus the Commission

> sees harmonization not as a standardization nor as the mere alignment of the various regulations and practices on those of the member country which would seem the most advanced in these matters, but rather as a progressive narrowing of differences between them in a common effort to make social progress within each country first of all and then in an integrated Europe, through co-operation of all the social forces in the six countries.[34]

This view was supported by the Social Affairs Committee. 'Your committee understands by "égalisation dans le progrès" that the rise in the standard of living must be accompanied by a lessening of disparities. The gap must be minimised through the provision of a higher social level.'[35]

The significance of this view is obvious although these institutions refrained from making it explicit. It implies that the Treaty of Rome required definite redistribution policies in order to ensure that a relatively more rapid improvement in standards occurred for those at the bottom. Furthermore, by recognizing that countries, groups or regions may be under-privileged in comparison with their peers it placed the treaty in the relatively new tradition of international responsibility for human beings. Such positive redistribution implies that it is not enough to rely upon economic growth or even upon the deepening of the process of economic integration. It does, however, presuppose the existence of some sense of European obligation. Whilst an effective social policy might be expected to help to create a European consciousness, it would seem also to be true that it requires a prior sense of European community based on a 'future of solidarity in which a better distribution of wealth may be considered an accompanying factor of expansion'[36] and which has led to the creation of political institutions with the capacity to translate this into policy.

The Commission was careful, however, not to claim too much in practical terms. Its inability to control wages, social benefits or levels of personal taxation[37] would in any case have left its policies of equalization heavily circumscribed. It preferred to attempt to establish effective co-operation with employers', workers' and other voluntary organizations in order to obtain general agreement on principles, active co-operation in applying them and to provide a forum for the examination of the results of studies made in order to see what moves would be necessary or desirable to establish a European labour law, collective bargaining at European level or harmonization of social security regimes.[38] 'To get general acceptance of these principles, to obtain from governments and the social partners their willingness to adhere to them and to apply them actively should be the principal aim of Community social policy during the next two stages.'[39] In the nature of things, the influence which the Commission might wish to exert on wage levels, working conditions or holiday pay required procedures whereby such matters could be exposed to discussion at European level and considered in relation to the objective of Art. 117. The conclusion was thus drawn that it was essential to establish employer-worker committees and to foreshadow the possibility of collective bargaining at Community level even if only on the broadest basis of model contracts or the principles of labour law.[40] Together with its study programme this formed the only practical means whereby the Commission might contribute to the levelling of wages and social security benefits which form a large element of those conditions relevant to the task of equalization.

The discussion on Art. 117, therefore, led to its weakening as the word 'harmonization' became a substitute for 'equalization'. Some may wish to argue that, in the absence of the ability to prosecute egalitarian policies, this can have made little difference to the work of the EEC. Against this, however, it may be said that states have taken their obligations under the treaty seriously. The redefinition in practice provided an escape route for them and one given, moreover, by those institutions which had social responsibility most at heart. The official British version of the Treaty of Rome, published at the time of accession, refers to the agreement of members to promote improved conditions for workers 'so as to make possible their harmonization while the improvement is being maintained'. As far as Great Britain is concerned, therefore, she accepted no egalitarian goal but a significantly weaker objective than that of the original treaty. Sir Keith Joseph's speech, to which reference was made a little earlier on p. 158, was careful to include the classic qualifications in the field of social progress. Although the treaty had little to say about social security and health, it allowed for 'close collaboration' in such fields although members were free to determine their own basic provision. Unanimous decisions on harmonization might in future be taken 'but there will be no obligation on us to change'. The term 'equalization' is not to be found.[41]

II Social Security

Within the framework of its harmonization activities, the EEC has paid most attention to the question of social security. At first sight it presents a promising field for the development of a European policy since it has been the subject of international agreements for many years, has been widely studied by the ILO, the Council of Europe and the European Communities as well as having been considered intensively as a possible barrier to international competition and to labour movement. The practical achievement of reciprocal social security arrangements, designed to facilitate employment flows has been managed by states without the necessity to establish uniform standards and the issues, although related, are better kept distinct. It is the latter aspect which is here considered. From this point of view a major question of definition at once arises. Although for certain purposes, such as international reciprocity, the emphasis has been on defined schemes providing cash benefits, most frequently on an insurance base, the development of social protection by the modern state either through or in addition to social insurance systems has meant that it is the totality of social care which can be the more significant. The term social security is often used in this wide sense and for some purposes this global interpretation is the more useful. The classic forms of social insurance are only one part of the way in which modern communities try to maintain social standards. Human needs are met by a gamut of health, welfare, employment and income maintenance services and the extent to which these facilities are incorporated into a formal definition of social security may be no more than a matter of historical accident. The United Nations Declaration of Human Rights made a very general statement.

> Everyone, as a member of society, has the right to social security and is entitled to realisation, through national effort and international co-operation and in accordance with the organisation and resources of each state, of the economic, social and cultural rights indispensable for his dignity and the free development of his personality (Art. 22).

> Everyone has the right to a standard of living adequate for the health and well-being of himself and of his family, including food, clothing, housing and medical care and necessary social services, and the right to security in the event of unemployment, sickness, disability, widowhood, old age or other lack of livelihood in circumstances beyond his control (Art. 25).

The attempts by the ILO and the Council of Europe to establish international standards of social security have necessitated a more precise definition. ILO Convention No. 102 was concerned to cover schemes, whether or not of an insurance nature, providing cash benefits and medical care in a defined range of circumstances, laying down the groups of the population to be covered and principles for the determination of minimum benefit levels. The Social Security Code of 1964 accepted by the Council of Europe adopted a similar approach. It specified a range of benefits, of which signatories must accept a minimum, and the necessary population cover with the twin objects of promoting higher internal standards and encouraging signatories to develop along the same lines in order to facilitate labour movement. Even this document, which is one of the more stringent international statements on social security, sheds little or no light on such problems as the level of adequacy of benefits, the proportion of national resources which should be devoted to social security or the relative importance of the different social security objectives themselves. No indication is given of the methods to be employed, of the importance to be attached to statutory and non-statutory schemes, or of how to co-ordinate health and income maintenance services so that the individual welfare is better served. So far the EEC has not attempted a comparable statement of social security standards of its own.

Attempts at quantitative studies of social security require yet tighter definition. The ILO has confined its work to schemes which fulfil three criteria. Objectives must be to provide curative or preventive medical care, maintain income or supplement income to meet family responsibilities. Systems must be based on legislation giving specific rights to individuals or specified obligations on institutions and be operated by a public, semi-autonomous or autonomous body.[42] The one exception to the last rule relates to compensation for industrial accident which can remain, as in Belgium, a direct liability on the employer.

The EEC has adopted its own definitions. Following the 1962 conference on social security, it began to collect detailed information concerning public social security schemes of a general and sectoral nature, which enabled it to produce comparative tables of coverage, benefits and financing. The series 'Tableaux comparatifs' provides detailed information of general, agricultural and mining social security schemes. No very rigorous definition is used and the attempt is made to include in the general tables all schemes for employed workers including those designated under occupational arrangements formally recognized by the state.

More recently the Statistical Office has attempted to develop 'social accounts' covering all expenditure entailed for individuals and households to meet a defined set of needs where there is a financial intervention by another source above that required from the beneficiary (Appendix Table 6.3). This definition has meant the inclusion of expenditures to meet circumstances of sickness, old age and death, invalidity, physical and psychological infirmity, industrial accident and diseases, unemployment, family charges, war, political and natural calamities.[43] Systems of social intervention are classified into social insurance, employers' benefits, systems to help victims of war and other disasters and systems of social aid and assistance. Of these the first two groups are of much the greater significance, and studies such as that on the economic impact of social security have ignored the effect of the latter two.[44] Capital expenditure, housing aids, the cost of industrial training and benefits such as special tax alleviations have not yet been included in the social accounts, which are thus wider in scope than the social insurance schemes of the *'Tableaux comparatifs'* but not fully inclusive of redistributive expenditure.

These problems of definition, of inclusion or exclusion in national returns which reflect differences in organizational structure and historical development make it necessary to exercise great care in drawing conclusions from international statistics and certainly do not allow a comparison of total living standards to be made; 'It is impossible to make an overall comparison of social service costs in terms of proportion of gross national product.'[45]

The diffused use of the term social security is closely linked with the historical process whereby social insurance schemes developed to take over increasing functions with the result that a process which normally began as a means of providing the industrial worker with a limited number of cash benefits and access to medical care became the preferred method of ensuring the satisfaction of a wide range of needs experienced by the bulk, if not all, of the population. Such extension of coverage, the introduction of family support, the wide definition of the family often used, access to health services for the dependants of the beneficiary, the integration of social insurance with social welfare services and preventive medicine all mean that the term can very easily be equated with the major part of modern social responsibilities. Indeed, it is possible to reach the stage at which the term social security 'thus includes practically all the activities of the *Welfare State,* that is to say the state which finds its justification and its goal in the well-being of its citizens. One ends . . . by associating social security and the *development of the human being.*'[46] Similarly, when Signor Levi-Sandri referred to social security as 'all those institutions and arrangements whose purpose it is, by providing suitable benefits, to cope with any hardship in which those who live solely by the fruits of their labour may find themselves',[47] he was using the term in a far wider sense than that necessary for the purpose of statistical comparison of insurance benefits, although not in a fully universal and comprehensive sense.

The growth of social security systems in Western Europe during the twentieth century was intimately linked with the development of an industrial system which revealed the inadequacy of individual thrift and mutual aid to deal with the greater variety of risk situations and the larger number of people exposed to them. With the identification of major needs it became possible to institutionalize methods of help and, although at first it was the condition of the industrial working class that caused most concern, greater experience of the problems involved and the broadening notion of the content of social security brought some degree of responsibility towards the bulk of the population on the part of the national state. One of the more noticeable trends of recent years has been the extension of the protection offered by social security schemes by the inclusion of wider groups of people, particularly the self-employed, agricultural workers and dependants and by the continuance of eligibility for benefits when work ceases in retirement. The movement has been away from the original interest in manual workers or, at best, those of employee status to much broader coverage[48] even if it has not yet reached the whole population. One example is the extension of the provision for maternity care, as shown in Table 6.1.

Table 6.1
Extension of Protection Against Maternity Costs[49]

	Number of persons (thousands)		Percentage of total population covered	
	1962	1968	1962	1968
Germany	49,000	52,972	86·1	88·0
France	39,760	44,790	84·6	90·0
Italy	43,212	46,798	85·8	86·8
Netherlands	8,901	9,483	74·9	74·1
Belgium	6,962	9,178	75·5	95·4
Luxembourg	274·7	329·3	85·1	97·9

The implications of this developing role are very important. There has been a steady growth in the proportion of national resources channelled into social expenditure. In its broad EEC nomenclature this accounted for between 13·8 per cent and 17·6 per cent of gross national product in 1962 according to country and by 1971 required from 18·4 to 21·6 per cent.[50] Of this about 90 per cent is absorbed by direct cash benefits. The importance of social security benefits themselves is shown in Appendix Table 6.5. With one-fifth of resources being used in this way, with significant influence being exerted upon both investment and redistribution policies, no state can avoid an active interest in social security schemes, the major users of such social expenditure, with their importance for the general management of the economy and the broad pattern of the return available for different social groups.

Is it a question of guaranteeing to everyone a certain degree of protection against a variety of social risks, a guarantee of which a more equitable redistribution of resources may be a possible *consequence* or method but by no means the *aim*? Or is it rather the contrary, in that the desired objective is exactly that of a more equitable redistribution of resources in which certain obligatory forms of protection against social risks may be only the *means,* indeed may serve as a pretext?[51]

This comment on the inter-war period is even more applicable today and draws attention to the severe difficulties presented to the process of international standard-setting which implies the passing to an international organization of responbility to determine those economic and social objectives which have hitherto been critical ingredients of the state's domestic role.

Statutory social security schemes are, furthermore, increasingly joined by occupational arrangements operative in the same field. In so far as the anxiety of modern governments to perpetuate economic growth brings the need for the state to check consumption and therefore to limit the growth of statutory social security schemes, modern conditions may be encouraging the transfer of demands from the political to the industrial arena and therefore the development of occupational systems. It is increasingly doubtful whether it is helpful to consider public schemes in isolation from the private sector, either from the economic viewpoint since occupational pension schemes are major investors in the economy, or from the social in that it is necessary to avoid the danger of the public system containing a predominance of the less well paid whose benefits cannot be improved for fear of disturbing the industrial sector. The debates on the reform of the French social security system in 1967 illustrated certain aspects of this problem. Thus tensions between the objectives of social security and economic constraints and between the role of public and private responsibility will continue, posing the question of priorities between one type of benefit and another, between one group in the population and another and between social institutions which are in some degree rivals rather than partners.

The broader view of the place of social security in the national life has been accompanied by an emphasis on the relationship between cash benefits and social services as a whole. The division has never been clear-cut for the earliest social security schemes were concerned to provide personal medical care if only for the recipients of sickness benefits or for the sufferers from industrial accident or disease, but with the passage of time the inter-relationship of welfare services has become more obvious. The enlarging concept of effective medical care, the need for the labour force to receive job finding and training facilities, the prevention of large-scale unemployment, the requirement of reasonable wages and conditions of work, the increasing number of the elderly with their heavy demands on health and housing services and the public interest in the quality of care provided by the family for the young have all helped social security schemes to burst out from the strict limits imposed upon them by the earlier view of their responsibilities. Even if national planning of the economy remains frail, the very process of collecting information and determining some view of desirable objectives and priorities highlights the question of the social return and the relative importance of various social objectives. Thus public pressures ally with the dynamics of operation of social security schemes themselves towards a wider concept of social welfare of which cash benefits are but a part and give point to the process of social budgeting in which France and Germany were pioneers and in which the European Community has become interested.[52]

The implications of these developments for social security schemes are by no means clear. One pressure is towards a view of benefits as part of the total wage bill of the employer and thus suitable for determination within the range of occupational welfare facilities by collective bargaining procedures. At the same time the integration of social security into social welfare suggests it is part of the whole process of the provision of a social standard of living which is the responsibility of the community at large rather than of employers, who are less suitable as agents for the provision of non-cash benefits or for meeting the needs of the non-employed or self-employed members of the community. In either case, the older view of the role of social security is no longer relevant. In the past the payment of certain limited, defined benefits at a level considerably below that earned by the industrial worker was, by virtue of its certainty, regularity and moral neutrality, a considerable advance on the poor law, indiscriminate charity and limited thrift. The constraints on earlier thinking, which arose because insurance schemes were largely designed as an alternative to poor law systems and based on a relatively strict application of insurance principles, are going. Instead social security schemes are becoming a major tool through which the population may be enabled to rear children, purchase ever costlier health care and, when retired, continue to live at a reasonable standard. The concept of the minimum has been swallowed up in that of the guarantee of a socially acceptable income.[53]

So far the enlargement of the purposes of social security has not proved incompatible with the retention of features peculiar to each national scene and which reflect its more limited origins, although the reconciliation of broad objectives with existing structures can give rise to serious problems. Historical inertia, the prevailing attitude to political and economic phenomena and the urgency of particular problems are all elements in the national environment which affect the nature of social security systems. At the end of the Second World War Great Britain became committed to viewing social security as a means of community solidarity in which state contribution would be relatively high and benefits would represent the responsibility to ensure minimum standards which citizens might themselves supplement. She was thus able to spread the cost of personal risks brought by the industrial system over the population as a whole and to retain, although not without difficulty, the concept of a universal health service financed from taxation. Social security can also be viewed, however, as a factor in industrial relations in which benefits are seen as a means of replacing wages rather than as a method of providing for all citizens. This approach has been common in the original common market countries in which both employer and worker have been accustomed to pay more in return for benefits more nearly related to wage levels. There is a long-standing view which claims that it is the employer's responsibility to bear the loss of income or the cost of the necessary reparation to the individual when the worker loses his job through ill-health, unemployment or old age. The relatively high employers' contributions levied in France and Italy and the low contribution from state funds is symptomatic of this philosophy (Appendix Table 6.4). The approach has led to the maintenance of special schemes for particular industries such as the mines, agriculture, railways or merchant marine which are now difficult to integrate into an all-embracing social security system (Appendix Tables 6.8, 6.9).

Finally, social security can be seen as a function of group solidarity. People who work in the same profession, or form the industrial wage-earning class, or are self-employed have traditionally found it advantageous to band together to help themselves in their misfortunes and in many countries – France is an example – social security is partially provided on a corporate basis and Belgium has adopted similar arrangements. There is, therefore, some degree of choice between the community, the occupation, the firm or the industry as the basis for public social security schemes and this choice will help to determine the method of financing adopted. The notion of the community obligation suggests general taxation, the industrial base the employer's responsibility and the occupational structure the extension of mutual aid.

The factors influencing the development of social security schemes have also affected the methods of administration. What in some countries is done by the public authority on a national scale may be done elsewhere by the descendants of local thrift societies brought into a public system or by a combination of the two. With their widening objectives, the need to establish priorities in expenditure and to work in conjunction with the medical and related professions, the achievement of decision-making methods acceptable to the general community and to organized interests has become a further issue which requires reconsideration.

Social security schemes must face a growing problem of finance in view of their extending role and rapid increase in costs. Resistance to the idea of acceptance by central government of a larger share of responsibility remains strong in many countries and efforts have been made to keep contributions from employers and the insured population as the main source of income. Even so, a trend towards a state contribution is evident in order to carry responsibilities more obviously of a general concern than those resulting from the process of industrial production. Sharing the economic cost of child-rearing, maintaining large numbers of the elderly, providing access to health care, incorporating the self-employed, the poorly paid and those who have not contributed to any scheme in the past are primarily community objectives whose cost has to be more widely spread than over industry alone. It is in the long-established special industrial schemes where the state has been obliged to step in most obviously, so that comparisons based on general social security schemes can give a misleading picture. 'The natural evolution of social security . . . logically demands national solidarity, that is to say a complementary financial contribution from the state as has already happened for the special regimes and the agricultural regime in certain countries.'[54]

There is general acceptance of the view that there have been common social security trends amongst the Community members to include greater coverage of the population and of circumstances eligible for benefit as well as improved benefit levels. This has not meant the adoption of similar priorities (see Appendix Tables 6.6 and 6.7). No longer is social security, however, a matter of covering the industrial wage earner for certain risks but of maintaining the living standards of man in industrial society.[55] This function seems to strengthen the case for increased state contributions to social security schemes. Yet very considerable variations in such responsibility continue to exist and from the financial point of view, which is likely to become an increasingly important issue, it is not easy to see that a common pattern has emerged. No economic imperative has been at work demanding uniformity of financial arrangements as shown in Table 6.2.

Table 6.2
Percentage of Revenue Raised from Different Sources, 1970[56]

Country	Insured	Employers	State	Misc.
Germany	26	50	22	2
France	20	61	17	2
Italy	14	55	24	7
Netherlands	37	43	12	8
Belgium	22	49	25	4
Luxembourg (1969)	22	37	32	0

The fact that social insurance has been a major tool in the development of social security schemes has coloured attitudes towards the provision of income maintenance services. It has led to the belief that benefits should come from a special fund made up of contributions, that the individual has some responsibility for contributing to the fund and that eligibility depends upon conditions which some people fulfil whilst others do not. Yet in many ways social insurance is less important than it once was. Its great contribution was to allow the development of organized systems of providing income maintenance in defined circumstances in ways acceptable to conservative elements in society and to the industrial working class. As schemes have expanded to include people whose working status is less orthodox or whose incomes are erratic or low, and as they have tried to cover less predictable risks, it has been necessary to move further away from the traditional insurance approach. Social security schemes today are thus normally a mixture of three systems. Social insurance, which may or may not include the government as a contributor, is supported by social assistance, designed to provide cash benefits for those below an income level and by the public service which provides for all by virtue of residence in which both membership of an insurance scheme and lack of means have become irrelevant. To these must be added the continued importance of the provident institution and employers' liability systems, both products of an earlier age, but which have continued to exist as accepted means of providing income maintenance.

For reasons, therefore, which include the absence of clarity of concept, the impossibility of separating social security benefits from the totality of welfare, the impact of social security schemes on the national economy and the social psychology of social security, there can be no easy optimism concerning the development of a supra-national social security system. Whilst it is not difficult to discern common trends in the role of social security in the modern state, the size, complexity and variations between national arrangements make them highly resistant to change, and the fact that they are facing similar problems such as the extension of coverage to the self-employed, rapid increase in health costs and doubt over administrative methods and financing is not in itself a sufficient reason for suggesting the time is ripe for a wholesale rationalization of existing measures on a European basis in the absence of adequate consideration of the much bigger problem of social standards generally and the role of the EEC in their imposition.

In 1962 the three European Communities held a consultative conference on social security which discussed the application of the harmonization concept in considerable detail. A number of specific questions had already been raised, including that of unequal burdens on employers, the possibility of harmonizing methods of financing, the impact of any such changes on national fiscal policies, the need to help the self-employed to enter voluntary social security schemes and to determine the terms to be offered to them and the role of supplementary systems. The conference brought together representatives of employers and workers as full participants, governmental experts, representatives from the medical and pharmaceutical professions, family welfare organizations, private insurance companies and benefit societies, international organizations, the European Parliament, the Commission and interested individuals.

The meeting showed how sensitive was the field with which it was concerned. Member states approached the discussions with considerable suspicion, so that Professor Hallstein was compelled to stress that '*les Etats membres conservent en principe leur autonomie dans le domaine de la politique sociale*' and to place the conference within the context of the non-binding clauses of the treaty, namely Arts. 117 and 118.[57] This fear of imposed harmonization continued, bringing reluctance even to participate in subsequent studies. Any suggestion of the right to expect such action was specifically repudiated by both France and Germany in 1964 when refusing to attend meetings to study the conclusions of a working party on the position of miners set up by the conference.[58] Additionally, a polarization of view between workers and employers at first threatened to become insoluble. Whilst the workers' representatives claimed that harmonization must logically mean identity of benefits, employers argued that the socio-economic context in each state was so varied that there was little to be gained in developing schemes further than their natural evolution demanded although accepting that some co-ordination of schemes might well prove useful. A common meeting-point was eventually found in the notion of 'equivalence'. Although this could be applied to each of the major themes of the conference it was 'the question of benefits which received most attention and which led to the adoption of the most passionate positions by the participants'.[59] Under conditions in which there was no internal uniformity of coverage, in which comparable groups were treated differently between one country and another and in which regional as well as national standards of living varied, it was accepted that identity of social security benefits had little value as an immediate, practical goal. However, since social security schemes bore strong resemblances to one another, being seen as predominantly employer–worker arrangements, heavily geared to the insurance model, levelling contributions and paying benefits linked to wage levels on a percentage basis, uniformity of *principle* seemed a less impossible idea. This might be used, it was thought, to answer questions such as the reasons for which invalidity pensions should be given, or the actual percentage of the wage which should be paid, without necessitating either fundamental changes in structure or an absolute uniformity in cash benefits. Later the Social Committee was to accept this view by arguing that differences in productivity could still find their expression in variations in wage levels and that it would be possible to establish uniformity of social security systems because of the principle of linking benefits to wages.[60]

The conference considered that the existence of a welter of schemes covering different people for different things in different ways, variations in sources of finance, differences in the relative importance of the various objectives of social security meant that a major task would be to identify and fill in the gaps.

> Since there will not be for a long time a simple conception of social security, since fundamental legislative differences will continue to exist and since direct pay of both employees and the self-employed will be very dissimilar it will be necessary to determine by precise study the exact significance of schemes in order to enable them to remove existing differences.[61]

Additionally it suggested that the first major attack on greater harmonization could come through consideration of the general scheme of social security. 'Our proposal is, therefore, to tackle European harmonization forthwith by taking the general regime as a guide since coverage for the least well protected social strata will have to be associated with the standards therein provided.'[62] The objects should be to incorporate in the general scheme those excluded by definition or by the existence of an income limit, to bring all employees, including agricultural, under the same provisions and to use the standards of the general regime as a guide to the provisions for the self-employed.[63]

Following the conference the Commission drafted a programme to form the basis of its work on the harmonization of social security systems. It fell conveniently into three sections. The first, and that which has had most obvious results, consisted of a wide range of studies in the field of social security thus extending and developing work already begun by the High Authority. Reports have documented the actual position in each state in ways which enable basic comparisons to be made, such as the studies of general systems and of coverage for the self-employed including craftsmen, tradesmen and members of the liberal professions. Further studies have analysed problems such as the economic effects of social security or redistribution of income and price levels, financing and coverage and agricultural systems. Special studies have been made of issues such as supplementary social security schemes in various branches of industry, drug consumption as it affects social security provision, the cost of hospital treatment under social security schemes and the relationships of the medical profession to social security institutions. It is a fair claim that the Commission has completed extensive basic documentation on social security schemes in members.[64]

Secondly, there was an active attempt at maintaining and improving consultation with members through meetings with officials from appropriate ministries to discuss the progress of harmonization, to exchange views on trends, finance and related subjects and, of course, to have detailed discussion with government experts, independent specialists, employers' and workers' organizations before the formulation of specific recommendations. The collection, and dissemination, of information from and to governments is also relevant here. Finally, there remained the question of the alignment of standards through positive action by the Commission, as was attempted through its recommendations on occupational diseases and the employment of young people. Even if the absolute value of cash benefits is to remain variable, the social case for uniformity on questions such as age levels for pension eligibility, waiting periods for unemployment or sickness benefit, conditions for family allowances is at least arguable and such matters seem suitable for an attack on the equalization of standards by defining subjects where the lowest levels of attainment might be improved. This programme of recommendations, though evidence of activity by the Commission, can hardly be said to constitute an effective attack on the question of the establishment of the uniformity of principle as it lacked mandatory power.

In sum it seems unlikely that the existence of the European Communities made more than marginal difference to the development of social security schemes in the substantive sense as opposed to easing the position of the migrant. The most fundamental question in the former category which was brought to the European level was that of finance for the miners' social security systems. In this case Community action was limited to *ex post facto* approval of government subsidies whose existence was independent of the ECSC. The Treaty of Paris did not question the rationale of the arrangements which existed in 1951, although there are no sound grounds for arguing that the particular division of costs which existed at that time must be perpetuated. The High Authority itself suggested that the direct incidence of economic integration on social security was less than on prices, wages and terms of employment[65] but this may be partly accounted for by the great complexity of the field and the rigidities of internal social security systems. The argument for the alignment of social security costs in the coal and steel industries became a dormant question overtaken by the more pressing problem of the relative burdens falling on mining as opposed to industry as a whole. Thus the underlying issue was in reality the relationship of such schemes to the national social security pattern and there was no evidence that government aid sprang from a desire to reconsider the philosophy and significance of special miners' schemes rather than *ad hoc* aid to an industry in economic difficulty. The example serves to illustrate what is generally true, namely that the pressures for social security development existed independently of the Communities although they may well have encouraged the interchange of ideas and, in so far as states provided advance information of intended changes, have prevented the development of further conflicting legislation.

Although the Commission itself looked forward to being able to 'direct future development of social security systems in a common direction',[66] it accepted the view that unification was neither necessary nor fundamental to European unity. Only where there was no justification for existing differences did the Commission consider it necessary to intervene actively, as in the case of its recommendations.[67]

III Direct Means of Harmonization

In circumstances compounded of treaty ambiguity, interpretative weakness and a growing recognition that harmonization of social security costs was not a matter of urgency for the creation of the common market, the Commission's direct approach to harmonization had perforce to be confined to the exploration of the process of collaboration. It was thrown on to activities in research, education and communication, not only in social security but for all those subjects covered by Art. 118 which foreshadowed deep and continuing discussion between the Community and its members on a wide range of labour issues, many of which were the subject of national legislative control and therefore thought suitable for the alignment of rules in order to conform to international standards and to abolish anomalies of provision.[68] In such a process the studies permitted under the article might be expected to reveal where improvements needed to be made, to assist the formulation of goals in related fields such as personal social services[69] and, together with the close collaboration procedures, to be part of the means of creating political acceptance of such standards.

Since there are few matters which are not linked, either directly or indirectly, to the working situation, there was always a tendency for the Commission to interpret objectives broadly to include housing, social service and family welfare. The *Action Programme* singled out a number of areas in which the Commission considered action was particularly necessary to promote the goal of harmonization. These were social security systems, legislation on the length of the working week, industrial health and safety provisions, family questions, housing policy[70] and the implementation of policies for agriculture and transport in their social elements.[71] The Social Committee had additionally referred to the possibility of encouraging uniform treatment of the unemployed through the terms upon which readaptation aid was offered, action to help increase productivity in backward regions through aiding investment, the establishment of European contacts between employers and workers, mediation by the executives when a member wished to modify its social legislation, the development of comparable statistics and intervention on the labour market on the basis of Art. 49. Special problems experienced by individual countries might be helped by mutual aid, such as the structural problems of the Belgian coal industry, the problems of the Italian South and the refugees in Germany.[72]

Together, therefore, the two articles appeared to give sufficient scope for the first steps towards harmonization and, although labour conditions are by no means the same as the full range of social policy, they form a large element in it, so that any Community influence towards greater uniformity and coherence would be likely to influence the pursuit of social goals generally in the same way. The essence of the Community's social policy appeared to be the creation of a common European framework of broad social goals, the establishment of minimum standards towards which members would aim, the close working together of all those institutions concerned with social policy and acceptance of the principle that the most disadvantaged should experience a relatively greater degree of improvement.

As has already been seen, the treaty prescribed different methods for the achievement of such purposes. Apart from its specific obligations with their defined procedures and the limited possibility of financial aid through the Investment Bank, the social fund and, in the case of the ECSC, the proceeds of the levy, direct means of fulfilling overall social goals rested upon the provisions of Arts. 117 and 118. Although the Commission accepted that 'harmonization cannot mean casting the various countries' legislation and administrative procedures in an identical mould',[73] which seems a logical view once strict uniformity of provision had been ruled out, Art. 117 opened a possible means of action in matters normally covered by social legislation whether in conjunction with Arts. 155 or 118. Some interest was expressed, too, in the development of Art. 235, which allowed the Council, acting on unanimous decision, to take action on matters which the treaty had not foreseen, but its use to aid the Italian sulphur miners was a retreat from, rather than a move towards, the development of a European policy. Whilst it may with justice be argued that the level of social security benefits is only meaningful in the context of general living standards which vary considerably within the Community area, other matters, such as the fencing of machinery or the prohibition of night work for young people, are more susceptible to standardized rules and where such matters are subjected to detailed legislative control it is harder to justify anomalies.

Although the improvement and equalization of standards thus received but limited encouragement in the treaty, the Commission hoped that members would accept an obligation to prevent subsequent changes in national legislation resulting in a further divergence of standards by means of both prior consultation with the Commission and strict regard to the need to inform it of changes which actually occurred.

> Another proposition of a general character . . . concerns the possibility which we shall call 'preventive harmonization'. Indeed, in several ways the opportunity has been taken to point out the need to avoid a situation in which future initiatives taken by states might lead in practice to greater disparities than those already existing between national systems. That is why states have been asked to provide advance information to the European Commission about the more important changes which they intend to introduce into their social security systems.[74]

In 1965, the Commission issued a recommendation[75] asking for notice to be given of intending legislation, implementing regulations and similar statutory action affecting the operation of the common market, but the system continued to cause difficulty since states did not always inform the Commission or provide sufficiently detailed information. It was thus necessary for the Commission to remind members from time to time of the importance of legislative harmonization which it could not influence if not kept properly informed.[76]

The realization that it would be difficult to use the treaty to establish European social standards meant that it was of continuing importance that members should ratify those formulated by other international bodies. A resolution of the European Parliament on 14 May 1963[77] urged states to ratify the European Social Charter, whilst in 1967 it pressed the need to accept agreements concluded within the framework of the ILO as part of the movement towards social harmonization and the establishment of common social principles between them.[78] Parliament considered, however, that there was a danger that the acceptance of such documents, appropriate for a wider and less closely-knit grouping, be used as an excuse both for delay in developing higher standards and for resistance to the creation of a social policy within the Community. The resolution therefore urged governments to consider, individually, together and with the executives, what action might be taken on such standards as remained unratified, in order to raise the level of harmonization in social affairs in the Community area.

The exploitation of Art. 118 was likewise hampered by uncertainties. It gave the Commission responsibility to promote close collaboration between members in a wide range of employment matters and to act in close contact with members through the promotion of studies, giving opinions, organizing consultations on problems at both national and international level. Since the reference was 'notably' and not 'exclusively' to the topics mentioned, it was possible to argue for an extension of Community concern as occasion arose and it has already been shown that the sentiments of the Commission lay in this direction. The most obvious, but also the most sensitive, of possible extensions was, and remains, into the field of wage levels.[79] However, it must be reiterated that the direction to states to collaborate closely fell well short of the establishment of a common policy and allowed states to retain their autonomy and to argue about how far such collaboration should be taken. Seemingly simple questions concerning collaboration, the application of its results, the organization of research studies or the extent of contact between the Commission and institutions other than national governments became sensitive political questions in which conservative views of social reform, reluctance to allow national governments to be shorn of welfare responsibilities and difficulties in interpreting and executing the somewhat anomalous provisions of the treaties mingled together to brake the generous interpretations that the Commission and Parliament had in mind. The treaty introduced a third party, of obscure mandate and powers, into matters which in any case involve tensions at national level about policy and who should control it. The Commission was not always successful in asserting its right to a role in influencing policy without appearing to usurp functions jealously guarded by those whose goodwill was essential if it was to achieve its objectives of positive and visible social progress within a context of harmonization. The attempts of the Commission to develop action on the basis of an uncertain and confused position was bound to lead to controversy as long as it remained unclear to what extent Art. 118 conferred the right of initiative upon the executive. Theoretically

> it is not part of the Commission's role to interfere directly in the play of forces which, within each country, combine to improve social conditions. But it has the right, and even the duty to define in an impartial way what seems to be the path of common progress and to evaluate the position of each country in a peaceful competition. Its duty includes the full exploitation of the institutional means given to it by the Treaty of Rome in order to help states reach the social objectives of the treaty as rapidly and as surely as possible. That the path of harmonious progress will be found through seeking a better equilibrium in regional development has been constantly reiterated by the Commission.[80]

It therefore continued to assert its right of initiative under Art. 118, including that of establishing studies and sending recommendations without prior unanimous agreement of the Council on the argument that if research work and consultation were not to be developed in conjunction with employers and workers except with the prior permission of all governments, no progress in social affairs was likely at all. Similarly, it considered that it had the right to use both Arts. 155 and 100 to pursue the subject matter of Art. 118.[81] The Commission thus found itself in a delicate position compounded of uncertainties of objective, feeble powers and anxiety to push the treaty to the uppermost to make a reality of its social goals despite the lack of adequate and coherent social policies to pursue them. This situation led to it becoming the subject of criticisms on all sides. Parliament and unions became impatient with the slow development of social policy, the limitation of the Commission's powers and perhaps suspicious that they were not always used to the full. States and employers, on the other hand, whose interests were neither necessarily strongly European in social matters nor in favour of increased social expenditure, argued that they were too great, complained that the Commission tried to do too much and, in pursuit of its ambitions, awakened hopes which could not be fulfilled.[82] The crux of the delicacy of the position lay in the Treaty of Rome itself, which neither committed states to a fully mature social policy nor made it clear how to apportion responsibilities. Whilst social affairs remained primarily a matter for national, not supra-national, governments, yet they could not be ignored by the Community. Thus a position of tension between states on the one hand and the Commission on the other was created in which a major objective of the members was to prevent trespass on their preserves and of the Commission to develop progressive activity.

The conclusion from these introductory years must be that the treaty did not give the Community an adequate legal base for its social development. This in turn was expressive of the fact that too little attention was given to social progress as a policy objective during the years of initial creation. There is no doubt that it would be extremely difficult to provide a firmer foundation, not only because of members' unwillingness to indulge in what would be a surrender of national powers and because 'égalisation' raises the question of the redistribution of wealth within states, but also because of the great complexity involved in any attempt to give the term a precise and practical meaning. The concept of the total social return to individuals, or to broad groups such as the young, the elderly and the workers, must be compounded of many elements each one of which is itself hard to define. A comprehensive notion of comparability of standards applicable over such a large area would contain a high level of abstraction. Even in the field of social security, which is perhaps an obvious starting-point for consideration in view of the degree of common interest and understanding, equivalence of benefits and financing did not commend itself as necessary or possible, although the inability to obtain agreement on the conditions of benefits seems due at least as much to the weakness of the Commission's powers as to the inherent difficulty of the subject matter. In such a confused situation the value of studies in clarifying issues was important and it was unfortunate that the Treaty of Rome did not make clearer the powers of the Commission to undertake them and to develop the collaborative process generally. The issue arises again in the following chapter.

Appendix: Social Accounts

1 General

Table 6.3
Social Expenses as a Percentage of Gross National Product[83]

Country	1962	1971
Germany	17·6	19·7
France	16·3	18·4
Italy	14·3	20·2
Netherlands	13·8	21·6
Belgium	15·5	18·4
Luxembourg	15·7	17·2 (1970)

Table 6.4
Sources of Social Revenue as a Percentage of the Total, 1971[84]

Source	Germany	France	Italy	Netherlands	Belgium	Luxembourg (1969)
Employers	50	62	57	44	48	37
Insured persons	26	19	14	36	21	22
Public authorities	22	17	23	12	27	32
Interest	2	1	3	8	3	9
Other	0	1	3	0	1	0
Total	100	100	100	100	100	100

2 Social security

Table 6.5
Social Security Benefits as a Percentage of National Income, 1971[85]

Benefit	Germany	France	Italy	Netherlands	Belgium	Luxembourg (1970)
Sickness	7·3	6·0	5·6	7·0	4·9	3·8
Old age, etc	10·5	8·8	8·1	10·4	8·2	13·5
Invalidity	1·2	0·3	2·7	—	1·0	—
Industrial accident, etc	1·3	1·0	0·8	2·2	1·1	1·5
Unemployment	0·3	0·3	0·3	0·8	0·9	0·0
Family charges	1·9	4·7	3·0	3·0	4·0	2·6
Other	1·8	1·5	1·6	2·4	1·3	0·7
Total	24·3	22·6	22·1	25·8	21·4	22·1

Table 6.6
Percentage of the Population Aged Under Twenty Years Receiving Family Allowances, 1970[86]

Germany (1969)	France	Italy (1968)	Netherlands	Belgium	Luxembourg
27	84	59	90	77	100

Table 6.7
Variations in Importance of Different Objectives of Social Security Expenditure Between Countries and Over Time by a Percentage of the Total Cost Devoted to Various Purposes[87]

Benefit	Year	Germany	France	Italy	Netherlands	Belgium	Luxembourg (1968)
Sickness	1962	30	24	21	28	15	16
	1970	33	29	25	33	22	16
Old age, death, survivors	1962	48	39	38	50	47	60 (including invalidity)
	1970	49	43	41	43	42	63
Invalidity	1962	7	2	9	2	6	—
	1970	5	1	14	9	5	—
Industrial accident and disease	1962	5	5	3	2	4	9
	1970	4	5	4	—	5	8
Unemployment	1962	1	0	3	3	5	—
	1970	1	1	1	2	5	—
Maternity	1962	2	1	1	0	0	1
	1970	1	1	1	0	0	—
Family allowances	1962	6	29	24	15	23	14
	1970	6	20	13	13	21	13
Other	1962	1	—	1	—	0	—
	1970	1	—	1	—	0	—

Table 6.8
Relative Importance of Different Social Security Regimes by a Percentage
of Total Expenses Absorbed, 1970[88]

Country	General	Special	Statutory	Complementary	Voluntary
Germany	77	5	17	1	—
France	48	17	22	9	4
Italy	70	18	12	0	0
Netherlands	74	1	15	5	5
Belgium	78	2	16	2	2
Luxembourg (1969)	80	—	19	1	0

Table 6.9
Main Sources of Revenue of Social Security Systems, 1970[89]

Source	Germany	France	Italy	Netherlands	Belgium	Luxembourg (1968)
I General regime						
Employer (including direct benefits)	49	78	66	42	50	36
Employee (	37	17	12	43	21	23
Non-employee (		2	0	7	5	4
Public authorities	12	1	16	6	20	26
II Special regimes						
Employer	14	14	41	88	2	—
Employee	8	5	14	4	2	—
Non-employee	4	32	18	—	—	—
Public authorities	73	45	15	—	80	—
III Complementary regimes						
Employer	43	62	28	52	96	33
Employee	17	33	39	17	—	19
Non-employee	1	—	0	—	—	—
Public authorities	3	0	3	3	—	1
Interest	34	5	23	28	4	46

7 The Attempt at Social Policy

I Institutional Attitudes

It must be borne in mind that the EEC was not a monolithic institution but one which expressed a complex balance of interests. It is not to be expected that Parliament, Council and Commission should have attached the same importance to the development of social policy, have assigned the same priorities to its elements or held the same views on its progress, and in the interplay between these bodies it is possible to find expression of the main issues concerning European social policy as they were identified during the period. The mechanisms of the EEC meant that the main burden of establishing policies fell to the Commission, in which it was actively supported by Parliament, whilst it was in the Council that the hesitations of member states were voiced and where national rather than Community viewpoints were defended. 'Why then should one be surprised if the ministers of social affairs consider it their duty to oppose community initiatives which they consider do not fall exactly within their national programmes?'[1]

The reasons for the reluctance of the Council to follow the lead of the Commission in social policy are not difficult to understand. In an organization which had many direct obligations in the economic field the relegation of uncertain social action to second place was inevitable, whilst the ambiguities of the treaty could be fully exploited whenever a particular proposal was unwelcome to a member. It was structurally easier for members of the Council to accept social measures with a direct significance for the economic objectives of the treaty and which were given a legal base than for them to consider uncharted developments. Thus at the Council session of May 1960 it was emphasized that, as part of the process of speeding-up internal integration, it would be necessary to pay attention to social measures such as vocational training, the free movement of labour, the application of the social security measures to those most immediately concerned and equal pay.[2] The tendency for the Council to view social affairs as an adjunct to economic goals was reinforced by similar thinking on the part of the employers, who also took a careful and orthodox view of the impact of the Treaty of Rome on social policy developments. Although accepting that the treaty contained certain social objectives and that 'neither governments nor the social partners can any longer determine their social legislation, their social policy or their collective agreements on the basis of considerations which are purely national but must allow community interests to have an equal influence', the real reason for this was that such social action was deemed to affect the harmony of economic change both nationally and within the Community as well as the competitive capacity of the latter on world markets.[3] Employers considered that the treaty limited the social action of the Commission to matters considered indispensable for the realization of economic union, amongst which issues connected with the labour force, notably the free movement of labour, had pride of place. They therefore accepted the need for further action to deal with the social and cultural needs of migrants and to improve knowledge of labour movement and associated problems. Employment and training policies would need to be co-ordinated at Community level and more effective use made of the European Social Fund. Whilst employers were thus not necessarily averse to particular social policy developments within a Community context they considered that economic expansion was the best means of improving standards and the placing of social objectives within an economic context would prevent their pursuit, adversely affecting price stability, productive capacity and the competitive ability of firms at home and abroad. For such reasons they welcomed the medium-term economic policy which linked social objectives with increasing productivity and thus ensured that their pursuit would not be allowed to endanger economic ends.[4]

In the main, however, employers held the belief that social policy grows from a complex of nationally based customs, history, traditions, of varying environments and political choices, besides being an area in which the treaty essentially preserved national autonomy. European social policy, therefore, as well as being limited to objectives relating to economic goals, should be based, in their view, on prior agreement by the states – the main role of the Commission being to promote close collaboration under Art. 118 by means of comparative and analytical studies. Whilst it could hold a watching brief for the co-ordination of those social policies which states believed could be achieved as modest, short-run goals, it should avoid establishing objectives incompatible with members' political opinions or beyond their economic capacity.[5]

However, examples are not lacking to show that even the process of creating economic unity did not depend upon Community social action in anything more than a limited sense and, indeed, the specific obligations of the treaty were often only fulfilled to a minimal degree. The equal pay policy was subjected to a hasty cover-up procedure in order not to hold up the ending of the first stage of the transitional period, and there was a striking discrepancy between the achievement of the price system for agriculture and the application of the common agricultural policies formulated by the Commission let alone their social features. Even the tremendous amount of work done to prevent the loss of social security rights can be seen as an evolution from the work already achieved by states, although, in general terms, the application of the free movement of labour policy is the clearest expression of the argument that social policy depends upon economic compulsion. It is, however, difficult to find evidence from this period strong enough to support the comfortable theory that the attainment of economic goals necessarily ensures the fulfilment of social objectives except in the most limited and immediate sense.

To differences of view concerning the proper substance of policy were added problems of whether Community machinery was being correctly used or of whether there was any right to establish a policy at all. The Council was the forum in which members could not only protect their interests against those of others and against Community decisions which might adversely affect them but also champion the general principle of national competence in decision making against supra-national bids. Finally, if one remembers that social action is costly, its results often diffuse and that studies, consultations and seminars at European level may have the effect of increasing demands from pressure groups at home, it is not hard to understand either the reluctance of the Council to accept action or the existence of a gulf of interest between it and the Commission. Action to establish a European interest in social policy was thus exposed to criticism by states seeking to protect their existing rights and expressing their hesitance to involve themselves in the evolution of a system of European standard-setting if this included definite rules.[6]

For reasons such as these the Council was dilatory in taking decisions in social affairs, and its opposition to European programmes was compounded both of the reluctance of members to adopt measures not in the immediate national interest when not demanded by the treaty and of unwillingness to allow the growth of the Commission's power. The possibility of clash was enhanced because, as has been seen, from the beginning the Commission insisted upon taking a dynamic view of its functions with respect to social goals, desiring to push the treaty objectives to the maximum and to create an active study programme in association with employers, workers and other experts as well as with international organizations. Its first report stated that the Commission would 'neglect no sphere' in which the promotion of collaboration under Art. 118 might be possible and announced its intention of working closely with governments, international organizations and labour associations.[7] Two years later it claimed wide liberty of choice and 'intends to make full use of this freedom. It will thus be possible, through close voluntary co-operation between the public authorities, the European Institutions and business organizations to take positive action to ensure that European integration shall not be effected at the expense of the less favoured social groups.'[8] This positive role included, it thought, the right to take the initiative in policy matters.[9] The Commission had a special responsibility for it was independent and capable of taking a broad, objective view of the Community's problems.[10] This was to be carried out through its work of 'co-ordination, harmonization and stimulation'[11] in order to achieve the approximation of social systems and the alignment of the social policies of the members.[12]

> Indeed it seems that one cannot entirely abandon to the natural course of events the responsibility to direct the social development of the Community towards that harmony and convergence which the Treaty marked out and . . . a better co-ordinated effort at harmonisation must be proposed to members . . . Agricultural policy is one of those whose application must favour an evolution towards harmonisation.[13]

Such objectives would require active collaboration between governments for the co-ordination of policies and the *rapprochement* of legislation and

> an essential role in the effort of harmonisation must fall to social policy itself but it must develop fully within the wide latitude given to it by the Treaty and, in particular, an active collaboration between governments must be gradually established on the basis of Art. 118 but with respect to the co-ordination of policies and the rapprochement of legislation. The effort of harmonisation began with the execution of the means foreseen in the Treaty . . . But it is clear that, however important such measures may be in this connection, harmonisation can be pushed further ahead if one agrees to look at the objectives that were set out as minimal and which a community social policy should try progressively to surpass.[14]

This dynamic view of potential development was reiterated the following year; 'the Commission intends to go further along the path which was marked out in a general way by articles 117 and 118 and to develop its social policy beyond the application of those measures whose elaboration constituted essential activity during the first stage.'[15] Only in this way, it thought, would it be possible to obtain the support of the workers in the task of building Europe and to fulfil the objective of improving living and working conditions.

> A dynamic social policy, not subordinate to other considerations of Community policy, is needed, not only to gain the support of all workers in the building of Europe, but also to achieve the main object of that process which, in the terms of the Preamble to the Treaty, is constantly to improve the living and working conditions of the peoples of the six countries.[16]

The collection of data in comparable form is an essential part of the scaffolding of a European social policy. 'As the High Authority has demonstrated in the social field, the power to enquire, to collect facts, and to make proposals, is often a most effective way of promoting action.'[17] Great importance was attached by the Commission to such investigatory work as an essential tool in determining the necessary facts concerning standards of living and their variations.[18] It was, therefore, considered necessary to undertake comparative studies of labour law, collective bargaining, wage rates, levels of real wages, the incidence of social charges, hours of work and extent of paid holidays since 'precise knowledge . . . is an essential pre-requisite' and would make it possible to single out those measures necessary to obtain harmonization, to find the best solutions to problems and to start on the right paths for solutions to future social problems.[19]

Such work was carried out in co-operation with other international organizations, within independent research institutes, in consultation with government experts, independent specialists and representatives of employers and workers.[20] It thus required direct contact between the Commission and national authorities in order to try to get material collected in a uniform way, and with employers, workers and other agents of social welfare in order to obtain the requisite knowledge, to get the studies made and to assess the results. Here it was following the precedent of the High Authority, which had organized meetings of the two sides of industry in order to discuss the results of investigations and possible lines of action at national level necessary to do away with obvious discrepancies.[21]

There is a theoretical distinction between such study and the translation of results into action although in practice this is harder to sustain. The Commission considered its responsibility to be

> to put the problems before national governments and the representatives of the various social groups in order to encourage them, through constant contact, to adopt solutions conforming to the general interest but it does not wish to usurp the proper responsibility of governments and of the social partners.[22]

However it naturally hoped that the results of its activities would be to encourage social developments to occur in the direction of more, not less, social harmonization.

> By their general responsibility of research and information provision and of its refinement and diffusion . . . through the organisation of colloquia, frequent meetings, working parties . . . by the adoption of recommendations leading more directly to community harmonisation, the European executives have helped governments and the social partners of each of the six countries to place their national activities more effectively in a context made up of both the social situation in other members and of the extra demands made at a Community level.[23]

In reality, the fine distinction is hard to draw. The very initiation of investigation is not neutral in its effects. The determination of subject, the choice of agents, the creation of committees to discuss projects all exert their influence through directing attention to certain problems and not others, exposing anomalies and subjecting matters previously hidden to wider influences, including that of the Commission. Parliament attached considerable importance to the existence of a wide range of contacts between the Commission and other agencies for the purpose, *inter alia,* of study programmes.[24] It is also unrealistic to suppose that studies of this nature can be carried on for long without raising the question of what action is to be taken on them. The attempts made by the Commission to give reality to Arts. 117 and 118 were never non-controversial in consequence. It was attacked for its actions in choosing subject matter not previously approved by governments[25] or which went beyond the scope of the treaty,[26] in making direct contacts with non-public authorities[27] and for the creation of committees not directly specified by the treaty. Experience in the ECSC joint committees on harmonization showed that their use was difficult.[28] Neither Art. 117 nor 118 referred to the creation of bipartite or tripartite committees on harmonization although many *ad hoc* ones were created. There was some suggestion that they should only be established on a tripartite basis.[29] All such moves by the Commission suggested that governments might be bypassed and action encouraged which was unwelcome to them. States and employers often did not wish to bind themselves to common rules of behaviour and disliked the recommendations of the Commission concerning the employment of young workers or the rationalization of invalidity allowances because of their extra cost.[30] Equally it was embarrassing to them for the Commission to issue recommendations which they did not intend to implement. It seems difficult to avoid the conclusion that the treaty structure itself made a clash of view inevitable. The Commission attempted to develop the treaty to the maximum and in this it was backed by Parliament and the unions who recognized that the treaty was weak on the social side and that social goals would not develop automatically.[31] States and employers, on the other hand, preferred a limited interpretation of the meaning of Arts. 117 and 118 together with a closely defined role for Community institutions in social affairs. Employers generally took the view, as has been seen, that the treaty was limited to economic development which was itself the way to improved living standards and in the early 1960s at least this view was in accord with that held by the German and French governments. The latter in particular held that '*égalisation*' was a short-term goal relating to ends with obvious economic costs such as overtime pay, paid holidays and equal pay and that social aspirations were much longer-term goals with no direct commitment towards such an end.[32] Whilst states were unable to refuse to collaborate under Art. 118 they were well aware that they retained the right to accept or reject the results.[33] It is not surprising that Signor Levi-Sandri believed that Art. 118 was the most difficult and sensitive area in social affairs for the very process of collaboration itself demanded some agreement on methods and principles.[34]

In the Council debate of 20 April 1964 some of the fears concerning the extension of the Commission's function were ventilated. Members unanimously took the view that competence to act under Art. 118 remained with governments and that the Commission should confine itself to promoting co-operation, organizing studies and issuing opinions. They thus found it unacceptable that the Commission should itself issue recommendations on the subject matter of Art. 118. The executive was warned to be prudent in its practice of associating non-governmental representatives with its studies in the field of harmonization of social legislation. A specific reference was made by West Germany to the need to limit the nature of the studies being undertaken on social security and pension schemes. However Signor Levi-Sandri defended the right of the Commission to issue recommendations under Art. 155 on all matters including social harmonization and considered that the Commission should reserve the right to contact both sides of industry directly despite its willingness to work through tripartite organizations wherever appropriate.[35]

On the other hand, strong pressure towards the maximum involvement of the Community in social affairs came from the European Parliament. In June 1963 the Commission remarked upon the 'active and vigilant support of the European Parliament, and more especially its Social Committee' in its work of implementing the few mandatory provisions of the treaty and improving the manner of their application.[36] Its members made considerable use of Parliamentary questions to draw attention to derogations from social standards occurring within the national context irrespective of whether any positive action might be taken by the Community or, indeed, if the matter was strictly of Community concern. It also took every opportunity to press for the development of a social policy at European level and to criticize the lack of progress made in the formulation of policy or in its execution in relation to particular issues. From the beginning it stressed the importance of finding a proper place for social issues as the Community developed,[37] and over the years its desire to see a proper place accorded to social achievement was maintained.

> We believe that the difficulties which are met with in the realisation of social policy, as well as their economic consequences, are so important that priority must be given to social policy in Council activities . . . The Council of a European community must attach as much importance to the search for a social organisation appropriate for the industrial society of Europe.[38]

Its resolutions recorded its disappointment with the slow progress made. In 1964 it additionally noted the absence of meetings held at European level between employers, workers and governments to discuss the harmonization of wages, working conditions and social security. This it attributed to the wish of governments to try to diminish the role of the Commission in social affairs and to exclude other parties from the work to be developed under Arts. 117 and 118.[39] In 1965 it again urged the importance of developing social action in expressing its fear that the merger of the executives might be used as an excuse for inaction and its wish that, in any change of competences as a result of the merger, the opportunity should be taken for equalization upwards. Any treaty resulting from the merger should include provision for a general Community social policy, both 'far-reaching and dynamic', based on appropriate legal and financial instruments.[40]

In July 1965 the Community plunged into a political crisis which not only ushered in a period of stagnation adversely affecting the likelihood of the development of overall policy but which meant the postponement of decisions on issues which had already become matters of Community concern. This caused Parliament great distress. 'We here wish to express to the Council our dissatisfaction with the total lack of activity in social policy and to insist that we can no longer accept its continued neglect in this field.'[41] During the debates of November to December 1966 it was pointed out that Ministers of Labour had not met for two years and that joint programmes at Community level were still needed.[42] Although Community measures under Art. 118 could have been taken, members still preferred to conclude bilateral or multilateral agreements for matters which required financial support.[43] Its resolution on the *Social Exposé* that year drew attention to the fact that, despite all efforts, the Community still had no positive social policy although it was necessary to prevent disparities in standards widening and important to evolve a Community employment policy.[44] Furthermore, considerable delays in taking action had occurred in a number of fields which had been of concern to the Community, notably the improvement in the use of the social fund, the development of schemes of accelerated vocational training, the extension of the social security regulations to seamen, a decision on the Italian sulphur miners, more effective implementation of the equal pay policy and the improvement and alignment of laws on industrial health, safety and hygiene. This sorry state of affairs it considered to be largely the fault of the Council which had not given a proper priority to social policy and which did not see its value to the process of European integration. A further resolution passed early in 1967 remained critical of the Council meeting on social affairs of the previous December and regretted the 'non-European' solution adopted in the case of the Italian sulphur miners. On the other hand, Parliament was generally approving of the Commission for having developed policies where the treaty had allowed for this and for having interpreted its functions broadly.[45] Nevertheless, as early as 22 January 1964 Signor Levi-Sandri had had to defend the Commission's record in Parliament by reminding members that it was unable to take a firm stand where the treaty was not clear and before definite policies had been worked out. The harmonization of social systems, for example, still largely remained to be settled as a policy. In some fields, such as housing, he pointed out that the Commission could not take action without considering the legal basis for its action which was not at all firm,[46] and this speech suggests that some members of Parliament were suspicious that uncertainties might be used as an excuse for inaction.

Responsibility for the initiation of general policy rested with the Commission in order to achieve social ends which were not automatic. A common procedure has been for it to establish guidelines as a basis for discussion and a declaration of the Commission's views. The first important statement was published in the *Action Programme*, which made it clear that the Commission wished to see a social policy develop as a matter in its own right rather than as a subordinate feature of the treaty system. Its essential objectives would be the creation of a policy of employment and vocational training and the levelling of living and working conditions in an upward direction. Vocational training was seen as the way into a common employment policy to which national policies would need to conform. Levelling upwards was to be applied in social security, the number of hours worked, industrial health and safety and indirectly through the creation of joint committees on an industrial basis at Community level and the conclusion of collective agreements. More attention should be given to housing and family questions, particularly through the study of requirements, the definition of adequate housing conditions and the possibility of financial co-operation among members to subsidize housing for migrant workers.[47] Finally, it recognised the need to pursue the social objectives of the agricultural and transport policies and for 'appropriate wage policies' to be framed either on the national or the Community level.[48] 'Initiative 1964' was largely concerned with measures designed to hasten the establishment of the customs union. It did, however, reiterate the need for reform of the social fund to give it a more positive character and to enable it to be used to develop occupational training facilities. Secondly, it stressed the importance of intensifying the close collaboration called for under Art. 118 as a means of pursuing the aim of levelling upwards.

The slow progress made in taking decisions in the social field and the apparent lack of concern shown by the Council for the development of social policy became particularly noticeable in 1965. By then the Community had reached the last year of the second stage, yet there was little sign of concrete decisions or of the willingness to create policy at a European level as the Commission had once hoped. Little had been done to develop the occupational training programme, accelerated vocational training schemes or to agree on common qualifications as a preliminary to the free establishment programme. The reform of the social fund had not been tackled and little attention given to the social aspects of the agricultural policy. Major steps had been taken solely with regard to the mobility of labour.

The French withdrawal from Community procedures on 1 July 1965 until the early months of the new year thus merely accentuated difficulties already being experienced. The crisis not only helped to build up a backlog of work, since no social decisions were handled during the crisis period under the procedure evolved for urgent matters, but accentuated the obvious reluctance of the Council to support the Commission's attempts to develop action under Art. 118.[49] Thus the Luxembourg meeting of January 1966 which resolved the political stalemate was not helpful for the development of social policy by the Community in that it curtailed the activies of the Commission which were of particular importance in a field such as social affairs where the lines of policy had to be created. Although it was agreed that the Commission retained the right of initiative, it was arranged that on important questions both the Council and the Committee of Permanent Representatives should be consulted at an early stage of formulating proposals, which in turn should not be made public until the Community institutions were in possession of them. Similarly, for the future, the Council was to be drawn into plans for developing contacts with other international organizations. In these ways the delicate area of Commission initiative in social affairs was curbed and it is not surprising that Parliamentary criticisms of the stagnation in social policy were not stilled. The Ministers of Social Affairs planned to meet in October 1966 but did not and it was not until the Council session in December that time was finally devoted to social affairs including the receipt of the Commission's guidelines for the future.

The meeting opened in an atmosphere of considerable mistrust. No Council meeting had been devoted to social affairs since October 1964 and by the end of 1966 it had become obvious that the subject of social policy was bedevilled by confusion of object, differences in treaty interpretation, conflicts of goals and priorities between members and disagreement over the Commission's role in social affairs. Of particular sensitivity were the twin problems of the extent of the Commission's powers under Art. 118 and its right to develop maximum consultation with employers' and workers' associations. The difficulties were well summarized in a memorandum of the President of the Council which referred to the difficulties in the way of developing social action and the meagre results obtained so far in social policy matters.[50]

The purpose of the meeting was to have a broad discussion on the question of the approximation of living and working conditions, to consider specific points awaiting decision and, in particular, to try to demarcate the powers of the Commission including its capacity to enter into relations with both sides of industry. It was at first unclear whether it would prove possible to achieve sufficient agreement between members either on future policy or on a definition of respective roles and the occasion was used for a statement of view both by the President of the Commission and each Minister. No grand strategy of social harmonization was adopted although Italy argued strongly for more positive action, notably for the reform of the social fund and the creation of an effective Community labour market. It was clear, however, that members were not ready to bind themselves to a policy of obligation on the basis of common rules. M. Veldkamp's memorandum expressed the prevailing mood of, at most, cautious development.

> It sometimes seems that approximation at the higher level is entertained, in other words that the most advantageous factors of social policy of one of the countries be combined with those of social policy practised by the other member states. It is obvious that no result can be obtained in this way. It is of the utmost urgency to cope with the problems of social co-operation in a more modest and in a more realistic way.[51]

The meeting adopted a middle-of-the-road view on the goals of social policy, which it considered should be confined to those expressly provided for in the treaty, to the provision of study material on common issues and to objectives previously agreed by governments. Thus, by implication, the Commission should not establish goals off its own initiative. A 'modest and realistic' programme of studies was unanimously agreed in social security matters. Firstly, a systematic study was to be undertaken of the advisability and possibility of harmonizing concepts and definitions as a necessary preliminary to their approximation should resources allow it. It was stressed, however, that such approximation would remain the responsibility of national governments and would be more the result than the condition of integration. A second study of the costs of social security, including the division of responsibility between the employer, the worker and the public authority, was agreed. A proposal that a timetable be established for the ratification by members of international conventions on minimum social standards was not acceptable to France. The Commission's guidelines were to be discussed in detail at a later meeting and it was further agreed to undertake studies of unemployment trends and of free movement of labour.[52]

The session must be considered a turning-point through its re-establishment of a degree of momentum in social affairs and recognition that they could no longer be ignored. At the same time the meeting made clear that the time was not appropriate for a bold step in social policy; 'Basically the attitude of the Council is tantamount to a partial rejection of the efforts of the EEC Commission to frame a kind of "Community legislation".'[53] Responsibility for social progress was to remain with states and in consequence members did not wish to see Community proposals which might encourage or justify claims they did not wish to satisfy.[54] The concept of a European norm was therefore not advanced. Five members were prepared to accept the principle that the Commission possessed the right to obtain all opinions it considered desirable and to establish links with both sides of industry provided such contacts were not used as a means of bringing pressure to bear on governments. France, however, considered that such consultation should be limited to the procedures laid down in the treaty itself, notably through the Economic and Social Committee and other committees whose creation was allowed for in the treaty. Other views on the form of consultation were expressed. Germany felt no hard and fast rule should be laid down but that each case should dictate its own procedure. Belgium suggested that consultations with governments should precede discussions with industry, whilst Luxembourg felt the Commission should be left free to act as it considered appropriate. The question remained unsettled.

Although the meeting provided new hope that social affairs would henceforth be given their due place in Council discussion since the intention of more frequent and regular sessions was expressed, it did not suggest any meeting of minds on the broad sweep of social policy, nor did it indicate that the Council was beginning to act as a Community institution in this respect or that states were prepared to push their 'close collaboration' further than hitherto. Few concrete decisions were taken and outstanding matters ranged from directives concerning purity standards in various food products and the manufacture and labelling of various dangerous substances to regulations on Community aid to enable workers in agriculture to move into new jobs in agriculture and to aid the setting-up of job information services for people working in agriculture.[55] The reform of the social fund, which had by now been before the Council for two years, was postponed for further discussion by the Committee of Permanent Representatives since only Italy was fully behind the Commission's proposals, whilst the suggested Community programme for adult vocational training in place of bilateral agreements was referred back to the Commission for new proposals.[56] Agreement on the allocation of aid to the Italian sulphur miners was reached but not within the context of a Community policy of rehabilitation, occupational training and regional development.[57]

In consequence the meeting received but a muted welcome from both trade unions and Parliament. Prior to the Council meeting M. Veldkamp had met with trade union delegates from the ICFTU and IFCTU and the importance of working out social goals by democratic means had been stressed. The two organizations welcomed the picking-up of momentum which the December meeting symbolized but argued that more needed to be done since industrial and economic developments were such as to make a European social policy more urgent. 'The absence of such a Community policy may well give rise to social tensions and disturbances which would constitute a serious threat to democracy in Europe.'[58] Although Parliament welcomed the signs of a new impetus in social affairs in the fact of the Council meeting and the publication of guidelines, it felt that much valuable time had already been for ever lost and that the concrete decisions of the meeting had been disappointing. The Social Committee tartly remarked that the studies approved by the Council were unlikely to do much to promote either the improvement of standards or their equalization[59] and a Parliamentary resolution[60] regretted both the nature of the decision concerning the sulphur miners[61] and the absence of one on reform of the social fund. As parliamentarian Mlle Lulling argued: 'In fact, this fund cannot fill, and you all know it, the role which ought to belong to it . . . the European social fund is only useful to the officials who run it.' After referring to the modest sums reimbursed she continued: 'Some people are even asking themselves if these very modest payments justify the costs of administration, control and financial assessment.'[62] Parliament protested against the Council's preference for inter-state arrangements and against the increased position of the Committee of Permanent Representatives as factors tending to undermine the role of Community institutions and wished to see stronger employer and worker participation in the work of elaborating a common social policy. It urged the Commission to undertake a study of industrial changes occurring in agricultural and underdeveloped regions and to make recommendations to help those unemployed in consequence.

The December meeting was made the occasion for the Commission to produce detailed guidelines for the development of social policy. These stressed the need to express the interdependence of economic and social objectives and the belief that social policy must be seen as a coherent overall programme and not just a list of specific items. It argued the case for taking decisions which would develop responsibilities beyond the essential obligations of the treaty which had hitherto received priority and ensure that no excessive social disparities remained by the end of the transitional period which would hinder the establishment of the common market although this did not imply exact uniformity of provision since national differences were held to justify variations. The prosecution of a medium-term economic policy would highlight social questions and, indeed, a major method of achieving social goals would be through paying adequate attention to the social aspects of other policies. The autonomy of the employer and worker must be maintained and their representation at European level would have to be strengthened.

Detailed suggestions were made with respect to obtaining greater knowledge of employment trends through periodic surveys, forecasts, joint reviews and sectoral studies. It was suggested that agricultural and building studies should have priority but special aspects of employment such as vocational training, the employment of women, the young, the old and the handicapped were also mentioned. Final obstacles to the free movement of labour should be removed and this should include seeing that Community provisions were in practice applied. Hence closer co-operation with national authorities was necessary and means should be devised to ensure a proper interpretation of the rules which might otherwise be 'robbed of their substance'. Better links between employment exchanges, more training courses for potential migrants, the improvement of measures to help to overcome the disabilities of migrants and the rationalization of recruitment policies for non-Community labour were required. Social security provision for migrants could still be improved through the inclusion of more benefits and its extension to classes of workers including the self-employed. To some degree the harmonization of schemes themselves was necessary in order to achieve this.

Vocational training of young people and of adults was susceptible to Community study to meet manpower needs over the whole area. Special reference was made to problems in rural communities, training for girls, multicraft training, the shortage of instructors and redundancy problems. The exchange programme for young workers could be stimulated and a co-operative scheme to exchange experience on vocational guidance developed. Many of these measures would be helped by a reform of the responsibilities of the social fund. Some convergence of national social policies would be necessary and this would require the fuller exploitation of Arts. 117 and 118, both in the form of positive action by the Commission and the willingness to interpret Art. 118 broadly. The treaty should not be held to limit activity to those provisions where specific directions were given.

Primary emphasis had been given in the past to studies of particular topics. These had already shown up both the importance of seeing each problem in its wider social setting and the need for more detailed investigations of certain problems such as wages, working hours and insurance schemes. It was no longer enough, for example, to study pensions without considering the whole range of problems faced by the elderly, and knowledge over a much wider area was therefore necessary. The resulting 'transparency' should not be under-estimated as a factor in harmonization, establishing a base for formal action under the treaty as an opinion, recommendation or a directive. 'Quotation and interpretation of the Treaty alone are not enough, analysis and implementation count more.'[63] The surveys of wages and working conditions would be continued and brought up to date. It should be possible to standardize the 'protective' aspects of laws on working hours. Regular information on new laws, regulations and collective agreements was essential whilst examination of such issues on consultative committees would have a constructive influence on social policy whether or not it led to formal agreements. Work in industrial health and safety would continue on the lines already established and could have a helpful effect on the free movement of labour and goods.

Since major inequalities resulted both from differences in individual incomes and from the lack of collective provision, social security schemes should be studied in order to see how effective they have been in removing social differences and how they might develop in the context of the European system. The possibility of minimum Community standards of provision was mooted and a large study programme in the field of social security laid down stretching far beyond the question of international labour mobility. Housing, social service provision and health problems were considered proper matters for Community concern. More attention would be given in the future to the social aspects of other Community policies, notably in agriculture, fishing and transport and to efforts to produce harmonized statistics.[64]

II Policy Developments, 1967–9

During 1967 the Commission's view on the most fruitful means of pursuing social ends crystallized into a tripartite attack. In the first instance the stress was laid on the social implications of other programmes.

> The first important method will be to treat social problems within the context of common policies and policies in other fields. It is essential in effect that social policy is asserted to the extent that new stages of European integration are attained. The new Commission wishes to seize the chance offered by the fusion of the executives to give to social policy a larger place and, in particular, to give developmental guide lines in the sectors where the single Commission intends to undertake new tasks: namely in policies for industry, energy, the regions and for scientific and technical research.[65]

This approach became steadily more important, had the virtue of being soundly based on treaty clauses in the first instance and the obvious attraction of allowing the achievement of social aims to benefit from the impetus of the application of more powerful policies.

The strength of this argument rests upon the fact that economic policies are bound to have social implications. The merging of the executives provided an opportunity for stressing this approach. From then on the Commission added to its arguments for the recognition of the social implications of agricultural and transport policies the importance of considering in the round any new policies that might be developed in the phase of positive economic integration.[66] It must not be forgotten in this connection that the creation of the new Commission made the expertise of the High Authority available for the generality of Community social policy. It was of direct relevance to the socio-economic problems of the declining areas and of energy production as well as to particular fields such as industrial safety in which the Authority had been active.

Both the transport and agricultural policies illustrate the possibility of inserting social provisions into wider programmes and to a degree support the Commission's view that this is a major method of achieving agreement on social ends. In the first instance, certain social standards were imposed on road haulage firms as part of the way of ensuring fair competition. During July 1968 the Council adopted a number of rules designed to introduce a competitive system in transport by rail, road and inland waterway including a draft regulation on social provisions in road transport. The text was finally adopted the following March but subsequently amended in order to comply with certain existing international agreements and to allow exemptions from such provisions in the case of farm vehicles.[67] It applied to the road transport of both goods and passengers in vehicles over a certain size on journeys between members and within them, including journeys made by vehicles registered in non-Community members. Daily and weekly breaks in driving and compulsory rest periods are itemized, minimum ages established for drivers and certain other crew members and supporting qualifications for the former laid down. The composition of crews on long and heavy vehicles was controlled and special provisions agreed where there were two crews. Members might continue to apply higher standards of their own. Inspection measures and penalties were agreed.

One result of the regulation was the necessity to check individual hours of work. This was done originally by the keeping of logbooks but in 1970 agreement was reached on the use of a mechanical monitoring device to be used in large lorries and in coaches. This will be compulsory for new vehicles and for certain goods vehicles from 1 January 1975 and must be applied generally by January 1978.[68]

A comparable example can be drawn from the field of agriculture. Policy here paid far more attention to the establishment of the price system and the bringing-in of rules to effect a common market than to the improvement of efficiency and ensuring a reasonable standard of living for agricultural communities through the diversification of employment opportunities, the improvement of community facilities or similar measures. By the late 1960s the farm fund aiding structural change was spending only about one-twelfth of the resources allocated to the agricultural support system.[69] The rapid fall in the number of those employed in agriculture cannot of itself mean an increase in efficiency on the part of the elderly farmers who are left with small farms and out-of-date methods whilst the young men swell the number of those crowding into the urban areas. These questions require solution through a policy of structural reform so that there will be fewer, larger units using more modern methods, adequately mechanized, supplied with support measures and allied with help to ease the transition from farm work to alternative employment. It is only very recently that direct incentives for those leaving the land or more efficient husbandry have been introduced. In March 1972 the Council adopted two measures[70] designed to supplement what most states were already doing and which may encourage Italy to adopt similar arrangements. The first scheme is intended to encourage farm modernization, through selective grants, so that at the end of a planned period, normally of six years, farms should be able to support one or two persons at a standard of living comparable with that obtainable in non-agricultural work in the region. The second aims to help states encourage elderly farmers to leave farming altogether provided their land is made available for community purposes or for amalgamation with other farms. Temporary aid to help states develop advisory services for farmers until the new social fund is able to take over was also agreed by the Council. Such procedures, if they are to be effective, need to be operated very closely with the work of the social fund to aid resettlement and retraining and of the investment fund to create alternative employment in agricultural areas. They therefore constitute something of a test case for the Commission's view that social improvements can be borne along by the impetus of the Community's broader policies.

Of considerable importance to the development of the view that social policy should be considered in the context of other policies was the introduction of economic forecasting. The first medium-term economic programme spoke of the inter-relationship of policies for competition and social welfare and devoted considerable attention to regional policies as well as to the question of labour shortage as a limiting factor on future economic growth. Thus it would 'also bring out the broad lines of a social policy at Community level' provided social objectives were taken into account from the start.[71] It suggested the importance of improving techniques of data collection in order to anticipate changes in job availability; the need to encourage workers to move from agriculture into industry, to enable the re-employment of labour in new processes and industries to occur whether through regional development or retraining policies, to develop both European policies and the greater co-ordination of national ones in order to overcome the many impediments to movement caused by national frontiers. To such questions the second programme added the development of incomes policies and the need to consider the return due to workers whether in the form of wages, contractual savings or property and share ownership.[72] 'In the definition and implementation of the medium-term economic policy, the Community possesses an instrument for information and for action which will make optimum social progress possible in all areas.'[73] The goal of economic and monetary union, mooted for the 1970s, with its inevitable restriction on national determination of questions such as subsidy and fiscal policy, taxation and income levels was a further Community development which demanded recognition of its social implications.

The second main emphasis in the Commission's approach to social problems was to be found in its encouragement to the formulation of employment policies and their manifold ramifications for occupational training and re-employment. The stress laid upon labour mobility and the provision of help to enable the worker to meet the demand for change by maintaining his income when unemployed, finding him new work through improved vocational guidance services and new training, suggests that the Commission accepted the view that it is not the responsibility of social policy to help to keep the worker in the same job with the same firm for ever but to enable him to meet the demand for change.[74] Primary stress in thinking was given to occupational training for adults needing refresher courses, social education or entering industrial jobs for the first time and for young people requiring a flexible training as a good base for the future. Skilled people were likely to be in increasing demand and here it was thought the Commission would have an important role in helping to overcome the grave shortage of training facilities,[75] to devise new teaching methods, encourage the alignment of training levels and to give further consideration to the importance of polyvalence as a base for future training. From this it followed that the reform of the social fund should become a major objective of policy for the Commission in order that it should be able to help more people at different points in the employment, or re-employment, process. It would, therefore, require new powers so that it would be able to act in a preventive and positive way, helping with the employment aspects of regional development policies and removing constraints on labour mobility through aid to retraining programmes, the building of training centres and social housing programmes.[76]

The recognition of the labour needs of the Community was seen, however, to provide a firm base for other activities of the Commission. More sophisticated employment services are a function of changing manpower needs. Workers require more vocational guidance, advice and information than hitherto if they are to respond to new employment situations without distress and this situation should provide the Commission with an acceptable role in helping services to improve. It was, of course, closely linked to the need to ensure the full implementation of the principle of free movement of labour, which itself ensured the Commission's work in relation to variations in social security systems which might adversely affect migrants, the social and cultural difficulties associated with labour movement and effective collaboration between national employment exchanges to provide up-to-date information concerning vacancies and to smooth the process of hiring workers from abroad. Full employment was seen as an essential prerequisite of an effective manpower policy and action to achieve it would need to be established communally under conditions of economic and monetary union.[77]

The third strand in the Commission's policy was to develop work designed to contribute to the improvement of living and working conditions primarily through its studies. The Commission considered that fuller information was required in order to monitor wage trends, social charges of employers and real incomes and to see how wages might become part of an overall incomes policy. Studies would show the position in members concerning the length of the working week, night and Sunday work, co-management and collective bargaining arrangements, the extent of health protection, medical services and industrial safety with a view to their gradual harmonization. Social security studies would be a particularly important element of this programme. 'The Commission will continue to promote close co-operation between the Member States in this field with a view to the "harmonization of the social systems" referred to in the treaty, in the light of Community requirements, the attitudes of Governments and the views of employers' and workers' organizations.' Such work, the Commission thought, would itself contribute to the argument for change. 'Work undertaken on the harmonization of the concepts and definitions used at national level will provide criteria for bringing the different systems more into line.'[78]

A vast field of work was opened up to the Commission in its study programme, particularly if the subjects under Art. 118 were to be supplemented with studies of wages, housing, the social services and related topics and if knowledge was to be collected in standardized form. However it is important not to under-estimate the difficulties. A great deal of such work was dependent upon the goodwill of members and yet always likely to meet resistance from them. Some of the difficulty related to the political reluctance of states to help to provide ammunition for those who wished to change the existing distribution of wealth and to share responsibility with a body such as the Commission which possessed progressive views on social policy. A public pronouncement such as that of Signor Levi-Sandri in 1968[79] that a modern social policy must consider not only wages but the total return to the worker including savings facilities and social investment in housing, leisure and health provision carried implications for the Commission's activities which were likely to be considered threatening by member governments. Other problems came from the sheer difficulty and inconvenience of attempting studies on uniform criteria which had hitherto been organized on a national base. This is particularly obvious in the case of the collection of official material such as census data which did, in fact, cause difficulty.[80] The programme carried, too, the implication that as many groups as possible should be involved in deciding programmes through a constant process of discussion, advice and general consultation, in order to achieve both a good understanding of the purpose of the work and to allow it to be influenced by the priorities favoured by employers and workers themselves.[81] The Parliamentary resolution on the social situation in 1966 supported this approach, expressing its approval of the Commission's attempts to develop contacts between both sides of industry within joint committees and to promote close collaboration under Art. 118 through joint working parties. Its further resolution on the 1966 guidelines referred once more to the importance of joint consultative committees and the general value of the consultations which took place with unions and employers.[82] In May 1968 the Commission called together a central group to examine the lines of future general action under Art. 118, to discuss the current stage of the work and to examine the implications of the medium-term economic programme. Subsequent developments designed to associate the two sides of industry with developing manpower policies have previously been mentioned in chapter 2.

1967, however, brought no solution to the fundamental issues of the determination and control of social policy and of the extent to which social harmonization should become a serious objective. In June the Council returned again to the substantive issues of the previous December. As before it was preceded by a discussion between the President and representatives from the ICFTU and IFCTU. Union members urged the need for greater effectiveness of Community policies, notably with regard to employment policies if free movement of labour was to be established, to the improved use of the social fund and an adequate policy of occupational training. They also argued for free consultation by the Commission of management and labour and for maximum exchanges of information in order to pursue the goal of social harmonization and to determine the general direction of Community social policy.[83] In particular the meeting devoted attention to the contentious subject of the content and methods of the studies to be undertaken by virtue of Art. 118, for which the Commission had drawn up a list of topics. Whilst a study of the economic effects of social security was agreeable to all, Germany was unwilling to explore the question of the definition of children for family allowance purposes, Italy felt similarly on worker participation in industry and France on studies of collective agreements.[84] The methods of study still caused concern in so far as they raised the fundamental problem of the independence and right of initiative held by the Commission.[85] France remained reluctant to allow the Commission a general right to consult management and labour preferring this to be done case by case and only with prior government agreement. She was therefore against any form of joint mixed committee at European level on the grounds that governments carried responsibility for national economic equilibrium and consultation might easily give rise to claims which would upset such balance. National situations were not identical and similar claims could give rise to different situations and repercussions. Furthermore, it should be sufficient for governments, who were in regular consultation with both sides of industry, to supply information to the Commission and any further consultation should take place through the officially constituted Economic and Social Committee. France did not believe that the Commission should possess the right to consult independent experts of its own choice but only those persons put forward under government sponsorship who could speak on behalf of their countries, nor did she believe in publication without prior government authorization.[86] General confusion was reported[87] on the right of the Commission to issue recommendations under Art. 155 to members on the subjects covered by the studies in order to begin to apply the findings and, although this was not formally discussed in June, it was clearly an issue likely to create further disturbance. The question of the Commission's right of initiative under Art. 118 was referred to the Committee of Permanent Representatives for further study,[88] but the argument demonstrated the continuing strength of the belief in national autonomy in the field of social affairs and the possibility of future conflict since the Commission continued to assert its right to consult employers, workers and independent experts and to proceed with studies.[89] Certain decisions were, however, taken. Ministers agreed to meet at least once a year to discuss the labour situation as a whole, announced their intention to give priority to labour from the Community over that from other countries as required by Italy, to develop more effective collaboration between national employment services and to take steps to prevent discrimination against Community nationals. In addition to such moves to make the free movement of labour policy more effective, certain directives on dangerous substances were adopted and agreement was reached on the need to examine the experience of the social fund with a view to its adaptation and reform.[90]

The new President of the single executive addressed Parliament on 20 September 1967 at a time when a new political *élan* was badly needed. He chose to consider the merger as a new stage along the road to European unity and not just an administrative improvement. Social goals he considered to be of the utmost importance to the new grouping. Fresh thinking would be required to effect both overall industrial policy and regional policy within a developing Community and a new impetus to policies conceived at Community level was necessary. 'I must also stress our particular interest in the social field. We believe that, in past years, despite the remarkable work done at Luxembourg, the Communities did not achieve enough. We are anxious to see if a new impetus can be given to social progress.'[91] Meanwhile Parliament continued to urge greater social measures. During the session November – December 1967[92] it complained that a common social policy had lagged and urged the Council to drop its 'reserved attitude' towards Community initiatives in this field. It felt that the Community had made no real progress in social affairs, considered that the Ministers of Labour should meet more frequently in Council to consider some of the Commission's proposals designed to lead to harmonization and urged the Commission to give greater attention than hitherto to the social requirements of common policies. It also wished to see the Commission do more to stimulate and co-ordinate members' efforts in publicly assisted housing, social services, family benefits and public health, to promote harmonization in social security provision and to call a tripartite conference on labour matters. It argued that the Commission should give more weight to the legitimate interests of consumers when considering social affairs and should take up the question of the needs of old people.

Discussions on social policy issues were resumed in the Council in December 1967 and again the following February. These two meetings were effectively the same discussion, the December meeting having had to be confined to declarations of view and discussion of general principle since the Dutch refused to co-operate further as a protest against the breakdown of negotiations for British entry.[93] As before the December meeting was preceded by discussion between the President of the Council, now Herr Katzer the Federal German Minister of Labour and Social Affairs, and union representatives as well as, on this occasion, with management. General agreement was obtained on the need both for a tripartite conference to discuss the employment situation of the Community and on the more effective use of the social fund.

Signor Levi-Sandri presented a report to the Council on the achievements of the Community's social policy during the previous six years drawing attention to the positive results obtained in those fields where the treaty had laid down definite objectives, notably the free movement of labour, the creation of the social fund and the maintenance of social security benefits for migrants. He referred to the real improvements in social conditions which had occurred over the Community area as a whole,[94] but argued that further activity was necessary in order to contain the social dislocations likely to develop in the wake of economic change.

It would be particularly important, he thought, for the Community to establish its own employment policies and to support occupational training schemes through the social fund. The meetings approved a number of studies to be carried out by the Commission. Studies of social security and of collective agreements, including the concepts and definitions used in social security, the assessment of incapacity caused by occupational disease and the definition of children for family allowance purposes were to be carried out in co-operation with national administrations; those of drug consumption within social security schemes, employment in building, shipbuilding and in textile industries were to use independent experts and studies of industrial health and safety were to be done with the help of government experts.

Discussion took place both of the possibility of the ratification by members of international agreements on social questions and of the general employment situation. The deterioration of the labour market meant that the Council was willing to devote time to the consideration of the Community interest in re-employment measures, such as the improvement of vocational advice, removal allowances, compensation for loss of wages and retraining courses. Members agreed to strengthen their co-operation in employment matters, particularly stressing the working together of their employment exchanges, the development of vocational guidance and free movement of labour policies including the need to give priority to the employment of Community migrants. The Council appealed to unions and employers to continue to remove the remaining obstacles to the full application of the equal pay policy and agreed on the need to improve the work of the social fund. It refused, however, to commit itself to specific reforms or to set a definite date for change.

General debate on the future development of social policy was initiated by a submission by Germany, supported by France, that the Council should stress the social aspects of other European policies in order to ensure they were considered in a positive, not merely a palliative sense and properly integrated into policies from the start so that aims were consistent.[95] Most importantly the Council agreed that this would mean consideration of a wide range of social matters and not just those specifically mentioned in Art. 118. The Commission was asked for a report on methods to facilitate co-operation which would examine the relationship between social and other policies to enable the Council and Commission to discuss together how far Community measures, or the alignment of national measures, was necessary.[96]

This meeting represented an important breakthrough for the Council. It meant that a new basis for social development was being established in that members had now positively accepted that economic and social goals were inter-related and that henceforth the latter would require adequate consideration. Whilst it is true that, on a theoretical level, the view was implicit that social goals derive their meaning from economic development under the treaty system, it nevertheless brought them into the main stream of European development in a way which had hitherto been lacking. However, this did not mean that attention had yet been given to the practical questions of how to overcome the limitations inherent in the treaty or of how to formulate social priorities and, although there were signs that the momentum in social policy might be picking up, yet the concrete achievements of the meeting suggested that states were only prepared to progress in the most gingerly fashion. A compromise on the consultation issue had been found through the meetings between the President of the Council and the two sides of industry which at least provided a means whereby their views might be heard although a long way from the full-blooded co-operation for which the Commission and Parliament had argued. The battle over the autonomy of the Commission and its right of initiative had gone largely in favour of orthodoxy since there was to be no right of recourse to independent experts except in special cases when governments would expect to be informed of the names of the persons approached, neither was there to be consultation of industry nor publication of the results of studies without prior permission of the Council[97] to whom studies were to be submitted for discussion. The question of Commission recommendations was left unsettled so that the drafts on maternity protection and family allowances remained in abeyance. Policy was still undecided on outstanding issues such as the reform of the social fund, the implementation of a common policy of occupational training and long-term means of consultation.

The Commission's report on the relationship between social and other policies was presented to the Council in July 1968, referred for discussion to the Committee of Permanent Representatives and finally approved by the Council at its meeting of March 1969. Employment questions were central to its thinking so that the major concern of social policy became the need to help the worker surmount a wide range of adaptation problems. This is, no doubt, a logical result of the policy to lay stress on the relation of social policy to other Community policies.[98] Here the report echoed the themes of the medium-term economic programmes, which had stressed the importance of an active employment policy to include aids to mobility, better training facilities, the improvement of forecasting techniques and more career guidance in order to deal with the impact of structural change. The Community's contribution to the solution of such problems was considered to come through its implementation of the free movement policy, the operation of the social fund, the development of the common policy of vocational training and the work to harmonize legislation in the fields of industrial safety and health. The construction of an occupational training system which would allow for the smooth transference of labour between industries, regions and members became, for the Commission, a major means of achieving this. 'Members should [agree] on a common approach to occupational training.'[99] This implied a considerable expansion of employment services, vocational guidance and of training and retraining facilities as well as the adoption of the principle of polyvalence for the training of young workers,[100] mutual recognition of training standards and a wide variety of social measures, including help with housing, to cover the personal issues involved. It was, therefore, essential to reform the social fund so that it was not limited to helping with unemployment after this had occurred but so that it could pursue a policy of 'preventive intervention'[101] and operate on a wider scale than hitherto. Financial support for retraining or for labour mobility, help towards the introduction of modern teaching methods in training centres and encouragement of job standardization were all ways in which the Community should be able to assist.

The report drew attention to the fact that the Community area was experiencing both industrial growth in the new technological fields and decline in the older industries of mining, textiles and shipbuilding. The latter would require particular help in the future and thus the problem of state subsidy would demand reconsideration. The Community should begin to study the use of various forms of national and international aid and the use of the social fund, the investment bank and agricultural guidance fund in this connection. The process of industrial change should be thoroughly discussed by firms and by workers so that the problems were fully understood and efforts made to carry out re-employment with the minimum of harm to individuals.

The report also referred to free movement of labour, which was required not only as a specific objective of the treaty but for modern employment policies. Here the Commission's function lay in dealing with problems which still acted as an impediment to mobility, notably the better co-ordination of social security provision, equality of representation of workers on social security bodies and in positions of responsibility in trade unions and the mutual recognition of qualifications which had hardly begun to affect employed workers.[102]

The process of economic integration deliberately introduced by the Treaty of Rome was designed to hasten industrial change and would, in the long run, demand many common policies. Some of them, for example regional, industrial, scientific, research and incomes policies, were neither fully worked out nor explicit in the treaty but as they became accepted would have a social incidence which would require consideration. In the meantime there were specific questions upon which to act. These included the agricultural, fisheries and transport policies, each of which had important social implications, the need to abolish technical obstacles to trade resulting from different rules of industrial health and safety and the aim to establish the statutes of a European company which raised the issue of workers' representation.

To handle the effects of industrial change in a satisfactory manner required the existence of a rational and ordered system of industrial relations in which workers had a stronger voice. This should form the context for the growth of a Community social policy which could help to strengthen patterns of employer–employee contacts. Change also meant that governments and employers were increasingly finding that they were concerned with questions of the reabsorption and retraining of workers, vexed by the problems of the elderly or incapacitated worker whose re-employment was difficult and who often had to suffer premature retirement and that they were involved in a wide range of projects, including the provision of cash benefits and pensions, on a growing scale. Such subjects would need co-ordinated action in a period of integration.

Parliament welcomed this report, with its stress upon an overall view of social policy and the importance of the integration with other Community policies,[103] but during 1968 and 1969 remained critical of the lack of practical decisions in the social field where nothing was done to reform the social fund, develop occupational training programmes or recognize qualifications as means of helping with employment difficulties.[104] Its debate in July 1968 spoke of the need for the Council to make 'binding decisions as soon as possible on concrete social policy measures and to lay down as a principle that such measures should provide considerable latitude for direct intervention by the Community'.[105]

Nevertheless the two meetings which the Council devoted to social affairs in 1969 displayed a strong sense of the willingness of members to accept social policy as a necessary part of the evolution of the Community. In March the Council examined the report on correlation[106] and, whilst it made plain that it considered social policy was here presented, not in its own right, but only as a result of economic measures taken or planned at Community level, it nevertheless agreed that it was not just a compensatory mechanism but one which had to be pursued along with economic objectives. It accepted that employment problems were of central importance and that it was impractical to suppose that workers subjected to special Community measures, as those in agriculture and transport, should find themselves in a position different from that in other industries. The common task of the Community had social implications and the Council therefore hoped that the Commission would submit plans for further co-operation in the fields of industrial safety and health where barriers to trade might exist and recommended that it produce a report on the social aspects of medium-term economic programming with a view to deciding what points required special action. It agreed that ways of improving information concerning the labour market, and of comparing training levels and recruiting policies were required. A further report was asked for on occupational training, migrant labour from non-Community countries and the problems of the employment of the physically handicapped, as a basis for detailed discussion of employment conditions.[107] The following November the Council agreed to the general lines of reform of the regulations concerned with social security for migrants, formally agreed to hold a conference on employment problems with employers and unions, discussed the labour situation, heard a statement on the reform of the social fund and received studies on the economic and financial aspects of social security.

Meanwhile the study and consultation programme of the Commission continued. The memorandum on agricultural reform of December 1968 dealt with a wide range of social measures, including the possibility of new job creation, vocational retraining and the grant of financial aid for improvement and compensation, whilst the transport regulations of 1969 included controls over employment, working conditions and industrial relations. February 1969 saw the submission of a memorandum on the social aspects of the coal industry within the context of the development of a Community energy policy. This called for a manpower programme for mining to take account of the recession in the coal industry, the effect of modernization and the importance of keeping a nucleus of production in being. In the following month the Commission held a general conference with the main labour organizations at which future social developments of the Community in the integrative phase were discussed. Studies of the economic impact of social security, of the financing of social security in agriculture, of the financial problems of social security schemes, of the German social security budgeting system, of services for old people and of public assistance schemes were undertaken during the year and the social aspects of company law considered. The following year the Commission's report on the employment prospects of the twelve million physically handicapped people estimated to live in the Community area was prepared[108] and an examination undertaken of the social objectives of the fisheries policy and of ways of harmonizing working conditions in agriculture. In the spring of 1970 the second report to the Council on the relation of social policy to other policies was submitted in draft form.[109] Its themes were the social aspects of the agricultural, fisheries, transport, industrial and regional policies and of the third medium-term economic programme then being prepared.

III The Hague Conference and After

The really important event of 1969, however, was the Hague Summit Conference in December which gave notice that members were prepared to progress beyond the initial stage of creation of a customs union towards a more effective and positive economic and monetary organization. The new impetus towards an integrated Europe through strengthened policies devoted unaccustomed attention to the place of social affairs within the broad sweep of development. Specifically the conference recommended the reform of the social fund.

The meeting marked a new importance for social questions in the European system, not because of any new initiatives but because of their recognition at the political level as a necessary component of developments as the Community took a surge forward into the future. Closer integration implied 'the necessary coherence between the economic and social aspects of the integration process [which] requires that social policies of the different Member States should be better co-ordinated at Community level, at least on certain points. . . .' Indeed the argument went further, for 'economic and monetary union must promote the achievement of the major aims of society'.[110] The detailed and patient work of the Commission to execute the treaties, to develop and interpret the clauses, to hammer home the significance of social policies here bore fruit in the political acceptance of social goals. It was this element which had been lacking at the time of the original signature of the treaties with the result that, during the transitional period, social affairs had been condemned to the half-light. The Hague meeting provided the basis for fresh thought to be given to the contribution the Community might make to social progress, lifting the debate beyond the tired rut of past controversies and the minutiae of treaty clauses to the analysis of the social fund along positive lines and to the creation of a standing committee on employment as a forum for co-operation and consultation between the Council, Commission, employers and unions.[111] It asked the Commission to begin to make studies leading to the drawing-up of a European social security budget and to undertake specialized studies of the effect of social security on costs and competitive positions and of the coverage of persons for social security purposes.[112]

The third medium-term economic programme, adopted by the Council in February 1971, and the preliminary guidelines for a Community social policy programme, issued by the Commission in March,[113] suggested the main directions for European social policy in the immediate future upon the assumption of a strengthened European unity. 'Now that the Community has embarked resolutely on the road to economic and monetary union, social policy appears in a new light.'[114] Whereas in the past it had been seen as an adjunct only to the process of creating the customs union, in the future the economic and social aspects of integration would become inseparable and integration would necessarily have to be pursued simultaneously in the economic, monetary and social fields. 'It is inconceivable that the Community should be built up and strengthened in its economic and monetary aspects without taking account of social requirements at a time when these are becoming increasingly important in the planning of economic life in all member countries.'[115] The Commission considered that the major social aims of the Community area could be summed up in terms of the search for not only full but better and more appropriate employment; greater social justice through a more equitable distribution of wealth and the protection of dependent groups; the promotion of a better quality of living through improvement of working conditions, health protection and provision for social and cultural needs. Furthermore members had reached the stage of being able to identify rather more precisely what particular objectives should be given priority in order to give effect to these general ideas. There was widespread acceptance of the importance of satisfying collective requirements through educational, health and housing provision even at the cost of holding down growth in private consumption in order to make such services more effective; of increased efforts to control the adverse effects of economic growth on the environment and to make those responsible bear the price; of a search for greater equality of opportunity through improved education and housing facilities and more fairness in the distribution of income and wealth; of the adaptation of social welfare systems with particular reference to the needs of those adversely affected by change and unable to play their part in the productive process.

Economic goals could not be formulated in a vacuum without consideration of these social objectives or in the absence of a firm structure of democratic discussion to allow their formulation and to determine priorities. In so far, therefore, as the Community was beginning to formulate economic goals, it necessarily followed that it must adopt social objectives and strengthen the process of consultation and debate. Joint social action by the Community and its members would be required, the former would be able to help through the financial aids it dispensed, through the formulation of structural policies, the harmonization policy and the work of helping to co-ordinate the policies of member states themselves, but there would have to be a shifting balance of responsibility between the European and the national levels as progress was made towards economic and monetary union.

It will come as no surprise to learn that the Commission pinpointed employment problems as the key factor in the pursuit of such aims at Community level. This is logical since the process of creating an effective common market for goods, capital and persons has obvious repercussions on levels of employment, job opportunities and mobility. An active employment policy to deal with regional divergencies, technological developments, special problems of the young, the elderly and handicapped, training and guidance and to improve the mechanisms of the labour market and forecasting techniques is essential under conditions of free movement for productive factors. Secondly, the report argued that the

Community has an important part to play in the establishment of greater social justice through helping to determine both the goals and the means of economic growth. This should be used, in part, to raise the standards of the least favoured sections of the population, encourage worker participation in wealth formation and to ensure that all those affected by distribution policies have an effective voice in their determination. Here the Commission defined a contradiction between the need to decentralize decisions with the need for the close co-ordination of overall economic growth at supra-national level. Economic and monetary union should bring a degree of economic stability by eliminating some forms of economic fluctuations and bringing the harmonization and approximation of legislation although not necessarily entirely uniform policies. It should therefore influence income trends. Social security schemes also require to be looked at afresh in the light of their effect on competition under new conditions and the need for fiscal harmonization and the emergence of new risks. A medium-term social forecast for the Community should evolve from the work beginning on social security revenue and expenditure during the 1970s.

Thirdly, there is the contribution that the Community can make towards a better quality of life. Controls over industry run the risk of distorting competition or of not being introduced for fear of competitive disadvantage, so that they must be considered by the Community. It has the capacity to play an important part through the analysis of working conditions and the encouragement of their harmonization through collective agreements at European level. Health protection measures, too, must be considered both from the competitive point of view and the need to improve standards. Minimum measures for the Community would include common standards of industrial health and safety, nuisance limits and medical services and comparable statistics to help with preventive work. Joint measures to help with rescue and emergency services in inaccessible areas or in natural and industrial disasters, special treatment for highly specialized problems and a drive to implement the free establishment policy for the medical profession should be undertaken. Agreement on pollution limits, joint research programmes into noxious substances and common purity standards would all help to improve environmental health and is work the Community could undertake. Indeed, in many such instances, only Community rules would be effective for 'every country and every entrepreneur is swayed predominantly by short-term considerations that have to do with competition'.[116] Thus an increased use of Art. 101 should be expected. Environmental controls also necessarily impinge upon the formation of rational regional policies designed to prevent the high social cost of over-concentration.

A programme for a Community social policy would have to be based on certain priorities. The guidelines suggested that these should consist firstly of the speedier achievement of the common labour market through improved transparency, greater comparability of data and forecasting techniques, the evolution of a more sensitive indicator than current unemployment figures, better mechanical means of supplying information about labour and vacancies, raising the level of skills, preventing discrimination against migrants and ensuring their better integration into new communities.

Secondly, there was a need to absorb the under-employed and those experiencing structural unemployment through more attention to regional problems and a concentration of aid facilities available through Community institutions towards vulnerable areas. Special questions of job training and retraining are to be found in underdeveloped areas and the social fund could be mobilized to help with them.

Thirdly, the introduction of the common market meant the need to consider jointly the improvement of safety and health conditions at work and outside. This work includes the imposition of common standards in fields such as disease prevention, dealing with industrial nuisances, food additives, pesticides and safety standards for consumer durables all of which are affected by the introduction of a common market.

Fourthly, the Community faced a major problem in the need to improve the working conditions of women. This would need to be tackled at a European level because of the fear of competitive disadvantage. Similarly the integration of the handicapped into active life, with a stress upon better employment opportunities, could be assisted through the work of the social fund. The Community should develop the notion of medium-term social forecasting out of the work beginning on social budgeting and should continue with its attempts to strengthen collaboration between employers and workers.

There was a two-fold theme in this document. It argued that the pursuit of certain social objectives was a necessary condition of further economic integration and that the members of the EEC had reached the point where it was no longer adequate to agree upon the necessity for economic growth but also upon the purposes increased wealth was intended to serve. The significant development since that date has been the attention given at the political level to such aims. The rejection of entry by the Norwegian electorate and the obvious reluctance of many people in Great Britain to accept membership demonstrated only too clearly that the Community had failed to appeal to the man in the street thus confirming the argument constantly put forward by the Commission of the necessity for a policy designed to make Europe a reality for the mass of the people. Speaking in October 1972 Herr Brandt articulated the theme that social justice should no longer be considered by the Community as an appendage of economic growth and that an effective social policy would enable people to identify more readily with the

European organization. He called for an action programme to include an information and statistical centre concerned with the Community labour market, common minimum standards for accident and disease prevention, improved conditions of work so that free movement might become a practical not a theoretical reality, effective participation of employees in decision making, an examination of the possibility of common basic conditions for collective wage agreements, the establishment of common principles of social security, vocational and adult education development, the creation of a regional fund and an environmental policy based on the principle that 'the polluter pays'.[117] The summit conference that month declared that a first aim of the future must be to reduce disparities in living conditions and to improve the quality of life. It also recognized the importance of 'vigorous action in the social field' and the need to involve management and labour in the evolution of economic and social life. States called for a social programme, including those 'concrete measures and corresponding resources' which had hitherto been lacking. The substantive fields mentioned in the programme ranged from a co-ordinated policy for employment and vocational training, improved working and living conditions and worker participation to consumer protection and collective bargaining at an international level. A conference of governments, unions and employers was arranged for the following year to work such proposals out more fully.

The significance of this statement lies in the stress laid upon the need for a definite programme. If this indicates a readiness to accept a strengthening in the responsibilities of the Communities it may refute the interpretation of the European philosophy as one which considers social progress as an adjunct of economic development rather than properly the subject of deliberate action by European institutions. At the time of writing it is still too early to pronounce upon the significance of the new developments. The Council adopted a resolution on a social action programme on 21 January 1974 designed to fulfil, in successive stages, the broad objectives of full and better employment, improved living and working conditions and greater participation of management and labour in the economic and social decisions of the Community and of workers in the life of the firms which employ them. The resolution expressed the political will to achieve a number of subsidiary aims by 1976 under these headings, for which detailed proposals are currently being developed by the Commission. Their achievement depends upon acceptance of each one by the Council under normal Community procedures.

By the early 1970s social policy seemed to have arrived at the point of being taken seriously. It had progressed from its original modest function in the ECSC as a means of compensation for those adversely affected by the common market to a place in the highest councils of the

Community and was making a bid to be considered as the essential purpose of its existence. Most activity in the past had related to employment matters, but the work of the Community demonstrated that it is not possible to draw a definite cut-off point between employment and other social questions. The 1971 guidelines marked a new stage in which a different type of issue was being posed as a responsibility of the Community for the future which bore little relation to the actual clauses of the Treaty of Rome, which appear out-dated and small scale in the light of the problems subsequently articulated. On the assumption that the Community had reached the point of the joint pursuit of social goals, its main problem for the future might be seen as that of finding a means of ensuring that such principles were translated into practical, meaningful and effective policies through the determination of priorities, the establishment of standards and the provision of adequate finance.

8 The Past and the Future

Twenty years is not a long time in the history of international organizations which set out on an unknown path with untried working methods. Any judgment must be tentative. It is helpful to bear in mind two levels of assessment. In the first place, there is the question of how far the Communities possessed a social mandate and whether this was adequate for their tasks or will be satisfactory for the future. In the second, there is the problem of how well the Communities fulfilled those responsibilities which had been given to them. The general answer is plain. In the broad sense, the Communities did not have the capacity to develop social goals comparable in importance to those pursued domestically. They were not political institutions with governmental structures of the same stature as the members. They were designed to produce economic integration and consequently dealt with those questions which appeared to have a direct relationship to this aim. Social affairs generally, as the Spaak report indicated, were to be ignored or left to the process of international co-operation as had always been the case. The movement for European unity has been largely an elitist concern, defining its task in political and economic rather than in social terms. The past shows, however, that, in their attempt to fulfil the social responsibilities which were given to them, those Community institutions primarily concerned found themselves unable to discuss social policy apart from moral ends and that the ability to execute the given tasks was constantly hampered by the inter-relationship of these goals to other factors over which they had no control. The two questions are, therefore, connected. Out of the experience of the past one might conclude that the treaties are inadequate for the future, that it is useless to expect a process of natural evolution from present social responsibilities to take care of social ends and that the first requirement is to face the question of whether the Communities are to evolve politically or not. Social policy developments are dependent upon this issue.

The assessment of the past, however, must accept the framework of the treaties. Here it is possible to see that, despite the fact that in social affairs their work was very closely related to that executed by other international bodies, despite the ambiguities of treaties which gave social matters limited attention, despite the feeling that, after enormous and

219

patient labours by the executives and a mound of documentation, comparatively little had emerged, the Communities were able to identify and respond to certain human problems. Albeit imperfectly, they had accepted a social dimension of economic integration which, through the labours of the executives, struggled to obtain more effective recognition even though this could not lead to the acquisition of fully mature social policies. If the period appears as one of gestation, this is also true of other aspects of the work of the Communities.

A number of themes stand out as the contribution of the European system to thinking about modern social policy. The outstanding factor was the recognition of the close interdependence between economic and social developments. The philosophy of the treaties was that economic and social progress go together and, since the emphasis of the time was on the economic advance that 'a more rational distribution of production' might bring, it was perhaps natural to stress the extent to which social improvements were dependent upon its achievement and were necessary in order to contribute to it. In theory there is no reason why the balance should not be reversed as a basis for future policy so that it becomes plain that economic development is not an end in itself but only important as a means to pursue worthwhile objectives. While at first sight the Community arguments for better vocational training, improved industrial safety and more favourable terms of employment often seemed to emphasize economic objects disproportionately, this thesis followed naturally from the treaties. For the Commission as the instigator of policy such an emphasis was the strongest argument available to it for the extension of social goals. At least this argument had the merit of insisting that any attempt at conscious control of human events by public authorities must be considered in the round and that social policy goals have a legitimate part in such planned development. The medium-term economic programmes of the Community showed this *leitmotiv* particularly clearly through their recognition that the process of structural change or the necessity to control the division of wealth also demanded facilities for vocational training, aids to mobility and special consideration of the problems of the backward regions as well as of the control of wages, investment and social security. It remains to be seen if the growth of medium-term programming will fill some of the gaps in the Treaty of Rome by demanding an incomes policy and by dealing more effectively with the redistribution of income. The effective consideration, not only of wages but of real incomes, of the level of social benefits, access to social capital and to savings mechanisms as part of economic policy would indeed form a vital part of the movement towards more coherent social objectives.

Community studies represent a strand in social policy which can be too easily overlooked. A pioneering function was performed here in that they collected in comparable form and on an international scale material which hitherto had not been available. Wages, social security schemes, employment conditions, industrial health and safety, vocational training programmes and housing projects were among topics subjected to detailed scrutiny. Allied with the consultation, conference and seminar activities they can be seen to form part of the slow process of clarification of issues and attitude formation whether at national or international level which is the first step towards active policy. Such work is not only the pre-condition for any effective development of social harmonization but is a contribution to a fundamental tenet of social policy, namely that a rational base for action may be established through greater knowledge and understanding. It is, therefore, unfortunate that states did not always co-operate fully in supplying the information for Community projects[1] and resented the contacts between the Commission and independent bodies and experts, for this only impaired the quality of the work done thus leading to the general loss. Only a beginning was made on the work of presenting information in a form which was truly comparable. Formal comparison of wages, for example, is of limited value; of more interest were those studies of real incomes produced by the Statistical Office allowing for wages, in cash and in kind, family allowances, income tax payments and social security contributions.[2] Studies designed to define and measure productivity, methods of wage payment, levels of real income, benefits in kind, health and welfare provisions are a necessary first step towards the definition of Community standards.

The notion of 'equivalence' was valuable but requires further precision for use as a policy base. The definition by the executives related too closely to the working situation to be entirely acceptable;

> All those economic and social factors which help to develop and fulfil the personality of the worker in his occupational environment including direct wages and social security benefits, . . . working hours, relations between employers and workers both inside and outside the enterprise, vocational and refresher training systems, promotion prospects, housing conditions, and other factors of all kinds.[3]

Given the existence of different wage and taxation rates, of variations in the cost of living and of social services, of differences in the size of firms, alternative employment opportunities and of the strength of employers' and workers' organizations, formal equality of living and working conditions seemed an unrealistic aim particularly for a Community which could not control taxation, wages, education or housing policies. Furthermore, 'the situation could not crystallize once and for all at a given level and thereafter develop in parallel for all countries from that level onwards'.[4] Thus the definition of 'equivalence' proved intellectually demanding. It is, however, not enough. The further issue is that of implementation of a policy aimed to ensure equivalent standards. The experience with the miners' charter, with the Commission's recommendations on industrial medicine and occupational diseases and its intended one on maternity protection, showed that there is no automatic process under the treaties whereby the formulation of standards ensures their acceptance. In the past the executives had no choice. They were not able to insist upon redistribution policies themselves and were wise not to waste time attempting to claim a responsibility they could not fulfil. Whilst more could be done to define 'equivalence' and also the notion that improvements should do proportionately more for the least well-off than for the rich, it was clearly for members themselves to decide whether they wished to pursue these goals as active policies. The Commission's function stopped at research and did not include imposition. Such work may well have contributed to the understanding held by workers, employers and governments about their problems, but this faith cannot be evaluated.

An important contribution from the Communities lay in their constant stress upon consultation procedures at all stages of the decision making and execution process as a necessary ingredient in social policy. 'Lastly, the High Authority has not forgotten that social progress leaves human beings dissatisfied if they do not themselves share in the formulation of those economic and social policies which provide the improvement.'[5] This view recalls to mind that social policy is not a matter solely for national governments but for employers, unions and voluntary organizations as well, and the European executives laid great stress upon the importance of establishing links with appropriate organizations and upon the importance of convincing them of the need to play a part in the process of European integration lest, by default, this latter process caused a fundamental change in the nature of Western societies without this being properly appreciated by those affected: 'European integration will be suspect if the action agreed by states is not accompanied, or even preceded, by action agreed by the relevant occupational organizations and social affairs comprise a vast field for such activity.'[6] The implication here is for more effective group organization at a European level. A constant process of discussion is vital if such associations are to be involved with the evolution of policy and the application of ideas at home which conform with the main outlines of European programmes. Real efforts went into this through the creation of an effective committee structure such as the joint advisory committees on the social problems in agriculture, transport and fisheries, the joint working party to examine the law on collective bargaining, the tripartite working parties for the study of protection for the working mother and for young people, in addition to the constant effort to seek the support of the formal institutions of Parliament and the Economic and Social Committee. If the executives put most stress upon the employers and unions in the consultation process this seems logical. The very nature of the grouping, centred upon economic change, made their interest and involvement vital. Solutions to problems of structural change in industry can only be found in conjunction with industry, whilst the Commission considered consultation to be essential if economic expansion were to lead to larger social justice.[7] It was therefore essential to ensure that employers and workers were committed to the process of European integration and, since it was the unions which were particularly wary, it was of especial importance to devote time to ensuring that their needs were not overlooked. One of the more remarkable changes with the passage of time was the realization by the main union organizations that the European executives were normally in favour of workers' demands and with the growth of confidence they became anxious to see more decisions and activity taking place at European level.[8] From their initial, generally suspicious, stance, unions moved to become broadly favourable to European integration as a means of creating a genuinely free and democratic society and therefore to stronger social measures within the treaty structure.[9]

Much of the work of the executives in the social field, such as the research and study programmes, could not be carried out without the active co-operation of employers and workers and their willingness to see sensitive issues ventilated, comparative studies begun and disparities brought to light. In consequence the European Communities pursued an information and publicity programme through seminars, scholarships and conferences.[10] Research projects can still be isolated by frontiers and language so that the encouragement of international contact, by introducing new ideas and comparative standards into fields traditionally dealt with on a national scale, should be beneficial academically. To the Communities, however, such activity had an additional aim. In so far as the participants came to value it or it led to action on a concerted basis or the Europeanization of concepts and standards, it strengthened the process of integration and its public support. The rapid proliferation of scientific, employer, worker and educational organizations at a European level indicated the importance attached to continuing contact with the executives and will have encouraged the habit of thinking in European terms. It can, therefore, only be considered unfortunate that in some ways recent years have brought a falling-off in the accessibility of material in the social field. The constant changes in the form of presentation of statistics make comparison over time difficult: the High Authority studies of social security in the six members and Great Britain have been discontinued, the social statistics available through the general and social reports have become less detailed with the advent of specialist publications, whilst the publication of research material is often very slow.

A particular aspect of the communication process was the opportunity given for a forum for the discussion of the mutual concerns of the two sides of industry at European level. With the growth of the multinational company, free migration of labour and more discussion of the broad sweep of economic policy by the Community some such meeting place is important. The work of the joint committees meant that issues could be discussed within a broader context than hitherto in which representatives from elsewhere within the Community and the executives could provide new insights into problems. The wide range of subject matter so discussed suggests that, over time, these arrangements may have been of considerable value in helping many people to a greater understanding of the complex issue of industrial relations at a time of economic change.

The period also showed the interdependence of social factors. It was difficult to deal with any issue in isolation from many others and it often appeared illogical to do so. Equal pay for women cannot be pursued without consideration of social and educational status, social security financing without taxation policy as a whole, sickness benefits without arrangements for medical care, mobility of labour without social integration. In many cases the pursuit of formal goals hardly seems worthwhile except as the first step towards their effective implementation through the removal of socio-economic barriers which prevent individuals taking advantage of the opportunities theoretically offered. The structure of the treaties did not allow for the development of actual policies to deal with the realities of these questions. The logic of facts was resisted by the reluctance of members to depart from a strict interpretation of the treaties. The Council recognition in 1968 that Community concern was not limited to those functions specifically mentioned in Art. 118 meant the first crumbling of the formal barriers preventing a generous interpretation of social policy, so that a consideration of the needs of the traditionally disadvantaged and the totality of human problems could be added to the initial preoccupation with the worker and his employment situation. Although the process of operating the specific policies of the Treaty of Rome drew the Commission inexorably into consideration of the social questions of dependency, whether these were seen as an offshoot of migration or of structural change in agriculture or health and retirement policies affecting the worker, practical action did not necessarily follow.

The sense of intellectual momentum is most easily seen in the comments of Parliament on social policy, for its thoughts did not have to be tied down by the treaty clauses, by lack of financial resources or the realities of political policies. These ideas provide, therefore, useful pointers to the way in which policy might develop in the future as new needs are felt even though such extensions appear in the immediate present as speculative and uncertain. The resolution on the *Social Exposé* of 1963, annexed to the seventh general report, is a good example. It referred to the need to obtain more information about incomes in order to determine the position of low income groups, the importance of establishing joint committees, of developing work under Arts. 117 and 118 as a means of achieving greater social harmonization and of furthering agreements at European level. It called for common standards of protection for young people and women at work, urged more action in a number of fields including vocational and equal pay and drew attention to the lack of low-cost housing within the Community which it was hoped the Commission might help to remedy. It stated the desirability of establishing a policy for old people and of standardizing syllabuses for technical training and education.[11] The following year Parliament called for the establishment of a European Youth Office under the auspices of the Community to provide a wide range of functions for young people including a greater concern with those living and working outside their own countries.[12]

At the same time the very process of operating the specific social goals of the treaty in a period of rapid development and experiment provided an impetus towards deepening conceptions. There is always more to be done once a process is started and this is clearly to be seen at work in the policy to create an international labour market which demanded consideration of many of the same problems met with in the national context, such as job definition, level of qualifications required for particular posts, matching and bringing together offers of jobs and labour and the need to overcome obstacles to the mobility of labour. They were, however, more difficult to solve. The Commission tried to overcome them through the use of comparative dictionaries of job content, job profiles, the establishment of collaboration between state employment services, the maintenance of social security rights and the adoption of standardized training systems. The extent to which such work spreads its way through into national structures is no doubt variable but is likely to operate everywhere to some degree particularly in those cases where a state is a receiver or supplier of migrant labour. In some cases the effects may be slow and the process had barely begun for skilled and professional posts. On the other hand, it is not easy to point to conceptual changes in social security resulting from the work of the Commission, but the need to encourage ease of transferability of benefits may encourage this in the same way that easing movement of labour or goods may encourage standardization of industrial medical services or of instructions for the use of machinery. As states come to revise their legislation, they may model provisions on work already done by the Communities thus helping to spread the adoption of standardized rules.[13]

However, it was not only the mobility of labour but the recognition of a manpower question which lay behind the interest of the Community in employment problems. The two worked together to enliven the debate on training, mobility, the integration of the migrant and the absorption of women and disadvantaged groups into the labour force. The operation of a reformed social fund, the establishment of new techniques made necessary by its wider use, the development by the Community of its own training schemes and more attention to the exchange of young workers were all matters which appeared as a natural development of what had already been done.

The broadening view of social policy was encouraged by the executives who, far from believing that economic growth inevitably brought social progress in its train,[14] stressed that man-made policy was necessary to ensure that increasing wealth was used in socially desirable directions and 'cannot confine itself to correcting the consequences of economic measures to social criteria'.[15] It was, therefore, essential for the executives to take whatever steps were possible under the treaties to ensure that economic progress was reflected in enhanced living conditions. Active policies aimed at some aspect of such improvement gave greater precision to the wide goals of improved and harmonized standards which, under the treaties, were both vague and indeterminate. If such aims now possess greater clarity this is in part due to the work of the High Authority and Commission in their definition and pursuit. The very range of work itself which was undertaken and the issues which were discussed at international level owed something to the initiative of the executives and their determination to pursue social ends as far as permitted to them.

A positive line of argument was developed in the late 1960s in the emphasis upon the social aspects of other Community policies. This seemed attractive as a method of enabling social policy to be carried along by the momentum generated by other Community goals. To rely overmuch on this process would be dangerous. In the first place, it may mean that the limited argument that social policy is essentially a compensatory mechanism for damage done rather than a means of contributing to the broad social improvement of the Community becomes accepted as its proper delimitation and, secondly, that the social implications of other policies are neglected whenever the latter are not clearly dependent upon prior solution of social problems for their achievement. As the Social Committee pertinently remarked: 'Market and price policies in agriculture have been 90 per cent realised whilst its social policy is still at death's door.'[16] Yet here was a case in which the treaty had specifically recognized the social needs of agricultural populations. Whilst, therefore, such a move carried the promise of greater attention to social questions in the future, it did not solve the real problems of turning aspirations into usable objectives. Above all, it bypassed the central question of the interpretation and application of Art. 117.

In brief, therefore, one may summarize the positive side of the social policy of the Communities as deriving from its stress upon the inter-relationship of economic and social policy and the vital importance of employment problems to human well-being, as well as upon the necessity to establish a factual base for action and to formulate policies as a result of a continuous process of consultation. Whilst the importance of pre-ventive work to guard workers against job loss and of a wide mandate for social policy because of the difficulty of dealing with any one problem by itself were both demonstrated by these experiences, their implications had not been fully worked out.

Material standards developed considerably in the Community area during the period under discussion as evidenced by high employment levels, increasing wages, more leisure time and better forms of social protection.[17] Whilst it is impossible to evaluate precisely the effect of the existence of the Communities, that is no reason for assuming that their contribution was irrelevant. Many factors contributed to such changes and their work may well have been one. The establishment of a free labour market, the growing protection of the migrant, greater support and help for the unemployed, more housing in coal mining areas and the general educational work of research and standard setting are all positive actions despite the blemishes and shortcomings. To evaluate the extent to which there has been a movement towards equality of con-ditions and, if so, what the Communities' contribution has been, is far harder except in this general sense. Real incomes have risen substan-tially since 1958, but

> there are still wide disparities in the distribution of incomes and wealth. Although the relevant data are inadequate, and sometimes completely lacking – a point which merits special attention over the next few years – it can be stated that all population groups have not benefited equally from the rise in incomes. There are still 'marginal' groups among both the active and non-active population. Whilst regional differences have narrowed slightly in certain cases, the dis-parities are still very considerable; the gap has even widened in the case of some regions. The wages pyramid, by branches, shows that the extreme range has widened, although the branches at the top or bottom of the wages scale are almost always the same in all countries at the same time. Furthermore, there is still a very marked difference between the wages paid to men and women with the same qualifi-cations.[18]

This quotation reminds us that a basic question for the Community is to decide whether its concern is with differences between people or with those between states. Much of our information relates to the latter and may not, therefore, be in the form that is really required. The stress on the protection against job loss, wage cutting and on better working conditions in the Treaty of Paris, on the mobility of labour and occupational training in the Treaty of Rome and the need to fulfil specific obligations such as equal pay all required that Community activity should be concentrated in a particular direction but limited by the actual powers delegated to these organizations.

It has been seen that both the High Authority and the Commission were intimately involved in the task of enlarging employment opportunities. The initial recognition that the creation of a new economic grouping might bring individual hardship which should properly be compensated was rapidly reinforced through the particular difficulties of the heavy industries which led to a development of the capacity of the High Authority to promote a variety of helping schemes. Its work was of sufficient importance for the Treaty of Rome to incorporate a definite institutional structure in the form of the European social fund with a mandate which was basically both wide and generous. Its limitations sprang from the narrow terms in which that mandate was confined and it is not to the credit of the Community that for so long it was unable to overcome the difficulties presented by its reform.

Closely associated with the provision of grant aid for retraining and better employment allowances was the creation of a common policy for occupational training designed to ensure the more effective operation of the Community labour market and utilization of labour potential in face of the changes occurring in industry. This work can be claimed as but a modest success. The lack of concrete results in terms of agreed training levels was particularly disappointing; at the most Community activity helped to make apparent the great importance of better training and vocational guidance facilities.

The programme for the exchange of young workers received comparatively little attention. This is unfortunate, for the original argument that it would be an effective means of establishing common attitudes and work practices still appears to be sound and it is perhaps time to blow the dust off the original idea. Reconsideration might be carried out as part of a drive towards making Europe a more meaningful conception for ordinary people and thus seen in the context of broader educational and training schemes than hitherto.

In contrast the free labour market, at least in a formal sense, was established earlier than strictly necessary together with action to protect the essential rights of migrants to social security protection, to equal access to employment and to the enjoyment of parity of working conditions. Great importance must be attached to these principles of non-discrimination and equality of treatment between individuals as elements of an effective social policy. It is not the claim that these principles worked perfectly and it was difficult for the Community to ensure that they did since it was not itself responsible for the immediate practical tasks of administration, and the strongest form in which it could express its views on the social problems of migrants was the recommendation. Whilst housing and social services were subjected to this process it was up to states to take the necessary action. Nevertheless, in the long run, an effective labour market may still prove the more important influence in establishing equality of living and working standards within the Community than direct action under Art. 117.

There is a striking difference between the achievement of the labour market and the programme for the establishment of the self-employed and for the supply of services. This took only the first and easiest steps. One has no wish to deny the importance of ensuring that Community workers can acquire property, join professional organizations, form companies or lease land in order to execute an entrepreneurial function. They are nevertheless dwarfed in size and importance by the questions of training levels, educational systems and entry thereto, access to public employment and contracts which require many more years of work before effective solution. An obvious first step is to extend transferability of social security entitlement to self-employed workers, the latest provisions being no more than a tentative nibble at a most complex problem. Arrangements at least need to be made to allow the self-employed to contribute to savings funds for old age whether in their own country, or in the country where they are working with adequate safeguards for transferability and tax relief.[19]

From a human viewpoint improvement in the position of the migrant worker should not be confined to those who are nationals of the Community as the 1974 social action programme recognized. On the contrary, the benefits established as a result of the treaties should be extended to all alien workers and serve as an example of how to overcome problems affecting individuals who move outside their own communities. The adjustment of national policies of recruitment to a Community framework may become increasingly necessary with the firmer establishment of the labour market and this in turn may encourage the formulation of a Community policy towards the treatment and condition of such workers.

After a scramble and with continuing reluctance the Community fulfilled its obligation to adopt an equal pay policy. This field, however, shows up clearly the limitations of Community institutions in attempting to apply any policy over such a large area and the persistence of severe anomalies in levels of pay between men and women[20] gives point to the Commission's view that the time has come to reconsider this issue in the broader context of action necessary to improve the general social position of women and enlarge their opportunities for satisfying employment.[21]

Although neither treaty contained a formal dedication to full employment, history shows the importance attached by the Communities to the practical right to work, both through making jobs available and through enabling workers to fit themselves to take the work on offer. A clear distinction was drawn, however, between the idea of a guarantee of a particular job and that of the acceptance of changes demanded by the evolution of the economy, provided continuity of work and wage levels was maintained and appropriate help given to workers required to make the transition from one position to another or to move home.[22] Great efforts were made by the executives to ensure mobility with minimum hardship through its policies to aid re-employment, to encourage mobility, to provide training, to stimulate housing projects, to finance more research into industrial health and safety and to build up the single labour market. Their work helped to clarify the many issues involved in the re-employment of labour. Although the Communities were responsible for giving certain workers better unemployment benefits than they otherwise would have had, the important lesson of the readaptation programmes was that of the value of taking a broad view of policy as they merged into regional redevelopment on the one hand and the free movement of labour on the other.

The key to the fulfilment of Community objectives for a manpower policy to meet the anticipated economic changes of the area lay in the development of vocational training, whether at local, regional, national or Community level. This required full consideration of educational systems and forms of training, the development of retraining and refresher courses and proper income maintenance for the worker undergoing training, but the treaties did not provide adequate strength here. It remains to be seen whether the new social fund will be able to make good the deficiency through supporting national schemes to improve training levels.

The emphasis upon the joint pursuit of economic and social goals brought clarification of the tasks the executives might pursue in the field of human betterment but carried the danger that in practice social policy would become the junior partner. Neither treaty could ensure that it would acquire a higher role, and it is clear that the social harmonization theme of the treaties cannot be dignified by the appellation of 'a policy' in the years up till 1972. In 1971 gross domestic product (gdp) per head ranged from 1876 US dollars in Italy to 3572 US dollars in Germany, and there were also still considerable differences in regional income levels. Industrial wages in the west of France were only 90·5 per cent of the national average compared with those in Paris which had reached 116·6 per cent and similar variations existed within other member states.[23] Although social security expenditures, as proportions of national incomes, are now more nearly akin, the variation in objective of such expenditure is very considerable and there is no sign of a greater uniformity in the pattern of financing.[24] Recent figures show that in Luxembourg 60·9 per cent of expenses go on pensions for invalidity and old age but only 36·3 per cent in Italy. Family allowances absorb 21·4 per cent of the total in France but only 7·7 per cent in Germany. Sickness benefits are more nearly comparable in importance but nevertheless range between 31·0 per cent in the Netherlands and 17·3 per cent in Luxembourg.[25] Any levelling-up process has been slow. In 1972 the Commission estimated that *per capita* expenditure through social security schemes in 1969 ranged from 444·5 units of account in Germany to 234·2 units in Italy.[26] The cautious words of the High Authority in 1962 should be remembered.

> While the position of workers in the ECSC industries has substantially improved since 1953, there is comparatively little evidence of any particular country's catching up on any other in social standards. The automatic levelling-up of living and working conditions which was earlier expected by some to result from the operation of the Common Market for coal and steel has thus not materialized.[27]

To argue that developments in social provision were rooted in economic changes is not to say a great deal. It is not surprising that areas which were experiencing similar problems due to the overall decline in the demand for coal and the need to close uneconomic pits should have responded in broadly similar ways, or that if the six members of the EEC were undergoing technological changes and alterations in industrial location at roughly the same time should find themselves facing similar problems. In this sense social policy is a function of the economic system. Nevertheless its content, range, enthusiasm and the speed with which it identifies and responds to such problems are issues which appear susceptible to human control. For the Communities the prime determinants of social policy in this sense were the treaties which, whether for practical or philosophical reasons, had seen social policy as a function of the economy and particularly for the individual industry or firm. There has probably been less tendency in the Continental member states than in Great Britain to think in terms of the community-based, universal service and more willingness to consider social policy as an extension of industrial relations, a view which the existence of the Communities can only have accentuated. 'Economic and social policy, though based on a single general concept, has always to be differentiated in accordance with the special features of the industrial sectors of the economy.'[28] The history of social security shows, however, that even in circumstances in which employers carry a large responsibility for welfare benefits it is not really possible to adopt a strict sectoral approach, and the domestic tendency towards alignment of benefits despite the continued existence of separate schemes suggests they may be losing their justification. The problem of the extent to which social advance is to be pursued in the political or the industrial arenas remains one of the major unspoken questions underlying the social thinking of the European treaties.

Opinion is generally agreed that it was where the treaties were precise and provided the institutions with the support of definite procedures and deadlines that social action was most successful.

> The most positive results were indeed obtained in those specific fields where the treaties gave to the Community executives – Councils, Commissions, High Authority – the powers necessary for the realisation of stated objectives, that is to say, in the context of the Rome treaty, the free movement of workers, social security for migrants and the social fund and under the Paris treaty readaptation aid and reconversion loans.[29]

Between these commitments and the broad generalities of the Preamble and Art. 2 of the Treaty of Rome lay a wide gap. To fill in the middle rung is the most urgent imperative of the time. Art. 117 is inadequate for this purpose since its lack of clarity was clearly a source of weakness rather than strength.[30] Here again one perhaps meets a difference between the British and Continental temperament. To the former, vagueness in a written document often appears admirable in that it allows scope for initiative and experiment, but to the latter it means that there is no mandate for action. Better, therefore, than hoping to interpret confusion so as to allow for Community development in a field in which members have shown themselves to be wary of such growth, is action designed to pin members down in the first place. Parliament posed the problems clearly enough in asking the Council for binding decisions on practical issues of social policy since social measures 'must not just be limited to the harmonization of state efforts . . . but must include an important role for direct Community intervention which is the sole guarantee that progress will occur in the Community on a par with economic expansion'.[31]

It was not, however, Art. 117 alone that wasted energy on fruitless debate. Institutional weakness also arose from the differences of view concerning the relative competence of the Commission and governments for the development of the occupational training programme, which was retarded by the argument that the Community should be limited to the formulation of general principles and that states alone should be responsible for their application. The same situation arose over the work to be carried out under Art. 118 where the issue of the right of initiative of the Commission and the interpretation of 'collaboration' remain dormant, unsettled questions. Such uncertainties concerning the competence of the European institutions helped to thwart the attempts of the Commission to play a part in the movement for social progress by involvement in the political argument concerning supra-nationalism. It is, therefore, not only the goals that need to be spelt out more clearly. More attention needs to be given to the techniques through which they may be achieved. Procedures based on the establishment of Community norms are suitable in certain cases such as industrial safety measures, inter-governmental co-operation may be more suitable in speculative and uncertain fields such as delinquency, whilst a basic European policy with a flexibility of application may be appropriate where there is already a good deal of common ground as is the case in social security provision. At the moment, however, none of this is clear, and the omissions of the treaty perhaps help to account for the noticeable distance between the advanced social thinking presented by the Commission and the practical achievements of the Communities. It is impossible for them to rest for ever on the preliminary tasks of defining goals, exposing the difficulties and finding out how far treaty clauses can be stretched. Moral aspirations have their place and if the Commission had not insisted upon recalling them to mind the Communities would no doubt be in an even more backward state than they are today with relation to the development of social policy. 'One of the most difficult and arduous tasks of our time is perhaps just that of resolving the old antagonism between social and economic imperatives in a synthesis operating at a higher level thanks to the establishment of an overall policy in which a balanced economic expansion permits greater social justice.'[32] It is difficult not to conclude that, in so far as the practical application of social justice requires action taken by public authorities to meet human need, social policy within the European Communities has barely begun and the range of activity so far attempted does not match widely-held views of the proper content of social policy. It is clear that the executives endeavoured to maintain a constant awareness of the need for social thinking and encouraged its re-evaluation and reinterpretation, but this needs to be backed up through the definition of middle-range goals that can serve as a working base for this purpose.

Associated with this lack of clarity in goals was a dilemma which goes to the heart of social policy today. There is no reason to doubt that the Commission genuinely believed that a wide range of persons and groupings must be involved in all stages of the decision-making process for this to retain its validity. To the formal Economic and Social Committee were added other advisory committees such as for the social security of migrants, the social fund, occupational training and the institutionalization of employer–worker committees in many fields such as coal and steel, agriculture, transport and fisheries. In relation to the large number of people living in the Community and their manifold associations these channels nevertheless appear narrow, and the Treaty of Rome is largely silent on the question of how a constant dialogue is to be carried on or how some form of decision sharing can be arranged. The institutional structure did not adequately reflect the multiplicity of social agencies existing within the Community with which it is essential for the Commission to develop links if its social policy is to have a real meaning for the people it is designed to help. Even the limited attempts made by the Commission to widen its relationships through the use of independent experts was on occasion resisted by national governments, so that any move to extend contacts much more widely is likely to be slow since the executives could not, and cannot, afford to offend members too bitterly as long as their formal position in social matters remains weak.

The issues of social harmonization and of sharing responsibility both therefore led back to the old question of state autonomy and the unwillingness of national governments to surrender powers either to an international organization or to other agencies within the state. 'Now social policy . . . has for some time been the dear child of national governments who do not wish it to appear that the realization of social objectives is, even in part, to the credit of another body.'[33] Yet the past suggests that if social harmonization is to be left primarily to a natural process of evolution it is likely to wait a very long time indeed. If it is to be taken seriously there seems to be no other choice than to strengthen the political capacity of the European institutions to ensure the pursuit of social objectives and to enable them to raise money for these purposes. Whilst this is difficult to do, it is not impossible. The treaties have already shown that there was sufficient agreement amongst states on protection against unemployment to allow them to incorporate this into an international document and to permit the establishment of a European system of grant aid. Other social purposes in the fields of education, health and housing are in reality agreed, so that it is not to expect too much to argue for a further step to be taken for the more effective pursuit of desired objectives.

The conclusions to be drawn from these experiences can only contain limited lessons for the future. The early years of the Communities were necessarily occupied with the preliminaries to action and the initial establishment of policies required for the immediate purposes of the treaties. Increasingly, it is true, the sense of urgency heightened as the transitional period drew to an end and the Communities began to look forward to the stage of strengthening their identity. The future will be very much a new situation. In order to discuss the social tasks of tomorrow one must postulate that the process of political and economic integration moves forward but in ways that are as yet unknown. Neither can the impact of new members be overlooked, for their absorption is bound to require considerable Community energy for some time.

Since the prime concern of social policy is with the redistribution of wealth it is useless to consider its possibilities in a Community which can neither assume the existence of a single economic unit nor possesses the political authority to take and execute social policy decisions. It is not adequate to rely upon the 'spontaneous development based on momentum coming from economic integration' which served the authors of the Rome Treaty.[34] Reasons to explain the lack of social progress in the past can be put forward, but they will be unconvincing in a strengthened system. It is, therefore, the future which will provide the testing time for the seriousness of social purpose of the Communities, in which the claim to apply the principle of social justice will need to be made good by its translation into specific policies.

> First of all, it can be stated that the construction of Europe, on the basis of the treaties of Paris and Rome, is motivated by principles of social justice. This is evidenced by the principles and arrangements of the treaties which underline the willingness of the six countries to achieve an improvement in the living and working conditions of the people and to ensure, along with economic progress, social development, particularly through reducing regional disparities and the slow advance of the less favoured.[35]

It must be accepted that the ability of the European Communities to translate this principle into viable policies is far less than that of the constituent members. It must always be remembered that there are fundamental differences between an advanced system of government, which stems from a well-knit, self-conscious national identity, capable of asserting its political, economic and social goals and which is supported by effective and long-established administrative systems on the one hand, and the Communities on the other which are of recent establishment and designed as inter-governmental systems although of a special, advanced kind. Their very creation has the air of an artefact which stemmed, not from 'the upsurge of economic forces',[36] but rather from the calculated decisions of a small number of people supported by governmental circles. It has been well said that the Communities are neither the Europe of peoples nor of states but of supra-national offices.[37] The European institutions are not the holders of unequivocal political authority, for so many fields of government, notably foreign policy and defence, remain outside their competence, yet the inter-relationship of policies, if only because of their competing claims on limited resources, is a commonplace at national level. To this frustration is added another. In so far as the objective of either treaty is defined as that of economic integration, it is understandable that social policy should be conceived essentially as a humane labour policy. But this brings difficulties for policy makers and is unsatisfactory from the human point of view. It is artificial to deal with conditions of work, levels of unemployment pay, the welfare of migrants and the like in isolation from the general social standards currently prevailing. These in turn are affected by a wide range of policies and socio-economic phenomena. The Communities are unable to exploit all methods of social progress and to adopt measures which, on an objective analysis, might seem the most appropriate. European social policy can only go so far before raising issues of priorities and redistribution which still lie within the competence of the members. To achieve 'common economic and social policies in this dimension necessitates a broad measure of political consensus among those concerned and a level of institutional and political integration which does not seem to exist in the Community at the present time'.[38] Future developments may ease but will not cure these difficulties.

The different priorities given by members to social spending or to one social objective rather than another, whether justifiable or not, are a given fact of life for the Community. Where such differences represent different needs uniformity would be harmful, whilst if it were ever attempted to insist upon uniformity at the highest level in all spheres each member would need to undergo a different reform process. Common sense suggests that the problem facing the German car worker, the Sicilian peasant or the French farmer are of a very different character and that local solutions to them are often to be preferred and likely to be more effective. European institutions can help to ensure that the problems are identified and tackled and can deal with those issues which present themselves at a European level including those which require a solution for the creation of an integrated Europe. Dual responsibility has to be established in order that more effective social progress can be made than would otherwise be the case.

A further limitation which must be expected to continue to operate in the future to some degree stems from the remoteness of European institutions. This is of particular disadvantage in the field of social policy which, in the end, must be judged by its effects on the individual, the family and the local group. The Communities are ill-placed to tap the ideas and innovating techniques of those concerned with handling day-to-day problems and are thus likely to be insensitive to change in a field where this is particularly important. This is not to deny that great efforts were made by the executives to broaden the basis of their decision making through constant contact with national officials, governmental representatives, industrial, professional, farming and labour organizations.[39] A complex and time-consuming process of discussion occurred between the executives and national experts in which not only the merits of a question but national positions thereon were thoroughly ventilated before proposals were ever formally submitted to the Council.[40] As a result there were 'thousands of national and Community officials involved in a continuous decision-making process'.[41] It is in this way that national attitudes to Community proposals have been influenced in the past so that the latter may be considered as something more than an international bargaining deal.[42] Unfortunately, as has been seen, the process was painfully slow[43] and attempts to strengthen the procedures in order to improve the contacts between the executive and social policy organizations would no doubt make the general issue of consultation worse rather than better. In relation to social affairs there may have been a vicious circle at work. In so far as policy at European level was weak and power remained with national governments it was perhaps not worthwhile for the agents of social policy to develop fully as pressure groups in Brussels but, in default of this, one of the main ways in which the Communities evolved was inadequately developed. At the same time the assumption that social policy operates essentially in the labour field meant that the executives naturally looked to the employers' organizations and unions for their contacts thus accentuating the limitation.

In the past the Commission was restricted by its lack of financial resources. Increasingly this will ease and some flexibility be incorporated, but the scale of Community financing must be borne in mind. Future resources will be modest in comparison with those of modern Western European governments which are accustomed to control about 30 per cent of gross national product. It would be futile to expect policies to operate on a scale comparable to that of which national governments are capable. European social policies will be supplementary, stimulating and co-operative but will not put member states out of the picture. The discussion is about joint programmes, or rather co-operative programmes, for the fact that social policy is not the prerogative of national governments but is shared with many other authorities at once implies that the concept of a transfer from a national to an international level is too simple. The argument is for the introduction of one more level of government into a highly intricate web of existing institutions.

> In most countries the authorities have only limited freedom in social affairs: they share their rights and privileges with the employers' and workers' representatives, who have responsibility and powers of decision either de facto or through legislation and the operation of the national institutions.[44]

Such inherent limitations suggest that one must be wary of expecting a full-blown social policy to emerge at the European level in the near future. In the past its benefit for human welfare may have lain as much in the influence it has had on the attitudes of governments, employers and unions as in its formal results. However, it is quite unrealistic to suppose that a Community increasingly concerned to control its economic development will be able to operate effectively or to obtain political credibility, without simultaneously sharing in the promotion of social objectives. The total return to workers, social investment in housing, leisure facilities and health services, the ability to save and own property, access to educational and training facilities are all matters of essential concern not only to the determination of economic policy but to social policy as well. Whilst in the foreseeable future European social policy seems likely to be on a smaller scale than that of national governments, it is not of a different kind. Its tasks are to ensure that resources are spent on social ends commensurate with their importance both by taking broad decisions to which national governments conform and by direct operations of its own in selected spheres. It will thus often be so intimately woven into the functions of national governments or industrial relationships that it may be hard to detect where one ends and the other begins.

The most obvious need for a European dimension in social policy arises from the ramifications of the creation of a single labour market. This is both a matter of finding ways of improving co-ordination between national employment services and labour systems generally and of recognizing that its establishment is bound to expose a host of social and economic difficulties which can only be effectively dealt with at European level. This is not just a question of those problems associated with labour migration but the implications of the creation of a European labour force for training policies and educational systems. Under such conditions the protection against unemployment which requires training and retraining schemes, mobility of labour both geographical and occupational and adequate social security is also a matter which acquires a European dimension. It is also politically inconceivable that any community in Western Europe could allow labour mobility to occur without showing that it is at least stimulating states to deal with the resulting problems through positive aid for housing, welfare services and whatever other facilities the future shows to be necessary. It is not, of course, suggested that the effect of a common labour market will be other than long term or that more than a minority of the working population is likely to move from one country to another, but it is through this minority that such changes are likely to come with the result that it will be increasingly difficult to confine the European interest to a group classified as 'migrants' whether potential, existing or past but will necessitate its extension to the standards of the population at large.

Secondly, it is necessary to consider the implications of the multi-national company whether this spreads eastwards across the Atlantic or results from the development of the European company as the entre-preneurial function becomes more mobile in Europe. As the firm increasingly liberates itself from the national framework so the attempts to counterbalance it with stronger union organization at international level will have to become more effective. The European platform, which provides a place for employers and workers to meet, seems a suitable one for allowing this to happen and for collective bargaining to occur within a political structure. So far the only examples of this process are the agreements to recommend the reduction in working hours in agri-culture, but the need to find ways of enlarging the possibility of such discussions may well be felt more urgently in the future. In the same way, if the Community finds itself able to take economic decisions, so management and labour will need to find ways of partaking in them.

Thirdly, both regional and agricultural policies are candidates for a European dimension. A major inequality of the time is that which exists between the advanced industrial region and the backward one. National efforts to handle this have so far not been fully effective and will become less so in a period of capital and labour mobility. The technologically advanced company, refused permission to develop in one overcrowded area, will not meekly settle in an underdeveloped region of the same country but move elsewhere within the golden quadrangle if it can. Similarly, the depopulation and impoverishment of some areas matched by the overcrowding of others which may result from the greater possibilities of migration can only be dealt with at a level above that of the member state. A policy of regional development in priority agricultural areas is of especial importance in relieving the problem of agricultural backwardness through the financial assistance which it could provide for medium- and small-sized firms willing to establish themselves therein to absorb surplus farm labour, allied with the resources of the agricultural and social funds to give incentives to workers to leave the land, rationalize holdings and prepare themselves for alternative employment.

The growth and speed of modern communications, too, will surely compel international action to deal with the noise of the jet, the siting of airports and the pollution of international rivers and maritime waters. Whilst some of these questions may be settled by international agreement of the traditional sort, many of them require highly controversial value judgments concerning the quality of life and responsibility for the cost of socially adequate policies. They appear to be of greater complexity than those involved in running the international postal system and to require political decision.

To argue the case in practical terms is not, however, enough. The essential distinction of social policy in the modern state is its acceptance of the worth of the individual and the promotion of his welfare. This is the quality that differentiates it from activities designed to promote economic growth or protect internal peace and order. The ability of the European Economic Community to develop social policy in this sense depends on Arts. 117 and 118 of the Treaty of Rome, whose weakness and ambiguity suggest that the full acceptance of this moral principle is still in an embryonic state. It may be argued that this is no more than a reflection of the relative weakness of international institutions generally in the field of human welfare. However, some direct recognition of the needs of individuals can be traced at least through the minority treaties, the creation of the ILO and the more recent protection of human rights, and it has already been seen that the European Communities were given a limited power to protect welfare directly. The credibility of the Communities to be more than an example of traditional international co-operation in the social field must depend upon the extent to which they pursue welfare goals, not only because it is necessary but also because it is right. This must raise the question of filling out the treaty so that social welfare objectives clearly exist. To put it in another way, more precise terminology is required in order to give an effective base for the pursuit of the aspirations of Arts. 117 and 118. Parliament and the Commission have contributed to this task through their discussions of the meaning of Art. 117, in which stress was laid on the inter-relationship of social and economic ends and on the belief that economic growth is neither an end in itself nor a phenomenon which automatically brings social progress in its train.[45] The multiplicity of immediate social goals arising from the implementation of the treaty and from the application of other Community policies has to be given coherence and identity through the pursuit of '*égalisation dans le progrès*' which alone can give purpose to the creation of the material wealth of which the Community is so proud. Limited objectives have their place but there are difficulties in pursuing one social benefit in isolation from another and a sense of overall policy is also required.

It would be helpful if it were made clearer that the social concern of the European Communities is with the whole of the population and not just the working members of it; there could then be no question but that the needs of the sick, the elderly or other disadvantaged groups are properly its concern. It is not really feasible to draw an effective dividing line between the workers and the rest of the population in relation to needs. Early attempts by governments to provide for the security of the worker quickly brought social security systems up against the question of family support and of the care of the worker in old age. The provision of health care and of public education was similarly linked with the evolution of the demands made upon the labour force, so that the well-being of the community and the welfare of its citizens have in practice become indistinguishable. It is relevant that such a high proportion of the money channelled through the social fund quickly came to the support of the handicapped, for there is no logical distinction to be drawn between those who have difficulty in finding work because of physical disability and those hit by the manifestations of technical change such as closures, mergers and rationalizations. All are casualties and the same principle should be applied generally through the open recognition of the needs of the whole community. A treaty which makes this distinction is artificial in conception and frustrating to operate.

The past has shown the existence of other blemishes. Their removal, in the light of the great problems which face European social development, seems small enough. A clarification and strengthening of the procedures of international standard-setting under Art. 118 is required.

This is most practical in the field of working conditions which are closely regulated everywhere but where investigation has shown that regulation leads to different results. Where the problem is to all intents and purposes the same one there is little reason, from the human point of view, for the continuation of such differences, and this can most easily be seen in matters such as the limitation of the number of hours worked by young people, the protection of the pregnant woman against dismissal from work or guarding the exposure of workers to harmful materials. Harmonization at the level of the highest should indeed be the aim in appropriate circumstances, although it is recognized that the application of this principle in less easily defined fields, although part of the process of integration, is bound to be a gradual and long-term process. New forms of employment bring new health and safety hazards, so that premature death and disability are not problems to be dismissed as having been the products of nineteenth-century capitalism but current social ills. If European society is to evolve common features as shown in its industrial processes and its urbanization and environmental pressures, it seems illogical that the citizens of Europe should not enjoy common protection against the adverse effects of these developments. The arguments produced to justify the suppression of Commission recommendations on relatively minor matters such as maternity protection have been those of cost or the difficulty of application for small employers and the adverse effects on those for whom help is intended by making them more difficult to employ. There is nothing new in these arguments. They are the ones which have traditionally been advanced and their acceptance would have meant the absence of any social progress at all. Where the imposition of controls causes genuine difficulty there is more of a case for providing help in finding solutions than in abandoning the policies of improvement.

The ambiguities surrounding a common occupational training policy have served no helpful purpose. The greater effectiveness of the European labour market and the demand for similar types of skills over a wide area suggest that there will be growing pressures towards similar trainings, but so far Community attempts to develop training facilities have not been given much support. It may be that the reformed social fund will be able to develop schemes which will show whether a stronger European base has in practice the value that logic suggests is the case. The development of the exchange programme for young people can also be suggested here as a further need if social goals are to be taken seriously.

None of these measures, however, is adequate to fill the gaps. There seems no alternative but to ask for an amendment of the treaty, or its supplementation, to enable specific goals in the fields of health, education, housing and welfare to be pursued and which would be subject to the same procedures for sanction as any other binding obligation of the treaty. Practical advance is more likely through setting targets in defined areas and meeting them over a period in new and expanding fields. Such objectives should include the duty of the Commission to undertake research work to identify the major problems and establish priorities, the obligation for it to submit proposals for action by the Council within an allotted timespan as has been used for other policies and the agreement by members that a proportion of the budget should be used for social ends. Such reforms entail both tighter national obligation to pursue social policies at home and the development of direct Community policies themselves to ensure that resources are in fact devoted to the pursuit of social goals. The example previously cited will suffice to suggest the difficulties. Despite her relatively high *per capita* wealth both infant and neo-natal mortality rates in West Germany have persistently remained the second highest amongst the original six members of the Community. Whilst this shows how inadequate it is to judge social progress in purely financial terms, it also raises highly complex questions of causality, including the distribution of wealth, access to and organization of health care and general inequalities in German society. Whilst the disparities shown by quantitative measures can obviously be used as indications of where special effort may be needed in particular countries, the very use of a *relative* index means that comparable effort in other members would be better directed into other spheres. It seems more appropriate for the EEC to think in terms of developmental policies which can be pursued by a variety of means and at several levels of political authority than to assume that the consequence of increased European responsibility in social affairs implies the application of rigid, detailed rules in every particular or the superficial judgement of national social policies against quantitative measures. In social affairs it is often essential to break down national statistics into component features to discover where the weaknesses really lie, and this is a further reason for the advocacy of strengthening the Commission's research work and its ability to work closely with non-governmental authorities.

Such a programme of social goals is a modest one. It does not expect the Community to be a more radical entity than its members by asking states to undertake activity which is novel or more far-reaching in its implications than that to which they are already committed. It does, however, suggest that social goals can no longer be fully achieved within the national context, that national endeavours can be stimulated and enlivened by being considered at the supra-national level and that national neglect of social responsibilities may be remedied both by the spotlight of international concern and by international help.

Reform of the treaty system needs to embrace three other factors. It is impossible to fulfil such an important and far-reaching objective as levelling upwards without giving the European Communities sufficiently powerful instruments to work towards it. The question of financial aid to enable the Community to pursue social goals by encouraging certain developments or establishing experimental schemes is an obvious one. Whether the scale of independent financing currently agreed on will be adequate to allow it to make a significant impact in the social field remains for the future. The past, however, shows very clearly that the High Authority was immensely assisted by its capacity to contribute to housing schemes, to research projects on industrial health and safety and to schemes to protect the unemployed. In contrast the work of the Commission was impeded by its lack of financial resources. Its work was hamstrung by the fact that, although it was able to define needs such as that for more training centres, the employment of social workers or housing provision for migrants, it was unable to do anything about them. Thus the willingness to allow the Commission a degree of control over income in order to pursue objectives which necessarily cannot be defined too precisely seems essential, and this cannot be divorced from the problem of formal controls of a supervisory and inspectoral nature. The previous system of *post facto* grants from the social fund was unsatisfactory to ensure preventive work, to influence objectives, to enhance the value of the work in operation or to assess its worth, but national experiences suggest that methods of supervision, ranging from an inspectorate to financial checks, are essential means whereby central governments in fact ensure that social measures are developed in a broadly acceptable direction and the same principle requires application for the EEC. One wonders, too, if more could be done to ensure that individuals in practice benefit from the provisions of the Treaty of Rome by the introduction of a system which allows the Community to participate in informal solutions in particular cases such as allegations of discrimination against migrants or against women with regard to pay rather than allowing the Community to shelter behind the principle that it is for members to ensure the application of the treaty rules. Recent Parliamentary questions on social problems have too often received the reply either that the Community has no responsibility for the subject or that enforcement of standards is a matter for state administrations. Examples include the abuse of child labour in Sicily, discovered by a delegation of the Social Affairs and Public Health Committee, the impossibility of Community intervention under Art. 118 in cases of industrial conflict, the inability of the EEC to adopt measures to combat drug-taking, to control illegal work done by the children of migrants, to prevent the employment of fourteen-year-old Dutch girls across the border in Germany resulting from a disparity in school leaving ages and at variance with the Commission's recommendation on the employment of young people, to interfere in the use of undesirable methods of employing labour in Italy allowing employers to avoid paying social security contributions or to influence the structure of trade union organization in the multinational firm.[46] Remoteness from the actual course of events is an impediment to effective policy objectives, efficient application thereof and to an appreciation of the contribution of the EEC by the general public.

Inextricably bound up with monetary independence is the need to define the right of initiative of the Commission. There should be no further doubt of its right to investigate, to call for information, to publish studies, to consult experts. The Commission has often been described as the 'guardian' of the treaty and in social policy it seems that it too frequently had to fall back upon this function as its powers of initiation were limited and governments were reluctant they should be exploited.[47] Thus behind the day-to-day work of execution of the treaties there always loomed the unsolved question of the role of the Commission in the growing field of social policy, and the inability to solve this question created a fundamental flaw in the Community's work. The Commission requires to be seen as the source of forward-looking optimism for it is clear that significant progress will rarely be started in the Council of Ministers unless it appears to favour a member's national objectives.[48] Although this indeed was the reason for the early completion of the free movement of labour policy under pressure from the Italian government, in the main it seems more likely to suppose that it will continue to be the Commission, drawing strength from union and Parliamentary support, that is the advocate of more advanced social policies.

The third factor is in some ways the most difficult of all, for it is the need to establish proper channels of communication with all those bodies, at whatever level, which play a part in social policy formation. Despite the efforts made by the Commission to create links with management and labour and with professional organizations, the Community has remained far from the consciousness of most people. Since so much of social policy is concerned with day-to-day events in individual lives, the problem is one of allowing it to make an impact at grass-roots level. Such a direct involvement with social groupings is in conflict with the fundamental principle that it is the states who are the members of the Community. The limitations of the Community's relations to those with members and with the organized interests represented on the Economic and Social Committee is inadequate, whilst the informal development of relations with interest groups able to maintain representation in Brussels does not fill the gap adequately in social affairs. It is particularly important to bypass the hierarchy of institutions, culminating in the nation state, in the field of social policy, which is not the exclusive concern of public authorities, but unfortunately, one of the more difficult tasks for an international institution is to find ways of involving individuals in decision making. This appears, however, to be a basic requirement for an effective social policy in order to meet current aspirations and to evolve viable policies. The Community can probably expect to play only a limited part in this process but just for that reason it should press to the limit those mechanisms of consultation, information and publicity that are open to it. Additionally it needs to come out of its shell by making an effort to meet local people in their own environments. The housing committees[49] which considered the use of High Authority grant-aided property are relevant here as a beginning. All social action with a Community aspect, such as house-building, the running of retraining centres or the payment of benefits, requires the setting-up of local committees to advise, to be consulted and perhaps to share in the administration. The Commission might be represented, if only occasionally, upon such committees. This would help, too, to make the Community's work more widely known, an essential requirement if allegiance is to pass, in some degree, from the state to a European grouping. A mutual sense of commitment is required if the claim to a social policy, in the full sense of the term, is to be substantiated.

> The allegiance of workers to a Europe in the process of being built will depend primarily on whether social legislation can be seen to give expression to the acts of the European Community so as to improve the economic and social situation of all the inhabitants of the Community . . . We believe, in this connection, that the ministers of labour and social affairs, if they were to meet more frequently, could contribute in an important way, to the realisation of a social policy programme.[50]

The achievements of the Communities so far are modest but not negligible. They are perhaps best viewed as the groundwork essential for the increasing momentum in social policy necessary if this is to keep pace with general development. They have often been overlooked because they deal with abstractions; their benefits are widely diffused throughout the area and their recipients may not appreciate that advantages experienced are due to the existence of the European Communities. Greater, and much wider, contact between them and the general public may help with this difficulty also. That it is a problem has been recognized. 'The gradual elimination of discrimination between nationals and workers from other member states is probably less easily discernible by the general public than the gradual elimination of customs duties on motor cars.'[51]

Additionally the canalization of the social urges of ordinary people can be helped by the development of existing institutions and their enlargement to ensure contact with a much wider range of social and occupational groups than has hitherto been possible.[52] A reconsideration of the general powers and of the initiatives and controlling functions of Parliament, the Economic and Social Committee and the advisory committees is required so that, instead of occasional debates in Parliament or reports on specific issues, a constant and steady pressure can be exerted in order to keep social policy active and to ensure that it has its due place in the political process. A broad, democratic base for the Community is an essential prerequisite to allow social policy to surmount extremely complex problems. This task is both large and long term. If one considers the political parties and the trade unions as the two institutions most likely, under existing arrangements, to demand more effective social policies, even they are not fully organized to operate at the European level. Much less is this the case for voluntary social organizations or popular groups. However the greater formalization which this implies encourages an arid institutionalism which alienates many people. This is why the involvement of European institutions themselves with local groupings seems equally important. The proposition may be made that the Community, no less than national governments, needs to join the search for new forms of government more appropriate for the age.

Even supposing limited reforms, the capacity of the European organizations to affect social welfare will remain less than that of national governments; 'In an overall sense, the treaty reserves responsibility for social policy to members.'[53] The sincerity of the Community's social objectives is therefore to some extent shown by its willingness to win the acceptance and support of members for its policies and not to insist upon schemes which can only antagonize them. The Community must also be a catalyst enabling national governments to be quicker and more effective in promoting human welfare at home. Since, however, social policies necessarily require states to take action that otherwise they might not and simultaneously requires the Community to strengthen groupings that governments often find awkward, it seems that the equilibrium established in 1966 is only a postponement, not a solution, of the supra-national issue. At the present time, however, the Community cannot afford to offend members by trying to ride rough-shod over their susceptibilities at the cost of delaying the introduction of beneficial measures. Social policy is a pragmatic exercise which requires to work in those ways best suited to achieve its ends, not a doctrinaire application of the ideology of Europeanization. The subject matter is controversial enough without adding further difficulties. Much of the forward-looking social activity of the executives of the past, such as the housing and readaptation policies, depended upon prior state agreement or upon the willingness of members to take the initial steps by applying for grant aid. In the same way, the study and research programmes required the willingness to co-operate through providing information, allowing experts to be consulted or even through doing work which might otherwise not have been done or done in different ways. It must be remembered that the Commission is still struggling with the collection of basic information in a comparable and usable form. As late as 1969 it was shown that states were not ready to accept definitions and methods of work for census collection which would be standardized over the Community area at the price of upsetting their traditional chronologies.[54] The disparity in national statistics, in the methodology of their collection and the criteria used in the definition of categories is such that it is small wonder the Commission considered that its best results were obtained by its own investigations,[55] but even these may be impeded by states if they withhold their co-operation. The length of the road ahead is indicated by the fact that the Commission is still aiming to obtain a Council decision which will ensure a greater standardization of basic population censuses to be established as far ahead as 1980.[56] The stress on 'transparency' takes on a new importance under such conditions and one becomes aware both of the difficulty and of the extent of the achievement lying behind the studies already completed. In the same way, the Commission will inevitably remain dependent upon receiving adequate and early information of intended legislation and national policy developments for its own work and general guidance to be of good quality.[57]

In practice, therefore, the Community will continue to be in a situation of tension in which it must rely upon the willing help of national states which simultaneously will regard its activities with a degree of suspicion. The goodwill of national governments and their willingness to pursue conforming policies at home, ranging from the full consultation of management and labour to the application of particular safety precautions in the mines, is essential. This fact gives the Commission a highly diplomatic role, for it needs to involve itself more closely in the real stuff of social policy and the activities of institutions prosecuting it without treading too hard on the sensitivities of states whose goodwill it also requires. The Community cannot just be interested in the alignment and development of social policies because this is necessary for its own reasons; if its concern with social improvement is genuine then it has to be ready to use whatever agents lie to hand to ensure it. In practice this means that the Community is in the hands of governments and is reliant upon their goodwill and co-operation. The growth of a European social policy, in the sense of the practical application of particular rules, will depend for a long time largely upon the willingness of states to align their policies in conformity with each other. There is no place, either, for the Community to stand upon its dignity for reasons of prestige and to insist upon Community solutions. If it is easier to obtain social goals through measures of inter-state co-operation such as the signature of instruments under the Council of Europe, then this must be accepted as a perfectly acceptable alternative to Community solutions. Intergovernmental co-operation may not be the sole method of achieving social progress but it seems likely to remain an important one for the foreseeable future even if it is less effective than Community procedures.[58] The first twenty years of the Communities' life span suggest that the habit of substituting Community for inter-governmental decisions was not established in social affairs. The work on reciprocity in social security under the ECSC, the rush over the introduction of the equal pay policy, the procedures for the help given to the Italian sulphur mines, the reluctance to accept the occupational training policy are all examples of this.

An effective Community role in the promotion of social welfare implies blurring of national responsibility for decisions. This may simply mean the willingness to discuss problems with state partners and with the Commission as under Art. 118, it may mean the need to adapt national procedures according to the wider interest as in some alignment of vocational training schemes, or it may mean the acceptance of decisions which will alter national structures in unwanted ways as in the equal pay commitment. Although some forms of action hurt more than others, none are painless. The conclusion of this study is that the time has come to take a further step towards a European social policy through allowing final determination on a wider range of issues to lie with the European institutions, however much it may be possible to disguise the fact by an emphasis on the alignment of national policies and by the sensitivity to the national interest possessed by the Council. Otherwise the challenge of *'égalisation dans le progrès'* is too daunting and at some future point it will become clear that social goals have gone by default. This question cannot be solved, however, in isolation from the future development of the Community as a whole. The growth of common policies requires recognition that it is an organization with larger objectives of social progress than the specific points written into the treaties in the 1950s. This is only to say that social policy is inextricably part of the future nature of the Community. If it is to level off on the plateau of a free trade area, albeit a complex and intimate one, its social activities will find it difficult to be more than the marginal adjustments made necessary to cushion the changes its creation has brought and to pursue international co-operation in social affairs in the traditional way. If, however, the Community is concerned to achieve political unity it is inconceivable that it could operate without acceptance of the social functions of modern government which both express and give deeper meaning to the human group from which it comes. In the end one is left with a sense that the instinct of the Commission to return to the need for moral purpose has been sound. Social policy is not, and never has been, solely about reciprocity in social security or the financing of adult training centres but about the nature of society itself, as the Commission recognized so clearly in its report for 1965–6.

> We must know how we wish to live in this new economic area and what future we desire. It is not only a matter of working out 'European' solutions to our economic problems. We must find a satisfactory

answer to the problems posed by the rapid evolution of the society in which we are living and by the greater responsibilities which the Community will assume towards the rest of the world.

Source Material

I *Publications Generally Consulted*

ECSC *Bulletin*
EEC *Bulletin*
European Communities Commission *Bulletin* (This replaced the two previous bulletins on 1 Jan 1968 and references to it are to Bulletin only)
European Community
Journal Officiel
Assemblée Parlementaire Européene (afterwards Parlement Européen) *Débats*

II *Unsigned Articles from Bulletins*

ECSC 'Merger Treaty' *Bulletin* No. 56 (1965)
EEC 'A Common Occupational Training Policy' *Bulletin* No. 12 (1961)
EEC 'The right of establishment and the freedom to supply services' *Bulletin* No. 12 (1961)
EEC 'Proposed regulations and directive on freedom of establishment in agriculture and aid to farmers to change occupations' *Bulletin* No. 3 (1965) Supplement
EEC 'Proposals regulations of 1965 for reform of European Social Fund' *ibid.*
EEC 'Proposals for measures to assist redundant Italian sulphur-mine workers' *Bulletin* No. 5 (1965) Supplement
EEC 'Guide Lines for the EEC Commission's work in the social sector' *Bulletin* No. 2 (1967)
European Communities Commission 'How the Community's social policies are related to other policies' *Bulletin* No. 6 (1969)
European Communities Commission 'Preliminary guidelines for a Community social policy programme' *Bulletin* Annex, No. 4 (1971) Supplement 2/71

III *Parlement Européen*

1 SESSIONS
1961–2 IV/62 No. 48 'Social Harmonization. Free movement'
1965–6 I/66 No. 82 'Debate on social situation. European conference on social security'
1965–6 III/66 No. 83 'Protection young workers. Compensation for industrial diseases'
1966–7 III/67 No. 89 'European social policy. Prevention industrial accidents'
1967–8 X/67 No. 94 'President Rey's speech 20 September 1967'
1971–2 No. 140 'Social situation in 1970'
      No. 146 'Social situation in 1971'
1972–3 No. 150 'Social situation in 1971'

2 DOCUMENTS
'Rapport intérimaire fait au nom de la Commission sociale sur l'égalisation des salaires masculine et féminins' Session 1961–2, *Doc. 68*
'Rapport fait au nom de la Commission sociale sur l'harmonisation social'

Session 1961–2, *Doc. 87*
'Rapport fait au nom de la Commission sociale sur les résultats des missions d'étude effectuées dans les pays de la Communauté en vue d'étudier les problèmes particulière de la libre circulation' Session 1963–4, *Doc. 118*
'Rapport fait au nom de la Commission sociale sur l'application des dispositions sociales prévues à l'article 118 du traité instituant la CEE' Session 1965–6, *Doc. 60*
'Rapport fait au nom de la Commission sociale conçernant l'exposé de la Commission de la CEE sur l'évolution de la situation sociale dans la Communauté en 1964' Session 1965–6, *Doc. 101*
'Rapport fait au nom de la Commission sociale sur les programmes d'action de la Commission de la CEE en matière de politique commune de formation professionnelle en général et dans l'agriculture' Session 1966–7, *Doc. 3*
'Rapport fait au nom de la Commission sociale sur les suites données par les Etats membres à la Recommandation de la Commission de la CEE concernant l'activité des services sociaux à l'égard des travailleurs se déplaçant dans la Communauté' Session 1966–7, *Doc. 11*
'Rapport complémentaire sur les propositions modifiées de la Commission de la CEE au Conseil relatives aux mesures particulières d'ordre social à prendre en faveur des travailleurs italiens licenciés des mines de soufre' Session 1966–7, *Doc. 45*
'Rapport fait au nom de la Commission sociale sur l'exposé de la Commission de la CEE sur l'évolution de la situation sociale dans la Communauté en 1965' Session 1966–7, *Doc. 130*
'Rapport fait au nom de la Commission de la protection sanitaire sur les problèmes de la prévention des accidents du travail dans la Communauté Session 1966–7, *Doc. 155*
'Rapport fait au nom de la Commission sociale sur les perspectives de la politique sociale européenne à la suite de la session du Conseil de ministres du 19 December 1966' Session 1966–7, *Doc. 171*
'Rapport fait au nom de la Commission de la protection sanitaire sur l'état actuel des travaux de la Commission de la CEE relatifs à l'application du droit d'établissement aux activités relevant de la santé' Session 1967–8, *Doc. 1*
'Rapport fait au nom de la Commission des affaires sociales et de la santé publique sur la communication de la Commission de la CEE au Conseil conçernant les lignes directives des travaux de la Commission dans le secteur des affaires sociales' Session 1967–8, *Doc. 138*
'Rapport fait au nom de la Commission des affaires sociales et de la santé publique sur l'application du principe de l'égalité des rémunérations entre les travailleurs masculins et féminins' Session 1968–9, *Doc. 26*
'Rapport fait au nom de la Commission de affaires sociales et de la santé publique sur l'exposé de la Commission de Communautés européenes sur l'évolution de la situation sociale dans la Communauté en 1967' Session 1968–9, *Doc. 57*

IV *Press and Information Service of the European Communities Community Topics*

No. 2 'Economic integration and political unity in Europe'
No. 6 'The right of establishment and the supply of services'
No. 11 'How the European Economic Community's Institutions work'
No. 15 'Initiative 1964'
No. 18 'Social Security in the European Community'
No. 20 'Sociale Policy in the ECSC'
No. 33 'Regional Policy in an integrated Europe'
Labor in the European Community. No. 11 (January 1966)
The Common Market (1961)
The Common Market and the Common Man (4th ed. 1972)

v *European Economic Community*

1 COMMISSION
1st to 10th General Reports on the Activities of the Community (periodical reports continued from 1967 by Commission of the European Communities, see section VIII)
Exposé sur l'évolution de la situation sociale dans la Communauté en . . . (annuel)
Les Problèmes de main-d'oeuvre dans la Communauté (annuel)
Memorandum of the Commission on the Action Programme of the Community for the second stage (24 October 1962)
'Rapport de la Commission au Conseil sur l'état d'application de l'article 119 au 30 June 1963' *Doc.* v/COM (64) 11 final
Direction Generale des Affaires Sociales 'Synthèse des rapports établis en 1960 sur la situation actuelle du service sociale des travailleurs migrants dans les six pays membres de la CEE' *Doc.* v/56641/1/60f
'Deuxième Rapport sur les suites données à la recommandation de la Commission aux états membres conçernant l'activité des services sociaux à l'égard des travailleurs se déplaçant dans la Communauté' *Doc.* 15157/v/67f
Commission Administrative pour la sécurité sociale des travailleurs migrants *Rapports* (annuels)

2 ETUDES: SERIE POLITIQUE SOCIALE
No. 1 'La formation professionnelle des jeunes dans les entreprises industrielles etc.' (1963)
No. 3 'Etudes sur la physionomie actuelle de la sécurité sociale dans les pays de la CEE' (1962)
No. 4 'Etude comparée des prestations de sécurité sociale dans les pays de la CEE' (1962)
No. 5 'Financement de la sécurité sociale dans les pays de la CEE' (1962)
No. 10 'Les salaries dans les branches d'industries . . .' (1965)
No. 11 'Etude comparative des normes législatives régissant la protection des jeunes travailleurs dans les pays membres de la CEE' (1966)
No. 12 'Les salaires dans les branches d'industries . . .' (1966)
No. 13 'La protection de la maternité dans les six pays de la CEE' (1966)
No. 21 'The Economic Impact of Social Security' (1971)

3 ECONOMIC AND SOCIAL COMMITTEE OF THE EEC
Rapport de la section spécialisée pour les questions sociales sur la 'Proposition de la Commission de la Communauté Economique Européene relative à l'établissement de principes généraux pour la mise en oeuvre d'une politique commune de formation professionnelle' CES/60/62/rb (17 February 1962)
'Opinion of Economic and Social Committee on the free movement of labour' *Journal Officiel* No. 298 (1967)

4 SIGNED ARTICLES, SPEECHES ETC. PUBLISHED BY OR CIRCULATED UNDER THE AUSPICES OF THE EEC
A Coppé 'The Social Horizon for 1980' *Bulletin* (1971) No. 1
Hans von der Groeben 'Approximation of Legislation: The Policy of the Commission of the European Communities' Address to Parliament (27 November 1969) offprint
L. Levi-Sandri 'The free movement of workers in the countries of the European Economic Community' EEC *Bulletin* (1961) No. 6
'The European Social Fund: the first phase' EEC *Bulletin* (1963) No. 3
'Réalisations et perspectives de la politique sociale de la CEE' reprint of speech to Parliament (24 November 1965)
Address to Quatrième Conférence Européenne des Syndicats Chrétiens, Amsterdam (October 1966) duplicated

'Les Aspects Sociaux du Marché Commun' Speech at Nice (21 March 1967)
'Pour une politique sociale moderne dans la Communauté Européenne'
reprint of speech to Parliament (13 March 1968)
'Free Movement of Workers in the European Community' *Bulletin* (1968)
No. 11
Discours to fifty-third session of the Conférence Internationale du Travail,
Geneva (17 June 1969)
J. Neirinck 'Social policy of the EE Commission. A general survey. Achieve-
ments and trends at the end of 1967' speech delivered at the University of
Louvain (December 1967) duplicated
G. Petrilli 'The Social Policy of the Commission' EEC *Bulletin* (1959) No. 2
L. Rosenberg 'The Activities and Importance of the Economic and Social
Committee' EEC *Bulletin* (1961) No. 3
F. Vinck 'L'action des Communautés européennes en faveur de l'harmonisation
de la formation professionnelle' speech to l'Institut européen pour la formation
professionnelle, Strasbourg (9 October 1968) Commission v/16357/68f

VI *European Communities Statistical Office*

'CEE. Salaires masculins et féminins' *Informations Statistiques* (1961) No. 1
'Coûts de la main-d'oeuvre CEE 1959' *ibid.* (1961) No. 3
'Revenus des ouvriers CEE 1959' *ibid.* (1962) No. 3
'Salaires CEE 1960' *ibid.* (1963) No. 1
'Salaires CEE 1961' *ibid.* (1964) No. 2
'Salaires CEE 1962' *ibid.* (1964) No. 5
'Salaires CEE 1963' *ibid.* (1965) No. 6
'Salaires CEE 1964' *ibid.* (1966) No. 5
'Budgets Familiaux 1963/4' *Statistiques Sociales* Série Spéciale (1966/7)

VII *Joint Publication of the European Communities*

CEE, CECA and Euratom *Conférence européenne sur la sécurité* Vols. I and II
(1962)

VIII *Commission of the European Communities*

General Report on the Activities of the Communities
Exposé sur l'évolution de la situation sociale dans la Communauté en . . .
(annuel)
*Exposé annuel sur les activités d'orientation professionnelle dans la Com-
munauté* (1967, 1968)
Les Problèmes de main-d'oeuvre dans la Communauté (annuel)
La Libre circulation de la main-d'oeuvre et les marchés du travail dans la CEE
(annuel)
Tableaux Comparatifs des Régimes de Sécurité Sociale 7th ed. (1972)
Occupational Rehabilitation and Placement of the Disabled (1971)

IX *Major Regulations, Directives, Recommendations*

1 REGULATIONS
No. 3 'Social Security for migrants' *Journal Officiel* No. 30 (1958)
No. 4 'Social Security for migrants' *Journal Officiel* No. 30 (1958)
Minor amendments to Regulations 3 and 4 *Journal Officiel* Nos. 42 and 52
(1961) and No. 9 (1962)
No. 9 'Social Fund' *Journal Officiel* No. 56 (1960)
No. 15 'Free movement of workers' *Journal Officiel* No. 57 (1961)
No. 16 'Amendments to Social Security' *Journal Officiel* No. 6 (1962)

No. 18/62/CEE 'Free movement entertainers' *Journal Officiel* No. 23 (1962)

No. 8/63/CEE 'Amendments to Social Security' *Journal Officiel* No. 28 (1963)

No. 35/63/CEE 'Family allowances for workers temporarily abroad' *Journal Officiel* No. 62 (1963)

No. 36/63/CEE 'Social Security for frontier workers' *Journal Officiel* No. 62 (1963)

No. 47/63/CEE 'Amendments to Social Fund' *Journal Officiel* No. 86 (1963)

No. 73/63/CEE 'Social Security amendments for seasonal and temporary workers' *Journal Officiel* No. 112 (1963)

No. 113/63/CEE 'Procedures for aid from Social Fund' *Journal Officiel* No. 153 (1963)

No. 130/63/CEE 'Amendments to social security' *Journal Officiel* No. 188 (1963)

No. 1/64/CEE 'Amendments to family allowances payments' *Journal Officiel* No. 1 (1964)

No. 2/64/CEE 'Social Security for frontier and seasonal workers' *Journal Officiel* No. 5 (1964)

No. 3/64/CEE 'Amendments to Social Security' *Journal Officiel* No. 5 (1964)

No. 7/64/CEE 'Definition of communes at French frontier' *Journal Officiel* No. 18 (1964)

No. 12/64/CEE 'Definition of prolonged unemployment for Social Fund rules' *Journal Officiel* No. 32 (1964)

No. 24/64/CEE 'Social Security for temporary workers' *Journal Officiel* No. 47 (1964)

No. 38/64/CEE 'Free movement' *Journal Officiel* No. 62 (1964)

No. 108/64/CEE 'Amendments to Social Security' *Journal Officiel* No. 127 (1964)

No. 188/64/CEE 'Organisation of inquiry into wage rates' *Journal Officiel* No. 214 (1964)

No. 80/65/CEE 'Amendments to Social Security' *Journal Officiel* No. 111 (1965)

No. 109/65/CEE 'Amendments to Social Security' *Journal Officiel* No. 125 (1965)

No. 117/65/CEE 'Definition of communes for free movement purposes' *Journal Officiel* No. 139 (1965)

No. 37/67/CEE 'Amendments to Social Fund' *Journal Officiel* No. 33 (1967)

No. 47/67/CEE 'Application of Social Security to seamen' *Journal Officiel* No. 44 (1967)

No. 1612/68/CEE 'Free movement of labour' *Journal Officiel* No. L257 (1968)

Nos. 2396/71/CEE, 2397/71/CEE and 2398/71/CEE 'New rules for Social Fund' *Journal Officiel* No. L249 (1971)

2 DIRECTIVES

Un-numbered 'Migrant labour' *Journal Officiel* No. 80 (1961)

Nos. 63/261/CEE and 63/262/CEE 'Free establishment in agriculture' *Journal Officiel* No. 63 (1963)

No. 63/340/CEE 'Lifting restrictions on payments for services' *Journal Officiel* No. 86 (1963)

Nos. 64/222/CEE, 64/223/CEE and 64/224/CEE 'Free establishment and supply of services in various intermediary activities in industry, commerce, crafts' *Journal Officiel* No. 56 (1964)

Nos. 64/220/CEE and 64/221/CEE 'General suppression of restrictions' *Journal Officiel* No. 56 (1964)

Nos. 64/240/CEE and 64/241/CEE 'Removal of restrictions on stay of workers and families. Also opinion of Economic and Social Committee' *Journal Officiel* No. 62 (1964)

Nos. 64/427/CEE, 64/428/CEE and 64/429/CEE 'Free establishment in various occupations' *Journal Officiel* No. 117 (1964)

No. 65/1/CEE 'Free supply of services in agriculture and horticulture' *Journal Officiel* No. 1 (1965)

No. 65/65/CEE 'Supply of branded pharmaceuticals' *Journal Officiel* No. 22 (1965)

No. 67/43/CEE 'Free establishment in various occupations' *Journal Officiel* No. 10 (1967)

No. 67/548/CEE 'Classification, labelling etc., of certain dangerous substances' *Journal Officiel* No. 196 (1967)

Nos. 67/530/CEE, 67/531/CEE and 67/532/CEE 'Free establishment in agriculture, access to credit and other facilities' *Journal Officiel* No. 190 (1967)

No. 67/654/CEE 'Free establishment in forestry etc.' *Journal Officiel* No. 263 (1967)

No. 68/360/CEE 'Free movement of labour' *Journal Officiel* No. L257 (1968)

3 RECOMMENDATIONS

Un-numbered 'Social workers for migrants' *Journal Officiel* No. 75 (1962)

Un-numbered 'Industrial medical services' *Journal Officiel* No. 80 (1962)

Un-numbered 'Adoption of standard European list of industrial diseases' *Journal Officiel* No. 80 (1962)

No. 64/412/CEE 'Import of educational material duty free' *Journal Officiel* No. 112 (1964)

No. 65/379/CEE 'Housing for migrants' *Journal Officiel* No. 137 (1965)

No. 65/428/CEE 'Notification of national legislation' *Journal Officiel* No. 160 (1965)

No. 66/462/CEE 'Compensation for industrial diseases' *Journal Officiel* No. 147 (1966)

No. 66/464/CEE 'Medical services for workers exposed to special risks' *Journal Officiel* No. 151 (1966)

No. 66/484/CEE 'Development of vocational guidance services' *Journal Officiel* No. 154 (1966)

No. 67/125/CEE 'Protection of young workers' *Journal Officiel* No. 25 (1967)

X   *Miscellaneous*

'Statute of the committee of the European Social Fund' *Journal Officiel* No. 56 (1960)

'General programme for free establishment and supply of services policy' *Journal Officiel* No. 2 (1962)

'Decision of Council 2 April 1963 on the general principles of occupational training' *Journal Officiel* No. 63 (1963)

European Court Case 6/67. Guerra v. Institut national d'assurance maladie-invalidité. Recueil de la jurisprudence de la Cour, Vol. XIII-3 (1967)

Decision 71/66/CEE 'Reform of Social Fund' *Journal Officiel* No. L28 (1971)

Bibliography

I Books, Studies and Reports

L'Année Politique Paris (annuel)

S. Barzanti *The Under-developed Areas within the Common Market* Princeton, Princeton University Press (1965)

W. Böhning *The Migration of Workers in the United Kingdom and the European Community* London, OUP (1972)

R. Broad and R. Jarrett *Community Europe Today* London, Oswald Wolf (1972)

W. H. Hartley Clark *The Politics of the Common Market* Englewood Cliffs, Prentice Hall (1967)

Commissariat Général du Plan d'équipment et de la productivité, France (1961) *Rapport du Commission des Prestations Sociales sur Vth plan* (unclassified and undated)

D. Coombes *Politics and Bureaucracy in the European Community* London, Allen and Unwin (1970)

J. P. Corbett *Europe and the Social Order* Leyden, Sythoff (1959)

Council of Europe *Social Services for Migrant Workers* (1968)

— *Study of Governmental Administrations dealing with Social Problems* (1968)

— *European Social Charter* Treaty Series No. 35

— *European Code of Social Security* Treaty Series No. 48

J. F. Deniau *The Common Market* London, Barrie and Rockliff 3rd ed. (1962)

D. Donnison *The Development of Social Administration* (an inaugural lecture) London (1962)

J. Doublet and G. Lavau *Sécurité Sociale* Paris, Presses Universitaires de France (1961)

Droit Social Paris (January 1968, November 1971)

Eire Government *Report of the Inter-Departmental Committee on Retraining and Resettlement in Relation to the European Social Fund* Dublin (undated)

L. Erhard *Prosperity through Competition* London, Thames and Hudson (1958)

European Journal of Sociology 2, 2 (1961)

M. Fitzgerald *The Common Market's Labor Programs* Notre Dame Ind., University of Notre Dame Press (1966)

J. Follows *Antecedents of the International Labour Organisation* Oxford, Clarendon Press (1951)

S. Graubard (ed.) *A new Europe* Boston, Houghton Mifflin (1964)

W. D. Halls *Society, Schools and Progress in France* Oxford, Pergamon Press (1965)

E. B. Haas *Beyond the Nation State* Stanford, Stanford University Press (1964)

— *The Uniting of Europe* London, Stevens (1958)

S. Holt *The Common Market, conflict of theory and practice* London, H. Hamilton (1967)

ILO 'Post-War Trends in Social Security' reprinted from *International Labour Review* LIX, 6 and LX, 1-3 (1949)

— *Approaches to Social Security* Studies and Reports. Series M (Social Insurance) No. 18, Geneva, 5th impression (1953)

— *Social Aspects of European Economic Co-operation* Geneva (1956)

— *The Cost of Social Security, 1961–3* Geneva (1967)

— *The Cost of Social Security, 1964–6* Geneva (1971)

C. W. Jenks *Social Justice in the Law of Nations* London, OUP for RIIA (1970)
U. Kitzinger *The Challenge of the Common Market* Oxford, Blackwell (1961 ed.)
W. Russell Lewis *Rome or Brussels* London, Institute of Economic Affairs (1971)
L. Lindberg *The Political Dynamics of European Economic Integration* Stanford, Stanford University Press (1963)
E. Luard (ed.) *The Evolution of International Organisations* London, Thames and Hudson (1966)
D. McLachlan and D. Swann *Competition Policy in the European Community* London, OUP (1967)
OECD *Employment of Women* Report of Regional Trade Union Seminar, Paris 26–29 November 1968 (1970)
M. Palmer and J. Lambert (eds.) *European Unity* London, Allen and Unwin (1968)
PEP *Regional Development in the European Economic Community* London, Allen and Unwin (1962)
P. Reuter *Organisations Européennes* Paris, Presses Universitaires de France (1965)
J. J. Ribas *La Politique Sociale des Communautés Européennes* Paris, Dalloz (1969)
B. Rodgers *Comparative Social Administration* London, Allen and Unwin, 2nd ed. (1971)
W. Röpke *The Social Crisis of our Time* London, William Hodge & Co. (1950)
Royal Institute of International Affairs, Chatham House: PEP European Series
    No. 1 D. Swann and D. McLachlan *Concentration or Competition. A European Dilemma*
    No. 5 G. Denton *Planning in the EEC*
    No. 6 D. Dosser and S. Han *Taxes in the EEC and Britain: The Problem of Harmonization*
    No. 7 D. Coombes *Towards a European Civil Service*
    No. 8 R. Mayne *The Institution of the European Community*
    No. 9 Action Committee for the United States of Europe *Statements and Declarations, 1955–67*
    No. 10 R. Colin Beever *Trade Unions and free labour movement in the EEC*
A. Sampson *The New Europeans* London, Hodder and Stoughton (1968)
A. Shonfield *Modern Capitalism* London, OUP (1965)
A. Spinelli *The Eurocrats: Conflict and Crisis in the European Community* Baltimore, John Hopkins Press (1966)
A. Thomas *International Social Policy* Geneva (1948)
L-E. Troclet *Eléments de Droit Social Européen* Brussels, Institut de Sociologie de l'Université Libre de Bruxelles (1963)
— *Legislation Sociale Internationale* Brussels, Institut de Sociologie de l'Université Libre de Bruxelles (1963)
L'Union des Industries de la Communauté Européenne *L'Industrie Européenne face à l'Intégration Economique et Sociale* (1966)
UK Government *Convention between UK, Belgium, France, Luxembourg, Netherlands* Cmd. 7911 (1950)
— *Convention on Social and Medical Assistance between the Brussels Treaty Powers* Cmd. 7973 (1950)
— *European Interim Agreement on Social Security schemes for old age, invalidity and survivors benefits* Cmd. 9510 (1955)
— *European Interim Agreement on Social Security other than schemes for old age, invalidity and survivors benefits* Cmd. 9511 (1955)
— *European Convention on Social and Medical Assistance* Cmd. 9512 (1955)
— *European Communities Secondary Legislation* (1972)
United Nations European Social Development Programme
— 'Seminar on the problems and methods of social welfare planning' France (September 1970)
— A. Hannequart (First Counsellor to the State Bureau of Economic Programming, Brussels) *The Scope of Social Welfare Planning* UN/SOA/SEM/37/WP1
— *Final Report* SOA/EDSP/1970/3
— *Methods of Social Welfare Administration* (1950) E/CN.5/224
D. W. Urwin *Western Europe since 1945* London, Longman (1968)

H. C. Wallich *Mainsprings of the German Revival* New Haven, Yale University Press (1955)
G. Williams *Apprenticeship in Europe* London, Chapman and Hall (1963)
F. Roy Willis *France, Germany and the New Europe, 1945–67* London, OUP (1968)
— *Italy chooses Europe* London, New York OUP (1971)
D. Zöllner *Social Legislation in the Federal Republic of Germany* Bad Godesberg, Asgard-Verlag (1964 ed.)

II   *Periodicals, Newspapers Generally Consulted other than Community Sources*

Industry and Labour
International Labour Review
Journal of Common Market Studies
Agence Presse Europe
The Times

III   *Signed Articles*

E. D. Brown 'International Social Law in Europe' *Yearbook of World Affairs* London (1965)
E. D. Brown 'Recent Developments in the Social Policy of the European Economic Community' *Common Market Law Review* (1965–6)
A. Campa 'The Organisation of General and Vocational Education in France' *International Labour Review* Vol. 82 (1960)
R. W. Cox 'Social and Labour Policy in the EEC' *British Journal of Industrial Relations* Vol. 1 (1963)
H. Creutz 'The ILO and Social Security for foreign and migrant workers' *International Labour Review* Vol. 97 (1967)
K. Dahlberg 'The EEC Commission and the Politics of the Free Movement of Labour' *Journal of Common Market Studies* Vol. 6 (1968)
J. W. D. Davies 'Immigrants in Germany' *Child Care Quarterly Review of the National Council of Voluntary Child Care Organisations* Vol. 23 (1969)
L. Erhard 'Policy statement on assuming office as Federal Chancellor' *German Economic Review* Vol. 1 (1963)
E. B. Haas 'System and Process in the International Labour Organisation' *World Politics* Vol. LIV (1962)
O. Kahn-Freund 'Social Policy and the Common Market' *Political Quarterly* Vol. 32 (1961)
P. Laroque and A. Zelenka 'International Balance in Social Security Costs' *International Labour Review* Vol. 68 (1953)
X. Lannes 'International Mobility of Manpower in Western Europe' Parts 1 and 2 *International Labour Review* Vol. 73 (1956)
P. H. Laurent 'Diplomatic Origins of the Common Market 1955–6' *Political Science Quarterly* Vol. 85, No. 3 (1970)
H. Niehaus 'Effects of the European Common Market on Employment and Social Conditions in Agriculture' *International Labour Review* Vol. 77 (1958)
C. O'Grada 'The vocational training policy of the EEC and the free movement of skilled labour' *Journal of Common Market Studies* Vol. 8, No. 2 (December 1969)
V. Petaccio 'The European Social Fund. Phase 1 in Positive Retrospect' *Journal of Common Market Studies* Vol. 10 (1972)
A. Philip 'Social Aspects of European Economic Co-operation' *International Labour Review* Vol. 76 (1957)
J. Pinder 'Positive and Negative Integration' *The World Today* Vol. 24 (1968)
R. Rifflet 'After the Hague' *Journal of Common Market Studies* Vol. 8 (1970)
R. Roux 'The position of labour under the Schuman plan' *International Labour Review* Vol. 65 (1952)
L-E Troclet and E. Vogel-Polsky 'The Influence of International Labour Conventions on Belgian Labour Legislation' *International Labour Review* Vol. 98 (1968)
N. Valticos 'Fifty Years of Standard-Setting Activities by the International Labour Organisation' *International Labour Review* Vol. 100 (1969)

P. van Praag 'Aspects économiques à long terme des migrations internationales dans les pays de la CEE' *International Migration* Vol. IX, No. 3/4 (1971)

F. Vinck 'Industrial Conversion in the European Coal and Steel Community' *International Labour Review* Vol. 91 (1965)

J. Wedel 'Social Security and Economic Integration: I: Freedom of movement and the social protection of migrants; II: Their interaction, with special regard to social cost' *International Labour Review* Vol. 102 (1970)

G. Zellentin 'The Economic and Social Committee' *Journal of Common Market Studies* Vol. 1 (1962)

IV   *Unsigned Articles and Miscellaneous*

Franco-Italian Labour Treaty 1904 *Bulletin de L'Office International du Travail* Paris (1904)

Industry and Labour Geneva, Vol. XXV (1961)

'Influence de l'intégration et de coopération internationale sur l'économic Belge – aspects sociaux' *Chronique de Politique Etrangère* Brussels, Vol. XXII (1969)

'Manpower Shortages and Active Manpower Policies in Europe in 1964' *International Labour Review* Vol. 92 (1965)

'Obstacles to Labour Mobility and Social Problems of Resettlement' *International Labour Review* Vol. 76 (1956)

'Social Aspects of European Economic Co-operation' *International Labour Review* Vol. 74 (1956)

'The Bundesrepublik – 20 years on' *Supplement to The Times* (14 June 1969)

'Women's Pay still Lags in France' *The Times* (26 August 1969)

'Workers and employers participation in planning in France' *International Labour Review* Vol. 93 (1966)

See also Source Material and Bibliography in the companion volume on the European Coal and Steel Community.

Notes

Chapter 1: The Treaty of Rome

1 *Manchester Guardian* (16 April 1955); *Le Monde* (23 April 1955); *The Times* (25 April 1955).
2 *Figaro* (27 May 1955); *Le Populaire* (1 June 1955).
3 *Financial Times* (5 February 1957).
4 *L'Année Politique* (1955) pp. 714–16.
5 *ibid.* pp. 716–17.
6 *Le Monde* (18 January 1957); *L'Humanité* (19 January 1957); *Financial Times* (26 January 1957).
7 L. Erhard *Prosperity Through Competition* (1958) especially pp. 211–17. See also *Le Monde* (26 May 1955).
8 W. Diebold *The Schuman Plan* New York, Praeger (1959) p. 442.
9 *Il Popolo* (24 December 1955); *Osservatore Romano* (30 November 1957).
10 Official Italian memorandum *L'Année Politique* (1955) p. 717.
11 P. H. Laurent 'Diplomatic Origins of the Common Market 1955–6' *Political Science Quarterly* Vol. 85, No. 3 (1970).
12 *Le Monde* (4 June 1955).
13 Comité Intergouvernemental crée par la Conférence de Messina *Rapport des Chefs de Délégation aux Ministres des Affaires Etrangères Bruxelles* (21 April 1956) (hereafter *Spaak Report*). It had three parts dealing respectively with the common market, atomic and conventional energy, transport and communications. Only the first part is discussed here.
14 *L'Année Politique* (1956) p. 263.
15 *Spaak Report* pp. 17–18.
16 *ibid.* p. 63.
17 *ibid.* p. 83.
18 See Spaak's comments, *Christian Science Monitor* (28 May 1956).
19 *Le Monde* (31 May 1956).
20 *Christian Science Monitor* (28 February 1957).
21 *Financial Times* (1 June 1955); *The Times* (29 May 1956).
22 *Le Monde* (6 May 1955); *The Times* (19 January 1957); *L'Humanité* (30 January 1957); *Figaro* (26 October 1956).
23 EEC *1st General Report* paras. 142, 165.
24 This was fixed at twelve years and ended on 31 December 1969. It was divided into three four-year stages. The passage into the second stage was the critical one, being subject to unanimous agreement that an adequate degree of balanced progress had been achieved. The transition from the second to the third stage was automatic (unless unanimously postponed). The customs union was completed on 1 July 1968.
25 M. Palmer and J. Lambert (eds.) *European Unity* (1968) p. 174.
26 European Communities *2nd Combined Report* para. 12. From 1967 the three European Communities issued a combined annual general report (hereafter *1st* [etc.] *Combined Report*)
27 W. Hartley Clarke *The Politics of the Common Market* (1967) p. 24.
28 EEC *3rd General Report* p. 17. On assumption of office Signor Malfatti re-emphasized the importance of the Commission's right of initiative as an aspect

of its political role which it intended to defend. *The Times* (9 July 1970).

29 *2nd Combined Report* para. 13.

30 *3rd Combined Report* p. 20.

31 Resolution on equal pay taken in Council, 30 December 1961. EEC *5th General Report* paras. 154–5. Declaration of intention to accelerate internal developments (including measures of a social character such as vocational training, free movement of labour, reciprocity in social security and equal pay) taken in Council, 12 May 1960. *Journal Officiel* No. 58 (12 September 1960) p. 1220. The important declaration of 2 December 1969, which expressed the intention to pursue the advance towards genuine economic and monetary union and to accept the close alignment of social policies this entails, resulted from a conference of heads of government meeting at The Hague outside the Community machinery.

32 The 1970 Commission was composed of F. Malfatti (President), S. Mansholt, R. Barre, W. Haferkamp (Vice-Presidents), A. Coppé, J. F. Deniau, A. Borschette, R. Dahrendorf, A. Spinelli (Commissioners).

33 EEC *1st General Report* Annex B, Q.19/68/*Journal Officiel*/C52 (25 May 1968).

34 i.e. including Euratom whose work is not dealt with in this study.

35 EEC *1st General Report* paras. 33, 34, 39. Joint symposia were held in the fields of industrial medicine, vocational training, joint meetings with national officials concerned with industrial health and safety. The Commission was represented on the joint committee for the harmonization of the terms of employment in the coal industry and on the technical committee for the application of Art. 69 (Paris) particularly with a view to a comparative study of ECSC and EEC systems for establishing the free movement of workers. Information was passed from the Commission to the High Authority concerning its views on state aids for the purpose of mining research. Common services included legal, statistical and press departments. ECSC *7th General Report* para. 9.

36 EEC *3rd General Report* para. 74.

37 EEC *1st General Report* para. 105.

38 *ibid.* para. 102.

39 *ibid.* para. 78.

40 Q.65/69/*Journal Officiel*/C91 (10 July 1969).

41 EEC Information Service *The Common Market* (September 1961) p. 15.

42 EEC *5th General Report* para. 50.

43 *European Community* (July/August 1968) p. 17.

44 P. Reuter *Organisations Européennes* (1965) pp. 311–12.

45 High Authority 'Les dispositions sociales dans les Traités de la CEE et de la CECA' Doc. 6487/60f. (16 November 1960) p. 6.

46 EEC *1st General Report* para. 7.

47 *Memorandum of the Commission on the Action Programme of the Community for the second stage* (24 October 1962) paras. 1 and 3 (hereafter *Action Programme*).

48 The European Conference of Christian Trade Unions, held in December 1960, drew attention to the problem of abolition of wage differentials, variations in welfare schemes, hours and conditions of work and of the application of a common policy of vocational training. ILO *Industry and Labour* XXV (January–June 1961) p. 164.

49 Trans. from Reuter *op. cit.* p. 338 (Quotations from non-English sources have, unless otherwise stated, been translated by the author.)

50 EEC Commission *Exposé sur l'évolution de la situation sociale dans la Communauté en 1960* p. 20, para. x (hereafter *Social Exposé*).

51 EEC *1st General Report* para. 103.

52 U. Kitzinger *The Challenge of the Common Market* (1961 ed.) p. 39.

53 The cost of an hour's work in April 1959 measured in new francs was 3·51 in France; 2·81 in Netherlands; 2·99 in Italy; 3·62 in Belgium; 3·84 in West Germany; 3·80 in Great Britain. *Community Topics* No. 5, p. 11.

54 Palmer and Lambert *op. cit.* p. 220.

55 'Conversion' meant conversion to the production of a different product and not

modernization or slowing down through loss of markets. *Doc. 6487/60f.* p. 7 note.

56 *Statut du Comité du Fonds Social* Art. 2. Committee members were nominated by the Council and chaired by a non-voting member of the Commission. *Journal Officiel* No. 56 (31 August 1960) p. 1201/60.

57 In practice it was, and is, widespread especially in lower-grade jobs. See, e.g., L-E. Troclet *Eléments de Droit Social Européen* (1963) p. 146.

58 EEC *2nd General Report* para. 176.

59 Troclet *op. cit.* pp. 147–8.

60 H. Niehaus 'Effects of the European Common Market on Employment and Social Conditions in Agriculture' *International Labour Review* Vol. 77 (January–June 1958) especially pp. 305–10.

61 D. McLachlan and D. Swann *Competition Policy in the European Community* (1967) p. 396.

62 L. Levi-Sandri, Parlement Européen, 1965–6, *Débats* 1/66 No. 82, p. 50. Speech of 24 November 1965 reprinted as 'Réalisations et perspectives de la politique sociale de la CEE'.

63 Thereafter by qualified majority vote.

64 From the third stage onwards this could be done by qualified majority vote where matters were for subordinate legislation.

65 After the first stage only certain matters had to be decided unanimously.

66 EEC *1st General Report* para. 8.

67 EEC *2nd General Report* paras. 159–60.

68 *Action Programme* para. 73.

69 *Social Exposé 1961* p. XIII and EEC *1st General Report* para. 102.

70 Levi-Sandri *op. cit* p. 56.

71 EEC *6th General Report* para. 184.

72 The Treaty of Paris created an Assembly (Art. 20) which in 1958 became common to the three European institutions and which formally adopted the name of European Parliament in 1962. Membership was enlarged to 142 delegates (14 for Belgium and the Netherlands, 36 for France, West Germany and Italy, 6 for Luxembourg).

73 Palmer and Lambert *op. cit.* p. 184.

74 It met for the first time on 11 March 1953 under the chairmanship of M. G. Nederhorst (Netherlands). ECSC *1st General Report* para. 8.

75 It is impossible to keep social aspects in a watertight compartment when other policies are discussed. Consideration of the freeing of international markets includes the right of establishment, of economic programming leads on to manpower questions, and so on.

76 EEC *1st General Report* para. 28. See also E. B. Haas *The Uniting of Europe* (1958) p. 89. The more vigorous labour policy pursued by the High Authority after 1955 owed much to the pressure exerted by trade unions and by the Assembly.

77 L. Major, Chairman of the Economic and Social Committee, speech on tenth anniversary of the committee. Economic and Social Committee *Ten Years of Activity of the Economic and Social Committee of the European Communities, 1958–68* pp. 11, 16.

78 Only agriculture and transport were specifically mentioned in the treaty but other sections, including a social one, were set up.

79 L. Rosenberg 'The Activities and Importance of the Economic and Social Committee' EEC *Bulletin* (1961) No. 3, p. 5.

80 e.g., 49 (free movement of labour); 54 (free establishment); 75 (transport policy); 118 (social collaboration); 121 (common social measures); 126 and 127 (social fund); 128 (occupational training policy).

81 e.g., the composition of the administrative committee for the social security of migrants; the draft directive on the free movement of workers; the adoption of a uniform list of occupational diseases; measures to improve industrial medicine.

82 Italy, France and Germany had 24 each; Belgium and the Netherlands 12 and Luxembourg 5. Members were appointed by the Council on a unanimous vote

for a four-yearly period.

83 G. Zellentin 'The Economic and Social Committee' *Journal of Common Market Studies* Vol. 1 (1962) p. 23.

84 Rosenberg *op. cit.* p. 6.

85 Zellentin *op. cit.* pp. 25–6.

86 EEC *1st General Report* para. 30.

87 Palmer and Lambert *op. cit.* p. 186.

88 *Ten Years of Activity op. cit.* pp. 14–15.

89 EEC *3rd General Report* para. 85. Examples of advisory committees include the joint advisory committees on social problems in road transport (first meeting 21 December 1966. EEC *Bulletin* [1967] No. 2, p. 36); on social matters in inland water transport (set up 28 November 1967, *2nd Combined Report* para. 311); on social problems in the sea-fishing industry (set up 7 June 1968, *ibid,* para. 372); on social matters in railways (set up 19 February 1971, *Bulletin* [1971] No. 4, para. 19). Other examples will be found in the text. Some of the more important private groupings were UNICE (union of employers' federations); COPA (committee of agricultural organizations); COCCEE (committee of commercial organizations); ICFTU (International Confederation of Free Trade Unions whose European body was the European Confederation of Free Trade Unions); WCL (World Confederation of Labour). The union organizations worked closely together on Community affairs. The French and Italian Communist-dominated labour federations, originally hostile, later maintained an office in Brussels and were brought into meetings held by the Commission with industry for the first time on 18 November 1969. *3rd Combined Report* para. 343. EFTA trade unions were also represented at Brussels. The international union of family organizations had its committee of family organizations of the European Communities. *Bulletin* (1969) No. 12, p. 56.

90 ECSC *2nd General Report* para. 6.

91 EEC *2nd General Report* paras. 3, 4; *3rd General Report* para. 85; *6th General Report* para. 188.

92 *Doc. 6487/60f,* p. 4. The scope of the Rome Treaty, being comprehensive over the economy, was wide enough to cover coal and steel, although the treaty itself did not modify the Treaty of Paris (Art. 232 of Treaty of Rome). The Treaty of Rome became equally applicable to the coal and steel industries provided it did not violate the earlier treaty, *ibid*, pp. 2–3.

93 N. Valticos 'Fifty Years of Standard-Setting Activities by the International Labour Organisation' *International Labour Review* Vol. 100 (July–December 1969) pp. 201–37.

94 D. Morse. Quoted in E. B. Haas *Beyond the Nation State* (1964) p. 178. See too ILO *Social Aspects of European Economic Co-operation* (1956) paras. 95–103. The general proposition must, of course, be distinguished from the particular position of any one industry at a given point of time.

95 E. B. Haas 'System and Process in the International Labour Organisation' *World Politics* Vol. LIV, No. 2 (1962) p. 334. See, too, his table, p. 335, showing the incidence of ratification of ILO conventions amongst the EEC members. This shows the relation of actual to possible ratification as a percentage and yields the following results: conventions on occupational hazards, 67 per cent; freedom of association, 89 per cent; anti-discrimination, 33 per cent; social security, 51 per cent; hours and vacations, 31 per cent; administration of labour legislation, 57 per cent; minimum age and protection of the young, 55 per cent. It appears that the relationship between the development of the international trading community and the acceptance of identical welfare standards at home is not an automatic one.

96 ILO *op. cit.* paras. 172–4.

97 *ibid.* paras. 90–3.

98 *ibid.* paras. 221–2.

99 A. Philip 'Social Aspects of European Economic Co-operation' *International Labour Review* Vol. 76 (July–December 1957) p. 248.

100 ILO *op. cit.* paras. 112, 115, 117, 152–3.

101 ECSC Common Assembly *Débats* (March 1956) pp. 339–43.
102 Valticos *op. cit.* p. 206.
103 ILO *op. cit.* para. 216.
104 Council of Europe *Assembly Debates* (21 October 1955, 22 October 1956).
105 ILO *op. cit.* paras. 214–15.

Chapter 2: Employment

1 The statistics presented in the first three paragraphs of this chapter are taken, or derived, from the following sources: *Social Exposé* (17 September 1958) Statistical Annex; *Report on the Development of the Social Situation in the Community in 1973* Statistical survey; Statistical Office *General Statistics* 12 (1973) p. 3; Commission 'Preliminary guidelines for a Community social policy programme' *Bulletin* (1971) No. 4, Supplement 2/71, especially pp. 13–15 (hereafter 'Preliminary guidelines . . .'); *European Community* (December 1969) p. 11; *Year Book of Social Statistics* (1972). The figures relate only to the six founder members and are best considered as illustrative of trends as the calculations are sometimes only approximate.

2 *Occupational Structure 1958–72** (percentage of total)

	Agriculture		Industry		Services		Unemployed percentage of civilian labour force	
	1958	1972	1958	1972	1958	1972	1958	1972
Belgium	9·4	4·2	47·5	43·4	43·1	52·5	3·4	2·4
Germany	15·7	7·5	47·6	49·5	36·7	43·0	2·9	0·9
France	23·7	12·9	39·0	40·3	37·3	46·8	1·0	2·4
Italy	34·9	18·2	35·4	44·3	29·7	37·5	(6.2)	3.7
Luxembourg	(17·9)	9·6	43·3	48·0	38·8	42·5	—	—
Netherlands	12·7	6·9	41·8	36·8	45·5	56·3	2·5	2·5

* See *Social Report* (1973) Statistical survey.

3 *Agence Europe* (28 December 1970) No. 713 (new series); *General Statistics* p. 7.
4 *Social Exposé 1968* p. 222.
5 *ibid.* pp. 225–7
6 *ibid.* p. 223
7 EEC *3rd General Report* para. 289.
8 Parlement 1965–6 *Doc. 101* para. 16. See also the opinion of the Economic and Social Committee on the free movement policies. *Journal Officiel* No. 298 (7 December 1967).
9 A. Coppé 'The Social Horizon for 1980' *Bulletin* (1971) No. 1, p. 7. See also *Social Exposé 1970* p. 9.
10 EEC *3rd General Report* para. 284.
11 *Journal Officiel* C5 (29 January 1968). The recommendations are to be found in *Journal Officiel* No. 241 (28 December 1966) p. 409 and *Journal Officiel* No. 159 (18 July 1967) p. 6.
12 *1st Combined Report* para. 264.
13 *Les Problèmes de main-d'oeuvre dans la Communauté en 1969* pp. 141–7.
14 *Débats* (10 May 1972) especially Mlle Lulling, M. Offray. *Agence Europe* (11–12 May 1972) No. 1044 (new series).
15 *Statistiques Sociales* (1972) No. 3 especially Tables 1 and 5.
16 A. Coppé *Débats* (9 February 1972) especially p. 77.
17 EEC *8th General Report* para. 143.
18 EEC *2nd General Report* para. 181, *3rd General Report* para. 304, *5th General*

Report para. 145, *7th General Report* para. 277, *8th General Report* para. 240, *10th General Report* paras. 232, 236.

19 EEC *1st General Report* para. 110, *6th General Report* para. 188, *8th General Report* para. 240, *1st Combined Report* para. 263.

20 EEC *3rd General Report* para. 303. It contained two representatives from each country from the Ministries of Economic Affairs and Labour and two representatives from the Commission.

21 EEC *Bulletin* (1960) No. 4, pp. 42–3.

22 *Les Problèmes de main-d'oeuvre dans la Communauté en 1968* Annexe II.

23 *Bulletin* (1969) No. 3, p. 95; *Bulletin* (1970) No. 1, p. 59.

24 *European Community* (1970) No. 7, p. 8.

25 *Agence Europe* (18 March 1971) No. 769.

26 *Bulletin* (1971) No. 1, pp. 76–7.

27 A. Coppé *Débats* (9 February 1972) pp. 76–8.

28 *European Community* (1972) No. 12, pp. 24–5; *Agence Europe* (31 May 1972) No. 1056 (new series).

29 J. Neirinck, Director-General for Social Affairs of the Commission of the European Community 'Social policy of the EE Commission. A general survey. Achievements and trends at the end of 1967' duplicated copy of speech delivered at the University of Louvain (December 1967) p. 14.

30 *Social Exposé 1961* p. IX.

31 *Social Exposé 1958* para. 27.

32 EEC *6th General Report* para. 188.

33 Parlement 1965–6 *Doc. 101* (19 November 1965) para. 29.

34 The European social fund found that the cost of retraining schemes of six to nine months' duration averaged 2,500 units of account per head in 1970 and had been increasing in cost by 20 to 25 per cent each year. Commission Preliminary Guidelines . . . Sec. (71) 600 Final (1971) p. 26.

35 EEC *3rd General Report* para. 289.

36 EEC *6th General Report* para. 353.

37 *Social Exposé 1959* p. 52.

38 Official statement on 11 June 1963, quoted in W. D. Halls *Society, Schools and Progress in France* (1965) p. 136.

39 Eire Government *Report of the Inter-Departmental Committee on Retraining and Resettlement in Relation to the European Social Fund* (undated) p. 23 (the committee was set up in 1962).

40 The National Employment Fund Act (18 December 1963) and three decrees of 24 February 1964. See also 'Manpower Shortages and Active Manpower Policies in Europe in 1964' *International Labour Review* Vol. 92 (1965) p. 15.

41 *Social Exposé 1968* para. 13.

42 Of 1960 and 1965 respectively. *ibid.* pp. 230–1.

43 ECSC *2nd General Report* para. 154.

44 Levi-Sandri *op. cit.* (November 1965) p. 4.

45 Le Comité Economique et Social (Rapport . . . sur la proposition de la Commission . . . à l'établissement de principes généraux . . . d'une politique commune de formation professionelle' CES/60/62 (17 February 1962) p. 3

46 EEC *3rd General Report* para. 289.

47 paras. 75, 76.

48 J. Wedel 'Social Security and Economic Integration' *International Labour Review* Vol. 102 (1970) No. 5, p. 470.

49 *Social Exposé 1968* Table 5, p. 261.

50 Troclet *op. cit.* p. 314.

51 Some held it was contrary to the treaty. Reuter *op. cit.* p. 342.

52 See below p. 202.

53 EEC *Bulletin* (1961) No. 12 Supplement. See too *European Community* (1961) Vol. IV, No. 8, p. 8.

54 EEC *5th General Report* para. 152.

55 The constitution of the Committee was agreed by the Council on 18 December 1963, its members appointed on 21 April 1964 and its first meeting held on 29

June 1964. EEC *8th General Report* para. 241. After its initial activity it fell rather into abeyance. *Agence Europe* (16 December 1966) No. 2581.

56 Troclet *op. cit.* pp. 315–16.

57 EEC *Bulletin* (1963) No. 4, para. 29.

58 *Agence Europe* (19 February 1963) No. 1485.

59 *Journal Officiel* No. 63 (20 April 1963).

60 J. J. Ribas *La Politique Sociale des Communautés Européennes* (1969) p. 224.

61 *Agence Europe* (21 February 1963) No. 1487.

62 *Agence Europe* (28 February 1963) No. 1204.

63 Neirinck *op. cit.* p. 21.

64 'Les actions entreprises en vue de réaliser les objectifs de la politique commune de formation professionnelle pourront faire l'objet d'un financement commun.' 10th principle, para. 2.

65 EEC *9th General Report* para. 233.

66 e.g., symposium on vocational training for experts from states, employers' and workers' organizations and scientific experts in November 1964. Visit of representatives to certain French centres in connection with the need to improve the training of teachers and instructors. EEC *8th General Report* paras. 241–2. Aid to study conference held by German Chambers of Commerce and Industry and Dutch vocational training institutions in 1965. Seminar for heads of official vocational guidance services. EEC *9th General Report* paras. 236, 233. Job analysis with a view to training schemes which emphasize common elements. EEC *10th General Report* para. 240. Study of teaching methods used in states. *Social Exposé 1966* p. 16; *1967* para. 13. Programme of seminars at the Turin Centre on vocational training from Africa and Latin America. *Social Exposé 1968* para. 18. Studies of polyvalence in the six member countries. *2nd Combined Report* para. 385. First seminar on a common vocational training policy was held at Turin in December 1969. *3rd Combined Report* para. 319.

67 Recommendation 66/484/CEE *Journal Officiel* No. 154 (24 August 1966).

68 This enabled the Commission to publish its *Exposé annuel sur les activités d'orientation professionelle dans la Communauté*. It was not until 1969 that the members, at a meeting of Ministers of Social Affairs in March, agreed to a definite exchange of information, via the Commission, on vocational guidance and training methods. *European Community* (1969) No. 4, p. 3.

69 *Journal Officiel* C81 (12 August 1971).

70 *4th Combined Report* para. 126.

71 *3rd Combined Report* para. 319.

72 EEC *4th General Report* para. 154.

73 EEC *9th General Report* para. 234.

74 Levi-Sandri *op. cit.* p. 6.

75 EEC *10th General Report* para. 238. *Agence Europe* (16, 20 December 1966).

76 Parlement 1965–6 *Doc. 101* para. 38.

77 EEC *Bulletin* (1961) No. 12, p. 7.

78 EEC *1st General Report* para. 116.

79 EEC *5th General Report* para. 153.

80 Ribas *op. cit.* p. 241.

81 *Journal Officiel* No. 78 (22 May 1964).

82 *1st Combined Report* para. 280. Examples are the conference of 17 July 1967 held for heads of organizations which engaged, or were likely to do so, in exchange activities. EEC *Bulletin* (1967) Nos. 9–10, p. 60. The meeting of employers' representatives to encourage them to increase places for in-service training for young Community workers. EEC *9th General Report* para. 238. Meetings of employers', workers' and international organizations. EEC *10th General Report* para. 241.

83 Details of the arrangements made by 1967, by no means uniform or sounding very effective, were given in reply to a Parliamentary question. Q.114/*Journal Officiel* No. 256 (23 October 1967).

84 Q.88/69/*Journal Officiel* C94 (19 July 1969).

85 *ibid. Social Exposé 1970* para. 6, p. 25.

86 *Journal Officiel* No. 182 (12 December 1963).
87 Q.88/69/*Journal Officiel*/C94 (19 July 1969)
88 Q.394/*Journal Officiel*/C18 (26 February 1972).
89 Economic and Social Committee *Report of 17 February 1962* p. 3.
90 *Social Exposé 1961* p. xxii, para. 25.
91 Economic and Social Committee *Report of 17 February 1962* p. 12.
92 EEC *1st General Report* para. 116.
93 Parlement 1965–6 *Doc. 101* para. 83.
94 C. O'Grada 'The vocational training policy of the EEC and the free movement of skilled labour' *Journal of Common Market Studies* Vol. 8, No. 2 (December 1969).
95 EEC *1st General Report* para. 116.
96 EEC *2nd General Report* para. 170.
97 EEC *3rd General Report* para. 291.
98 L. Levi-Sandri 'The European Social Fund: the first phase' EEC *Bulletin* (1963) No. 3, p. 5.
99 Ribas *op. cit.* p. 251.
100 Accepted by the Council on 11 May 1960. EEC *3rd General Report* para. 293. It was discussed by both the Economic and Social Committee and Parliament; the report of the latter foreshadowing the need to extend its scope. The Regulation became effective on 20 September 1960.
101 Regulation 12/64/CEE *Journal Officiel* No. 32 (1964).
102 EEC *8th General Report* para. 251.
103 Levi-Sandri *op. cit.* (1963).
104 Regulation 47/63/CEE *Journal Officiel* No. 86 (10 June 1963).
105 EEC *9th General Report* para. 239.
106 *1st Combined Report* para. 281. This is easily accounted for by the complexity of the task and the longer time necessary for training.
107 Regulation 47/63/CEE widened the definition of allowances with the extra costs involved in training the handicapped particularly in mind. Regulation 37/67/CEE increased the limits for resettlement allowances to permit separation allowances up to a maximum of three times the average weekly wage actually received by the worker during his first six months of new employment plus twice that wage for each dependant. A maximum of fifteen times the wage received was imposed.
108 The list, and changes therein, was published by the Community. By 1966, 70 agencies had been accepted: 46 in Italy, 15 in Germany, 5 in Belgium, 2 in France and one each in Netherlands and Luxembourg. *Journal Officiel* (1 February 1962; 10 February 1965; 17 March 1966). It is probable that considerable variations in standards, competences and modes of work existed between agencies.

109	General Community Expenses (figures are percentages)	Social Fund
Germany	28	32
France	28	32
Italy	28	20
Netherlands	7·9	7
Belgium	7·9	8·8
Luxembourg	0·2	0·2

110 8,636 persons in 1967; 180,000 in 1968. *1st Combined Report* para. 281. *2nd Combined Report* para. 387, note to Table 16.
111 Information supplied by the Commission.
112 *4th Combined Report* Table 8, para. 128.
113 EEC *10th General Report* para. 251. Over two-thirds of the 1967 retraining

applications came from Italy. *1st Combined Report* para. 282.

114 EEC *9th General Report* para. 239.
115 See *Journal Officiel* No. 196 (29 October 1966) announcing Commission decisions on certain social fund payments. They included 1·3 million units to Germany for schemes during the period from 30 April 1958 to 31 December 1962; 89,574 units to Italy for schemes during the period from 19 July 1962 to 27 June 1964; 33,697 units to the Netherlands for schemes during the period from 1 January 1963 to 30 June 1964.
116 *Agence Europe* (16 December 1966) No. 2581.
117 *European Community* (1969) No. 7/8, p. 6.
118 The only application it received was one from the Belgian government in 1964. A Ford subsidiary at Anvers was changing from car to tractor production, a process which required laying off about eleven thousand workers for six months and a certain amount of retraining. The Belgian government agreed to meet 90 per cent of the cost but applied to the social fund for a 50 per cent grant totalling about £189,000. The request was rejected on the grounds that there was no obvious need for increased tractor production and there was plenty of alternative employment in the area. The request was an embarrassing one for conversion aid had hardly been intended for the support of a wealthy, international company.
119 *Agence Europe* (16 December 1966) No. 2581.
120 EEC *Bulletin* (1965) No. 5, Supplement, pp. 51–60.
121 Under Art. 127 the Council could decide both the regulations to give effect to the social fund and the terms of assistance.
122 The 4th principle of the occupational training policy allowed the Commission to make proposals and the 10th expressed members' agreement to consider special problems and stated the possibility of common financing.
123 EEC *Bulletin* (1966) No. 3, p. 41.
124 Q.56/*Journal Officiel* No. 212 (21 November 1966) referring to the objections held by some members to the Commission's proposals.
125 *Journal Officiel* No. 246 (31 December 1966) p. 4168.
126 *1st Combined Report* para. 280.
127 *Agence Europe* (18 December 1970) No. 710 (new series). *4th Combined Report,* para. 130. *Bulletin* (1972) No. 12, p. 67.
128 *Journal Officiel* No. 153 (24 October 1963).
129 Q.18/68/*Journal Officiel* C53 (31 May 1968) p. 3 relating to alleged frauds on the fund by certain training centres in Italy. The Commission had no part in the resulting inquiry. See too Q.495/69/*Journal Officiel* C59 (22 May 1970).
130 Levi-Sandri *op. cit.* (1963) p. 6.
131 *Social Exposé 1961* p.IX.
132 Ribas *op. cit.* p. 261.
133 EEC *3rd General Report* paras. 286, 287.
134 *European Community* (1963) No. 2, p. 16.
135 L. Levi-Sandri quoted in EEC *Bulletin* (1965) No. 8, p. 59.
136 Neirinck *op. cit.* p. 24.
137 *Agence Europe* (16 December 1966) No. 2581.
138 *Bulletin* (1969) No. 8, p. 33.
139 *Agence Europe* (21 December 1967) No. 168.
140 *Agence Europe* (10 September 1968).
141 'Reform of the European Social Fund' *Bulletin* (1969) No. 8, pp. 33–6.
142 *3rd Combined Report* p. 13.
143 *Bulletin* (1970) No. 1, p. 16.
144 Decision of the Council 71/66/CEE *Journal Officiel* L28 (4 February 1971). The new fund became operative in May 1972.
145 *Agence Europe* (24 June 1971) No. 835; (29 September 1971) No. 892.
146 *ibid.* (25 June 1971) No. 836.
147 *5th Combined Report* para. 229. The original rules for the fund now only operate in a residual, transitional sense.
148 Regulation 2396/71. Art. 1. *Journal Officiel* L249 (10 November 1971).

149 Regulation 2396/71; 2397/71. *Journal Officiel* L249 (10 November 1971).
150 Regulation 2398/71. *Journal Officiel* L249 (10 November 1971).
151 *Journal Officiel* L94 (28 April 1970).
152 R. Broad and R. Jarrett *Community Europe Today* (1972) p. 186.
153 Commission *Doc. COM (72) 812 final* (12 July 1972).
154 *Agence Europe* (20 September 1971) No. 885.
155 Directive 72/159/EEC; Directive 72/160/EEC (17 April 1972). HMSO *European Communities. Secondary Legislation* Part 15, Agriculture.

Chapter 3: Wages and Working Conditions

1 Troclet *op. cit.* pp. 192–3. He suggests equality is expressed or implied in Arts. 2, 3, 48, 51, 117, 118 and 119 and that indirect pay is covered by Arts. 51, 118, 120 and 121 of the Rome Treaty.
2 O. Kahn-Freund 'Social Policy and the Common Market' *Political Quarterly* Vol. 32 (1961) No. 4, p. 398.
3 *Social Exposé 1965* p. 11, para. VIII; *1968* p. 234, para. 18.
4 *Social Exposé 1968* p. 238, para. 26.
5 Troclet *op. cit.* p. 191.
6 *Social Exposé 1958* p. 49, para. 1.
7 *Social Exposé 1968* p. 232, para. 15.
8 *2nd Combined Report* para. 414.
9 The working parties on labour relations, working hours and wages had joint membership with government experts assisting; those on the protection of young people and women at work were tripartite; government experts were used to study imbalance on the labour market; independent experts to study the economic impact of social security and social security for migrants. EEC *6th General Report* para. 192. *3rd Combined Report* para. 303, EEC *Bulletin* (1964) No. 7, pp. 31–2, Levi-Sandri *op. cit.* (1965) pp. 8–9.
10 EEC *7th General Report* para. 229.
11 *Bulletin* (1971) No. 7, pp. 55–6.
12 Neirinck *op. cit.* p. 31.
13 *Bulletin* (1970) No. 8, Supplement. Proposed statute for the European company.
14 Troclet *op. cit.* p. 194.
15 *Action Programme,* para. 86.
16 *Social Exposé 1968* Wages and Conditions, pp. 17–18, para. v.
17 EEC *3rd General Report* para. 55.
18 Twenty or more in Luxembourg. Wage costs were held to include direct and indirect costs, bonuses, paid holidays, contributions to social security, social charges, costs of vocational training, benefits in kind and other social contributions for manual workers paid by the piece, the hour, the day or the month if employed exclusively on manual work.
19 Results are in *Statistiques Sociales* (1961) No. 3; (1962) No. 3; (1963) No. 1; (1964) Nos. 2 and 5; (1965) No. 6; (1966) No. 5.
20 *Statistiques Sociales* (1961) No. 3, p. 45.
21 *Statistiques Sociales* (1962) No. 3, based on the original fourteen industries. Incomes were adjusted to allow for income in kind, family allowances, social security contributions and income tax.
22 *ibid.* Table 17. Also *European Community* (1963) No. 2, p. 12.
23 *Statistiques Sociales* (1964) No. 5, Statistical Annex, Tables M/2.
24 'Budgets Familiaux 1963/4' *Statistiques Sociales* Série Spéciale (1966/7).
25 Regulation No. 188/64/CEE. *Journal Officiel* No. 214 (24 December 1964). This was based on firms employing ten or more workers. It included information on the gross wage, supplements to wages and family benefits deriving from collective agreements and duration of work. It demanded close collaboration between the Commission and national statistical offices.
26 Regulations 100/66/CEE; 101/66/CEE. *Journal Officiel* No. 134 (22 July 1966). Results relating to particular industries are periodically published in *Etudes: Série politique sociale.*

27 *Statistiques Sociales* Série Spéciale, No. 8.
28 *Agence Europe* (26 October 1971) No. 911.
29 Parlement 1961–2 *Doc. 68* (11 October 1961) para. 6 (Motte Report).
30 See the comments on the real progress of equal pay in Italy by A. Codazzi 'Problems of Equal Pay for Men and Women Workers' in OECD *Employment of Women* Report of Regional Trade Union Seminar held at Paris 26–29 November 1968 (1970) (hereafter OECD *Report*). Despite the acceptance of the principle in the constitution there was little effective breakthrough until 1960, with the collective agreement of 16 July between the confederation of employers and confederations of workers applying to the industrial sector and affecting 1·3 million women workers. The significant change was the agreement on a single job classification (p. 135). 'More progress has therefore been made from 1960 to 1968 than from 1948 (entry into force of the Constitution) to 1960 since the "right" has passed from the legal stage into practical application' (p. 133).
31 EEC *Bulletin* (1964) No. 7. Parliamentary resolution on progress towards equal pay.
32 EEC *3rd General Report* para. 22.
33 EEC *Bulletin* (1960) No. 6/7, p. 44.
34 Reply to Q.79 of M. Troclet on the application of Art. 119 to the payment of family benefits to employed married women. *Journal Officiel* No. 186 (19 October 1966).
35 Parlement 1961–2 *Doc. 68* para. 18. The report accepted that progressive implementation would be the best now attainable; para. 25.
36 Council meetings of 30 and 31 May 1961. The working party was composed of two Commission members and two representatives from each member. It started work in June 1961 and was advised by a group of experts in collective agreements composed of representatives of employer and worker organizations and assisted as necessary by expert statisticians. The working party continued to meet periodically to receive information on the application of Art. 119; to analyse the legislative position in members and the extent to which the principle might be protected through the courts; to receive reports from national groups and to furnish a periodical report on the situation in association with the Commission's staff. Q.45/*Journal Officiel* C60 (15 June 1968) p. 3.
37 EEC *Bulletin* (1961) No. 12, p. 44.
38 Troclet *op. cit.* p. 206.
39 Council meetings 30 December 1961. Members acted as governmental representatives and not as the Council. The text of the resolution is in ECC *Bulletin* (1962) No. 1. Members agreed that by 30 June 1962 the differentials between male and female wages would not exceed 15 per cent; by 30 June 1963 10 per cent, and be abolished entirely by 31 December 1964.
40 Parlement 1968–9 *Doc. 26* (8 May 1968) para. 24, p. 9.
41 *ibid.* para. 16, p. 7.
42 E. Toffanin in OECD *Report* p. 176. The Belgian industries of chocolate and confectionery manufacture, fruit canning, glucose and maize flour production were particularly mentioned. '1st Report of the Commission on equal pay' *Agence Europe* (22 January 1963) No. 1461. However in Germany a legal ruling established that pay disparities which victimize women are incompatible with the Constitution. EEC *Bulletin* (1963) No. 2, p. 54.
43 Troclet *op. cit*, p. 213.
44 Ribas *op. cit*, p. 298. See also EEC *Bulletin* (1965) No. 9/10, p. 36.
45 Neirinck *op. cit.* p. 27, *Social Exposé 1968* para. 29, p. 240, Parlement 1968–9 *Doc. 26* para. 24, p. 9.
46 Q.150/*Journal Officiel* No. 256 (23 October 1967). The question was repeated the following year and the reply was the same. Q.213/*Journal Officiel* C3 (22 January 1968).
47 EEC *6th General Report* para. 194.
48 Resolution of Parliament on the report of the Commission on the state of application of Art. 119 at 30 June 1963. EEC *Bulletin* (1964) No. 7, pp. 34 and 60.
49 Parlement 1968–9 *Doc. 26* pp. 3, 5.

50 Quotation from the Netherlands Minister of Finance. Parlement 1968–9 *Doc. 26* para. 24.
51 *Social Exposé 1968* para. 29, p. 240.
52 *Year Book of Social Statistics* (1970) Tables 111/9–111/15.
53 *Bulletin* (1970) No. 8, p. 111.
54 A direct result in Belgium of Art. 119. L-E. Troclet and E. Vogel-Polsky 'The Influence of International Labour Conventions on Belgian Labour Legislation' *International Labour Review* Vol. 98 (July–December 1968) p. 409.
55 Parlement 1968–9 *Doc. 26* p. 14. Part of the opinion of the Legal Committee given in 1968. In Germany the right derives from Art. 3 of the constitution; some Länder constitutions have specified the right to equal pay and labour tribunals have upheld it. In France the minimum wage applies equally to men and women; since 1950 collective agreements must include methods of implementing the principle before being extended; in Italy the right is written into the constitution and has been upheld by the courts; in Luxembourg there has been a statutory minimum wage applicable to both men and women and acceptance of the principle of non-discrimination since 1963. In 1965 the minimum wage for skilled workers was applied to men and women and legislation on collective agreements took up the question of methods of implementing equal pay. The Netherlands introduced legislation for an equal minimum wage for men and women in 1968. OECD *Report* p. 178.
56 Q.82/*Journal Officiel* No. 186 (19 October 1966).
57 e.g. Q.85/*Journal Officiel* No. 208 (28 August 1967) from M. Vredeling on the Dutch decree on minimum wages for 1967. The Commission considered this partially conformed to the policy.
58 Levi-Sandri *op. cit.* (1965) p. 9.
59 'Women's Pay still Lags in France' *The Times* (26 August 1969). See too *Year Book of Social Statistics* (1970) Table III/11 showing the range of discrepancies in various industries.
60 This does not, of course, solve the old question of whether such standards should be fixed at minimum or maximum levels. See M. Troclet, Parlement 1965–6 *Débats* III/1966 No. 83, p. 14.
61 EEC *7th General Report* para. 232.
62 EEC *3rd General Report* para. 32. *6th General Report* para. 196.
63 *Journal Officiel* No. 28 (17 February 1967) pp. 446–7. Resolution adopted after discussion of Parlement 'Rapport sur les problèmes de la prévention des accidents du travail dans la Communauté' 1966–7 *Doc. 155* (24 January 1967) (Hansen Report).
64 Levi-Sandri *op. cit.* (1965) pp. 7–8.
65 EEC *6th General Report* para. 196.
66 Parlement 1966–7 *Doc. 155* para. 2.
67 EEC *10th General Report* para. 262.
68 Parlement 1966–7 *Doc. 155*, para. 18.
69 *ibid.* para. 34, p. 9.
70 *1st Combined Report* para. 324.
71 EEC *8th General Report* Table 7, sub-section VI, p. 96.
72 EEC *9th General Report* Table 8.
73 *Journal Officiel* No. 196 (16 August 1967) p. 196/1. In 1971 the operative date was laid down as 1 January 1972.
74 *European Community* (1969) No. 7/8, p. 8.
75 'Etude comparative des normes législatives régissant la protection des jeunes travailleurs dans les pays membres de la CEE' *Etudes: Série Politique Sociale* No. 11 (1966). See too Parliamentary Debate of 18 January 1966 expressing support for a Commission recommendation on the subject.
76 *Journal Officiel* No. 25 (13 February 1967) pp. 405–8.
77 See the Commission's report on the situation at 30 June 1965. 'La protection de la maternité dans les six pays de la CEE' *Etudes: Série Politique Sociale* No. 13 (1966).
78 Adopted by the Commission on 12 January 1966 and approved by Parliament

and the Economic and Social Committee later in the year. EEC *Bulletin* (1966) No. 3, p. 42; No. 12, p. 48.

79 EEC *6th General Report* para. 197.
80 Parlement 1962–3 *Doc. 16* (7 April 1962) (Report Mariotte).
81 *Journal Officiel* No. 80 (31 August 1962) p. 2181.
82 *ibid.* para. 17.
83 *ibid.* para. 12.
84 *ibid.* para. 15.
85 EEC *8th General Report* para. 261.
86 Q.268/*Journal Officiel* C12 (21 February 1968); Q.3/*Journal Officiel* C41 (4 May 1968).
87 Q.269/*Journal Officiel* C12 (21 February 1968); Q.4/*Journal Officiel* C41 (4 May 1968). A first report, sent to Parliament on 29 October 1965, provided information on industrial medical services up to 1964.
88 *Journal Officiel* No. 151 (17 August 1966) p. 2753/66.
89 Q.35/*Journal Officiel* No. 208 (10 December 1965).
90 Recommendation on protection of workers exposed to special hazards, para. 3.
91 *European Community* (October 1962) p. 3.
92 EEC *5th General Report* para. 149.
93 *Journal Officiel* No. 80 (31 August 1962).
94 A year later the Commission reported that several countries had extended their own lists or reported the intention of doing so. The 'two stage' list had been adopted in Germany and more information about diseases was being internationally exchanged. EEC *Bulletin* (1964) No. 2, pp. 35–6. Considerable use was reported of the 'European' list. EEC *9th General Report* para. 250.
95 Recommendation 66/462/CEE *Journal Officiel* No. 147 (9 August 1966).
96 The recommendation was sent to the Economic and Social Committee which approved the general approach but wanted three, not two, categories of disability. The texts of the recommendation and of the Committee's report are in *Journal Officiel* No. 208 (15 November 1966).
97 Neirinck *op. cit.* p. 31.
98 EEC *8th General Report* para. 260.

Chapter 4: The Movement of the Working Population

1 Levi-Sandri *op. cit.* (1965) p. 5. See also the opinion of the Advisory Committee on free movement quoted EEC *8th General Report* para. 246.
2 L. Levi-Sandri 'Free movement of workers in the European Community' *Bulletin* (1968) No. 11, pp. 5–6.
3 *Agence Europe* (14 December 1970) No. 706.
4 Parlement 1963–4 *Doc. 118* (20 January 1964) para. 20 (hereafter *Storch Report*). *Agence Europe* (28 December 1970) No. 713.
5 Commission *La Libre circulation de la main-d'oeuvre et les marchés du travail dans la CEE* (1968) p. 33 (hereafter *La Libre circulation*).
6 *Storch Report* para. 42.
7 *The Times* (19 December 1962).
8 See the suggestions contained in the opinion of the Economic and Social Committee *Journal Officiel* No. 298 (7 December 1967) especially pp. 10, 11.
9 *Social Exposé, 17 September 1958* para. 22.
10 EEC *1st General Report* para. 111.
11 EEC *3rd General Report* para. 116.
12 EEC *4th General Report* para. 39.
13 Regulation No. 15 *Journal Officiel* No. 57 (26 August 1961).
14 *Journal Officiel* No. 80 (13 December 1961).
15 L. Levi-Sandri 'The free movement of workers in the countries of the European Economic Community' EEC *Bulletin* (1961) No. 6, p. 7.
16 *Débats* IV/62 (24 November 1961) No. 48, p. 115.
17 Q.13/*Journal Officiel* No. 43 (7 June 1962). See also Troclet *op. cit.* p. 156.

18 *Social Exposé 1965* pp. 23–4.
19 *La Libre circulation* . . . (1968) p. 73.
20 EEC *10th General Report* para. 247.
21 Troclet *op. cit.* p. 151.
22 Mme Schonwenaar-Fransen *Débats* IV/62 (24 November 1961) No. 48, pp. 112–13.
23 *Journal Officiel* No. 183 (13 October 1966) gives the composition of the two committees for 1966–8.
24 EEC *5th General Report* para. 28.
25 *La Libre circulation* . . . p. 76.
26 Regulation 117/65/CEE *Journal Officiel No.* 139 (29 July 1965) established a list of communes in areas near the frontiers between France and other members for the purpose of defining a frontier worker.
27 Regulation No. 18 concerning procedures for applying Regulation No. 15 to entertainers and musicians. *Journal Officiel* No. 23 (3 April 1962) p. 722.
28 *Journal Officiel* No. 62 (17 April 1964).
29 *ibid.*
30 *Journal Officiel* No. 56 (4 April 1964).
31 See K. Dahlberg 'The EEC Commission and the Politics of the Free Movement of Labour' *Journal of Common Market Studies* Vol. 6 (1968) pp. 310 *et seq.*
32 EEC *8th General Report* para. 244; *9th General Report* para. 241; *1st Combined Report* para. 297.
33 Q.116/*Journal Officiel* No. 243 (7 October 1967).
34 *2nd Combined Report* para. 400.
35 Art. 53 of the Regulation accepted that members still had special relations with non-Community territories although it agreed that if workers consequently entered one member state they would not be able to invoke the regulation in order to move on elsewhere.
36 *1st Combined Report* para. 295.
37 *Journal Officiel* L257 (19 October 1968).
38 *European Community* (1969) No. 12, p. 12.
39 *Social Exposé 1970* para. 14, p. 32.
40 EEC *9th General Report* para. 243.
41 *2nd Combined Report* para. 399. Opinion of the Consultative Committee.
42 Regulation 1251/70 *Journal Officiel* L142 (30 June 1970).
43 Parliament asked for the issue of indefinite residence permits. EEC *Bulletin* (1970) No. 7, p. 97.
44 The demand for new foreign labour in 1968 was estimated between 420,000 and 440,000 workers, whilst estimated availability from Italy was only 150,000. *La Libre circulation* . . . p. 83.
45 P. van Praag 'Aspects économiques à long terme des migrations internationales dans les pays de la CEE' *International Migration* Vol. IX, No. 3/4 (1971) p. 128. The average yearly number of work permits issued to Community nationals during the years from 1961 to 1966 was 271,000. *European Community* (1967) No. 5, p. 14.
46 EEC *Bulletin* (1968) No. 1, p. 35.
47 'Preliminary guidelines . . .' p. 19. The foreign proportion of the paid active population is approximately 2 per cent in Netherlands, 7·5 per cent in France, 7 per cent in Belgium, 5 per cent in Germany, 27 per cent in Luxembourg. Van Praag *op. cit.* p. 128.
48 Q.590/*Journal Officiel* C49 (18 May 1972).
49 EEC *9th General Report* para. 242.
50 Guidelines on social policy submitted to the Council by the Commission on 22 December 1966. EEC *Bulletin* (1967) No. 2, Supplement.
51 See Parliament's opinion on the new regulation. *Journal Officiel* No. 268 (6 November 1967) p. 7.
52 See advice of the Economic and Social Committee on the need for a uniform and restricted definition. *Journal Officiel* No. 298 (7 December 1967).

53 The Committee's Work Programme. *Bulletin* (1969) No. 5, pp. 82–3.
54 EEC *4th General Report* para. 42.
55 Directive 68/151/CEE *Journal Officiel* L65 (14 March 1968). *Bulletin* (1969) No. 2, Supplement.
56 EEC *6th General Report* para. 353.
57 *Journal Officiel* No. 2 (15 January 1962). See also *European Community* (1961) No. 8, pp. 4–5.
58 EEC *10th General Report* para. XIII.
59 Directive 63/340/CEE *Journal Officiel* No. 86 (10 June 1963).
60 Directive 64/220/CEE *Journal Officiel* No. 56 (4 April 1964). For restrictions for purposes of public order and health see Directive 64/221/CEE, page 109 above.
61 EEC *Bulletin* (1964) No. 9/10, pp. 22–3.
62 Directive 67/43/CEE, Art. 6. *Journal Officiel* No. 10 (19 January 1967) p. 140.
63 *4th Combined Report* (1970) para. 54. The description of procedures here is illustrative, not a comprehensive discussion of action in all occupations.
64 Directives 64/223/CEE; 64/224/CEE; 64/222/CEE. *Journal Officiel* No. 56 (4 April 1964).
65 EEC *8th General Report* para. 35.
66 Directives 64/429/CEE; 64/428/CEE; 64/427/CEE. *Journal Officiel* No. 117 (23 July 1964). Directive 69/77/CEE. *Journal Officiel* L59 (10 March 1969).
67 *Bulletin* (1969) No. 5, pp. 39–40.
68 Directives 63/261/CEE; 63/262/CEE. *Journal Officiel* No. 62 (20 April 1963).
69 Troclet *op. cit.* p. 183.
70 EEC *5th General Report* para. 41, *8th General Report* para. 36.
71 Directive 65/1/CEE. *Journal Officiel* No. 1 (8 January 1965).
72 Directives 67/530/CEE; 67/531/CEE; 67/532/CEE. *Journal Officiel* No. 190 (10 August 1967).
73 Directive 67/654/CEE. *Journal Officiel* No. 263 (30 October 1967).
74 Directive 68/415/CEE. *Journal Officiel* L308 (23 December 1968).
75 *Bulletin* (1971) No. 2, p. 48.
76 EEC *7th General Report* para. 54; *9th General Report* para. 40. *Journal Officiel* No. 152 (11 September 1965).
77 *European Community* (1970) No. 11, p. 19; No. 12, p. 18.
78 EEC *5th General Report* para. 43.
79 Parlement 1967–8 *Doc. 1* (7 March 1967) para. 11.
80 EEC *3rd General Report* para. 123.
81 See above, page 120.
82 EEC *8th General Report* para. 266.
83 EEC *Bulletin* (1967) No. 7, p. 40.
84 Parlement 1967–8 *Doc. 1* para. 17.
85 *ibid.* para. 19.
86 EEC *9th General Report* para. 259.
87 *Journal Officiel* C54 (28 April 1969).
88 *Journal Officiel* C54 (28 April 1969).
89 Parlement 1967–8 *Doc. 1* para. 35.
90 *Journal Officiel* C156 (18 December 1969).
91 *Journal Officiel* C18 (12 February 1970).
92 *Journal Officiel* C155 (5 December 1969).
93 Directive 65/65/CEE. *Journal Officiel* No. 22 (9 February 1965).
94 *European Community* (1969) No. 5, p. 20.
95 EEC *10th General Report* para. 95.
96 This was despatched. *Bulletin* (1969) No. 6, p. 37–8.
97 *Agence Europe* (22 December 1967) No. 2827.
98 *Journal Officiel* C46 (9 April 1969). *European Community* (1969) No. 11, p. 26.
99 *Journal Officiel* C54 (28 April 1969).
100 *4th Combined Report* para. 67.
101 EEC *7th General Report* para. 44; *6th General Report* para. 35; *10th General Report* para. 35.
102 *Bulletin* (1969) No. 6, p. 35.

103 *Journal Officiel* C21 (19 February 1970).
104 H. von der Groeben 'Approximation of Legislation: The Policy of the Commission of the European Communities' address to Parliament (27 November 1969) p. 7.

Chapter 5: Supportive Social Services

1 J. Follows *Antecedents of the International Labour Organisation* (1951) pp. 169–70.
2 CECA 'La Sécurité sociale des pays membres de la Communauté et les travailleurs migrants des pays tiers' *Doc.* 4657/66f, para. 5.
3 ECSC *14th General Report* para. 396.
4 Commission Administrative pour la sécurité sociale des travailleurs migrants *6th and 7th Rapports* p. 59.
5 EEC *1st General Report* para. 118.
6 Regulation No. 3, Arts. 43 and 44, setting up the Administrative Commission, were operative from 19 December 1958.
7 Commission Administrative pour la sécurité sociale *6th and 7th Rapports* p. 63.
8 Vaasen–Göbbels case. Affaire 61–65. Recueil de la Jurisprudence de la Cour, Vol. xii–4 (1966) p. 377.
9 *Journal Officiel* No. 47 (1964) p. 746/64.
10 EEC *6th General Report* para. 185.
11 Provided he had thoughtfully obtained form E6 from his local insurance office before leaving home.
12 EEC *5th General Report* para. 32.
13 *Journal Officiel* No. 28 (23 February 1963).
14 Regulation No. 3, Art. 33 and Annex C. In consequence other members only accepted the principle for coal and steel workers in respect of French and Luxembourg nationals.
15 Regulation No. 3, Annex E.
16 *Journal Officiel* No. 86 (31 December 1961).
17 *Journal Officiel* No. 1 (8 January 1964).
18 *Journal Officiel* No. 62 (20 April 1963).
19 EEC *5th General Report* para. 32.
20 Regulation 108/64/CEE. *Journal Officiel* No. 127 (7 August 1964).
21 *Journal Officiel* No. 125 (9 July 1965).
22 e.g., Belgium–Italy; Germany–Italy; Germany–Netherlands; Belgium–Netherlands; Italy–Netherlands.
23 Examples include discussion with national authorities of a standard form of certification to be used by employers sending workers to another member for several short stays; methods of implementing arrangements under Art. 47 concerning the receipt of information by an authority not immediately competent to act; discussions of ways of simplifying the formalities necessary to claim benefit.
24 *Agence Europe* (19 February 1963) No. 1485.
25 There are considerable delays in publication.
26 In 1967 the Court gave its opinion to the Belgian Conseil d'Etat that the social security authorities must accept documents, presented in Italian, designed to support a claim to widow's benefit.
27 Regulation No. 3, Annex 3.
28 *Journal Officiel* No. 62 (20 April 1963).
29 *Journal Officiel* No. 5 (17 January 1964).
30 *Journal Officiel* No. 112 (24 July 1963).
31 Regulation 7/64/CEE. *Journal Officiel* No. 18 (1 February 1964).
32 Ribas *op. cit.* p. 169.
33 *Journal Officiel* No. 44 (10 March 1967).
34 Not all issues have been dealt with here. See the amending Regulation 419/68/CEE, *Journal Officiel* L187 (8 April 1968), which brought certain changes required because of changes in Dutch laws concerning disablement and resulting

incapacity for work and in French laws of support for the elderly. Regulation 80/65/CEE, *Journal Officiel* No. 111 (25 June 1965), defined the social security position of unestablished officials of the European Communities.

35 *Journal Officiel* No. 194 (28 October 1966).
36 EEC *9th General Report* para. 246.
37 *3rd Combined Report* para. 334.
38 Regulation CEE/1408/71. *Journal Officiel* L149 (5 July 1971). Supplemented by the amendment to Annex 1 of Regulation CEE/36/63, *Journal Officiel* L159 (16 July 1971), concerning social security for frontier workers and by Regulation CEE/574/72 on administrative procedures. This last was adopted by the Council on 21 March 1972 but had not been officially published at the time of writing.
39 *International Labour Review* Vol. 106 (1972) No. 1, p. 96.
40 A collective agreement of 31 December 1958, later made obligatory, set up a national scheme covering industry and commerce comprising regional funds grouped in a national union (UNEDIC) and financed by employers and workers.
41 Q.472/69/*Journal Officiel* C62 (28 May 1970); Q.142/70/*Journal Officiel* C122 (7 October 1970).
42 *Bulletin* (1972) No. 10, p. 80.
43 Regulation 130/63/CEE. *Journal Officiel* No. 188 (28 December 1963). This 'withdrew' certain provisions in existing bilateral agreements covering mine workers which had become less favourable.
44 A. Coppé 'The Social Horizon for 1980' *Bulletin* (1971) No. 1.
45 Parlement 1968–9 *Doc. 158* (20 November 1968) pp. 17–18.
46 EEC *1st General Report* para. 122.
47 Neirinck *op. cit.* pp. 34–5.
48 *Social Exposé 1958* pp. 95–6.
49 *Social Exposé 1968* paras. 39–40, p. 246.
50 EEC *5th General Report* para. 36, *7th General Report* para. 233.
51 para. 82.
52 HMSO *Report of the Working Party on Social Workers in the Local Authority Health and Welfare Services* (1959) para. 616.
53 *Social Exposé 1968* para. 42, p. 248.
54 A conference of social service specialists was held in December 1958. The first meeting of experts to deal with family questions in February 1960 brought together government representatives, leaders of family movements, workers from international organizations and from workers' and employers' organizations. A general seminar on social services was held in July 1960 and a further meeting on family affairs in March 1961 followed by a seminar on the relationship between social security and social services arranged in conjunction with the Belgian government, the European Office of the UN and the ILO. Consultations with family, employer and worker organizations were undertaken preparatory to the family budget survey of 1962–3 and comparative material on aids to the family collected. In 1965 a meeting of organizers of hostels for young workers was held, etc.
55 *Storch Report* para. 4.
56 Ribas *op. cit.* p. 203.
57 *Storch Report* para. 7.
58 All Community members were, or were about to become, signatories of the UN Convention on the Recovery Abroad of Maintenance (1956). EEC *8th General Report* para. 263.
59 Ribas *op. cit.* p. 196.
60 *The Times* (13 and 14 February 1970).
61 *Storch Report* para. 27.
62 *2nd Combined Report* para. 427.
63 ECSC *Obstacles à la Mobilité des Travailleurs et Problèmes Sociaux de Réadaptation* Luxembourg (1956).
64 Explanatory memorandum attached to the recommendation of the Commission to member states concerning the housing of workers and their families moving within the Community. *Journal Officiel* No. 137 (27 July 1965).

65 EEC *Bulletin* (1965) No. 9/10, p. 8.
66 *Doc.* v/com/65/28.
67 *Journal Officiel* No. 137 (27 July 1965).
68 Ribas *op. cit.* p. 202.
69 *Social Exposé 1968* paras. 245–6, p. 157–8.
70 All created in 1964. France *Décret* 24 April 1964. Luxembourg *Regulation* 2 May 1964. Netherlands *Arrêté* 10 September 1964. See also EEC *Bulletin* (1966) No. 12, p. 39.
71 *Doc.* 15157/v/67/f, 'Deuxième Rapport sur les suites données a la recommandation de la Commission aux états membres conçernant l'activité des services sociaux à l'égard des travailleurs se déplaçant dans la Communauté' (hereafter 'Deuxiéme Rapport . . .' para. 24.
72 *ibid.* para. 24.
73 *ibid.* para. 8.
74 J. W. D. Davies 'Immigrants in Germany' *Child Care Quarterly Review of the National Council of Voluntary Child Care Organisations,* Vol. 23, No. 1 (January 1969) p. 30.
75 *La Libre circulation* . . . pp. 72–8.
76 Council of Europe *Social Services for Migrant Workers* (1968) p. 42. See this report for further details concerning services provided, at home and abroad, for migrants and their families.
77 'Deuxième Rapport . . .' para. 8.
78 'Sythèse des rapports établis en 1960 sur la situation actuelle du service sociale des travailleurs migrants dans les six pays membres de la CEE' *Doc.* v/56641/1/60f (hereafter 'Synthèse des rapports . . .'). This summarizes the social service situation at that time.
79 *Journal Officiel* No. 75 (16 August 1962).
80 *Débats* (21–23 September 1971). Text of Resolution in *Journal Officiel* C100 (12 October 1971).

Chapter 6: Social Harmonization

1 D. Zöllner *Social Legislation in the Federal Republic of Germany* (1964) p. 5.
2 A conference on the social problems of agriculture was held in 1961 to discuss particular measures to equate the social conditions in agriculture with those of the rest of the population.
3 Parlement 1961–2 (14 November 1961) 'Rapport fait au nom de la Commission sociale sur l'harmonisation social' Introduction *Doc. 87*
4 EEC *3rd General Report* para. 282.
5 *Parliamentary Debates* (1970–1) Vol. 823, Cols. 1115, 1123.
6 *Conférénce eurpéenne sur la sécurité sociale* Vol. 1, p. 196, para. 7. Although this was intended to include the self-employed.
7 L. Levi-Sandri 'Les Aspects Sociaux du Marché Commun' speech at Nice (1967) p.7 (author's italics).
8 *ibid.* p. 3.
9 'Social Aspects of European Economic Co-operation' *International Labour Review* Vol. 74 (1956), pp. 101, 112.
10 Levi-Sandri *op. cit.* (1967) p. 7.
11 Parlement 1961–2, *Doc. 87* para. 48.
12 EEC *1st General Report* para. 102.
13 Levi-Sandri, *op. cit.* (1967) pp. 5–6.
14 Parlement 1961–2, *Doc. 87* para. 13.
15 *ibid.* especially paras. 13, 14, 30, 48.
16 *Social Exposé 1960* p. 21. See also *Débats* IV/1962, No. 48, p. 123 for M. Nederhorst's recognition of the importance to be attached to the fact that the Commission held this view because of its implication that a positive social policy is necessary.
17 *Conférénce européene sur la sécurité sociale* Vol. 1, p. 197, paras. 8, 10.

18 Nederhorst *Débats* IV/1962, No. 48, p. 119.
19 *Year Book of Social Statistics* (1970) Table 1/5 p. 46 for infant and neo-natal mortality.
20 G. Petrilli 'The Social Policy of the Commission' EEC *Bulletin* (1959) No. 2, p. 6.
21 Parlement 1961–2, *Doc. 87* para. 13.
22 *ibid.*
23 *ibid.* para. 14.
24 Resolution of the Assembly (28 February 1958) quoted Troclet *op. cit.* p. 321.
25 *Social Exposé 1967* p. 15.
26 *ibid.* p. 20.
27 Quoted Troclet *op. cit.* p. 325.
28 Parlement *Doc. 87* para. 28. *Débats* IV/1962, No. 48, p. 119.
29 *Conférénce européene sur la sécurité sociale* Vol. 1, p. 197. See also Parlement *Doc. 87* para. 30. This, too, used the notion of working to bring standards closer so that they are equivalent. See also Parlement 1965–6 *Doc. 60* para. 54 which continued to accept that harmonization does not necessarily lead to a uniformity of benefits but to a state of 'equivalence' between workers.
30 *Débats* IV/1962, No. 48, p. 119.
31 L. Levi-Sandri *European Community* (1963) No. 2, p. 16.
32 *Débats* IV/1962, No. 48, p. 118.
33 EEC *2nd General Report* para. 160.
34 EEC *5th General Report* para. 147.
35 Parlement *Doc. 87* para. 14.
36 Petrilli *op. cit.* p. 5.
37 The Commission did not consider harmonization of taxation necessary for the purpose of the free movement of labour. Q.309/70/*Journal Officiel* C150 (23 December 1970).
38 Parlement 1965–6 *Doc. 60* para. 1.
39 *Social Exposé 1960* p. 22.
40 *Débats* IV/1962, No. 48, p. 120. See also *Action Programme* paras. 79–82.
41 *Parliamentary Debates* (1970–1) Vol. 823, Cols. 1113, 1115.
42 ILO *Costs of Social Security* (1964) p. 2.
43 'Comptes Sociaux' *Statistiques Sociales* (1967) No. 5, p. 13. See also *Statistiques Sociales* (1972) No. 2, pp. 87–91.
44 'The Economic Impact of Social Security' *Etudes: Série Politique Sociale* No. 21 (1971) para. 23.
45 Joseph *Parliamentary Debates* (1970–1) Vol. 823, Col. 1118.
46 M. Dupeyroux *Evolution et tendances des systèmes de sécurité des pays membres des Communautés Européennes et de la Grande Bretagne* ECSC (1966) p. 13.
47 *European Community* (1963) No. 2, p. 16.
48 *Social Exposé 1968* p. 242.
49 *Social Exposé 1970* Annex 4, Table 10.
50 'Comptes Sociaux' *Statistiques Sociales* (1972) Preliminary Results 1962–71.
51 Dupeyroux *op. cit.* pp. 99–100.
52 Commission 'Preliminary guidelines . . .' Sec. (71) 600 Final, p. 79.
53 *Social Exposé 1968* p. 243.
54 *Conférénce européenne sur la sécurité sociale* Vol. 1, p. 203.
55 'La Politique Sociale de la Haute Autorité etc' *Notes d'information sur les événements sociaux dans la Communauté* IX Année, No. 5, para. 150.
56 *Statistiques Sociales* (1972) No. 2, p. 67.
57 *Conférénce européene sur la sécurité sociale* Vol. 1, p. 23. See also *Agence Europe* (17 December 1962) No. 1438.
58 ECSC *13th General Report* para. 439.
59 *Conférénce européene sur la sécurité sociale* Vol. 1, p. 752.
60 Parlement *Doc. 87* paras 17, 21, 25.
61 *Conférénce européene sur la sécurité sociale* Vol. 1, p. 197, para. 11.
62 *ibid,* p. 200, para. 18.

63 *ibid,* p. 201, para. 21.
64 EEC *6th General Report* para. 201.
65 ECSC *10th General Report* para. 543.
66 EEC *1st General Report* para. 120.
67 Neirinck *op. cit.* p. 32.
68 *Débats* IV/1962, pp. 120–1.
69 EEC *1st General Report* para. 122.
70 The Commission had wished to offer 'every possible assistance' in the construction of dwellings for workers. EEC *1st General Report* para. 122.
71 *Action Programme* paras. 78–82.
72 Parlement *Doc. 87* paras. 36–44 and 24.
73 *Action Programme* para. 78.
74 *Conférénce européene sur la sécurité sociale* Vol. 1, p. 754.
75 *Journal Officiel* No. 160 (29 September 1965).
76 Q.115/*Journal Officiel* No. 262 (28 October 1967). The Commission stated that both Belgium and Germany had let it know of certain intentions but France, Italy and Luxembourg had not yet done so, although it should not therefore be assumed that they were necessarily violating the spirit of the treaty. The Commission reported that, when it became aware of impending changes but thought it unlikely to be informed, it reminded states of the importance of harmonizing standards. See also Q.174/*Journal Officiel* No. 312 (21 December 1967). This referred to a recent French ordinance allowing workers a greater share in the profits of the firm. In reply the Commission stated that it had not been consulted about the proposal but expected to be so increasingly when such national action was taken.
77 *Journal Officiel* No. 84 (4 June 1963) p. 1577.
78 Resolution on the Commission's guidelines for work in social affairs. *Bulletin* (1968) No. 1, p. 104.
79 Parlement 1965–6 *Doc. 60* para. 6.
80 *Social Exposé 1961* p. v.
81 Parlement 1965–6 *Doc. 60* paras. 14–6.
82 Neirinck *op. cit.* p. 7. Levi-Sandri *op. cit.* (1967) p. 3.
83 'Comptes Sociaux' *Statistiques Sociales* (1972) Supplement, Resultats Preliminaires, Table B.
84 *ibid.* Table F. Luxembourg 1969 *Statistiques Sociales* (1972–z) Table M.
85 *Social Report* (1972) Section C.
86 *Social Exposé* (1971) Annex 5, Table 11.
87 *ibid.* Table 4.
88 *ibid.* Table 2.
89 *ibid.* Table 7. Luxembourg 1968 *Social Exposé* (1970) Table 7.

Chapter 7: The Attempt at Social Policy

1 Levi-Sandri *op. cit.* (1967) p. 13.
2 EEC *3rd General Report* para. 22, p. 38.
3 UNICE *L'Industrie européenne face à l'intégration économique et sociale* (November 1966) p. 9.
4 *ibid.* pp. 8–9.
5 *ibid.* See also *Agence Europe* (22 November 1966) No. 2560.
6 *Agence Europe* (16 December 1966) No. 2581.
7 EEC *1st General Report* paras. 103, 104.
8 EEC *3rd General Report* p. 23.
9 Parlement 1965–6 *Doc. 60* para. 5.
10 EEC *1st General Report* para. 8.
11 Petrilli *op. cit.* p. 7.
12 EEC *4th General Report* para. 147.
13 *Social Exposé 1960* p. 21.

14 *ibid.* pp. 21–2.
15 *Social Exposé 1961* p. XIII.
16 EEC *6th General Report* para. 184.
17 PEP *Regional Development in the European Economic Community* (1962) p. 80.
18 Neirinck *op. cit.* p. 29.
19 EEC *1st General Report* paras. 108–9. See also Levi-Sandri *op. cit.* (1965) p. 9.
20 Petrilli *op. cit.* p. 7.
21 ECSC *5th General Report* para. 249.
22 Petrilli *op. cit.* p. 7.
23 *Social Exposé 1967* p. 15.
24 See its resolutions on the *Social Exposé 1966* and the Commission's guidelines for social policy submitted to the Council in 1966. *Bulletin* (1968) No. 1, pp. 103–4.
25 Parlement 1965–6 *Doc. 60* para. 34.
26 Employers, for example, objected to the study and discussion of wages. *Débats* IV/1962, No. 48, p. 119. Parlement 1961–2 *Doc. 87* paras. 8, 9.
27 Parlement 1965–6 *Doc. 60* para. 34. *Agence Europe* (21 April 1964) No. 1823.
28 Parlement 1961–2 *Doc. 87* para. 40.
29 Parlement 1965–6 *Doc. 60* para. 18. This document lists, in an annexe, all groups constituted in social matters. Groups created under Art. 118 were bipartite, tripartite and purely governmental.
30 *Agence Europe* (16 December 1966) No. 2581.
31 Parlement 1961–2 *Doc. 87* para. 6.
32 *ibid.* paras. 8, 9, 12.
33 Parlement 1964–5 *Doc. 75* para. 188; 1965–6 *Doc. 79* para. 152; 1965–6 *Doc. 85* paras. 53, 78.
34 Levi-Sandri *op. cit.* (1967).
35 *Agence Europe* (21 April 1964) No. 1823; (6 November 1964) No. 1976. Ribas *op. cit.* p. 287.
36 EEC *6th General Report* para. 184.
37 Parliamentary session 26 March–2 April 1960. See too EEC *3rd General Report* para. 14, p. 34.
38 Parlement 1966–7 *Doc. 130* (28 November 1966) para. 77.
39 Resolution on *7th General Report.* EEC *Bulletin* (1964) No. 12, p. 73.
40 Resolution on the social aspects of the merger of the executives. EEC *Bulletin* (1965) No. 7, p. 64.
41 Parlement 1966–7 *Doc. 130* (28 November 1966) para. 72.
42 EEC *Bulletin* (1967) No. 1, p. 51.
43 Parlement 1966–7 *Doc. 130* para. 71.
44 *Journal Officiel* No. 232 (16 December 1966) p. 3918.
45 *Doc. 130* para. 69.
46 EEC *Bulletin* (1964) No. 3, p. 41.
47 *Action Programme* para. 74.
48 *ibid,* para. 86.
49 *Doc. 130* para. 70.
50 A summary of the memorandum by M. Veldkamp of the Netherlands is to be found in *Agence Europe* (17 December 1966) No. 2582.
51 *ibid.*
52 For a summary of conclusions see *Agence Europe* (19 December 1966) No. 2583, and EEC *Bulletin* (1967) No. 2, p. 33.
53 *Agence Europe* (19 December 1966) No. 2583.
54 *ibid.*
55 Parlement 1966–7 *Doc. 171* (25 January 1967) p. 9.
56 *Agence Europe* (19 December 1966) No. 2583.
57 *Doc. 171* paras. 6–13.
58 EEC *Bulletin* (1967) No. 2, p. 54.
59 *Doc. 171* para. 22.
60 EEC *Bulletin* (1967) No. 4, pp. 65–6.
61 Clearly Parliament was unconvinced by the statements made to it by official

spokesmen. Signor Levi-Sandri denied that the Italian decision meant a return to bilateral action because of the executive role given to the Commission. He was supported by M. Servais (President of the Council of Ministers): 'I do not share the point of view of those who believe that the agreed solution may be tainted with a spirit of bilateralism,' on the grounds that the credits for the scheme were to go through Community accounts. *Débats* III/1967, No. 89, pp. 101, 105.

62 *ibid.* p. 86.
63 Neirinck *op. cit.* p. 42.
64 The guidelines were published in EEC *Bulletin* (1967) No. 2, Supplement.
65 L. Levi-Sandri 'Pour une politique sociale moderne dans la Communauté Européene' reprint of speech to Parliament (13 March 1968) p. 8.
66 *Social Exposé 1967* pp. 16–17.
67 *Journal Officiel* No. L175 (23 July 1968). *Bulletin* (1968) No. 9/10, p. 38. Regulation 543/69. *Journal Officiel* L77 (29 March 1969) p. 49. Regulation 514/72; Regulation 515/72.
68 Regulation 1463/70. *Journal Officiel* L164 (27 July 1970).
69 *3rd Combined Report* (1969) paras. 140–2, *5th Combined Report* (1971) paras. 278–80.
70 Directive 72/159/EEC and Directive 72/160/EEC of 17 April 1972. HMSO *Secondary Legislation* Part 15. See also *Bulletin* (1972) No. 4, pp. 15–18.
71 EEC *8th General Report* paras. VII and 254.
72 *Social Exposé 1967* No. XI, p. 21.
73 EEC *10th General Report* No. XXIII, p. 33.
74 Levi-Sandri *op. cit.* (1968) pp. 6–7.
75 Ribas *op. cit.* p. 377.
76 Levi-Sandri *op. cit.* (1968) p. 10.
77 *Social Exposé 1970* pp. 9–10.
78 EEC *10th General Report* p. 33.
79 Levi-Sandri *op. cit.* (1968) p. 7.
80 In 1968 Luxembourg and in 1969 the Netherlands refused co-operation in certain population studies because of the problems involved in making the returns. Q.79/69/*Journal Officiel* C90 (9 July 1969).
81 *Social Exposé 1968* pp. 20–1.
82 *Bulletin* (1968) No. 1, pp. 103–4.
83 *Agence Europe* (5 June 1967) No. 2695.
84 *Agence Europe* (2 June 1967) No. 2694.
85 *Agence Europe* (5 June 1967) No. 2695; (6 June 1967) No. 2696.
86 *Agence Europe* (2 June 1967).
87 *ibid.*
88 *Agence Europe* (6 June 1967).
89 Q.36/68/*Journal Officiel* C68 (9 July 1968).
90 *Agence Europe* (5 and 6 June 1967).
91 J. Rey *Débats* X/67, No. 94 (20 September 1967) p. 11.
92 Resolutions on the *10th General Report*, and on the guidelines for the Commission's work in social affairs. *Social Exposé 1966. Bulletin* (1968) No. 1, p. 101–5.
93 The account of the Council meetings is based on *Agence Europe* (20 December 1967) No. 2825; (21 December 1967) No. 2826; (13 February 1968) No. 31; (22 February 1968) No. 38; (6 August 1968) No. 153; and the Agency's Europe Documents No. 466 (29 February 1968).
94 Unemployment had fallen from 2·75 million in 1958 to 1·5 million in 1966; there had been a notable increase in wages, a drop in working hours and the coverage provided by social security schemes increased. *Agence Europe* (20 December 1967) No. 2825.
95 *2nd Combined Report* para. 368. *European Community* (1968) No. 5, p. 6.
96 *Agence Europe* Documents No. 466 (29 February 1968).
97 *Agence Europe* (13 February 1968) No. 31.
98 Q.43/69/*Journal Officiel* C71 (9 June 1969).

99 *European Community* (1969) No. 5, p. 8.
100 Parlement *Débats* No. 101 (13 March 1968) p. 64.
101 *Agence Europe* (6 August 1968) No. 153.
102 The Communities' Work Programme. *Bulletin* (1969) No. 4, Supplement, pp. 6–7.
103 Parlement 1969–70 *Doc. 58* (17 June 1969).
104 *ibid*. See also *Bulletin* (1968) No. 9/10, pp. 59–60.
105 *3rd Combined Report* para. 497.
106 The Council's view of the report is summarized in 'How the Community's social policies are related to other policies' *Bulletin* (1969) No. 6, pp. 17–23.
107 *Bulletin* (1969) No. 5, p. 64.
108 *Agence Europe* (21 December 1970) No. N.711. See reply to Q.301/70 stating that no comparable statistics concerning the numbers of physically and mentally handicapped exist, that the opportunities available to such people vary considerably and that the Commission's programme is designed to further their social integration by setting both short- and long-term objectives. There is no immediate intention to attempt the co-ordination of national legislation but to encourage development by educational activities. Q.301/70/*Journal Officiel* C150 (23 December 1970). The report is now published. Commission *Occupational Rehabilitation and Placement of the Disabled* European Symposium, Luxembourg (May 1971).
109 *Bulletin* (1970) Nos. 4, 12.
110 Coppé *op. cit.* p. 10.
111 See above, page 46.
112 *Social Exposé 1970* pp. 33–4.
113 'Preliminary guidelines . . .' Sec. (71) 600 Final (17 March 1971). See summary in *Bulletin* (1971) No. 4, Supplement 2/71.
114 'Preliminary guidelines . . .' p. 2.
115 *ibid*. p. 71.
116 *ibid*. p. 69.
117 *The Times* (20 October 1972).

Chapter 8: The Past and the Future

1 Q.91/69/*Journal Officiel* C112 (28 February 1969). Q.309/69/*Journal Officiel* C9 (23 January 1970). Q.471/70/*Journal Officiel* C33 (7 April 1971). Dutch refusal to participate in surveys of the working population.
2 See, e.g., ECSC Etudes et Documents *Comparison des revenus réels des travailleurs de la Communauté* (1956).
3 ECSC *7th General Report* para. 262.
4 ECSC *10th General Report* para. 541.
5 'La Politique Sociale de la Haute Autorité etc' *Notes d'information sur les événements sociaux dans la Communauté* IX Année No. 5, para. 23.
6 L. Levi-Sandri, Address to Quatrième Conférence Européenne des Syndicats Chrétiens, Amsterdam (7–10 October 1966) duplicated, p. 4.
7 Parlement *Débats* No. 101 (13 March 1968) p. 65.
8 'La Politique Sociale . . .' *op. cit.* para. 19.
9 L. Rosenberg 'European Integration – A Necessity' *European Community* (1971) No. 5, p. 15.
10 Q.71/69/*Journal Officiel* C94 (19 July 1969).
11 EEC *Bulletin* (1965) No. 1, pp. 73–5.
12 *Journal Officiel* No. 96 (28 May 1966).
13 *Social Exposé 1968* para. 46, pp. 250–1.
14 *Social Exposé 1967* p. 19.
15 The Communities' Work Programme (20 March 1969). *Bulletin* (1969) No. 4, Supplement.
16 Parlement 1967–8 *Doc. 138* para. 59.
17 Levi-Sandri *op. cit.* (1968) p. 62. See also Ribas *op. cit.* p. 664.
18 'Preliminary guidelines . . .' Sec. (71) 600 Final, p. 28.

19 Q/276/*Journal Officiel* C23 (20 March 1968). Q.64/68/*Journal Officiel* C68 (9 July 1968). Questions on non-availability of tax reliefs for Frenchmen working in Belgium of contributions paid to French savings funds.
20 *Year Book of Social Statistics* (1970) Table III/11.
21 Q.190/68/*Journal Officiel* C120 (16 November 1968).
22 *Social Exposé 1967* p. 19. 'La Politique Sociale . . .' *op. cit.* para. 145.
23 'Preliminary guidelines . . .' p. 34.
24 See Chapter 6, Appendix.
25 *Year Book of Social Statistics* (1972).
26 *Agence Europe* (17–18 April 1972) No. 1028.
27 ECSC *10th General Report* para. 485.
28 ECSC *Policy Report* (1965) p. 14.
29 Levi-Sandri *op. cit.* (1968) pp. 4–5.
30 Levi-Sandri *op. cit.* (1965) p. 53.
31 Parlement 1969–70 *Doc. 58* (17 June 1969) para. 10.
32 Levi-Sandri *op. cit.* (1965) p. 56.
33 Levi-Sandri *op. cit.* (1967) p. 13.
34 Coppé *op. cit.* pp. 5–6.
35 Levi-Sandri *op. cit.* (1967) p. 5.
36 A. Spinelli *The Eurocrats* (1966) p. 7.
37 *ibid.* p. 25.
38 D. Coombes *Politics and Bureaucracy in the European Community* (1970) p. 65.
39 Spinelli *op. cit.* p. 64.
40 See especially Spinelli *op. cit.*; Coombes *op. cit.*; L. Lindberg *The Political Dynamics of European Economic Integration* (1963).
41 Lindberg *op. cit.* p. 62.
42 Spinelli *op. cit.* p. 63.
43 A Parliamentary question on the examination of loans for industrial conversion drew attention to this problem. Q.384/69/*Journal Officiel* C22 (22 February 1970).
44 ECSC *5th General Report* para. 262.
45 *Social Exposé 1967* p. 19.
46 *Journal Officiel* C91 (10 July 1969); *Journal Officiel* C147 (17 November 1969); *Journal Officiel* C154 (2 December 1969); *Journal Officiel* C5 (13 January 1970); *Journal Officiel* C16 (7 February 1970); *Journal Officiel* C69 (11 June 1970); *Journal Officiel* C56 (11 May 1970).
47 Neirinck *op. cit.* p. 43.
48 Levi-Sandri *op. cit.* (1967) pp. 12–13.
49 Q.371/69/*Journal Officiel* C20 (14 February 1970).
50 Parlement 1966–7 *Doc. 130* (28 November 1966).
51 Levi-Sandri *op. cit.* (1967) p. 12.
52 *Social Exposé 1967* p. 22.
53 M. Servais *Débats* III/67, No. 89, p. 103.
54 Q.79/69/*Journal Officiel* C90 (9 July 1969).
55 Levi-Sandri *op. cit.* (1965) p. 53.
56 Q/269/*Journal Officiel* C115 (13 November 1971); Q/270/*Journal Officiel* C118 (24 November 1971).
57 This still does not work well enough. Q/174/*Journal Officiel* No. 312 (21 December 1967). Q/203/68/*Journal Officiel* C122 (23 November 1969).
58 Levi-Sandri *op. cit.* (1965) pp. 50–1.

Index